DATE DUE

BRODART   Cat. No. 23-221

Debating the Good Society

Debating the Good Society
A Quest to Bridge
America's Moral Divide

Andrew Bard Schmookler

The MIT Press
Cambridge, Massachusetts
London, England

© 1999 Massachusetts Institute of Technology

This book was set in Sabon and Officina Sans Book by Achorn Graphic Services, Inc.

Printed and bound in the United States of America.

Library of Congress Cataloging-in-Publication Data

Schmookler, Andrew Bard.
   Debating the good society : a quest to bridge America's moral divide / Andrew Bard Schmookler.
      p.   cm.
   Includes bibliographical references.
   ISBN 0-262-19414-7 (hc : alk. paper)
   1. United States—Moral conditions. 2. Social values—United States. 3. United States—Social conditions—1980– . I. Title.
HN90.M6S347   1999
306′.0973—dc21   98-31588
                                                                        CIP

All the characters in the Internet discussion forum herein (with the exception of the author)—and all of the e-mailed messages—are fictional.

Contents

Introduction: The Design from Argument   **1**

1   **The Nintendo Dilemma**   3
     The Good Order Group   3
     Trust but Verify   5
     The Noble Savage   6

2   **Constructing Some Frames**   15
     A Consultation in the Garden   15
     Ideas Growing Out of the Soil of Experience   20
     The Dance of Polarization   21
     Time for Us to Listen   25
     Historical Currents   28
     Signs of Disorder   30
     Let's Mix It Up   35

3   **Spinning a Few Threads**   37
     Checking in on Business   37
     Back Out from My Court   39
     Do They Need to Be Pushed, or Will They Jump?   43
     All of a Piece   45
     Who Are You to Judge?   47
     Is Anything Really Good?   49
     For Whose Good?   52
     The Power of Ideas   56

Interlude: Another Meeting in the Garden   **61**
     Overwhelmed by Complexity   61
     The Challenge of Creation   62

I   **The Crooked Timber of Our Humanity   67**

4   **From the Ground Up:**
     Does the Well-Ordered Soul Develop Naturally?   69
     Nature Isn't a One-Story Building   69
     Higher Faculties   72
     Foundations and Superstructure   76
     If You Will   78
     As Water Flows   80
     Visions of the Kingdom of Reason   82
     The Greatest Teacher   83
     A Somber Empiricism   87
     Reality Check   88

5   **Found Wanting:**
     The Question of the Adequacy of the Human Being   91
     Creatures of Habit   91
     Rigged Experiments   95
     Pressed into the Mold   99
     The Critique of Reason   101
     Following Tradition   104

Interlude: Bitter Lessons   111

II   **Word from On High   121**

6   **Bow Down:**
     Must People, to Be Good, Submit to Authority?   123
     Gate-crashers   123
     Law and Order   124
     Minding Our Betters   127
     The Anarchist Vision: A World without Coercion   131
     A Story of a Delayed Splash   136
     Overarching Order   137
     Submission to the Will of God   138

7   **Built upon Sand:**
     Can a Good Order Be Based on Hierarchy?   143
     Issues of Might and Right   143
     Hungry for the Undeniable   146
     Plant Hierarchy, Harvest Injustice   147

Doing Violence   153
Back with a Pitchfork   157
Coming to Grips Together   159

Interlude: Handling Wild Creatures   161

III Under Construction   169

8   In What We Trust?
Do We Have the Moorings We Need?   171
Where Are We?   171
Go with the Flow: Taoism Revisited   173
Zeno's Paradox   176
God's Place   179

9   A Passion for the Whole:
When Bad Things Happen Because of Good People   183
The Moral Culture of Liberalism   184
Interrupted by Business   186
The Self at Sea   188
Beyond the Small Self   190
Tired Questions   194
Old Virtues   197
Would We Have to Invent Him?   206

Interlude: A Colonel of Truth   209

10 The Idiocy and Theodicy:
What Does This Creation Say about the Creator?   219
God's Moral Accounting   219
The Scene of the Crime   225
Free to Be You and Me   227
The Question of Compassion   232
Providence   238

Interlude: A Hand in the Miracle   247
The Creature in the Creation   247
The Magic of It   252

11 Under Construction:
An Evolutionary View of Order   259
The Darwinian Ban on Skyhooks   259

A Crane Is Not a Pyramid   261
A Call to Order   266
What's So Good about It?   273
The Direction of Our Grain   280
The Unfinished   288

Interlude: The Creature and the Creation, Revisited   295
The Spell of the Ideal   295
The Mind of the Breadbaker   300

**12 The One Truth and the Many:
How Can Good Order Be Built from What We Can Know of
Truth?   303**
A Missing Dimension?   303
Heresy   309
The Missing Capital "T"   314
Fears of Chaos   317
A Necessity for Idols?   323
The Tower of Babel Problem   328

Conclusion: Choices   337

13 Choices   339
My Son, My Adam   339
We May Grow   350
When Push Comes   354
Terra's Visit   357
Beyond the Standards of Apedom   360
Progress and Entropy   364
More than Sacrifice   368

Notes   375

Introduction
The Design from Argument

1

The Nintendo Dilemma

Was it just a coincidence? I have no idea. But it certainly seemed to me serendipitous that the very day that our new Internet discussion group was up and running my deep confusion about how to deal with Nathaniel's Nintendo mania crystallized into a deeply probing question. So, naturally, I brought my question to the group.

The Good Order Group

This group consisted, at the outset, of a half dozen people with what we sensed to be a common interest. We had met at a conference, "A Better Future for America," at which some of us had been brought as invited speakers, while the others had been attendees. The conference was in California, sponsored by a group that was keeping alive the old counterculture's flame of liberation. During the several days we had been together, these several of us had found ourselves continually engaged—backstage, as it were—in the liveliest of conversations on a variety of themes I would call "moral." Then, as our time together was coming to an end, several of us expressed regret that we'd have to give up these invigorating discussions, and the idea was born: we would set up a forum on the Internet through which we'd stay engaged.

The group would consist of the dozen or so of us who felt already engaged with one another in discussion, with each of us deputized to recruit any additional members we thought might enrich our exploration of our issues.

When we tried to come up with a title for our group-to-be, we found that we had as many notions of what our conversations had been about as we had members. One declared the topic to be "the meaning of true freedom," another proposed it was "what are God's commandments in a godless universe?" while a third suggested it was a quest to understand the place of the human saga in the evolution of the cosmos. My own way of encapsulating the theme was the question: "What are the sources of 'good order'?" All this disagreement did not disturb us in the least. Despite our different slants on the subject, we knew that we shared some basic concerns: the shaky condition of American society as the twentieth century comes to a close and, at a more philosophical level, what it means to be a "good" human being and what it takes to create a "good" society. And even in the absence of accord on what the question was, we already knew that it would be worthwhile—and fun—to seek the answer together. So we officially called ourselves "Inquiry," agreeing that we trusted the process of free inquiry to unfold in a constructive direction.

Although we set up our Internet list as the "Inquiry Group," I've never used that name, even in my own mind. I call us the Good Order Group, and so I plan to call it here. Some may accuse me of usurpation of powers in imposing my own title—and thereby also my agenda—on an unconsenting group. But hey, it's not for nothing that "author" is more than halfway to "authority."

And speaking of author, I had gone to California already having some sense that my daemon, or my muse, was pulling me toward writing a book on the subject of "good order," and our intense discussions had solidified that commitment. I'd asked for, and been given, permission to use whatever material our forum might generate that would be useful for my literary enterprise. One idea I had, which I was eager to try out, was to be more or less the secretary for a cyber-meeting that, as the discussion evolved in its own organic way, would spontaneously yield well-formed fruit.

So, by coincidence, or whatever, it was on the very day that our more technically competent member managed to get our list set up and helped us all link up by subscribing to the forum, that I felt compelled to confront this problem from my family life: how to deal with—or at least, how to understand the challenge of how to deal with—the passion of my son, Nathaniel, for playing Nintendo. Sensing that it was a problem that would be appropriate to bring before the group, it occurred to me that the

Nintendo Dilemma might be a suitable vehicle for launching our forum discussion.

Trust but Verify

Here's what I wrote.

Subject: My Nintendo Dilemma

Hello, friends. As it happens, a puzzle has just descended on me, and I would like to consult you guys (to be understood as inclusive of gals) about it. It grows out of my life—in this case, in my role as a father—and I think it bears directly on our concerns here (assuming I know what those are!), so I don't think you'll regard my personal quandary as "out of order."

As you probably recall—some will remember the portrait in my wallet I beamingly showed around—I have a son who's seven years old, almost eight. Like a lot of boys his age these days, he loves video games. At first, I thought his playing them was fine. I remembered how I was as a boy, and I know that if these had been around then I'd have loved them, too. And I got pleasure from seeing him learning each new game, being so serious and engaged in working toward mastery of it, thinking and talking about it even when he was doing other things.

But after a while, my wife (April) and I started feeling concerned that his lust for Nintendo was getting out of hand. Too much time spent on the screen, so much that he seemed reluctant to do any of the other things he's enjoyed in the past, things like reading, and hanging out with me in the garden. And the activity itself, while not so passive as watching TV, seemed unnaturally unphysical. I mean, how much exercise is it to push buttons countless times so that Mario will jump and shoot his way from one world to the next? Then there's the quality and magnitude of the spiritual space the games provide. As inventive as the game-makers may have been in some ways, the games themselves involve the kid in a rather narrow little world. Not much poetry, or depth of spirit, or any of a thousand other vital dimensions of our reality are to be found in them.

April and I both felt that, in pouring so much of his energy, and time, and attention into the realm of his Nintendo games, Nat was choosing an unbalanced way of living. We encouraged him to move toward greater balance. "Got some great books for you from the library!" "How about you and [your friend] Zack turning off the game and going out exploring in the woods or something?" But simply encouraging did not seem to avail. Left to his own decisions, Nathaniel clearly was inclined to choose video games more than April and I felt was right. If we let him be free, it seemed clear, he'd make what we thought were some wrong choices.

Now, let me be clear about what the question is that I want to ask you, and what it is not. It is **not** how we should deal with the problem, though I actually would be interested in hearing your ideas about that. At long last, we've handled it by imposing our decisions on Nathaniel: we've limited his time on the video games, we've set up ways for him to earn the right to play (so much reading, so much exercise, etc.), so that at this point his life appears to be in reasonable balance (his "life" in the sense of how he spends his time, but not in terms of his desires: I fear that even while climbing trees, he hears the siren call of the Nintendo). The issue that I want to bring to this forum from this Nintendo Dilemma of ours is not "How is a parent to deal with this?" but rather "Why should a parent have to deal with it at all?"

By that question, what I mean is, why doesn't Nathaniel—and here I am using him as a representative of *Homo so-called sapiens*—just do the right thing on his own? Why can't we trust his apparently healthy little organism to find its own balance? Why doesn't the little bugger just stand up on his own, after say thirty minutes on the screen, and say, "Enough of this stuff. Time for some deeper spiritual explorations, or some more thoroughgoing exercise of my multidimensional being"? When we give him freedom, why doesn't he just naturally use it wisely?

It is this question that has hit me like the proverbial ton of bricks just today. I saw that it had taken me so long to assert my parental authority against the Nintendo obsession because of my beliefs around this issue—beliefs concerning why the imposition of my authority should not be necessary. And that therefore if I'd concluded it was right to intervene against my son's own natural inclinations—and my actions declare that I reached that conclusion some months ago—that meant I was obliged to look more deeply into my underlying assumptions about the natural wisdom of the human being.

Looking forward to hearing your thoughts. **Andy**

The way these Internet forums work, I would send my message to the list, and it would automatically distribute it to the e-mail inboxes of all the subscribers. And the answers my fellow members would send would likewise be seen by all the others.

The Noble Savage

The first response I received back was from George Thomasson, or Reverend George as we called him in our little group. Rev. George is a minister in one of the more liberal Protestant denominations, and his talk at the conference was entitled "Salvation in the Gospels as a Metaphor." He was something of an anomaly in our little group because of his placing traditional religious beliefs at the core of his understanding of the world and of the human condition. But at the same time, his holding of those beliefs was somewhat loose—as though he thought such things as "Jesus died for our sins" to be true, but also not necessarily actually true, as if Jesus might just as well be a character in a work of fiction. When I tried to pin him down about what he thought was "really true," I thought him elusive, but I got the impression that he thought there was some Ultimate Truth that was so far over our heads that we wouldn't "get it" even if it were handed to us on a silver platter (or a printed page), but that nonetheless his tradition had a meaningfully illuminating image of it.

Anyway, almost immediately after I sent off my message to the group, I got this response from Rev. George:

Subject: Re: My Nintendo Dilemma
Andy, let me respond to your question in the manner of your venerable tradition, i.e. with another question. Why on earth should it surprise you that your boy—four or five years out of diapers, his mother's milk scarcely dry on his lips—would choose badly? Or, put slightly differently, what is the belief that leads you to expect that a child would be trustworthy to use freedom wisely? **Rev. George**

Subject: Re: My Nintendo Dilemma
Good question, George. It spotlights precisely that part of my belief system that this Nintendo business has compelled me to question. I've believed that the human organism possesses a natural wisdom, that it knows what it needs, knows what is good for it, and that it naturally is drawn to seek those things, to grow, to become **what it should be**. **Andy**

Andy, your faith in the organism seems more naive than I have found you to be, *Rev. George responded*. Do you think Nathaniel—or any other kid—will just "naturally" do all the right things, never lie or steal, never be selfish or cruel? Haven't you ever heard of Original Sin?

Which elicited from me:

You're right, George, to press me. Let me confine my expression of faith in the innate goodness and wisdom of the human organism somewhat. I have always hesitated to assert that the human organism naturally will seek to grow into "what it should be" with respect to every aspect of "the good." You mention selfishness, for example. That leads into the question of how "moral" the human creature naturally is, and I'm not sure I'm ready to address that. But what the Nintendo dilemma compels me to question is another dimension of "should," and that has to do with **the creature's own needs**. I've thought that we've naturally evolved to possess the inclination to seek our own full development, our self-actualization.

As for the doctrine of original sin, I've long rejected this assertion of our fundamental defectiveness. My cosmology is not Eden-based, but evolutionary. And look what evolution has wrought! Look at the marvelous intricacy of the creature, the ordering of matter and energy down to the molecular level—all to meet the challenge of maintaining life's lead in the race with death. Everything functioning together, harmoniously, telling us to avoid what hurts and go for what feels good. And what has felt good? Eating the food that nourishes us, maintaining health, being embedded in harmonious connectedness with others. A natural wisdom that leads the newborn to suck, the toddler to develop his skills in walking and climbing and running, to inquire into everything and learn about the world, to absorb the language of his group.

So, why can't the kid be trusted, apparently, to turn off the Nintendo when it would seem to be best for him to do so? **Andy**

This brought a response from a third member, Eleanor Flowers, a practicing clinical psychologist. At the conference, Eleanor—or Flowers Child, as we dubbed her—gave a talk entitled "Overcoming a Legacy of Abuse." In her view, our history can be understood substantially as an illness or an injury from which we need to be healed.

Re: My Nintendo Dilemma

Andy, I entirely concur with you about the natural wisdom of the organism, but to expect the human child's actual choices to embody that wisdom is to expect her to emerge from the development process unscathed. I hope you won't take my comments amiss if I suggest that this expectation is simply unrealistic in today's world. I don't know your son, of course, but knowing you I imagine he's a neat kid. Nonetheless, we're all carrying our historical burdens—you and your wife doubtless included—and besides we're raising our kids in a society that discourages our flowering, that continually frustrates our self-expression. It's no wonder that so many young boys are addicted to video games these days. **Eleanor**

And I replied:

I'm not offended, Eleanor, at your suggestion that my boy might have suffered some damage that would impair his natural wisdom, but neither am I satisfied with that as a way out of my dilemma. It's funny, but though Nat is my third child, it is with him that I find my beliefs tested. My first two children were from a marriage that ended with much *Sturm und Drang,* and though both have grown up to be very fine people, I've always been painfully aware that the circumstances of their upbringing were less than optimal. If they've grown up strong and well put-together—and I think they have—it is probably like those trees one comes across in the forest with some interesting bend in the trunk that shows the effect of having some large neighboring tree collapse on them when they were saplings, requiring them to take a hitch and a detour in order to gain the space to take their natural course skyward.

But with Nathaniel, it has been rather otherwise. I fear you'll think me immodest, and I'm rather sure you'll think me deluded, when I say that Nathaniel is quite simply a healthy child, the fruit of a happy marriage, a child whose needs have been well met all along the way from La Leche nursing practices on. His spirit is quite clearly undimmed. His burdens, such as they are, seem to have come with him from the womb. I think him to be a good limiting case for our shared belief in the creature's natural inclination to do what's good for itself. I'm not saying we've done perfectly, but I don't think the resolution of this dilemma is to be found in whatever imperfections there have been in his upbringing.

Though I don't expect you'll be persuaded by my testimony on this—I know that I would not be driven to question my own assumptions about our natural wisdom based on anyone's self-serving testimony—I nonetheless feel that a satisfactory answer to my question will need to take my assertion as a given. So I ask you folks to assume that injury has not disabled this particular boy's natural wisdom. **Andy**

Rescue Mission

In the course of the next several hours, my inbox filled with a variety of messages from other members of the group, all extending the thread entitled "My Nintendo Dilemma." My buddies offered me a variety of ways out of my dilemma.

Boy, I've been there, too, Andy, *wrote Keith, a clinical psychologist with a special interest in the issue of self-esteem.* We went through the same thing with our boy when he was that age. (Now he's twice the age of your son.) Here's how we handled it. (I'm not criticizing what you and your wife have done, just reporting our experience.)

We just let him work it out on his own. It was tough. He did little but play that damned video game for four months—other than eat, sleep and go to school (we made him do that!). But eventually, he got tired of it. On his own. Just decided that he'd had it, and went on to other things. So I felt confirmed in my belief in the natural wisdom of the organism. We didn't have to exert any kind of parental authority; we let him learn on his own that there's more to life than jumping on video turtles and avoiding flying video monsters. **Keith**

The response from John, a social worker who did a lot of work with communities and schools, was more challenging:

You speak of whether Nathaniel does the "right" thing. You talk of the way he "should" be. A person listening would think, from your language, these moral categories were objective realities, like a loaf of bread or a stone in your shoe. But nothing is **really** right or wrong, good or evil. These dimensions, which so many people like you treat as important, aren't part of the cosmos at all. You can scan the universe all you want, and you'll find no "good" and no "evil" embedded in it. "Should" your kid play video games less? On this subject, the cosmos is silent.

Our notions of right and wrong are, therefore, just concepts that we invent. They're just our own constructions. There being no objective basis for distinctions between good and bad, right or wrong, we develop such ideas from our own subjective preferences. **John**

You are looking at your boy's video game playing too narrowly, *began Cynthia's response to my query.*

Cynthia was a woman in her mid-forties, a biochemist with a special concern about world peace, someone of whom I'd become quite fond during our time together at the conference.

We've gone through something similar with our daughter. Megin was read to since she was first able to understand, maybe even before. My husband and I have continued reading to her even after she could read perfectly well to herself, choosing for our sharing some of the best of children's literature. *Winnie the Pooh,* for example, and the *Little House* books. And she became an avid reader on her own, with an active and inquiring mind. She knows good stuff, she enjoys employing her mental faculties. But then in recent months, we noticed with alarm that she's choosing to read a whole series of these ghastly (in more senses than one) *Goosebump* books. There's nothing terrible about them, but it's still shallow literature; very little here to feed the soul, or give much food for thought.

We were disappointed. Like you, we believed that our healthy and alive child should—would—naturally challenge herself to grow. We thought that if you put such a child in front of a bookshelf with nourishing books on subjects of interest to her— in her case, books about sea animals, desert life, that kind of thing—she would quite spontaneously and on her own gravitate toward them in preference to fluff and trash.

Like you, we tried encouragement. Like you, we found it insufficient. But then we discovered that this reading of the *Goosebump* books was going on in a social context that put the whole issue in a very different light. ***All the other kids*** were reading these books, and talking about them, and trading them. Not to read them was to exclude oneself from the social discourse of her peer group. If she were reading a book on chameleons, she'd not have the same social connections growing out of it, no shared world, no synergistic excitement.

What we came to understand, then, was that what looked to us like Megin making bad choices in her reading was really Megin making sensible choices about her membership in her society. Given that the other kids have not been nurtured as fully, perhaps, or at least not exposed to such intellectually and spiritually worthwhile worlds as Megin has, Megin is forced to choose between what is intrinsically wise in terms of reading material, and what is extrinsically wise in terms of her peer group participation. It's like the Sufi who ends up drinking the water that makes a person crazy because everyone else had done so, and until he drank it, too, everyone else thought him crazy: it's too lonely to be out of step with the rest of the world, however out of joint that world may be.

When we considered the importance of that participation, we felt able to respect and embrace Megin's decision. **Cynthia**

Then came Fred, a social activist in the San Bernardino Valley, jovial by nature, with long hair and beard, turning white, but with also a penchant for playing the *enfant terrible*.

You write about the child growing into "what it should be," and you have intervened in your son's choices because you don't see them as the best way for him to become that creature you think he should. But ***who are you to judge what he should be?*** Oh, I know—you are his father. But what right does that give you to put your trip on him. You think he "should" be doing something more thoughtful, more vigorous. Sounds like you're saying he should become more like you. I don't suppose you like it when the Christian Coalition goes around telling people how they should live, what they should or shouldn't be doing in their own bedrooms. I ask you: what's different about what you are doing to Nathaniel?

Your "trust" in the creature's wisdom, evidently, extended only as far as the means. As for the ends—as for the question of what the creature should become—you evidently are willing here to arrogate for yourself the right of imposing that on him. This power trip has been going on for thousands of years, and as far as I can see, it's the root of all our difficulties. It's hard for us, I realize, not to carry inside ourselves some of the contamination of this infernal authority trip in us. But the solution is not, as you seem to think, to reimpose the hierarchical approach on the choice of means—e.g. forcing the kid to turn off the video game—but rather to complete the liberation process. That means to expunge what remains of the top-down mentality and put all your faith in the free bottom-up flowering of the creature. Let *him* decide what he should become!

Your child, like every other human being, is a mystery and a miracle beyond your comprehension, and therefore beyond your capacity to control. You should therefore give up all these hierarchical notions of order in which some ruler—benign or otherwise, enlightened or otherwise—will make great judgments and shape the lower stuff into the right shape. How can you know what the natural shape of this growing being "should" be, i.e. what it will naturally become, if not meddled with by people laying their trips on him? Stand back and watch him grow: that's the only way you'll find out how he's supposed to develop! **Fred (the Anarchist)**

Yes, the creature comes equipped with a natural wisdom, but by the nature of the evolutionary process, that wisdom can only be backward looking.

This was Larry. With Larry, one had the feeling that he was often checking his map, making little adjustments on it to make sure that he stayed well-oriented to the terrain at hand.

It cannot anticipate unfamiliar options. In other words, your kid—like the rest of us—was born ready to thrive, and be wise, in a Stone Age environment. He wasn't ready for Nintendo. It's like sweets: we're born to like them because we're evolved in an environment where sweet means good ripe fruit, not Snickers bars. So it is that we parents find ourselves having to limit our kids' devouring of Twinkies, unable to rely on the wisdom of the body to just say no to refined sugar.

So, likewise, I suggest, we're born wired to like the stimulation of mazes and other such challenges, but we lack the necessary "off" switch that might enable us to limit our appetite for a pure and refined stimulus like the video game. Indeed, I suspect that video games and TV both have ways of plugging directly into our central nervous system, bypassing our natural capacity for higher judgment, and hooking into our addictive centers. **Larry**

I saw that Eleanor had posted another message:

To Andy and George: I think Andy gave too much ground too readily in answer to your challenge, George, about lying and stealing and such. Andy staked out his position about natural inclination toward the good on the narrower grounds of the creature's own needs. I'm willing to defend the whole battlefield: I say that the child, if properly nourished and supported, naturally grows up to go for what is good in a moral sense as well as Andy's narrower sense of knowing what is good for its own flourishing.

A child that is loved will naturally be loving. Stealing from another is not loving. A child whose own inner nature is supported, not thwarted, will be happy and caring. It's the kid that's been abused that will be abusive of others. It's the one that's deeply frustrated that is full of rage. The one whose being is respected will naturally give respect to others in return.

Our image of the moral person is, I would maintain, itself an immoral image. It is of a person divided against her- or himself. On top there sits this harsh judge issuing his stern pronouncements, uttering his "Thou shalt nots." Below are the natural desires of the human creature—innocent in nature but made into sin.

I propose a more truly moral person, one who is all of a piece. This person is not ruled by some harsh voice taken in from above to stand as a colonial ruler in a conquered land. Her desires are not labeled bad and forbidden. She does what is good because her heart is good.

I say, therefore, that Original Sin is a calumny against our humanity. It is the soured and spoiled fruit of a human culture that is based on trampling on human needs. I say that all the goodness we want of humankind is there in the seed. **Eleanor**

Thus ended the first exchange. I looked it over and said to myself, "Hey, this is good stuff!"

2

Constructing Some Frames

The next few hours gave me chance and occasion to clarify just what it was that I was trying to achieve by confronting this Nintendo Dilemma, and indeed by committing myself to the process of inquiry with my new forum.

A Consultation in the Garden

Immediately after reading those messages, I had to hurry off to see a friend of mine, Mr. Godachi. Well, he had become a friend, but in the beginning the relationship was one of master to apprentice, more or less, and the realm of our interaction was over the practice of gardening. His place is about a mile from my place, along the same ridge on the western side of Virginia's Shenandoah Valley. My walk over to his place two or three times a week was always a treat, the journey as well as the destination.

I treat most people with a degree of respect, I think, but I must confess that respect is not my long suit, at least not in the old-fashioned sense of deference. But with Mr. Godachi it was rather otherwise. Part of that, certainly, was that our discussions were on a topic on which he was an undoubted master. In addition, there was the fact that he was my senior by enough years that the expression "old enough to be my father" fit pretty well, though as a Japanese-born American he was not naturally well cast for that role. (Indeed, he reminded me more than anything else of Mr. Miagi in the *Karate Kid* movies.) But beyond that, over time I'd recognized in the man a degree of wisdom that is far from common. And because of that, I had been happy when our conversations evolved beyond gardening into a variety of other subject areas.

On this day I was eager to share with Godachi my excitement about the gathering discussion in my Good Order group.

When I came into his garden, the exquisite beauty of the place stunned me, as it usually does. The plants were so healthy, their blossoms so abundant and colorful, their arrangement so perfect. Sometimes it was enough to make me despair of my own gardening, so far were my own flower beds from such perfection. But usually the effect was to inspire me to work harder to progress further, albeit only by a few baby steps, in that direction.

My master gardener was deftly pruning a dwarf mulberry when I found him. The tree looked as though it was one of those traditional Japanese ink-brush drawings come to life, first reaching up stalwartly toward the blank sky and then drooping languidly off to one side. Godachi himself looked as he always did, a man of seventy or so years but who looks as though he could go on forever.

After he and I had discussed a problem I'd been having with a butterfly bush that had been hard hit by the previous winter, I told him about the forum conversation as it had transpired thus far. My account gave considerable detail, as I was eager to hear his evaluation of the various rejoinders I'd elicited, and especially to know what he thought my Nintendo Dilemma revealed. But as usual, he deflected my more direct efforts to reach his point of view and instead challenged me to carry my own thinking process further.

"How would you put what to you is the Big Underlying—or Big Overarching—Question?" Godachi asked me.

"Sometimes the question seems clear," I replied, "and sometimes I feel awash in a whole chaos of questions whose interconnections appear and vanish in turn. Here, let me try.

"One way of putting my question is, 'What is the source of good order?' How do things get made right? Where does good come from? And then," I continued, "the Nintendo Dilemma helps crystallize the issue into two rather basic competing perspectives: there's the top-down view and there's the bottom-up view.

"Top-down I see as the traditional view: Goodness has to be imposed from above, and the stuff below is regarded as fundamentally flawed or incompetent. So God hands down commandments, as the traditionalists see it, and society is ruled from the top of a hierarchy with the mass of people kept mute and passive, and parents are supposed to impose the forms of righteousness handed down to them from above onto their children who come from nature made of base and sinful stuff.

"I've tended to resist that perspective my whole adult life, believing that the real roots of good order lie in meeting the needs of that which is below, allowing a natural unfolding to flower forth. This means the politics of liberty and autonomy. 'Question authority' is a good bumper sticker, and 'If it feels good, do it' at least has the validity of honoring the natural wisdom of the organism, the idea that our design is quite a piece of work in the service of life. And when it comes to parenting, one honors that masterpiece that nature has handed up to us parents to raise, and we do our raising largely through—as one of my correspondents put it—watering and fertilizing."

"Yes, I certainly agree that watering and feeding are indispensible. Any gardener who wants healthy plants does not make war on them."

"But, Mr. Godachi, I see you are certainly not above pruning them."

"Yes, I prune. I weed, too."

"But from the bottom-up point of view," I resumed, "the members of my tribe would say, 'See the thriving of the forest. It is not pruned, nor is it weeded. Yet Nature has so ordered things that it grows forth magnificently and full of health and vitality.'"

"Quite true," Mr. Godachi agreed. "If I died, or just went away, there would be plenty of life still here in the garden. After a while, it wouldn't be a garden, of course. But it would still be alive, and it would still reflect a kind of perfection and beauty."

"So does that mean that my anarchist fellow is right when he says we parents could just keep hands off, just water and fertilize, and our children will develop spontaneously into a form of goodness?"

"Not necessarily," Mr. Godachi said, pinching off some buds from one of his rose bushes. "A human being is not a tree. Nor is a healthy human society ordered like a healthy forest."

"In what way is it not? Is it our being social animals? Are you talking here about our freedom? our indeterminacy? What is the essential difference?"

"Yes, yes. Good question," he replied, meaning, I knew, that he was not going to give me any answer to it.

"Do you approve of the way April and I are 'pruning' Nathaniel in his video game addiction?"

"Children definitely do need some pruning. Watering and fertilizing are not enough."

"Does that mean, Mr. Godachi, that you hold with those who say that good order must be imposed from the top-down, that it cannot be trusted to emerge naturally from the bottom up?"

Mr. Godachi immediately gave out a hearty laugh, so suddenly that I was somewhat startled. Then he came over to me, regarding me with an intense and inquisitive look, brandishing his pruning shears now toward my face, then down toward my fingers. "Let me see," he muttered, as if talking to himself, "just what is it here that needs pruning?" And then I laughed, too. "I can barely tolerate being edited," I said, "but that kind of pruning would definitely go against the grain."

"Against the grain, eh? Maybe you *are* a tree."

We chuckled together, and then he invited me over to a little garden table where somehow, miraculously, a pot of still quite hot Japanese green tea was sitting, along with a couple of those tea cups that have no handles.

"So just what is it in my thinking," I asked after a few minutes, "that needs pruning?"

"Top-down, bottom-up: not a bad dichotomy. It highlights some genuine differences. For example, between your e-mail friends on the one side and our Bible Belt neighbors on the other. Your division of perspective helps illuminate some important differences in the ways they think about goodness, and order. But don't reify your dichotomy. It's not the continental divide."

"Are you saying that one does not have to choose between the two, that there's some kind of integration? I'd like to believe that, but at this point, I just don't see it. Either human nature can be trusted or it can't, it seems to me. Either God handed the Ten Commandments down on Mount Sinai or He didn't. No?"

"Well, let me just give you a little advice on how to proceed with your inquiry. May I?" He looked over for permission, and when I nodded, he continued. "In all your discussions to come, make an effort to bring in the concrete examples, the real-life situations. Abstractions are fine. They're necessary for any good understanding. But they are always in danger of floating off into unreality. Bringing things down to true examples—your Nintendo Dilemma was a fine example of this, by the way—will help you keep your feet on the ground. Then your inquiry will have a good chance of building. Trust reality. There's nothing like it!" And again he was off into his uproarious laughter, and after a hesitating start, I took off too.

"Well, what do you think of the forum discussion as a means for me to sort these things out?" It was when we'd settled back down to sipping our tea that I asked.

"I'm sure it can be quite valuable. I would observe to you that given the way you have described your fundamental question, your present group of interlocutors—although stimulating—are somewhat skewed to one side for your purposes. Of the responses you've described to me, I can't think of one that is not fundamentally bottom-up. It's as though in your search for knowledge, you're taking a variety of bites from the same side of the apple.

"And in addition, you will find that with people from that side of the apple, a crucial kind of moral energy is often lacking. There are exceptions, to be sure, and they are very important resources. But the bottom-up crowd contains a lot of people for whom the questions about how things *should* be, about the gap between the way they are and the way we should work to make them, are just not very alive and vital. Oh, they *care,* but it's often not from the gut. Their caring about whether the wider world is in 'good order' is not so great that it makes it impossible for them to turn away from that challenge if it gets in the way of their own pursuits and their comforts. 'Hey, I know what's happening in Bosnia is terrible, but gee, what can I do? I realize that there are people in my community that could use a home visit, or a Big Brother, or maybe even some food: and I sure hope there's some agency that'll take care of it.'

It's more often the top-down people, folks from the churches, whom you'll find in the soup kitchens, and living among the jungle peoples suffering from dengue fever and yaws.

"I suggest you look into the roots of this. But my main point is that you may need people from the other side to join the conversation if you want it to come alive with the numinous energy it warrants.

"But you've got to go with what you have. What else can you do but use the material at hand? You can't just make something out of nothing. Maybe the missing elements will be developed out of the dynamics of the group in its search and through the process of disputation. But in the meanwhile, I think if you can keep your attention on your purpose, on what it is you are looking for, and then turn to each message to discover what opportunity may lie within it to achieve your purpose, it will be quite worthwhile. Even exciting. Please promise me you'll keep me posted."

Which of course I was happy to do.

Ideas Growing Out of the Soil of Experience

Stick with reality, Godachi had said, and of course it was my sense of some distressing realities that had driven my whole concern with "good order."

"Good order" sounds pretty abstract, but ideas don't come out of nowhere. They grow out of the stuff of life. A fellow like Thomas Hobbes wrote his *Leviathan* more than three centuries ago, talking about such abstractions as anarchy and authority, out of his flesh-and-blood experiences of the bloody chaos of a country riven by civil war. Likewise, my own concern about "good order" grew out of an increasing distress that my own society—America in the late twentieth century—was in danger of devolving into disorder, was indeed perhaps already in the process.

My tribe—the children of the counterculture—had not worried much about disorder. Our worry had been on the other side of the cultural divide, with tyranny, with rigidity, with repression of what is natural and alive. Order was something we took for granted. It was also part of the banner of those on the 'law-and-order' right wing who would seek to preserve their privilege and power, and to impose upon those who still possessed vitality the same kinds of psychic wounds by which they themselves had been disabled. Order, as we saw it, was part of a power trip.

But a quarter of a century had gone by since we'd waved our own banners of "Make Love Not War"—a bumper sticker that, as a text, might be read as calling for obedience to sacred natural impulse over misguided hierarchical commands. In that quarter century a lot had happened, not all of it good. Some of our countercultural revolution had succeeded, and some of it had failed. No surprise in that. But what was surprising to me, as I paid attention to the daily realities in the world around me, was that even our successes did not always look like good news. More and more I sensed that my countercultural tribe, which, like all the others, had thought our vision of things offered a solution to the ills of the world, had become in many respects just another part of the problem. I watched as many of the ideas that seemed so "liberating" in the '60s seemed to bear fruit in the form of a contribution to the unraveling of the moral order.

In response to that perception, already several years before this "Good Order" forum got started, I began to work toward new thinking, to develop new understanding to address the problems that were just becoming visible to me. My inquiry took me along three tracks.

The Dance of Polarization

On one track, I tried to address the problem of the polarized and strident nature of America's current public discourse. We did not seem to know how to talk with each other. And it seemed to me that neither side of our intensifying "culture war" had as much of the truth as its adherents thought, that our polarization was a challenge to us to seek some higher truth that somehow integrated the seemingly contradictory insights of the counterculturalists and the traditionalists. (Thus Godachi's suggestion that I prune out too dichotomous a view of the issues fell on already fertile soil.)

On this theme, I wrote and published (in the *Baltimore Sun*, April 30, 1996, and the *San Francisco Chronicle*, September 28, 1995) a piece called "The Dance of Polarization, and the Next Step Beyond." Here's how it went.

For those of us who feel ourselves to be participants in America's present culture war, it is difficult to understand the conflict other than as a battle between an "Us" who are right and a "Them" who are wrong. Whether the issue is law and order, the expressions of human sexuality, the balance between rights and responsibilities, or any of today's other charged and divisive issues, we see ourselves as embodying wisdom and virtue and our opponents as misguided and possibly even evil.

This view of our cultural polarization leads naturally to a view of how the conflict should be resolved: by the victory of our side in the arenas of persuasion and political power. On the right, for example, Pat Buchanan has used military images of fighting house by house, street by street, to "take our culture back." Progressives on the left are calling for mobilization to block the advancing forces of the Christian Coalition.

For the combatants, the culture war is about division. But let's look at the polarized sides as components of a cultural whole and inquire how polarization occurs in human systems and what a better alternative might be.

Polarization is something we can see happening constantly in human relationships, on scales large and small. I have observed some relatively benign examples in my own life.

When I drive with my mother—who can envision accidents occurring at every turn—she voices the need for caution to a degree I regard as extreme. In response, an impulse arises in me to drive less carefully than I usually do. In the presence of what I see as my mother's over-cautiousness, I have to work to maintain my more typical prudence. This dynamic leads to a division of labor concerning the polarity of caution and daring.

Something analogous happens between me and my 18-year-old son. To my mind, he procrastinates too much; I lean on him to take care of business more promptly and reliably. His tendency toward procrastination may have developed in reaction to my tighter relationship with my inner Taskmaster. But whatever its origin, when I am in his presence, I tend to become even more like myself than usual: my taking-care-of-business muscles get tighter than even I am comfortable with.

You have probably noticed how married couples can polarize in various ways—between the slob and the compulsive straightener, the spendthrift and the miser, the one who does all the feeling and the one who is always rational and controlled, etc.

When people divide on an issue, unless they find a resolution, they tend to push each other further out toward the opposite ends of the spectrum. Each end represents a value that is legitimate, but that also must be balanced against another value. Polarization is one way the system preserves balance, but it is an unstable and conflictual balance. Far better if the actors in the system, instead of dividing into mirror-image opposites of one another, could achieve the healthier balance of integration.

But such integration is difficult. It represents that high human achievement: **wisdom**. In the absence of wisdom, people are compelled to struggle in their folly.

Each side, wedded to its half-truth, sees the other as the problem. But the problem is a property of the system: the polarization and conflict are symptoms of the failure to find a way to bring together those values that are in tension.

The polarization of our culture around a variety of "hot-button" issues—such as whether or not to prohibit the burning of the American flag, to stigmatize the birth of children to unmarried women, to teach the canon of the Western tradition, to execute criminals, to accept homosexuality, to allow religion into our public institutions—represents a failure to integrate a deeper polarity that has always been at the heart of the American experiment. On the one hand, we cherish the value of the free flowering of the human spirit; on the other hand, we also honor the value of a coherent social order.

The present battle between the defenders of the traditional social order and the advocates of more countercultural values is a message to us of a challenge yet unmet by our present civilization: to find an integration at a higher level of human wisdom than either side of that war has yet attained.

The idea that "the truth lies between the extremes" would be the cliché it appears to be if it meant only the need for a mechanical compromise, a splitting of the difference. But the real truth lies not between but above the extremes. The great spiritual leaders of humankind—a Buddha or a Jesus or a Gandhi or a St. Francis or a Dalai Lama—are people who have integrated values that seem to be in tension into a form that is not just a compromise on a lowest common denominator. At their level of integration, one might be at once freer than the libertines and more disciplined than the straightlaced. One might be both a better warrior than the hawks and a better peacemaker than the doves.

The best resolution of our culture war is not to be found through our present mode of conflict. Neither is it to be found in mere centrist political compromise. The real challenge is for both sides to work together toward an integration at that higher level where opposites no longer seem so irrevocably opposed, where the expressions of our liberty and the requirements of our civilized order achieve a fuller harmony.

No easy task. But the more quickly we can move out of our stance as partisan combatants into a position from which we can see how we are in this dance of polarization together, the sooner we can get to the real work.

The question raised in my mind by the Nintendo Dilemma seemed to point toward part of the heart of our polarized cultural visions: the question of whether human nature can be trusted or how much it needs to be combated.

Deeply embedded in the development of civilization, I have thought since I first had the vision that bore fruit as my first book, *The Parable of the Tribes: The Problem of Power in Social Evolution,* has been a fundamental distrust of—and distaste for—human nature. Original sin. The idea of the flesh as corrupt and corrupting. Goodness as somehow a disembodied force that reigns—or should reign—from some spiritual realm above, and removed from, the material plane on which our natural and living bodies move about. Like St. Paul's saying he is at war with "the law of sin which is in my members."

And, thus, much of civilization grew up as a structure to wage that war, creating cages to keep the wild animal from expressing its inherent destructiveness of good order. How is a person to be made to conform to the good? Keep him in his cage, whip him when he strays. If four strokes of the whip don't rectify his rebelliousness, try five. Fence the creature in with a wall of "Thou shalt nots," and make sure that he gets the message that his natural inclinations are misguided, perhaps even evil.

Living as I do in Virginia, on the fringes of the Bible Belt, I know well how strong remains this fundamental cultural thrust. In the schools hereabouts, the young students are kept regimented—little kindergartners are not seen in the halls except in straight lines closely monitored. It is an educational environment that rewards coloring between the lines, not self-expression or originality of thought. The traditional culture's apotheosis of discipline reaches its apogee a little south of here at the state's famous military institute, where the newcomers are subject to a torrent of abuse and of arbitrary demands from anyone above them in the hierarchy. Cultivated there are obedience and self-control, the distinguishing characteristics of those whose crude human ore has been refined and tempered into "a few good men."

But on the other side of the cultural divide is the onrushing current of liberalization, which over time has come to reveal dangers that had previously escaped my notice. Dangers of self-indulgence and softness, of a decline of standards of morality and achievement, of a disintegration of the larger social body. We had worked to sow the seeds of true freedom, of celebration of our natural humanity, of a social order liberated of the taints of coercion and conformity. But as was said of old, "By their fruits shall ye know them." And I began to wonder, How much of the cultural ugliness and distress now around us is the fruit of our own beliefs? What do we think of the nature of the pornographic imagination, now that it has been loosed to market itself without restraint? What do we think of the breakout from the cages of conventional family life, now that we see the waves of illegitimacy and of inadequately raised children? What do we think of the breakdown of discipline in political parties, now that we see how easily demagoguery and opportunism, rather than an informed popular will, can fill the vacuum thus created?

If both the right and the left have defective visions, therefore, it would seem that some greater humility and openness in discussion is called for, that both sides might benefit from a conversation more about learning than winning. Maybe with this group on the Internet, and beginning with a core question like the Nintendo Dilemma with its focus on the nature of the human beast, such a conversation could be initiated.

Time for Us to Listen

If the strident quarrels between those who would war upon our nature and those who would indulge our every impulse made me eager to seek ways of fostering a more constructive conversation, the discovery of the inadequacy of the countercultural vision of "If it feels good, do it" made me eager to embark on the second aspect of my evolving inquiry: to challenge myself, and members of my countercultural tribe, to rethink our ideological assumptions about how the world works.

I myself found it invigorating, as well as at times distressing, to turn the old slogan of "Question Authority" upon myself, and question the authority of my own established beliefs. But invigorating or not, it seemed to me to need doing.

Along these lines, I wrote and published (in the *Christian Science Monitor*, April 1, 1994) a piece called "A Time for Us to Listen." It read thus:

This is a message to members of my generation who helped launch the progressive movement called the counterculture 25 years ago:

Have you noticed the moral energy these days is on the cultural right? The most impassioned social analyses are not from those trying to create a new society, but from those trying to restore traditional values.

This is not how it was when we formed our political attitudes. Confronted by a society in need of self-examination, we in the counterculture had something to say. We managed with our fervor to change the terms of cultural discussion and some of the directions of America's development.

Racism and sexism didn't disappear; but they ceased to be acceptable notions. A self-congratulatory historical self-image was made to incorporate a darker side, as we disinterred the hearts at Wounded Knee and exposed lies and crimes in the White House, the CIA, and the FBI—institutions that were supposed to safeguard our democracy.

Much of what we had to say needed to be heard, to correct what had gone wrong.

The situation today is different. Now in many arenas, it is the very forces we helped unleash, taken to extremes, that threaten the health of our country.

These excesses have spurred conservatives to do something they seemed incapable of a generation ago: think with clarity and depth about American society, and argue for values that make sense and serve real human needs. Not all their arguments are reactionary "backlash." To gain a more balanced vision of a better society, progressives must listen. . . .

• We were right that judgments of right and wrong are often heavily tainted with prejudice. But that doesn't mean that judgments of right and wrong are wholly relative. It is one thing to acknowledge that the American way of life is not the only way; it is different to say that Auschwitz was acceptable because it was a matter of Nazi values. Our culture may have needed shaking; but moral relativism may dash it to pieces.

William Kilpatrick makes a good case, in *Why Johnny Can't Tell Right from Wrong,* that the effort to bring a more tolerant moral vision into American classrooms has fostered the idea that morality is purely subjective, like one's taste in ice cream flavor. This has helped create a morally confused generation of youth.

• We were right that society stigmatized differences and enforced conformity in unjustifiable ways. But such stigmatization should not be replaced with the idea that all differences are to be celebrated equally.

A child should not be made to feel less worthy if he or she comes from a "broken home." But there is no point in denying that the increasing number of single-parent households is bad news. Barbara Defoe Whitehead and James Q. Wilson make a good case that America has seen an erosion of "family values," and that this abandonment of traditional understanding has helped set the stage for some of the frightening violence now being played out in the schools and on the streets.

The list goes on: A much-needed movement to increase the respect women are afforded and the power they wield has led to the denigration of men and the virtues they have traditionally embodied. Some of these virtues we have depended on for our survival in a dangerous world.

Appropriate critiques of Western civilization have turned into a demonization of our cultural roots, as if profound flaws are not found in all human cultures. And an appreciation of cultural diversity has wrought a disregard for the importance of a shared core culture to hold us together.

It is not surprising that efforts to correct the deficiencies of the established order failed to produce a pure social wisdom. That is not the way human affairs work. Instead, one extreme view gives rise to another; the pendulum swings. Encountering conservative values in a toxic form, many of us found it difficult to discern how those values, cleansed of their contaminants, are essential to a healthy society.

No one side of our cultural dispute has a monopoly on truth. The challenge is to find ways of integrating various truths. How will we do so?

On the right—where immutable truths are supposed to be handed down—admitting errors is regarded as a sign of weakness. That world view, with its virtue of steadfastness, has the defect of making self-correction difficult. Those who believe that the answers to life's questions must be found through honest exploration can see the admission of errors as a strength.

It may be up to progressives, therefore, to lead the way out of a polarized moral discourse. To heal our cultural rift, we can begin listening to the impassioned critiques of our excesses.

My posing of my Nintendo Dilemma—especially with a group like this, with a heavy representation of "New-Agey" thinking—seemed a good way to delve into an absolutely crucial part of our ideological foundation: our benign assumptions about human nature. If the human being is by nature wise and good, then our traditional cultural apparatus of restriction and constriction is worse than superfluous. On such assumptions about our inborn nature, much of what our moralities and polities do in the name of goodness appears instead to be the root of evil.

In its extreme form, this view appears in the form of anarchism: forms of governance that the conservative apostles of order see as indispensable to keeping what Shakespeare called the universal wolf from holding sway are themselves seen, in the anarchistic vision, as the predators upon the innocent human flock they tyrannize. But one need not travel in that direction all the way to the anarchistic extreme to see the same basic ideological structure. On closer inspection, a great deal of what is most distinctive about our modern culture, growing out of the Enlightenment, incorporates some of these optimistic assessments of human nature, and with it some of the same deep antagonism toward structures of power and the institutions of social control, whether they be in the realms of moral beliefs, religious dogmas, legal regulation, or political power.

The liberal mind bristles at the enforced conformity of prayer in the schools. The conservative's patriotism of "My country right or wrong" seems the antithesis of genuine duty, a fruit of the manipulation of the sacred individual into cannon fodder. The unthinking adherence to traditional ways—"If it was good enough for my daddy, it's good enough for me!"—seems to those who abhor all tyrannies over the mind of man a denial of the crown of our humanity: the capacity for autonomous judgment.

With its democratic polity, its scientific approach to knowledge, its individualism, the culture of liberalism has sought to create a different, more open, less restrictive approach to human life. But at what point does the liberty of separate individuals add up to chaos in the society? What is required for free thinking to be consistent with a culture's capacity to render human life in meaningful terms? Is there a way to combine a respect for the sanctity of human desires with a process of oversight by moral judgment so that the idea of the "good life" does not devolve into an unprincipled lust for pleasure?

Much of our cultural tension, it has seemed to me, revolves around the question of whether, and to what extent, this historic experiment in liberty, this more open approach should supplant the older traditions of tighter control.

A challenge to my own benign assumptions about human nature, I therefore concluded, could provide a good tunnel into the larger cultural confusion about how human affairs should be governed. The Nintendo Dilemma presented such a challenge and, as you will see in the chapters to come, did open the way into exploring such pressing contemporary issues.

Historical Currents

After I had embarked upon the process of challenging myself and my own presuppositions on moral and cultural issues, I expanded my exploration by leading conversations on talk radio about the controversial issues of the day. It was through trying to get to the core of these disputes with people of very diverse ways of thinking that I began to discern that underlying all the many little disagreements was one central, but rarely articulated, dispute. This dispute is about what I called earlier "the sources of good order."

The questions underlying today's cultural confusions about order and freedom are big ones. What does it mean to be a free human being? Can free human beings live together in peace and harmony, or will they eventually break apart like the builders of the Tower of Babel? Will a society of free people, unfolding over the generations, lead to an elevation of its humanity, or will they expend the moral capital of their preliberal traditions and lapse into moral bankruptcy? To what extent, if any, must people be subject to an external authority that can, by coercive means or otherwise, constrain them from acting according to their wills and desires?

The tension between liberty and order has been there from the outset of the American experiment. We in the 1960s counterculture, I came to see, were players in a long-running drama about this tension. One of the blindspots in our understanding of our cultural roles, in fact, was a failure to see how profoundly embedded we were in a larger historical process. Seeing ourselves as the vanguards of liberation, we thought that erupting around us and through us was a whole new vision of human possibility. But more than we recognized, our movement could be seen as an extension of that liberal tradition which had begun before America and which had helped to bring our country into existence.

We spoke about "doing our own thing" and "letting it all hang out," but in the larger sweep of history, these ideas were part of our own distinctive political and cultural heritage. "Life, liberty, and the pursuit of happiness" is a phrase that preceded the Free Speech movement in Berkeley. The idea of the autonomous individual, in possession of rights to create his own way of life and to fill his mind with his own beliefs, untrammeled by any authority above him, was likewise a part of a long-running historical current that had borne us baby-boomers onto the shores of the brave new world of the Age of Aquarius. What I now believe is that we were a vanguard of liberty at a time when the tide of liberalization was at a crest.

This deep connection, for the most part unseen by my countercultural tribe, between our ideas and the historic currents of American civilization meant that by rethinking the counterculture—by working through the gaps and contradictions and fallacies in our understanding of how goodness and order relate—we might help illuminate the challenge faced by the much larger project of American civilization: the challenge of reconciling the values of order and liberty.

My intention in paying the value of order its due has not been not to abandon the dream of liberty, but rather to salvage it. Liberty may be something with which we were endowed by our Creator, but I have come to believe that bringing it forth into a healthy and viable form is not a birthright, but a difficult achievement. When Fourth of July speakers talk of the price each generation must be prepared to pay to secure our liberties, they seem to have in mind the risk of shedding our blood on battlefields against foreign enemies. But these days, the task I see before us to secure those liberties is to fight a philosophical battle against our own glib and shallow understanding of precisely what they require.

Signs of Disorder

It was, then, to explore such questions of order, and of the possible limits to the proper scope of liberty, that I had initiated the conversation on the Nintendo Dilemma. And now, on the dirt road leading from Mr. Godachi's back to my place, I was thinking about how, as he had said, I might create something out of the stuff at hand, how I might find in the responses provided by my e-mail buddies a way toward the exploration and understanding of those problematic social realities. I worked to conjure up in my mind an image—as clear and as grounded in the concrete as I could—just where our culture was most seriously struggling with the problem of good order, an image I figured I should bear in mind as I composed my responses to the e-mail messages I'd received a few hours before.

I could think of three main arenas in which signs of disorder call into question some of the ideology of the countercultural liberal outlook.

(1) One of these arenas concerns how we rear our children. So many children seem to be growing up without an adequate moral compass, without a sense of discipline or responsibility, without a sense of purpose to help supply meaning to their lives. Even if this observation is correct, admittedly, an ideology of excessive liberty would not be the only contributor. For example, some parents just don't have, or choose to give, their children the time they need. Work in the marketplace seems to be absorbing an ever-increasing proportion of adults' attention. At the same time, a lot of marriages break up, and a good many never occurred in the first place. But for all that, my intuition told me that the ideological dimension—what people believe that children need—was important enough to be worth exploring.

Now, I wondered, what would be a good concrete example of the possibly "disordering" role of "liberal" beliefs? I recalled a discussion I'd had with a soccer coach.

He was a nice fellow, always full of encouragement for his players. We were talking about how we should conceive the purpose of soccer for the seven- and eight-year-olds in the league where he coached and where Nathaniel played. He was speaking disparagingly of that macho and authoritarian approach to sports in which winning isn't the most important thing, it's the only thing. Then he went on to say that all that matters is that the kids should have fun, that they should feel good about themselves out there and come back for more. I said that all sounded good, but I wasn't sure it was the whole thing. Then he told me a little story from his experience.

"I was coaching this team and there was a girl, maybe eight, positioned over near the sidelines, and the ball starts coming her way. Now, she was standing real close to her family, and they were yelling like crazy, 'Here it comes, Lucy' or whatever her name was. 'Now's your chance.' And the ball's heading straight for her, and Lucy sees it. Then, just before the ball gets there, Lucy spies this flower—a dandelion it was—and she stoops over to pluck the thing and exclaims, 'A dandelion!' And the ball whizzes by her and out of bounds!"

His voice seemed to be saying, "Was that kid cute, or what!" "Yeah . . . ?" I said to him, not yet getting his point. And then I asked: "So how'd you deal with her?"

"The point is, that was just where she was at that point in her development. She was into dandelions. I didn't hassle her. When she's ready to skip the dandelion and kick the ball, I figured, she'll do it. But I wasn't going to chew her out and make her feel bad."

I said to the coach, "Well, if I were her coach, I wouldn't want to make her feel bad, but I would want to convey to her in some effective way that there's a time for dandelions and then there's one hour a week when it's her job to take care of business on the soccer field." I spoke mildly, but in my mind I'm jumping up and down and shouting, "Hey, this kid's part of a team. She owes something to her teammates. She's got a job to do. It may not be about 'winning,' but sports are about something that goes beyond just having fun and doing whatever one feels like on the whim of the moment. An eight-year old is old enough to take on some responsibility."

(2) In addition to child-rearing issues, I have thought I discerned a more general problem in our society about standards and ideals. These are ideas that people hold *above* themselves to measure themselves by, hoping they can rise to meet them. Essential to such standards and ideals is the idea that some ways of being and doing are *better* than others. Standards (at least collective versions of them) are eroded by such notions as "Everything and everyone is equal," and "Each person and only that person knows what is best for him or her," and therefore, "No one is entitled to pass judgment on the choices of anyone else." Ideals are undermined by the idea that all desires and all pleasures are of equal worth. Such notions gained a strong footing in the counterculture but, again, their roots go much further back—for example, to the "utility" of the economists of the market ideology, and to Bentham's utilitarian "greatest good for the greatest number." Such relativism seemed to offer a way out of the opinionated and narrow-minded conventionality of the uptight and self-righteous guardians of the One True Way. But now, after more than a generation, this view of morality seems to be draining the moral core out of our civilization, the way a spider leaves its prey stuck in its web looking intact but really reduced to a dry and brittle exoskeleton.

A concrete example? Maybe the world of our celebrities and entertainments offers some of the most striking illustrations. When I was growing up, there was a wide difference between fame and notoriety. Now the two seem converged. If you get caught up in some scandal, like Gordon Liddy or Oliver North, you become a hero to a lot of people, and you get your own radio show, too. For at least a part of our culture, the crucial difference has become that between being a Somebody and being a Nobody.

Our movies represent an important part of our collective imagination, and the mirror they hold up to us is not a pretty one. Perhaps all societies have images like those of Hannibal Lechter, the monstrous criminal in *Silence of the Lambs,* and the various other barbarities of films like *Seven,* and *Natural Born Killers,* and dozens of others. But our society seems to have succumbed to wallowing in them, to holding them up for such continuous scrutiny that it becomes a form of celebration. Our lust for

sex and violence in the crudest and most graphic terms is routinely gratified, as if whatever pleasure we might get from such sensationalism must
be equal to any other we might get from a thoughtful film like *Wild Straw-
berries*. "'Higher' pleasure? Oh, please: don't you know that nothing is
higher than anything else. In the land of equality, we have leveled all."

(3) A third area that came to me was more strictly political: our democracy seems troubled.

What a wonderful idea it is: government with the consent of the governed. "Power to the people!" was a vision born long before our '60s'
protests. Our cultural ancestors knocked the crowns off the kings who'd
claimed a divine right to rule, and those democratic revolutionaries in
whose debt we stand placed a piece of it on the heads of every citizen.
It may have taken until recent generations to extend more fully the "sovereignty" of the people to all—regardless of gender, or race, or property—but the logic has worked its way, creating the opportunity for real
bottom-up governance: "of the people, for the people, by the people."

However—setting aside our failure as a people to reclaim our democracy from the depredations of private wealth—how wise and how good
is this sovereign? When the "voice of the people" speaks, does it help
create good order in the body politic? I worry.

That same lack of discipline that might lead or allow a girl to pluck a
dandelion when she should be handling—or footling—a soccer ball also
seemed for years to allow the American people to tell their leaders that
they want the budget deficit closed, and they want their taxes reduced,
and they want all their government programs preserved. When a political
leader tried to speak sense to them, he was roundly punished.

"Sacrifice" is a word that leads to the sacrificial offering of him who
speaks it. And then the people complain about the scoundrels they've
elected: they break promises, they don't speak plainly, they don't solve
our problems. As if anyone who did would win at the political contest,
a contest in which the winner is he who best persuades the people that
he offers what they want, even if their wants represent an insoluble set
of simultaneous equations.

How much is this dysfunction of democracy a reflection of the indulgent culture of hedonism, the one that tells us that "You can have it
all!"? How much is the burden of debt we are leaving to our children

and grandchildren a manifestation of a culture of unbridled desire, one which believes in the sovereignty of gratification, that has bought into the individualistic focus in which "You only go around once, so you gotta grab all the gusto you can" constitutes a kind of creed?

My heart still belongs to the idea of liberty. But it seems to me that the idea of liberty as we find it now coursing through our culture has become a rather primitive one. It's in need of a closer look. "The human being who is free"—but from what and to do what? Is there a structure of governance within the sovereign and autonomous individual to replace the external governance—the traditional hierarchies of dominance—that has been dismantled? Can we thrive in liberty with no work on achieving proper order, and if not, what does that proper order require of us?

If the open society does not provide the means to hold the precious fluids of meaning and security, it has seemed to me, people will flee from openness and cling blindly to whatever will give them the moorings they need.

I see signs of this in a recent development that that has astonished me: how in these days the backward forces of creationism seem to be advancing. As a boy, I thought it amazing that the Scopes Trial could have been so recent as to be within my parents' lifetime; and now, seven decades after that famous trial, the Tennessee legislature is again trying to buttress the image of God's made-to-order world against that of the gradual unfolding of life's adventurous experiment. Even as the mountain of evidence piles up through the free inquiry of science, I see to my astonishment that antievolutionary arguments are appearing even in intellectual journals.

I think of Churchill's remark that "the lights are going out all over Europe," and I know that there are some lights from the Enlightenment that I cannot bear to imagine going out. The free-thinkers of the Enlightenment may not have seen everything, but at least they had their eyes open.

As I come down my driveway, and stoop by one of my flowerbeds to do some weeding, I realize where it is that I get my sense of urgency about these questions of good order. If we of the liberal culture fail to meet the challenge—philosophical and emotional and political—of maintaining a good order that preserves liberty, the choice may ultimately be between the chaos of anarchy and the rigid and authoritarian structures favored by traditional conservatives. Having watched places like Lebanon in the 1980s and Somalia in the 1990s, I am far from convinced that when the choice is between tyranny and anarchy, it is the latter that is to be preferred. But while we still have enough "archy" to retrieve and rebuild good order, I think we have some serious work to do to make sure that we and our descendants do not face that dismal choice.

Let's Mix It Up

When I returned home after reviewing these dimensions of my concerns, I sat down to read once again the several responses I had received from my forum-mates to my query about the Nintendo Dilemma, and to think about how I might answer them in order to lead the conversation the next step forward in the directions I wanted to go. I found that, in my absence, Rev. George had posted another message, apparently after reading the substantive rejoinders of the other members.

Subject: More to Be Said

Hey, gang. This is great! Such a diversity of ideas. At the same time, I hope you recognize that all your responses attempt, in their different ways, to rescue the fundamental premise: that goodness just naturally comes out of us human beings, that all you've got to do is water and fertilize and presto! you've got humanity making things right. Evolution's put it all in the seed, and so it all springs spontaneously up from the ground.

Well, there *is* another point of view on this business. And I think we'll benefit from having it represented here in our discussions. Oh, I know, you think that with me in here you've got the right wing covered, since I'll use words like "sin," and "divine forgiveness," and such. But believe me, even if one Daniel in the den with you liberal lions would be enough, I'd not be he. So I am going to exercise the prerogative we all agreed upon at the founding of this group—the one where each of us founding members can invite anyone else to join in if we think that they would find our issues of interest and that their participation would enrich the discussion.

As said John the Baptist, he that cometh after me is mightier than I. Well, maybe "mightier" is not the issue. At least deader-set against your heathen notions. (Don't worry, I'll stick to the more civilized among my more orthodox compadres.) By this means, I'll rescue you from your rescue mission. After all, you won't have a very complete discussion if you're all biting from the same side of the apple. **Rev. George**

I almost choked when I read that "same side of the apple" image. It was precisely the same one Godachi had used in our conversation a short while before! How could that be? Were they in communication? Seemed impossible. I'd never mentioned either to the other, certainly not by name. And George lives on the other coast, in Oregon. But that image—different bites from the same side of the apple—seemed an unlikely one, not so strongly dictated by the context that one would expect it to emerge independently from different minds, not like the calculus wafting in the Zeitgeist and germinating simultaneously in the soils of the minds of both Newton and Leibniz. I pondered the puzzle awhile, felt completely bewildered—and then I turned away from the inexplicable, dismissing it, to go on with the pursuit of my purposes.

Spinning a Few Threads

Checking In on Business

Before I could boot up my computer and get to work on responding to the first batch of messages, the phone rang. It was my agent, Lila Davenport, returning my call. I was eager to tell Lila about the book idea I'd started working on. Before the California conference, the idea had not yet fully taken hold of me, so I'd kept it to myself: why should Lila have to witness my fits and starts? But now the book was in my blood. I didn't know just what it would look like, but I knew that at the core of my new inquiry was a question with which I was determined to grapple until I'd learned what I could.

I gave Lila the basic outlines of what I had in mind, and I summed it up: "I think there's a really basic confusion in our culture right now on the question of morality. As a people, we're uncertain how to think about right and wrong; we seem beset by half-baked ideas concerning how to make ourselves and our world the way we and it should be. There's something quite fundamental here that, as a culture, we are really misunderstanding. And this misunderstanding is hurting us, demoralizing society (literally); our confusion is leading many souls to become lost; it's sapping our cultural health. I feel certain I can do something in this book that will at least help us get clearer, get more grounded and more whole in our moral understanding."

I said it with a lot of passion, and I was hoping Lila would share my excitement.

"Well, Andy, I'm sure you'll have a lot to say. I'll be happy to take it to the market for you." I didn't hear the kind of excitement I'd heard from her about my previous book, which she had served so well that she earned a place in my pantheon of exceptional professionals.

"You've got reservations?" I asked.

"No, you go ahead and do it if that's what you're clear you want to do." Lila paused, then added, " I just think it will be a hard sell."

"Why? What's the problem with it?"

"The subject—it's kind of *philosophical*. I'm not sure the editors up here will go for something so reflective, so much about how we *think* about things."

"Goodness isn't something we just *think* about. I mean, we've got real *feelings* about right and wrong, too. But how's this any different from *Living Posthumously*? That book is pretty philosophical, too."

I was referring to my previous book, which, while beginning with my own experience with a chronic illness, dealt with how we think and feel about the discovery that we will not be able to keep our vital powers forever. Lila had always been very enthusiastic about *Living Posthumously,* and believed the book would find a wide readership. "Yes, but you see, that book really *spoke to me*," Lila tried to explain. "It speaks to a lot of people."

"Yeah, but what's the difference between that book and this one?"

"Andy, that book talked to me about my *mortality*. That's very close to home. It felt very meaningful to walk through your reflections on that one. But this idea—about good order, about how we go about making the world as it should be—that's kind of interesting, but it's remote. It doesn't hit me where I *live* like my mortality, or like whether I'm sick or healthy."

"Remote." I paused to think a little about this. "But it *is* close to home. The subject bears upon the whole question of how we live our lives. And I'd say our confusions about morality are matters of life and death, or sickness and health. Our confusions on this question *are* killing people, are leading to real pathologies in the lives of millions."

"How's that?" Lila asked.

"Look at all the ways our society suffers from people not doing the right thing. The rate of murders, the packs of sociopathic kids, the millions of babies being born without families or communities to give them what they need, the multiplying rates of teen suicide, the degeneration of our politics into spin and manipulation and scandal-mongering . . . I mean, the list could go on and on."

"Yes, Andy, but it still feels remote. None of those lives you say are being destroyed are mine, or my family's, or anyone's I'm likely to be close to. I care about those people, those problems you're talking about. But I don't have a whole lot of time to think about them, or what they have to do with me, and I'm just afraid that the editors I deal with will feel that way, too. I mean, these are very busy people, and they've got this stack of manuscripts to get through, and they've got to ask what's alive enough here that it's going to sell. They've got to be asking, 'What are the readers out there going to shell out hard cash for?'

"But, Andy, if you'll do up the proposal, I'll give it my best shot. You know that."

"Yes, I know. Well, thanks. I'll get a proposal together as soon as I see the shape of it."

We hung up, and I turned my attention from the business of selling ideas in a world run by what grabs editors, or rather, what the editors think will grab their readers, back to the task of finding which ideas would help lead us out of the wilderness I believed us to be in.

Back Out from My Court

I felt challenged and gratified by the diversity of responses I'd received. I wasn't sure whether any of them offered me a satisfactory way out of the immediate dilemma I'd presented, that is, the question of whether I needed to modify my old ideological leanings in the face of my experience of parenthood. That question remained open in my mind. But what these various messages undeniably did do was to open a variety of avenues into some of the important questions I was eager for our group to grapple with. So I sat down to compose a few responses that might help move these conversations forward.

Subject: Who's to Judge?

Fred, you wrote: "Oh, I know you are his father, but what right does that give you to put your trip on him." Gosh, I didn't think of it as a right, but more as a responsibility. Actually, I didn't conceive of it as putting my trip on him; I saw it more as safeguarding his development to make sure it comes out all right.

You ask what's the difference between my imposing on my son my beliefs about what's right, and the Christian Coalition's imposing its beliefs on society. Doubtless, there's a lot to be said on this topic. But just for starters I would say that it's widely thought that an adult's moral standing is rather different from that of a child. Adults are held responsible for their own actions in a way that children are not. And adults are considered, in a society like ours, more capable of making their own reasoned judgments about what the good life is, and how they want to go about leading their own. Children, in this view, are in need of adult guidance—most appropriately, parental guidance—in coming to understand what they need and what is required of them. I'm not ready to endorse in its entirety that distinction between children and adults, but I do think there's enough to it to justify my imposing some of my judgments, in some ways, on my child.

Now, if your point is that the judgment of a parent—about what the child needs and how it should develop—is fallible, of course I will agree. Parents have done some terrible things to their children "for their own good," to paraphrase Alice Miller's title for her book about systematically abusive pedagogy. But I don't think we have any choice except to raise our children using the very best judgment we can achieve.

Of course, if one could be certain of the validity of your assessment that human nature unfettered will blossom into perfection, then we would have an alternative. (I wonder, upon witnessing your apparent certainty, if you've raised any children.) I do not share that certainty, however, and I would rather risk imposing on my child my faulty judgment than abdicate my responsibility to provide the guidance my child may need. **Andy**

Subject: Is Goodness Something We Just Make Up?
You raise a rather fundamental question, John. And it's probably one that's useful to confront at the outset of our discussions. If we're going to try to explore the sources of "good" order (as I've proposed we do) or, as where we all first met, a "better" future, it certainly makes sense to ascertain whether we're talking about anything "real" or if it is all just so much invention, or delusion, or whatever you are suggesting that it is.

I'm willing to concede that goodness is not objectively "real" in the same way that the sun is. It doesn't rise in the morning and set in the evening, nor bend planets into orbit around it or cause heliotropic plants to sway following its course. But the fact that it is not a thing to be found in the cosmos does not necessarily mean that it is not real.

You say that it is just our personal preference. Does that mean you think that our attaching of good and evil to certain phenomena is wholly arbitrary? merely idiosyncratic? If so, what do you make of the tremendous—not complete, certainly, but nonetheless substantial—agreement that exists about good and evil? And I don't just mean between individuals within the same cultural stream (one would expect all believing Christians working from the same texts to have substantial agreement), but even among extremely diverse and independent cultures.

If there were not some **Reality** to which all these peoples were responding, would you not expect to find greater randomness of moral beliefs than the historical and anthropological record reveals? The compassion taught by Buddha and the Golden Rule taught by Jesus—and the adoption of those teachings by whole peoples over millennia—seem to me strong evidence that morality is something more deeply grounded in the nature of things than your account allows. **Andy**

Subject: On the Idea That People Do Bad Things Only if Bad Things Were Done to Them in Their Formation
You write, Eleanor, that "It's the kid who has been abused who will be abusive of others." I am imagining this to be a shorthand way of saying that you believe that a person will grow up to be a good person unless the world treats him or her badly.

The question arises, if you are correct about that, does this understanding have any bearing on how we deal with people who do terrible things in the world? Is every torturer and murderer automatically entitled to the "abuse excuse"? **Andy**

Subject: Will Our Children Challenge Themselves to Be All That They Can Be?
I'd like to send two responses, Cynthia, to your posting, as in my mind it raises two different questions.

Your account of your daughter and the *Goosebump* books I found quite interesting. Not least because *Goosebump* books represent another domain, in addition to Nintendo, where April and I have wrestled with the question of allowing versus interfering in Nathaniel's choices. And yeah, it's not irrelevant that all the other kids are reading them. Same with that abysmal TV show, *Scooby Doo*. (Has your daughter gotten into that?)

But for this first proposed thread, I'd like to challenge the adequacy of your explanation. Or, rather, to stay within the confines of my experience, I'd like to say that the explanation you propose for your daughter does not seem sufficient to settle my mind about my son.

Nathaniel's being drawn to these things seems to go beyond what is required for participation in his peer group. Some people follow the football world so that when guys at work say, "Hey, whaddyathink of those Redskins?" they can join in the conversation. But Nat could play a great deal less of Mario Brothers than he has and still be entirely able to connect with his fellow vidiots.

In addition, this particular kid—according to his teachers—shows a remarkable sense of knowing his own mind, and being willing to go his own way even when the other kids go theirs. He likes soccer better than kickball, for example, and so for several months, even when his friends went off to play kickball during recess, he'd practice his soccer (sometimes joined by a couple of other kids, sometimes just on his own). If he were willing to do this while actually with his peer group, I cannot explain his playing video games, or watching *Scooby Doo,* etc., **in the privacy of his own house,** just in terms of social membership.

What it looks like to me is a kind of laziness. I hate to say it, partly because I can't explain it, but his choices somehow seem to be the easy choices. What I can't explain is: **why doesn't he challenge himself to do the things that would make him grow?**

Scooby Doo is pure formula. If you've seen one, you've seen them all. Like already-chewed food. Something on the Discovery Channel would more likely be something you could really sink your teeth into. Same with *Goosebump* versus some real literature (for children, of course) like the *Little House* series: one goes down without any work and gives little nourishment; the other requires some chewing and digesting, but helps build strong minds twelve ways.

I don't get it. He seems healthy and vigorous in both mind and body, but also seems not to challenge himself, not to choose to stretch to develop his capacities. So, if you'll grant me that he's not damaged, what I observe seems to challenge my assumption that our appetite for life and for self-actualization will naturally lead us to challenge ourselves to be all that we can be.

What do you think: Is there anything wrong with this assumption? What is the meaning of this laziness? **Andy**

Subject: Should We Not Challenge Our Children to Strive Toward an Ideal?
Next, Cynthia, I'd like to raise a question based on the premise that you are right that your daughter's reading of mediocre books was motivated by the more worthy purpose of fitting into her peer group.

I can see how that would reassure you. And I can see how you might respect and accept her choice more than you otherwise would. But I'd like to raise the further question of whether our respect and acceptance of such choices should not still be limited by our having some higher image of how our child should be than the image provided by the consensus of our social environment.

More generally, whenever our child is not realizing what we see as his or her potential—regardless of the reason—should we inculcate a higher ideal toward which we expect that child to strive? If your daughter starts to place too high a value on the clothes she wears and to become too caught up in being voted "most popular," do you accept these standards or do you hold up what you think are higher values of, say, spiritual development or service to others? And if holding them up is not enough, do you go beyond that to require that she at least try out some steps in the direction of living what you see as that higher life? **Andy**

I sent out these messages, wondering how these themes could be fit together, wondering whether I'd managed to ask the right questions, wondering whether my friends out there in the ether would feel that the directions in which we were heading were worthwhile.

Do They Need to Be Pushed, or Will They Jump?

Larry was the first to get back on my first response to Cynthia.

Subject: Will Our Children Challenge Themselves to Be All That They Can Be?
You are probably worried, Andy, that I am offended that my posting was not one of those you chose to honor with a response. Don't. Really, I handle rejection quite well. I'll just use your message to Cynthia to reiterate my evolutionary perspective.

You're afraid your kid is lazy. Plays Nintendo instead of romping around in the woods tracking squirrels. I know that in my previous posting I said that Nintendo was beyond the scope of our evolved apparatus to deal with wisely, and at one level that's true. But at another level, I would suggest, what your kid is really doing *is* romping around the woods tracking squirrels, or is at least an analogue of that.

What would he be doing if he were living in the Stone Age world he was born expecting? He'd be with his pals out practicing his hunting skills, learning his way around in a complex world, forming mental maps in his mind, gathering goodies and bopping real or imaginary prey, and fending off real or imaginary dangers.

Now, take a look—a real look, not one of these parental judgmental looks—at what's going on with him on the video screen. What's he doing? The same damned thing. Have you ever watched a kid play a video game he's experienced at? It's amazing how much they've memorized very detailed and complex arrangements: they know where the coins are buried, they know which routes are cul de sacs and which lead to the next level, they know just what they have to do to get past particular dangers. All this they have learned by romping around in that virtual world.

Where else can a kid in our contemporary world immerse himself in such a complex and challenging set of circumstances? Maybe on the athletic field. Certainly not in our two-dimensional schools.

Kids lazy? I bet as a two year old your son didn't seem lazy. I know mine couldn't get enough of practicing his climbing skills on the sofa. Up and over, again and again.

Our heads would be spinning from the continual repetition of the movements until he had mastery. That, I suggest, is what evolution has crafted as the nature of the beast. And your seven year old with his Nintendo screen is still doing the same thing!
Larry

Then Rev. George weighed in, having written his posting evidently before Larry's had been distributed around.

Subject: Re: "Do Our Children Challenge Themselves to Be All That They Can Be?"
So, your Nathaniel gravitates toward what is easy, and eschews what is difficult. Quoth the parrot in *Aladdin,* "Why am I not surprised?"

Did you think that the Catholic Church named sloth one of the seven deadly sins just to snag a few slugs among us? Sloth is one of our tendencies. It is not always to be found in its most obvious forms: lounging around eating bonbons, say, instead of piling up firewood for the winter. Sloth is a spiritual state, which can as readily be found in the busy and industrious as in the sluggard. (Indeed, for many workaholics, keeping busy is a form of laziness.) It is a state of failing to do what really needs to be done, not attending to the genuine business at hand—which, of course, is God's business, including the business of tending to the state of our own souls.

Laziness is a part of the nature of the human being. I would suggest that it takes some "higher power" to goad the naturally slothful human soul into the kind of work that is most needful. For a seven-year-old boy, who perhaps takes the too-easy path of spending his time on the video games, a good earthly father might serve as such a higher power. **Rev. George**

In this batch, there was another posting. This was from Donna, a woman who attended our California conference, a pleasant person big on what used to be called "good vibes." Her clothing, as I recall, was at once flowing and shapeless, her hair long, and she had a chain around her neck with a crystal the size of my little finger as a pendant.

I just wanted to say that you don't have to worry about your son being "all that he can be." He's just perfect the way he is. Not just your son, Nathaniel, of course, but all of us. The whole universe is just the way it should be right now, and as things change, they are changing just as they should change.

I can't tell you how wonderful is the peace of mind I have enjoyed since I have come to this realization about the cosmic order. I wish I could just give to you that same peace of mind. **Donna**

Even with just words on the screen, I felt that I was back in Donna's palpable presence. I felt that same combination of goodwill toward her along with a difficulty in taking her entirely seriously. This idea that everything is perfect as it is, just as it should be, just did not make much sense to me. Not with all that I know about what happens in the world: the massacres in Rwanda, the rape camps in Bosnia, the starvation in Somalia, and plenty right here in the USA, too, with aimless and sometimes even vicious youth, miserable marriages, untrammeled greed, and the despoliation of the landscape. It doesn't look the least bit perfect to me.

The comforting New Age belief in the cosmos being just as it should be reminds me of the equally comforting article of faith among the more conventionally religious that everything that happens is God's Will. And in neither case do I see any intellectually credible—by which I mean rational and empirical—way of coming to that belief.

All of a Piece

I had no desire to engage Donna on her faith in this being the best of all possible—or conceivable?—worlds, but chose instead to address what Eleanor had written earlier about the moral person's having no ruling part, no colonial ruler, sitting in judgment from above.

I appreciate, Eleanor, your bringing the conversation back to the question of the moral person. It is, indeed, the moral dimension of what is good that interests me most, and I now see that the Nintendo Dilemma, while it is good for raising some basic questions about human nature, does not represent the kind of dilemma that would take us to the heart of the moral dimension. But thanks to you and George, the moral realm has surfaced readily anyway.

You write about your vision of a person who is all of a piece, contrasting that with our usual more hierarchical image of how a moral person operates, with an internal judge. You propose that a truly moral person—one I guess whose formation is not itself a record of some external interventions in the name of a socialization process you regard as immoral in nature—will not be divided against herself.

I love the idea, but I don't see just how it works. A person inevitably has a lot of desires, not all of them consistent with morality. Desires will conflict. The desire to have what one intensely wants will conflict with one's desire to do right, to be loving, to serve justice. Given such inevitable conflicts, I'm not sure what "all of a piece" could mean. But more importantly, if your psychological model rejects the notion of any natural hierarchy within us, I don't see how your natural person will be equipped to cope with such conflicts.

By that I mean, without some capacity that, in a sense, sits "above"—like a judge, if you will—how does a moral person decide which of the conflicting desires should get its way, and which be overruled? To say that a person who lacks such a governing part above will reliably choose morally would seem to be to say that the desire to be moral will reliably be more intense, more powerful, than any conflicting desire. That just doesn't seem plausible to me.

For example, you have proposed that the well-nourished child will grow up to be loving. OK, I can grant that. But what happens when that loving child becomes a grown-up man who finds that he has a powerful loving desire to spend the night in bed with his friend's beautiful and wonderful wife, who is also his friend? And if that desire comes into conflict with his desire to be moral and not commit adultery, can we be sanguine that the desire for the woman will be weaker than the the desire to do what is right? And if not, by what means can this person who is all of a piece move in any direction but toward adultery? **Andy**

Eleanor shot back quickly.

You assume that what you call "adultery" is some kind of a sin. I say it is a label that our patriarchal culture has put in our heads. The man in your question loves this woman, and let's presume she loves him too, and they have a natural desire to express that love with one another. Now here comes patriarchy, with its sense of the woman as a sexual possession, and says, "No, thou shalt not. It's adultery!" It takes more than name-calling to establish that something is wrong. **Eleanor**

To which I responded:

Your characterization of adultery as one of patriarchy's forms of oppression raises, in itself, a good many interesting questions. But I will resist my impulse to pursue them now, following instead the voice of my better judgment that tells me that I should stick to the immediate point at hand. So let me replace my adultery example with one that should not trigger your counter-patriarchical immune response.

Let's say that your well-loved, unrepressed child has grown up to be a loving and all-of-a-piece kind of man. And he finds that his loving energies are strongly drawn to a neighbor girl of, say, fourteen years of age. His desire to woo and caress and bed this young woman—and nature has already crowned her a woman—is opposed by a moral sense that she is too young, too unready, too vulnerable for it to be appropriate for him to follow his very powerful desires for her. How will this all-of-a-piece guy, blessedly lacking in an internalized judge who renders verdicts about which of his desires are worthy and which should be kept in check, manage to do the right thing? **Andy**

Who Are You to Judge?

Andy, I don't question your good intentions with respect to your son, *Fred then wrote*. "But I still find your willingness to impose your views on him rather more like than different from the Christian Coalition's moralizing to the rest of the country about whether a woman has a right to an abortion, about whether homosexuals should be allowed to live unharassed by the heterosexual majority, and so forth.

You cite the difference between children and adults, but that strikes me as a difference more reflective of power allocation than of any fundamental change during the course of the human life cycle. You may recall the famous Magna Carta as a document in the history of the development of liberty: it extended only to the peers of the realm—a rather select group of nobility—some rights in relation to the Crown. The mass of the population was left unprotected, without rights. I'm sure they had some rationalization about how the nobles deserved rights that would be misapplied if extended to the vulgar masses. But the reality is, they got the rights because they had the swords. Eventually, thanks be to the Void, those rights became extended to all men, and now to women also. So now we adults have the vote, and now like the nobles of old we say that **we're** different, and that children should remain under our sway.

I would say that children and adults are alike human beings, alike in having the innate capacity to find and define their own good. Each person is entitled to make of his own life a project to discover **what's right for him**. Each person is a unique expression of the Life Force. For another person to believe that he can judge what is right for someone else is an act of great presumption. Live and let live, I would say, is the most important moral principle.

I think both you and your son would be better off if you let go not only of your ideas about what kind of person he should be, but even of the idea that you should take it upon yourself to have such ideas. **Fred**

This posting from Fred produced a couple of interesting responses before I'd had time to figure out just what I might wish to say in reply to him.

Cathy was an educator who had attended the conference. She'd been a New Age hippie, as I recall, back when a lot of us were in a state of rebellion. But since then she had spent a couple of decades in the trenches teaching high school, and more recently in administration at a teachers college in California. In response to Fred, she wrote:

I feel a little reticent about entering into this discussion because I'm not as intellectual, and certainly not as philosophical, as you fellows. And I'm not sure I'm really equipped to deal with questions like who has got what "right," and just how autonomous each person is or should be in defining what is good and right for him- or herself. But I do have some practical, hands-on experience that seems germane to the question about whether we adults should guide young people or allow them to follow their own path.

Where the rubber hits the road on this issue in my bailiwick is the question of required courses. I remember how I felt about required courses when I was an undergraduate in the late '60s: they seemed like an imposition, an authoritarian slap in the face, or at least an obstacle to my free expression. I resented having to choose one from column A and one from column B, especially since column B might be math and science, which I didn't want to trouble myself about.

I wonder how many of us who went to college back then, or before, know how much things have changed in higher education since our day. The answer is: a lot. It's the kind of changes I would have applauded. Students can create their own programs with an ease that was unimaginable back then. They can practically invent their own curriculum. "Requirements" sounds like a foreign word. Just go and read the college catalogues: all over the place, including at many of the most top-notch schools, the message to the students is, "Come here and tell us what you want and that's what you'll get."

So, we campus radicals got what we wanted. The future we dreamt of is here. And now that I have seen the future, I can report to you: it doesn't work. It really doesn't. Oh, there are a few students who can take the ball of such freedom and run with it. But they are quite the exception. Lord knows just where they got the wherewithal to make the sensible judgments they make. But the great majority of the students can't use the freedom wisely because **they don't know what they don't know!**

How is some kid, coming out of the usual high school, going to know whether her life is going to be enriched if she learns something about the history of civilization? Nothing in high school has given her an idea of what that will be like. How is someone who wants to enter a profession or some other field of work going to know what areas of knowledge are pertinent? He has never worked in that profession.

When wagon trains came West across the prairies, they hired scouts to guide them, fellows who'd been through that way many times before and could tell them where the water holes were and where hostile tribes might be confronted. Without the scouts, the folks from back East would have been in pretty dire straits. It seems to me that we adults have to act like those scouts for the generation coming up behind us, or a great many of them will leave their bones bleaching in the sun. **Cathy**

The other response to Fred came from an unexpected direction.

Hello. My name is Carl, and I was encouraged by George Thomasson to join your group. I've been reading all your postings with considerable interest, and I hope you won't mind if I join in your discussion. Though I wasn't there with you folks "at the creation" and, as you will see, my convictions are rather different from yours, the questions you are discussing are of a kind that I've been thinking about for years, and I'd like to participate.

I am a biblical Christian, and I am concerned that liberal ideas about human autonomy are gaining such a profound hold on people's notions these days that as a society we're all stumbling out into the wilderness. You see, to my understanding this notion of the autonomy of the individual is founded on a fundamental illusion.

Well, doubtless there will be time to get into some of that later. In the immediate context, let me say that with Fred I have one basic agreement, and one basic disagreement. Where I agree is with Fred's assertion that between children and adults there is, morally speaking, a basic similarity that the usual liberal distinction between minors and majors doesn't recognize. Where I disagree is that whereas he sees people of all ages as being able to find their own way, to decide "what's right for them," to determine their own life-plan wisely, I say that none of us is able to do that for ourselves.

To me, to be human is to be fundamentally incapable of finding one's way on one's own. It is to rely on the grace of God for guidance, and on God's word for instruction.

I would ask any of you who believe in the liberal idea of each person—as an autonomous being embarked on a "life project"—just what is it that you believe that adults possess that would enable them to discover the good on their own and to enlist their will—entirely by their own powers—to walk upon that self-discovered good path? I am challenging you because I disagree, but I also would really like to know how you come to believe what seems to me so clearly and profoundly false. **Carl Stoessel**

Is Anything Really Good?

John responded to the message in which I'd suggested that Jesus and Buddha—and the cultural currents that had flowed out of their teachings—taught rather kindred moral visions, using that as a major example of what I'd said was the general tendency of consensus among humankind about the good.

You suggest, Andy, *John wrote,* that diverse cultures have arrived independently at rather similar ideas about the good, and that this tendency toward moral universality is evidence that the Good or the Right or the Moral is something "out there" that people are actually in touch with. It's an interesting argument, but I think it fails.

Of course there are areas of agreement among different groups. But just as you point out the universals—none of which is really universal—I can point out profound differences. Diametric opposition. In one moral vision, the good man turns the other cheek when struck. But in another, such turning of the cheek would bring terrible shame; in that context, the worthy course of action is the defense of one's honor.

Which one is right? Is there any possible basis on which one could persuade the other that his view was wrong? And if not—and I think the answer to that second question is indubitably no—then I challenge whether you can establish any meaningful answer to the first question. In other words, whatever answer you come up with—whichever side you choose—will only say to me that it better corresponds with *your* subjective viewpoint, not that one is more valid than any other.

Differences among moral visions are at least as striking as their overlaps. One society inculcates a belief in impersonal ethics, in principles that are applied justly to all parties, like Justice with her blindfold. In another society—such as heroic Greece— the path of virtue is to grab all you can for yourself and your group, and to disregard or actively tear down the welfare of those outside your circle.

What **can** either of these visions be but a social construction, an idea imposed on a valueless objective reality by a group of people we call a culture who have constructed such a notion to live their lives by? We construct the idea of the "good" the same way that we make up words. But then when we speak with others whose mother tongue is ours, we can begin to actually believe that "stone" or "tree" is what the object is, rather than just being an arbitrary sound. Like those religious mystics who play games with the words or letters of Hebrew or Sanskrit, as if the arbitrary signs of a human language were somehow a map, drawn up by God, showing the way through the mysteries of the cosmos.

The good, therefore, is not something real or fixed that we can meaningfully see ourselves as trying to grasp, or understand, or achieve. It is, rather, something arbitrary that we can speak of together only because—or only if—we have agreed to impose such an image on our reality. **John**

I wrote back:

I don't want to downplay the reality of the profound intercultural moral differences you point out. But I am still not willing to take the leap you propose from the fact of difference to the assertion of the arbitrariness and basically illusory nature of the

Good. It still seems to me that there are all kinds of evidence requiring us to recognize that there's something beyond the differences, beyond the opinions and beliefs. (A stone can be called a "stone" or a "Stein" or a "pierre," but despite all those different and arbitrary labels, there is still such a thing as a stone.)

Let me leap over the idea of universal content, which evidently did not impress you as much as I hoped it would, and call attention to the universality of the notion of morality per se. I hope you will grant that wherever one looks among the hundreds of known human cultures, one will not find any functioning social group without **some** notion of the good, of virtue, of there being a difference between the right way and the wrong way of conducting oneself. That being the case, does that not in itself suggest to you that there is something in the **essential nature** of human life that needs morality? And does that in turn not suggest that all these different moralities are engaged in serving a purpose that is not arbitrary but is inherent in what it is to be a human being? **Andy**

And John replied:

It doesn't seem to me that you've adequately dealt with my challenge that all people's ideas about the good are arbitrary constructions. You can say, probably correctly, that wherever there is traffic there are rules to govern it. But tell me, is it right to drive on the right side of the road as we do in America, or is it right to drive on the left side of the road, like the British? I think the question is meaningless, for the determination is arbitrary. **John**

To which I said:

If this were chess, John, and I were a gentleman, I would ask you if you wanted to take that move back. But as it is not, and I am not, and as—once you click your "Send" button—you have taken your hand off your piece, I will consider the move made, and will now move to take your piece. (I make no claim that it is checkmate, mind you.)

Of course it is arbitrary whether we drive on the right or the left, but in both Britain and America the traffic is regulated to achieve a nonarbitrary good, which is the orderliness of the traffic and therefore the safety of the people and their efficiency in achieving their destinations. This is the Good that transcends the differences.

With moralities, of course, the many kinds of traffic that need to be regulated are infinitely more complex, and the room for arbitrariness is correspondingly more vast. But I think the same kind of underlying, nonarbitrary purpose obtains. There is a fundamental human Good to be achieved: the good of making human social life possible, of allowing people to find meaning and fulfillment, of keeping order within society, of perpetuating the culture from generation to generation. In short, the good of meeting human needs over time.

A variety of strategies may be employed to achieve these purposes. Not all these strategies are necessarily equally effective. And not all the components of the good are in full harmony with each other. But for all those failures and difficulties, it seems to me that the fundamental reality of the Good that morality serves is clear. **Andy**

For Whose Good?

Then came a challenge from a slightly different direction. The writer was a woman named Maria, with whom I'd become acquainted only slightly at the conference. My recollection was that her work involved helping people become spiritually freer in some way.

Andy, I am concerned, like Fred, with your apparent willingness to impose on your child a bunch of "shoulds," but my concern is not so comprehensive as his. I want to build on a differentiation you already made between teachings directed at what your child needs to find his own fulfillment and teachings of a moral nature that seek to manipulate the child into being willing, for the sake of Gaia-knows-what, to sacrifice what he wants for himself.

In my view, a parent's "shoulds" should be confined only to the first sort. Go ahead, teach the kid ways of being that will help him achieve his purposes. These include such obvious things as "You should not play in the street" (after all, he'll not achieve any of his goals if he's flattened by a truck) and "You should get a good night's sleep" (a young child may lack the wisdom to understand the trade-off between the good time he'll have tonight, and the lousy feeling he'll have all day tomorrow). And these child-serving "shoulds" can include making a child learn various forms of discipline. For example, if a child deeply wants to become a basketball player, but then wants to quit going to practice because the coach looked at him cross-eyed, I'd be willing to compel him to keep going, imposing on him my understanding that the momentary obstacle should not weigh so greatly against his long-term goal.

But when it comes to telling a kid to do what he should in ways that are not for her own sake, I say No. I would not tell my child she "should" kiss her Aunt Sophie because Aunt Sophie expects it, or that she should become a doctor and go to Africa because people are suffering there, or that she should tithe her earnings to charity.

I agree with Fred in rejecting this kind of imposition of one's own trips on children. They have a right to pursue their own paths, to find happiness in whatever way seems right to them. **Maria**

I dashed off a quickie.

Maria, I'd just like to know, if your five-year-old daughter were finding happiness by jumping up and down in your lap, would you tell her she should cut it out?

And she replied:

Yes, I would. I left out that I do think that adults are entitled to define their own boundaries and their own individual needs. In such cases, all I'd say is that it should be made clear and explicit that these limits, these shoulds, are being imposed for the sake of the parents. And that they should not be presented as if they were for the sake of the child's proper development ("It'll be good for you to grow up to be a considerate person"), or that they represented some cosmic moral imperative ("You should honor your father and mother").

Let me make it clear what I am opposed to. It is the whole approach to people that has traditionally been so deeply established in this civilization in which people are taught to think of themselves as the means to achieving ends that do not serve them. My vision of "a better future for America," is of a society where people are not manipulated to sacrifice themselves for so-called larger or higher purposes. **Maria**

Before I had a chance to think through just how I might respond to Maria's position, a posting from Karen came through. Karen was practicing clinical psychologist who had been a speaker at the conference. Her talk had been entitled "Visualizing the Human Potential," and as I recall, she really seemed to be a person who walked her talk. Her role in our conversations always seemed a positive one, encouraging people to say more fully and from a deeper place whatever it was they were venturing to present to us.

Karen wrote:

I really resonate, Maria, with your remarks about "shoulds." The respect you are expressing for the individual person's own purposes informs everything that I try to do in my work as a therapist.

When someone comes to me, I try to find out what he wants to achieve by working with me. What's going on in his life? What does *he* want to change, or simply to examine? What are *his* goals? And then I try to help the person achieve the purposes that grow out of his own needs and desires.

In doing this work, I believe that I am fostering what **should** happen at some deep level. I don't see myself as being just some amoral hired gun, like a lawyer who will hire out to anyone to achieve just any purpose. As I see it, the purposes that come from inside the person are not just any purposes, but they are the right purposes for that person. The purpose I am speaking of is self-actualization.

And my role is not entirely neutral: what I bring into the situation is a positive value on awareness and on free choice. So many people are just on automatic pilot— unaware, programmed from long ago to see things and do things in certain ways, not even seeing that they might have other choices. What they are, in other words, is not really their own true selves. By fostering that missing consciousness, I help the people I work with choose a path that really belongs to them, really serves what *they* want out of life. And that, I think, is how it "should" be. **Karen**

Karen's description of her role as an unjudging midwife to other people's self-actualization, in combination with Maria's opposition to the idea that a person should ever regard herself as a "means to achieving ends that do not serve" herself personally, helped crystallize some questions in my mind. The idea of self-actualization had always seemed to me a positive and important one. At the same time, it was not entirely clear to me how it fit into the larger scheme of things. So I quickly composed a message to raise that question.

Let us imagine a world where everyone follows only his own inner voice, the voice of his own desires—whether they be seen as frivolous or wise or whatever. I am wondering: what will a world composed of such people be like? How well will they fit together? How well will they be able to communicate together? How well will they be able to work together to do all the things that need doing for a healthy society?

Does good order require people to subordinate, in any way, their own individuality? Is self-actualization an adequate purpose for individual development, if we also care about the analogous realization of the good potential of the social whole that these individuals comprise together? And finally, how much can the self-actualization of the individual be understood separately from the question of how well-ordered is the larger social world around them? **Andy**

When I logged on to send that message, another response to Maria arrived from Ralph, a professor of history who had attended our conference. I'd enjoyed meeting him, and in fact he and I had spent a stimulating hour together climbing some cliffs near the beach one afternoon. Our discussion that day, as I recall, was of a study he'd done on the rhetoric Lincoln had used from the time he'd first become unalterably opposed to slavery through the end of the Civil War. I felt drawn to him because, even though he was in some respects cut from rather different cultural cloth from me (he wore a bow tie to the banquet the first night!), I sensed that—unlike some who were cut from the tie-dyed fabric of my tribe—Ralph was a guy whose promise you could put in the bank.

Ralph wrote:

I find it remarkable, as I read some of these messages, just how profound is the apparent repugnance toward the whole idea of morality on the part of a number of the people on this forum. To me, it is virtually inexplicable. I'm trying to imagine just what could lead people whom I know, from having met you in the flesh, to be good and decent people to have such an aversion to something so necessary as basic morality.

The image that has come to my mind is of my own experience of developing a hatred of cottage cheese. Cottage cheese was something I liked, but one night I came down with a serious flu shortly after I'd eaten a bowl of the stuff. The flu made me nauseated, and I'll spare you the details. Suffice it to say that my experience of the return trip of the cottage cheese left me with a visceral feeling of repulsion at the very thought of eating it, even though it has been thirty-five years since that traumatic night. So I find myself wondering: did someone stuff morality down your throats so that you gagged on it?

Anyway, I myself would not like to contemplate a future of America in which everyone thought that self-sacrifice was a form of pathology, and that the individual's pursuit of his own fulfillment was the be-all and end-all of human existence. I'm reminded of a speech given by the Gregory Peck character in an old World War II movie, *Twelve O'Clock High*. He's addressing a group of young American flyers who are under his command at a base in England, and he says something like: "I expect there are some of you out there who think that your hide should not be risked up there because it is just too special." And then he proceeds to disabuse them of that notion.

It's a tough thing, and it doesn't fit into the self-centered notions fostered in us these days that the universe is here for our own amusement and pleasure. But if there were no people prepared to hold something—like their country, and like the welfare of their families, and the rights of their descendants to life, liberty, and the pursuit of happiness—there would be no America. We would not be on-line here together freely expressing our visions of a better future.

The burden that fell on young men like those depicted in *Twelve O'Clock High*, the majority of whom in real life never survived to come back to the land of the free and the home of the brave, is an extreme instance of a rather general dimension of our lives as members of things larger than ourselves. I'm sorry, but there are "larger" purposes, and "higher" ones too, than seeking only what fulfills our own desires or even what serves our own purposes. All kinds of questions arise in the course of our lives as individuals and as a society that require us to consider obligations that may conflict with the comfort of our own hides.

Does a parent leave his kids for long hours at day care so that the progress of a career will not be delayed? Does an adult inconvenience herself to take care of an aged parent? Do elderly citizens vote to support a school bond, even though their own children are grown and they will never benefit directly from what their tax money buys? Do we as a people willingly cut back on our consumption of fossil fuels, because there's a good chance that otherwise, after we're dead, the climate of the planet might be disastrously altered?

If we don't teach our kids the importance of "shoulds" that don't pay off on their own bottom-lines, what kind of world do you think all our children will inherit—or create? **Ralph**

Another message then popped in.

All you people are being seduced by Satan. You will all rost [*sic*] in hell.

It was unsigned, and the return e-mail address (slbaum@morph.net) seemed to indicate a name wholly unfamiliar to me.

The Power of Ideas

Before I left the computer to go up to meet Nathaniel's returning school bus, I noticed that there was another message from Ralph. It had the subject line "Too far out," and when I opened it, I saw that the message had not been sent via the forum, but was a back-channel communication only to me.

Dear Andy, *Ralph wrote,* I'm somewhat disturbed by some of the views being put forward, and I'm asking myself whether they are worth the trouble of engaging. What I'm referring to are these notions I'd call extreme, questioning whether goodness is real, proposing that all morality is relative, talking about bringing up kids as if parents neither have nor should exercise authority. What a crock!

I'm wondering: how many people really believe this crap? If I think about the people I know—and I'd say that, at this level, I must know several hundred at least—I can't think of anyone who thinks it's not **really** wrong to torture people. Have you ever seen parents who'd never tell their children that they **should** do something just because it's the right thing to do? I haven't. So if our friends here on Inquiry represent some kind of philosophical fringe, it then occurs to me to inquire of myself, why should I spend my time and energy dealing with them and their ideas—ideas which I, for one, have trouble taking seriously.

Come to think of it, it's hard for me to believe that even these guys really believe what they're saying. I remember what a nice bunch of people they are. If moral beliefs are so arbitrary, how come these guys just arbitrarily happen to choose to live by moral beliefs pretty much in line with the Golden Rule? (This argument I just put forward runs parallel with your Jesus-and-Buddha consensus point, only this version of it strikes perhaps still more tellingly.) So if even the proponents of this relativist/constructionist/whatever view of morality are just playing with these ideas, why should people like us bother to engage them?

Hope you don't mind my turning to you with my distress. Of the people here, you're the only one who I feel confident hears a drum enough like the one I'm marching to that he'll understand why I think this St. Vitus dance our friends are doing represents—like St. Vitus's dance of old—a form of pathology in the central nervous system. **Ralph**

In response to this, when I returned with Nat from the school bus stop, I wrote back to Ralph, also of course back-channel:

Dear Ralph, No I don't mind in the least your turning to me, and in fact I very much appreciated not only the substance of your inquiry but also your reminding me that this back-channel mode of contact is available to us. I can imagine that given all the diversity we'll have in this group—did you notice that some of George's friends are entering this discussion?—there will be times when the needs of diplomacy will make a wise person hesitate to go public until he's had a chance to exercise considered judgment on how it might best be done. And deliberating together with people we feel understood by is a good way to work toward such judgment. So, better you should tell me you think they're full of crap than just blurt it out on our public forum!

Though I'm not as certain as you seem to be that some of these views are so vacuous that we can just dismiss them, like you I find disturbing this treatment of right and wrong, of good and evil, as less than wholly real. Then there's the question you raise about whether ***anyone really believes these notions,*** and if not whether those ideas are worth our bothering ourselves about.

That's a question that plugs into some serious thinking I've done in other contexts about "the power of ideas," including ideas that are perhaps held less than completely, or with less than complete seriousness. My answer, in a word is, "yes": it is important for us to take these ideas seriously, whether one believes (as I do) that they may point toward some bigger truth, and thus be worth exploring, or whether one thinks they are a complete crock.

The key to this answer is located in the question, "What do we mean when we ask if someone *really believes* something?" The answer to that question, I would suggest, is rarely a simple yes or no.

Think of the propaganda campaign from the tobacco industry over the last three decades directed at the mass of the American people who make up their potential customers. At one level, we can say that **everybody has long known** that tobacco is a serious threat to a smoker's health. That was pretty clear, I think, even before the Surgeon General's report. After that report came out, one would think, knowledge of tobacco's deadly effects became inescapable. The warnings on the cigarette packs repeat the message, and meanwhile new research is continually being reported on the news showing all the ways cigarettes can kill you. Anyone who is not a moron "knows" tobacco is bad stuff.

But if that's the case, what sense would it make for the tobacco industry to employ their glib and good-looking spokespeople to promulgate all their pseudo-science? Why would they spend good money to put forward the idea that no such link has been established between smoking and one disease or another, to declare there to be substantial doubt where the unbiased scientific community finds none? If people "really know" the contrary, then there's no room for them to "really believe" what the industry is saying. Which would mean that this blowing of smoke by the tobacco industry is just a waste of its time and money.

But whatever else the tobacco moguls are, they're not foolish about their money. And it is safe to assume that they've known what they are doing by sowing these doubts. What those doubts do is coexist in the same minds as the knowledge the doubts are intended to undermine. The same minds are entertaining contradictory notions. And the doubts, we can assume, influence behavior: the tobacco companies can get a pay-off only if there are a lot of people who start smoking, or who fail to quit, who would do otherwise in the absence of the industry's multimillion dollar campaign.

So do people "really believe" that it is not yet established that smoking can kill you? No, I expect they know better. But also, yes, enough that the space occupied by the ideas they pick up from the Tobacco Institute can make the difference between smoking and not smoking. Even "unserious" ideas can be powerful, can be determinative at the margins.

That's why I think that even *extreme* ideas that are propounded by only a small philosophical minority can be important in the functioning of a society and are therefore important to be addressed. If we went around asking people questions like "Are some things really right and wrong?" or "Are good and evil simply arbitrary inventions?" or "Should parents exert authority to shape their children into being good people?" I imagine you're right about what we'd find. There'd be no large number of people who would proclaim positions like some of those we've been hearing in our forum, calling into question some of the most fundamental notions about morality and authority. But that doesn't mean those ideas don't also exist in their minds, and that they don't exert an important influence.

As with tobacco, the moral ideas a person doesn't "really believe" probably have their impact at the margins. When a tough decision is hanging in the balance—a guy is seriously tempted to commit adultery, say, or some woman is thinking of stuffing a stack of her employer's cash into her purse—just having that voice echoing someplace in one's mind saying "Nothing is **really** right or wrong" can make the difference. If the space for that idea didn't exist, the person might simply say, "No, I can't do that, it would be wrong." But fringe ideas running around in a society can open up new possibilities—sometimes for better, of course, but sometimes also for worse.

So I wouldn't dismiss these "extreme" and "fringe" notions as insignificant, but rather I see them as purified and undiluted versions of ideas that exist in more shadowy form in a lot of people's heads. I hope my sharing these thoughts is helpful to you.
Andy

Funny, when I completed this message to Ralph and hooked up to my server to send it out, the following came into my inbox through the forum.

Hey, let's get real here. Nobody raises their kids how you're describing. Parents are parents, whatever they say they think. From the time our little ones are old enough to get into trouble, we're all telling them "Don't do this, don't do that." If you guys tell me that when they were about two years old, your kids didn't walk around chiming out with "No!" all the time, I won't believe you. And of course, that "No!" was just a delayed echo of the word they'd heard most.

It has always bothered me when I've heard the conservatives beating their drum about "permissive parenting," trying to blame us liberals for everything that has gone wrong. I've always thought it a figment of their uptight imaginations. Now that George has gone out there recruiting his legions of the Bible Belt, I'm afraid you guys are going to lend credibility to the permissiveness myth. **Jeff**

A little while later, Len—a professor of philosophy I'd taken an instant liking to at the conference—posted this in response:

Would that you were right, Jeff. But your challenge compels me to come forth with a mea culpa. I see myself as a perfect example of an entire generation of parents who failed to exert proper authority, who were permissive and who thus failed to establish for their children clear limits.

I figured that this parenting thing should be "natural" and not require anything beyond "going with the flow." My example should suffice, I thought, a little encouragement would do, and so forth. Now, my wife and I must endure the heartache that comes from that failure.

Our children are now 18 and 21. Our daughter (18) had a fairly unhappy junior-high through high-school experience, experimenting too early with everything, not listening to our advice, etc. She all but dropped out in her first year of high school. On my analysis, when she reached the very beginnings of adulthood (13 years), which are difficult enough, especially for girls with their hormonal thing blazing, she was not equipped with a sense of **boundaries** and **limits,** of what is proportionate, etc. My son had much less difficulty, though he is narrowly self-centered and individualistic. He may now be growing out of that a bit through a relationship with his girlfriend.

I've noticed a tendency on the part of both of my children to want to drop out when the going gets tough, or to lose motivation when they have to put out real effort or when they have to forgo immediate pleasures and comfort for the sake of more distant and more noble goals. This of course is somewhat typical of youth, but among our duties as parents is to instill in our children—through practice—the virtues of discipline, patience, and prudence, etc. I think that I failed there and my children have suffered for it, and I suffer to see them that way. I was too worried about being a bad father, overbearing. I had heard too many stories from friends about how horribly totalitarian their fathers were. So, I moved in the other direction a bit too far. It will be interesting to see what kind of parents they will be. **Len**

Interlude

Another Meeting in the Garden

Overwhelmed by Complexity

It was already clear at this point in the conversation that our explorations together were stretching out in many directions. But in the course of the next week, the plethora of threads proliferating from the single germ of the Nintendo Dilemma became truly overwhelming.

Some of the issues were psychological, while others were uncovering essential problems of social order and political governance. Some of the participants approached the inquiry from a naturalistic perspective, while for others the foundation of understanding was laid upon the rock of religious revelation—and not all of them from the same revealed tradition. And to the whole question of the meaning of morality and the status of evaluative statements generally, the disagreements were substantial and highly involved. On all these matters, some people liked to ground the discussion in their own personal experiences, others had their eye to the salient aspects of the contemporary scene (nationally or globally), while still others perceived these issues through the long lens of history, especially (but not only) the history of ideas.

It was a rich stew but, in the form in which it poured in, rather indigestible. As the days went by, and the conversation spun out in a myriad of shining strands of inquiry and insight, like so many dendrites and synapses in a neonatal communal brain, it became clear to me that merely assembling the transcript of our multifaceted discussion would not comprise the meaningful fruit, the coherent vision, that I wanted.

It was while I was pondering this particular challenge that I made my next visit to Godachi. In fact, truth be told, the question I was bringing about pruning apple trees was more the pretext than the actual reason for my dropping over. The real text was the challenge of this text.

The Challenge of Creation

Mr. Godachi and I spent a while up in one of his most mature apple trees, with him demonstrating for me the difference between the good, more obtuse angles and the bad, more acute angles for branching to occur in apple trees—the better to withstand the stresses of weather and of fruitbearing. When this little clinic had concluded, we dismounted. When Mr. Godachi landed after me on the ground beneath that big apple tree, the spry old guy turned to me with a mischievous expression. "Enough of apples," he said. "How goes your search for the knowledge of good and evil?"

I laughed: "Gosh, Mr. Godachi, you certainly have a serpentine way of turning the conversation. Actually, I do have something I wanted to discuss with you."

Mr. Godachi gestured me over to a small stone bench nestled by the side of an arch of wisteria vines, and after we were seated, facing east across the valley towns stretched along the distant and invisible interstate, he motioned for me to continue.

"We're only a few moves into the inquiry on this forum of mine," I recounted, "and already we seem to be all over the map. Start with Nathaniel and his Nintendo, and the conversation takes off in all different directions. Or maybe I should say, the conversations, because already there are several threads that have been established, each one already many-faceted. Each one is interesting, each posting is provocative and stimulating, each question eminently worth pursuing. The brew is as rich as I'd hoped for.

"But there are so many questions, so many seemingly arbitrary twists and turns, how can I get it all to hang together? As you know, I want to use these discussions to create a book that will help people get a clearer view of the fundamental issues we are wrestling with in our moral disputes. I had hoped, I guess, that the book would more or less write itself. The group mind would be so much more than the sum of its parts that it would all come together. But if anything, the centrifugal forces seem—

at least now, at the outset—more powerful than those pulling things toward some center. I feel overwhelmed.

"What do you think," I concluded, "that I can, or should, do?"

"What would be surprising," Mr. Godachi replied, "is if you were surprised at this overwhelming complexity. How could it be otherwise? Think about it. Just what are you asking? You are asking, how does someone become a good person? What is goodness, and what entitles it to be called good? How do justice and good order get established in a society? Right? There's also the relation between the natural and the good, which brings you to confront issues of evolution and the possible relationship of good order to a Creator. What did you expect? That it was going to be simple?"

He reached over and gave me a playful dig in the ribs. I was always surprised, at moments like this, when this seemingly very spiritual being would suddenly get physical with me. "I guess I expected the conversation would simply display some natural kind of integrity," I replied, flicking an acorn in the direction of Mr. Godachi's foot.

"Integrity, yes," he replied, "but on what scale? The earth curves, but if you walk across the land you have no sense you are walking in a circle. You and your steps are too small. Likewise with this huge question you are asking."

"I guess I was hoping that the conversation on the forum would somehow somehow just unfold, relieving me of the burden of putting it all into an intelligible order."

"'Somehow' is right," Mr. Godachi shot back. "Your pious hope in the powers of the group to just spin out clarity reminds me of these people who think that the World Wide Web is going to create instant wisdom for the planet. The mind of Gaia will somehow automatically compose itself by knitting together all these individual neurons we call human beings, with instantaneous firings of e-mail messages through the ether of the Net. Hah!"

"I gather, Mr. Godachi, that you are not so sanguine about the possibilities from all this interconnection?"

"Possibilities. Yes, there are possibilities. But what is going to govern which of those possibilities will come into being? More possibilities are not always better than fewer. Isn't that the lesson of the human story to this point? Wonderful things, yes. But also has there ever been such misery in the world as that which human beings have brought about? Have there ever been such terrible evils as those that have sprung from the great human range of possibilities?

"Well, the Web has great possibilities. But where is the judgment that will separate the beneficial from the malevolent? And from where will come the structure and the forces to assure that it is good judgment that will choose, that from among all the possibilities it is those that will make the world better that will prevail?

"Such quaint faith in the benign powers of self-organization." At this point, Godachi stood up and started wandering over to one of his flower beds, and I followed. He knelt down in front of a stand of phlox that were now in bloom, and started weeding among the stalks.

"That's your problem, too, is it not?" he said when he resumed speaking, his fingers still active upon the surface of the soil. "As an author, you have the power to govern the cosmos as it takes shape beneath your fingers. You'd hoped that you could just set your creatures loose in the garden of the forum and they'd make everything right on their own. But it turns out that you have to exercise your power and put things in order, right?"

"But I'm overwhelmed by the complexity of it all," I lamented.

He smiled at me as he stood up, his fingers caked with the clay of our ridge. It was a warm smile, filled with a paternal benevolence I could really use just then. For me, to feel overwhelmed instead of lucid and on top of things is a rather stressful experience; and a part of the stress is the feeling of failure in my effort to live up to my father's ideals for me. My late father was many things, most of them good—definitely better "late" than never—but one of the foremost of those was this: as a son of the Enlightenment, he manifested great clarity and worked to cultivate it in me. So part of my anxiety, doubtless, at confronting the difficulties of ordering my text clearly—once I saw that my compadres on the forum would not be doing it automatically on their own—was the unconscious sense of my father looking over my shoulder and saying, "Hey kid, this isn't good enough." Which I would interpret at some level as meaning, "You're not good enough." So a benevolent paternal smile from Mr. Godachi was just what this Dr. Schmookler would have ordered, if he'd had the insight and judgment to know what he needed and the power to summon it up from wherever our ancestors go for their eternal sleep, or for their watch over us.

"Making a cosmos of any kind is no easy task." As he spoke next, Mr. Godachi put his hand gently on my shoulder. "Just do what you can. That will be the definition of good enough."

"Thanks," I said, truly moved. "Both for your kindness and your wisdom."

"You are entirely welcome. It is good for me, as well. You give me some contact with a dimension of my own life—the creative spark—that is more quiescent now than it was in my own more youthful, less formed earlier days. And for that, you have my gratitude."

As we passed his rose bushes, Mr. Godachi whipped his pruning sheers seemingly out of nowhere, clipped a long branch with several luxuriant, blood red rose blossoms erupting at its ends, and handed it to me. "For the lady," he said, referring to my wife, April, with whom he had a sweet if slightly inarticulate relationship, full of kind gestures.

I left to go and, just as I got to the gate, I heard his voice again. "Oh, and by the way, Andy, it is OK that you should feel overwhelmed. It is part of what it is to be a human being confronting his reality honestly. If you can come from that honest place, even your failures might be useful for your readers. I think it is good for people to experience just how in over our heads we all are. Useful for little creatures on a speck of dust floating among the galaxies to remember how much their sense of *terra firma* is based more on wish than on reality."*

---

* To repeat the disclaimer artfully hidden on the copyright page, all the characters in the Internet discussion forum herein (with the exception of the author)—and all of the e-mailed messages—are fictional.

I

The Crooked Timber of Our Humanity

From the Ground Up
Does the Well-Ordered Soul Develop Naturally?

Len had posted his soulful lament about his paternal abdication. He had believed, he'd told us, that his children would develop as they should more or less naturally, without requiring the exercise of his paternal authority. And now, he and his wife must taste the bitter fruit, he said, of his failure to provide them with the guidance and discipline they apparently needed.

This led us into a rather challenging discussion of how, if at all, a person should be organized, and how that organization develops. The thread began with Larry posting a response to Len.

Nature Isn't a One-Story Building

Len, I was very moved, *Larry began,* by your repentant story of your being too little of a father—too reluctant to be authoritative—because of your belief that it would all just happen naturally. Some mistakes in life certainly hurt a lot to acknowledge, because once they are made, they can't be unmade. It's like trying to put Humpty Dumpty together again.

Concerning that issue we've been nibbling at, the one about "natural order," it's not self-evident just what your experience teaches us. I, for one, would **not** want the lesson to be interpreted as indicating that what happens "naturally" just wasn't enough. This leads to a thought that I had some impulse, which I resisted for a time, to articulate in answer to Andy's original Nintendo Dilemma. But now that there are two reasons to say it, I'll put it forward: there's more to nature than just individual organisms being born with impulses and either endowed or not endowed with sufficient natural wisdom.

You left something out of your evolutionary model, Andy. For the millions of years that our children have been entering the world, they've not done so in a vacuum. They don't plop down in the midst of nothing, or even grow up with a den of wolves like Kipling's Mowgli. No, they are born with parents, families, groups of people who are older than they, who have been around their particular block before them. And thus part of the natural wisdom that is to guide the child is embodied not in the child himself but in the larger group that naturally will be there to provide the guidance. And part of the child's natural wisdom is to know to look to those older and wiser people for that guidance.

So, I would suggest to you, Len, that as a father you were a part of a natural hierarchy. Your reluctance to play what I would call your natural authoritative role seems, from your report, to have grown out of your having some ideological image of "totalitarian" fathers. You cite your having heard of friends' experiences, but I also wonder what there was in your own experience that made you so susceptible to rejecting the idea and role of paternal authority. But in any event, I see that rejection as not a choice to align with nature but a misunderstanding of the nature of nature. Nature herself does not construct only one-story buildings. **Larry**

Among the responses that followed, one was from Peter, who described himself as moderately conservative in political and cultural terms, as a lawyer and as a friend of a friend of Rev. George, who had evidently appointed himself our "minister to the right."

This fear of totalitarian fathers, *Peter mused after his self-introduction,* what is to be made of it? It seems to be part of the larger phenomenon of the culture-wide assault on patriarchy. Certainly, patriarchy has entailed a great deal of tyranny and brutality. But in America today, it seems that we have less a problem with totalitarian fathers than with those who are absent. By absent fathers I mean not just the many who never marry the mothers and who fail to assume responsibility for their children. Nor even those many who become cut off from their children because of our tragically high rates of divorce, rates much higher than in earlier eras of American history. No, I also mean the fathers so caught up in the demands of their careers, and perhaps so emotionally inaccessible, that the children grow up feeling there was no whole person where their fathers should have been. (Like that old popular song of a couple of decades ago, "Cat's in the Cradle.")

Does that explain the disrepute of authority? Maybe some, but why the fear of too much authority, as if we were still living under the thumb of benign dictators like Clarence Day in *Life with Father* or George Banks in *Mary Poppins?* **Peter**

Meanwhile Len had also replied to Larry's statement that nature does not construct only one-story buildings, and that the authority of the parent is a part of nature:

You're right, Larry, human beings do not begin life floating by themselves in the sea like some fishes' spawn. We're born into families. We're little and our parents are big. We're new and they, as you say, have been around the block (or around the savanna). I can see now how flawed my image was of what it meant to let things happen "naturally" (though my insight into why I fell into that flawed way of seeing things is rather limited).

To introduce some levity into this discussion—and since it is my heartache that's on the table, I guess I'm the one who'll do it if anyone will—let me share a joke that somehow connected in my mind with what you were saying about a parent's exercise of authority being a part of the natural design. One of the great things about this medium is that I can say "Stop me if you've heard this" secure in the knowledge that I'll get to tell the whole joke.

It's the one about a man whose house is being overwhelmed by a flood. As the waters rise he goes onto the roof and perches there. Some neighbors, in the same predicament, come in a rowboat to within shouting distance of our man on the roof and call out offering him a spot in their boat. "No thanks," the man says, "I know the Lord will take care of me." A while later, a sheriff's boat out to rescue stranded people comes motoring up to him and invites him to come with them, but again he declines, expressing confidence that the Lord will provide. Finally, with the waters almost up to the man's waist, and with him clinging to the chimney to keep from being swept away, a helicopter hovers overhead and drops him a ladder. Again he declines, expressing his faith that the Lord is looking after him.

Finally the guy drowns, and goes up to heaven. When he meets God the man complains, "Lord, I thought you'd look after my safety." And God responds, "And who do you think sent you those neighbors, the sheriff, and the helicopter?"

I think I was like that man. I was looking to nature to provide, and somehow always seeing my authority as something that was not from nature. I bet that over the years, my failure to recognize precisely your insight, Larry, led me to override many of my own "natural" feelings about guiding and correcting my children. **Len**

Larry's thoughts, together with those rejoinders, got me wondering along lines akin to Peter's questions. Why *is* it that so many people in America these days are so skeptical about the very idea of authority, so inclined *automatically* to equate authority with abusive authority? And why have the social worlds of a great many young people (much more than seems to have been the case with earlier generations) become so caught up in their horizontal relations—in the culture, say, of their junior high school peers—rather than with their vertical relations, with parents and teachers?

If the other kids think something is "cool"—in music, or literature, or in attitudes toward school—then surely it must be so. If the adults have a high regard for the value of something—like manners, or diligence—it makes little impression. It was not always thus, was it, I wondered? At least not to this extent.

If Larry is right that the human being is born to look to its elders for guidance, I wondered, what does it mean that these days one finds neither the elders much inclined to fill the role nor the children much moved to look to their elders for wisdom about how things should be?

While I was musing thus about fathers, and about Peter's reference to some Victorian figures in the popular imagination, I tried to think of examples of powerful and positive paternal role models, of elder men who serve as mentors, from the images of our present-day popular culture. Have there *been* any fathers? Did Forrest Gump have one? I couldn't remember one. The only father I can remember from the *Dead Poets Society* drove his teenage son to kill himself.

Only two positive male mentors from the past couple decades of movies readily came to my mind: Obi Wan Kanobe (and, later, Yoda), the Jedi teachers to Luke Skywalker in the *Star Wars Trilogy,* and Mr. Moragi, the Okinawan karate-and-life teacher to Daniel in the *Karate Kid* trilogy. In each case, the boy has grown up apparently with no father, and the mentor is a figure from a culture entirely alien from the boy's own, introducing him to a spiritual tradition foreign to his upbringing.

Hardly the image of the continuity of tradition that my rural Virginia neighbors have in their conservative minds.

Higher Faculties

The exchange between Larry and Len about the natural authority of fathers brought forward this message from Herman, an older member of our group, part of whose training had been in psychoanalysis.

I find Larry's comment about "natural hierarchies" most interesting. One implication of his point, I think it can be shown logically, is that the development of the individual psyche also must **naturally** entail the construction of a second floor, as it were. The psychoanalytic concept of the **superego,** as many of you no doubt know, incorporates the notion of a **parental introject.** In other words, it is a voice that originally belonged to an actual parent, another person existing independently outside the boundaries of the self. As the child's psyche evolves, that parental figure gets incorporated—with or without significant distortions—within the psyche itself. It ceases to be "out there" and becomes instead a part of the psyche—Freud called it the superego—one that is perched, we might say, in a position above, from which to judge and evaluate the person's thoughts and feelings and actions.

At first glance, the emergence of the superego as a parental introject seems like an "unnatural" development for the psyche, an imposition of an alien spirit onto a creature with its own inborn nature. It resembles the image of a hostile occupying force that Eleanor employed. (Indeed, Freud himself used a similar image.)

If, however, we adopt Larry's insight into the natural hierarchy of the parental role, then this second story assumes a more natural, more benign countenance. For if the parental authority is understood as part of the natural wisdom that evolution has provided for the growing organism, then the subsequent introjection of that authority is likewise natural. The psyche is built from parental contributions in stages: one stage is genetic, being made before birth; the other is cultural, being transmitted during the child-rearing process. It is like the way the tiny marsupial nursling in the pouch has in some respects already been born but is also in some meaningful way still part of the mother's body—almost, but not quite, the way his not-yet-born placental cousin would also be at that stage.

The boundaries of the self are more fluid in nature than our too-individualistic ideological conception would have it.

I think of an image from Lewis Thomas's *Lives of a Cell* about ants: he sees them not so much as separate creatures but rather as components of a superorganism, stupid by themselves but rather smart when the bits of wits are woven together into the single larger ant-society. Our individualistic perspective, I fear, tends to blind us to such naturally occurring larger wholes. **Herman**

Herman's proposal for a natural hierarchy in the psyche, with the parental introject as the governing authority, evoked a response from a man named Kenneth, whom George confirmed to me via back-channel was one of his colleagues, a minister from one of the more conservative denominations, as well as a part-time teacher on ethics and society in a seminary in Oklahoma.

It is difficult for me to know how and whether to enter this conversation, *Kenneth wrote,* coming as I do from a very different understanding of the world from that of almost everyone who has posted here thus far. Most of you evidently see us human beings as phenomena embedded in, or at most growing out of, a naturalistic system shaped by impersonal mechanisms. You see us in a continuum with the primal ooze, and with ant societies, all comprised of matter and energy that has congealed, as you see it, by chance, into life. It is a view according to which we emerge out of what is below us, and as for what may be above us—about that you say nothing. (That old phrase comes to my mind, from the philosopher Protagoras, when ancient Greek civilization was starting its slide into disintegration: "Man is the measure of all things.") In your map of the cosmos, we are on top of this mundane dungheap—a dungheap with no purpose of its own—and find nothing whatever above us to which we might look for guidance, or bow down in obedience.

Yet for me—and for more people than you could ever find to join you in a conversation based on your naturalistic terms—that which is above us is absolutely key to all the questions of our lives. It is from Him that all order comes, and all purpose, and all definition of what is or is not good for us.

Believing the gulf between your mechanistic universe and my God-centered cosmos too great to be bridged, I have held my peace as you have groped for a way to understand how authority might fit into such things as raising children, and the ordering of the soul. Now, I find in Herman's comments a small link upon which I can seize to speak a bit of my truth to you, perhaps for my own sake—in bearing witness—as much as from any thought that it will avail anything for your sakes.

What I would like to say is that this natural space in the developing human soul—the one Herman suggests is provided for the "introjection" of an image of the parent—might be understood in a different way (a difference that, I believe, makes all the difference). Namely, it is not for some primate parent that we are born ready to make room in our hearts and souls in order to know the good, and to walk the path of righteousness. That space is there, rather, for the Holy Spirit which was there from before a human creature ever walked this earth. It is when we allow that space within us to be filled as it was meant to be filled that we become aligned with the good order that gives our lives meaning, and that makes us the instrument of God's good purpose.
Kenneth

Eleanor had also sent a quick response to Herman's proposal of the natural hierarchy of the mind, with the introjected superego sitting at the top.

I expect that the Hierarchy Party will come out on top here, as it generally does. But I will not join, and I want at least to bear witness in favor of the wholeness of the organism itself, without the intrusion of introjects to keep order where some kind of chaos would supposedly otherwise reign. I do not believe there is any such chaos in the natural creature itself. No need for a ruler to keep the disorderly natives in check. This parental introject is about guilt, and the condition of guilt is not a natural state but the sign of a sick creature. Like one of these Irish boys one meets in Irish literature plagued with guilt that he's been selfish and a disgrace because he masturbated.

Give the kid love, the way the mother kangaroo keeps the nursling warm and nourished, and it will naturally grow up to be orderly. (Do you imagine that the marsupial must somehow "internalize" the pouch to become a functioning creature on its own?) I do not see why the natural wholeness of the organism should be shattered by a second-story construction of any kind. **Eleanor**

Then a fellow named Victor, apparently recruited by Fred, posted something under the heading "Graffiti for the Moment." It read:

Rousseau said that the words "obey" and "command" should be banned from the child's vocabulary.

To which a fellow who did not sign his message said,

Isn't it typical of these great left-wing liberators like Rousseau that in order to spare the child the burden of the responsibility to obey, he is willing to tell everyone else just what words should be banned, for being "pedagogically incorrect," from use in homes all across the land. With liberators like these, who needs tyrants?

When I read that, I realized there *were* indeed some paradoxes here I'd not fully recognized. I'd thought of left-right as mapping fairly well onto a spectrum of bottom-up and top-down. But then there's the way the "right," in our country at least, is most vociferous in opposing "Big Government," and the left constructs the bureaucratic state. What accounted for this paradox, I wondered?

Very soon, several other messages appeared in quick succession. First, Ralph responded to Eleanor's recent posting opposing the "Hierarchy Party's" assumption that, within the psyche of the child, the unruly natives needed to be held in check.

Eleanor, your rejection of the second story is consistent with your earlier assertion that we are or should be "all of a piece." But you haven't met the challenge Andy posed to you last time around concerning how different desires are to be sorted out, how the psyche is to function without some kind of executive, as it were, to adjudicate among different factions in the body politic. Where's the voice going to come from to tell the lustful, natural kid he shouldn't just jump the girl across the street or, if that's not his style, just sweet-talk her into the bushes?

I'm wondering: in your psychology, does the word "temptation" have any meaning?
Ralph

Foundations and Superstructure

The backlash against the hierarchical vision continued with the next posting, a message from Frank. Frank was a therapist whose practice combined deep energetic work on the body with attention to emotional release. At the California conference, he had given a talk titled "Freeing the Life Force," and there were clear echoes of that talk in his present message.

It is sad, but not surprising, *Frank wrote,* that even among a comparatively liberated and humane group of people such as this, the image of good mental health is infested with images of control and suppression of natural impulse. What we should want for our children, and for ourselves, is not such despotism, however benign, but a freeing of the natural energies of the body. Trust the organism. Its essence is Eros, and Eros is the source of life.

This understanding of our essential nature grows out of the work of Wilhelm Reich, and after a fashion out of Freud, of whom Reich was a maverick disciple. It was Freud who demonstrated the sexual springs of our basic vitality and desires, and then Reich revealed the fundamentally fascistic nature of the regimens of impulse control that our so-called civilization foists upon us. (Freud himself ultimately sided with that fascist struggle, and it is no wonder that his vision of life was so grim, seeing nothing better possible for us than to accept the inescapable misery of our lot.)

Freedom is our birthright. We need but to trust the body to serve our good: our bodies are what we are, and its desires are our needs. The healthy human animal—the well-ordered organism—is one in which the flow of sexual energies is unencumbered by mechanisms of control or suppression or repression. From the liberation of sexual expression and its flowering in orgasmic fulfillment comes everything else that we value in the "good" human being: the capacity to love, harmony with the world, and peace of mind. **Frank**

Frank's words brought an interesting and thoughtful rejoinder from Fred, whose anarchistic tendencies would have led me to predict a more supportive stance toward Frank's message calling for the liberation of sexual impulse.

It has been a long time, Frank, since I've heard articulated this vision of human architecture that places natural impulse—specifically, sexual energy—at the foundation, and depicts everything else as superstructure. But this idea was once a very important idea in my own life.

At a crucial time in my young adulthood, I too believed that the free flow of sexual energy was like a Holy Grail of human development, that one could gauge the overall wholeness of the person from how clear or impeded were the channels of sexual expression and pleasure. I myself was coming to grips with my own imperfect freedom, the various "hang-ups" and inhibitions that impaired my own celebration of the pleasure principle. As I searched for my perfect mate, my quest was advised by this sex-as-foundation notion of what a healthy structure in a person looks like.

This council proved disastrously flawed. I'll be mercifully brief in my account of it here. I found a woman whose so-called foundation was as solid and healthy as could be. Believing that meant she must be a whole lot better put-together as a person than I, I was foolishly slow to recognize that her so-called superstructure—her character as a human being, how she lived, how she dealt with others—was seriously defective. I learned the hard way that the capacity for healthy and intense sexual expression tells you nothing about a person's ability to be a responsible and caring, just and self-aware human being. Eventually I learned the other, happier side of the same lesson, finding a truly fulfilling relationship with a woman of great character who, in addition, was as imperfect as I in the Reichian Olympics.

It's not just my own experience. Talking with a variety of other people has confirmed the lesson: the worship of natural impulse is folly; and while the capacity for free bodily pleasure is a blessing, it by no means assures the healthy development of good character. **Fred**

Fred's powerful personal account brought forth two quick replies. One was from Kenneth, the minister who'd written not long before about how what Herman had called the superego occupied a "space" within us that was intended less to be occupied by an introject of our biological father than by the Word of our Heavenly father.

I feel compassion, Fred, for the evident suffering your misguided belief in the paramountcy of sexual impulse brought you, *Kenneth wrote.* More generally, I'd like to express how sad I find it that, though we have in the Bible a complete guide to how we are to live, so many people today simply disregard the divine guidance we have been given. Maybe what happens is even worse than "disregarding" that gift, for what is this deification of natural impulse except a rebellious turning of God's word on its head? This idea from Reich sounds to me like a justification for Sodom. As if we hadn't already been taught that when the fires of sexual appetite are not strictly contained, neither will anything else be in good order. Was it not the Sodomites who menaced the visiting angels-in-disguise, thus showing their contempt for the sacred rules of hospitality? **Kenneth**

The second message was from Ralph:

In your response to Andy's initial Nintendo question, Fred, you argued very forcefully that he should just allow the natural creature to unfold in its own way. I'm wondering how you have related your unhappy experience with the natural-impulse-as-foundation theory to your evidently still-strong belief in the rightness and sufficiency of the "natural" person. **Ralph**

Fred wrote right back:

You know, Ralph, I'm not sure that I've ever held these two ideas—the discrediting of the freely-expressed impulse as the key to the whole, and the preserved commitment to the natural—in my mind at the same time. This is something I'm going to have to take a look at. Thanks for the push. **Fred**

If You Will

Next came a posting from Cathy, the educator who had previously told us of the problems she saw with letting students design their own education as if they already knew just what it was they needed to know.

The idea of a person as "all of a piece" seems to me impossible to sustain, or even to conceive, *Cathy wrote*. If we were that simple we would not be human. If we were human and all of a piece, without any governing element, we'd be paralyzed. Obviously, something inside us must govern. But why should it have to come from outside? Are we to imagine that without importing something from the outside, the magnificent organism that is a human being would be incapable of making plans, executing decisions, choosing among options?

I don't think so, and so I don't propose that we think of ourselves as being commanded by a superego.

What I propose as a "higher" faculty is an old-fashioned concept, but I think this oldie is still a goodie. I mean the "will." The will as in willpower. It can be moral, as in steeling oneself against temptation like jumping the girl across the street. But it can also be just a brute power by which one pulls oneself toward achieving one's purpose, whatever that willed purpose may be.

And this will comes way before morality. I've seen it in an infant, determined to turn itself over no matter how many times it tries and fails. The determination is palpable. The child's will will prevail. And I've seen it in the faces, and the characters, of many people of great achievement. The determination to work one's will. It can be a force for good or evil, I suppose, depending upon the character of the will.

But however it is used, it is there. It is stronger in some than in others, but it governs to some degree in all of us. It's the quarterback that calls the play in the huddle of the mind. Its natural role in the organization of the creature's behavior seems to me another instance of the "natural hierarchy." **Cathy**

I was tempted to post some thoughts in response to Cathy's statement about the will—because her message both intrigued and frustrated me—but I refrained. I wasn't clear enough in my own mind about whether the will was an important and illuminative concept or not. Cathy's ideas seem to me to bring us to the doorstep of an important issue without getting us across the threshold.

One question that came to my mind was, "What is and what is not 'the will'?" If a heroin addict goes to great lengths to feed his habit, is that a manifestation of the power of his will? Or does the fact that he is a slave to his addiction signify a failure of will?

Cathy had observed, though only in passing, that the will is stronger in some people than in others. Why is that? Is it an inborn thing, like the way some people have bigger feet than others? Or is it a function of training and the formation of character, the way you can recognize a competitive swimmer by his pectoral muscles not because he was born part fish but because he has submitted his body to the discipline of daily sessions of specific exercises in the water?

Strength of will does seem to be an issue that captures some part of the moral flabbiness many of us sense in today's world. The ads for potato chips say that you can't eat just one. I have difficulty imagining the Victorians using such an ad as a positive inducement to buy their product. For many people, I know, the experience of being slaves to their cravings is a real and disturbing one. St. Paul's lament came to my mind: "For the good that I would do, I do not: but the evil which I would not, that I do." And surely, the recently reported fact that fully a third of adult Americans are significantly overweight, obese, up from a quarter of us just a decade ago, seems to suggest a problem of weakness of will.

But strong will, by itself, does not guarantee a psyche in good order. How does it come to be that some people exert their wills in destructive ways, while others choose to harness their wills toward serving the good—the actor's own good (as in eating sensibly instead of bingeing on junk foods) and/or the good of the wider world (as in resisting the temptation to betray a trust, to get away with murder)? Whence comes that "will" that chooses whether to harness one's will for good or ill? How does it come to be that some strong-willed people are wise, while others are such fools that their great powers of will can only be a liability to them?

Though I did not post these puzzling questions, and no one else pursued the question of will further, at this point, it was not long—as you will see in the following chapter, where the critique of the natural man and the advocacy of the imposition of order began for a time to dominate the discussion—before these issues returned for some further illumination.

In the meanwhile, a new message from Maria—who had previously proposed that "shoulds" should only be imposed when they are for the good of the child—brought a challenge to the whole concept that we ought to be governed by will of any kind.

As Water Flows

Anyone who studies the history of ideas, *Maria wrote*, or the belief systems of diverse cultures, cannot help but be struck by how often it is the case that communities of people will be completely convinced of the self-evidence of ideas that turn out not to be true at all. I gather from what I've been reading that to many of you it is self-evident that a human being—and, I am guessing, other aspects of our world as well—simply could not function if there were no controlling part to make and enforce decisions. Here's the concept of order as "the triumph of the will," to summon up an image that you'd probably think unfair for your ideas to be associated with.

But let me call your attention to another, very deep and venerable tradition of understanding that sees the order of things rather differently. This is the tradition of Taoism. Lao-Tzu says of the Tao, "It loves and nourishes all things, but does not lord it over them." If this is the way of the Tao, are we to believe that we ourselves should be ordered otherwise?

A lot of the talk here is of ordering things so they are as they should be. But Lao-Tzu employs the concept of *tzu-jan*, that which happens spontaneously, of itself, without having to be made to be. As I understand this vision of things, it accords well with Eleanor's affirmation that the natural self—far from being chaotic—naturally reveals a wonderful kind of order. Things happening rightly, "like water flowing downhill."

Cathy writes of the will, but a Taoist master said that "by intending to accord [with the Tao], you immediately deviate."

Are you willing to entertain the possibility that the order you are seeking is one that just is, that involves no willing or arranging or forcing? **Maria**

This Taoist critique of the dominance of will was quickly picked up by Karen, the therapist who had previously told of her own mission of facilitating her clients' formulating and achieving their own goals.

I appreciate Maria's bringing in the Taoist vision, *Karen wrote.* This notion of the natural wholeness of things that we humans—out of our lust for power, or our folly, or our greed, or whatever—have subverted is absolutely vital, I believe, to our finding our Way. But it is *so foreign* to the view of the world with which we have been indoctrinated that anyone with such a vision really is in the position of that Sufi who hasn't drunk of the waters of madness.

To descend for a moment from the sublime to the ridiculous, I'd like to share with you a recollection this exchange brought to my mind. A while back I took my then five- and six-year-old kids to see Disney's film, *The Lion King.* I don't know how many of you are familiar with this film, but it is a mixture—like so many of the movies made in this country—of incredible achievement with equally incredible sloppiness in its treatment of ideas and themes. Part of the incredible achievement of this film is visible in the very opening sequence: breathtaking animation combined with very pleasing music combining African elements with the music of Elton John. But right here in the opening sequence, there is this absolutely fundamental contradiction that I expect the Disney people never dreamed of noticing.

This beginning sequence is a celebration, as the opening song says, of "The Circle of Life." This is a marvelous, and quite core idea: that we are part of a seething, living Whole in which things move in cycle, in which—as in Arthur's **Round** table—no one thing is higher than another. Rather they all fit together with their complementary roles. But **at the same time** as this Circle of Life is being sung, the occasion is also this wonderful event that all must attend: the birth of a lion cub. **The King of Beasts!** And here are all the other creatures come to pay homage and adoration, a bestiary version of the shepherds come to the manger to marvel at the birth of Christ. And later in the film, disorder among the ruling clique of the lions somehow afflicts the whole ecosystem with such terrible systemtic distress that even the trees have lost their leaves. Some circle!

The circle of life is just reduced to another version of an irredeemably hierarchical order. The hierarchical understanding of order apparently so permeates our understanding that an ecological, or a Taoist, vision cannot really register in our minds. As with the Disney people, so also perhaps with many of us in this discussion. When we try to imagine a Way for the human being, we cannot envision the wholeness of that way designated by the Taoists as *tzu-jan,* but instead feel compelled to imagine some kind of King of Beasts upon his throne above the rest of the psychic order. **Karen**

A posting from Victor—who had posted a previous "graffito" about Rousseau—now informed us of some interesting linguistic connections which seemed to bear upon what Karen had just said about *The Lion King.*

The Greek word for order—*taxis*—contains an ambiguity: it can mean either "possessing a pattern" or "having been forced into a pattern." And the kind of "force" implied there—*tasso* in Greek—derives primarily from "the setting up of an army in order of battle." **Victor the Graffiti Artist**[1]

Visions of the Kingdom of Reason

At this point, Jeff returned to the discussion. Jeff had previously declared that he did not imagine that anyone actually raised children in the way that some seemed to suggest. (It was this declaration that led to Len's unhappy confession of his failure to give his children adequate guidance as they were growing up.)

"Will" smacks too much of power and dominance, a creature at war with itself, *Jeff wrote.* But I like your proposal, Cathy, that the well-ordered psyche can develop without our having to imagine that colonial ruler coming in from the outside. Hey, we modern liberals believe in self-determination of peoples, don't we? Well, that should be true for our individual peoplehood, too, I figure.

What I propose as a "higher power" is something different from Herman's superego or Cathy's will. I propose reason. The idea of there being a "natural reason" has a distinguished pedigree, which should be pleasing to some of the more conservative folks lurking out there on the fringes of this discussion. I mean it as a natural capacity of the mind—in Freudian terms, maybe like the ego with its sensible relationship to the "reality principle"—to perceive clearly, to think logically, to draw conclusions and make decisions based on reasonable assessments.

The reasonable person recognizes the reality of other people, and can thus grasp how an ethical principle like the Golden Rule conforms to reason. Using one's reason, one can understand "If being treated inconsiderately would give me pain, and if this other person gives every evidence of being a creature like me, I can reasonably conclude that if I treat this other person without consideration, that would cause him or her pain as well." Additionally, reason enables one to foresee consequences. I may want to seduce the girl down the street, but my reason tells me that all kinds of negative consequences may fall upon my head if I succumb to that temptation, and thus a well-ordered psyche will listen to the voice of reason and keep the impulse in check.

Finally, reason is equipped with a powerful epistemology, which means that over time a person's decisions will be based on an ever-sounder base of knowledge. The person with the well-ordered psyche—the reasonable person—thus grows to become the wise person. **Jeff**

The Greatest Teacher

At this point, Larry posted a message.

I've been excited to watch this unfold. The different positions presented in this disputation all seem to me to have some validity. But I'm reminded of the Jewish story about the rabbi who meets with a couple who have been quarreling. When he hears the wife's side of the story, he says "You're right." And when he hears the husband's side of the story, he says, "You're right." Then the rabbi's disciple, who has been watching all this, asks the rabbi, in exasperation: "How can they both be right? They contradict each other!" To which the rabbi responds, "You're right, too!"

My own predilections lean toward those who oppose an order that is based on hierarchy and dominance. Something in me just resists the notion that order has to be top-down in any way. But obviously, we are not born ready for prime time. It is not only physically that we have to develop in order to become the autonomous individual who can be whole and stand on his or her own two feet.

But when we mature from babyhood to adulthood in physical terms, we do not need something outside and above us telling us how to progress. Why should such intervention be necessary for the development of a well-ordered, mature psyche, able to make choices consistent with health, well-being and morality?

I've been thinking about some way of perhaps integrating Maria's lovely Taoist concept of *tzu-jan* with Jeff's notion of a natural, in-house executive called reason. Out of that effort to reconcile the purely-like-water-flowing-downhill with the benign ordering-without-dominance, I'd like to propose something rather simple and even obvious but that might offer us a way forward: it's the idea that ***we are by nature creatures who learn from experience.***

The world is continually speaking to us, *Larry continued,* and we are by nature formed to listen and to learn. As our experience unfolds, we discover which paths lead to which outcomes; we learn what works and what does not. Our discussion here has been about the issue of subordination: is there something to which we must submit? This is a highly charged issue in a group of people like us, so dedicated to the values of liberty and autonomy. Here is a benign resolution of that conflict: we submit to the truth as we discover it; we subordinate ourselves to reality.

And what a marvelous instrument we human beings have evolved to possess, one that allows us to process the continual flow of information, to remember, to infer causal connections, to see patterns, to test different hypotheses. The crown of life's creation—the human capacity for reason—equips us to become truly *Homo sapiens.* Man knowing, man the wise.

And all this without resort to the ugly and corrupt structures of power. It is indeed a kind of *tzu-jan,* this learning process we undergo through our life's experience. Like the very evolutionary process that, over the course of two billion years, crafted the structure of the living cell that became our building block, like that same evolutionary process that in the subsequent billion years has made the human neocortex possible, our learning process is itself highly evolutionary. If you are familiar with learning theory, you may recognize the analogy that can be made between learning in a particular organism and the process of evolution. Even the word "extinction" appears in both systems!

Experience provides the data that constitute the variations of possibilities, our reason exercises the mechanism of selection. We enjoy freedom and autonomy—free to choose, to employ Milton Friedman's title for his book about the market system. And like the freely competing creatures evolving in the biosphere, our evolving structure is not chaotic or anarchic, but is governed by the realities of the world around us. Freedom with order. Can you dig it?

Let me bring this down to earth with a couple of illustrative cases. My kid went to the fair last year and really pigged out on the junk food to be had there: cotton candy, pronto pups, that sort of thing. At home that night, he felt miserable with cramps and bloating and the rest of the indigestive unpleasantness. Let me tell you, some substantial one-trial learning occurred! When we went there this summer, he was abstemiousness itself. Quoth he: "I'm not going to make that mistake again."

Here's another example. When I was a teenager, I used to play the field with the ladies in a rather cavalier fashion. I enjoyed the conquest; I broke some hearts. After a few rounds of this behavioral pattern, I took stock of what was happening. I saw that this way of dealing with sexual intimacy was not really scratching my own itch, and that the pain I was causing other people, even when I tried to disregard it, was a drag upon my own spirits. And I said to myself, "So, this is what I get by taking that trail, I don't want it any more." And I cleaned up my act.

In living, we inevitably do our experiments. And our knowledge and wisdom grow in a free yet orderly way. **Larry**

I find your idea very exciting, Larry, and nicely articulated, *wrote Cynthia.*

This was her first posting since she had reported, near the beginning of these exchanges, how she and her husband had come to appreciate why their daughter would choose to read literature of low quality that all the other kids were reading. In this instance, however, she seemed to be reflecting not her experience as a parent so much as her professional background as a biochemist.

I believe you capture there an essential element of the human adventure. And not just at the individual level, of learning through a lifetime, but also how we as humankind have become so adept at interacting with the reality around us to the point where our base of real knowledge grows almost exponentially. Once a sizeable piece of humankind broke out of the cages of rigid and stifling beliefs, once the fetters of superstition were broken, the powers of human reason were unleashed to discover how things really work, what the order really is of which we are part.

Think of it. Without the breakthrough—especially in the West in the past half millennium—to the rationality of the Enlightenment and the rise of science, we could hardly have conducted a conversation like this. And I don't just mean technologically, although humankind was certainly, five hundred years ago, almost inconceivably far from being able to weave together anything so marvelously interconnected—ordered—as the World Wide Web that enables us to have this spontaneous interaction across thousands of miles. I mean also even our concepts: who would have known of the marvelously complex microcosm of the cell, let alone been able to talk about the eons of evolutionary unfolding that perfected its order?

The rise of science is therefore also a huge leap in the evolution of the role of consciousness in furthering the creation of order in the universe. Science is about *free* inquiry, with all questions on the table, with complete openness to hear what the cosmos might disclose to us, and at the same time maintaining the openness of all the questions, regarding no answers as final. Once we embrace such openness, we discover that the sky is the limit! Paradoxically, once we approach our knowledge with the humility of scientific skepticism, we are rewarded with an unprecedented cocreative role in the cosmic order.

This has long been true, of course, just as human rationality is no new invention. Ten thousand years ago, for example, our ancestors were scientific enough to grasp the possibilities of their gaining control over the forces of the living system on which we'd always depended for our survival, and to engineer the stuff of life to serve their own purposes. Seeds were no longer just gathered, but were now sown. Animals were no longer just hunted, but were made into captive herds. Nature the selector of order was supplemented by Man the selector of a new, more useful order.

But the co-creator role we achieved then was but the seed for what has sprung forth in recent centuries, up to now when we are even able to engineer the genetics of that cell of whose existence we were ignorant just moments ago, in historical terms.

And of course, all of this has coincided with a birth of similar openness at the social and individual levels. The Enlightenment that came with science also came with the liberal notions of the autonomous individual endowed by his creator with the right to pursue his good by the light of his own reason. And with this liberty came a corresponding shift in the concept of government. Government was no longer understood an instrument whose legitimate purposes were those of a "higher power," whether that power be God or be a Sovereign King to whom we all exist as subjects. No, with the new liberal breakthrough, the real purpose of government became to be an instrument of those under its rule. The "consent of the governed" meant government "for the people." And suddenly, the new openness has freed the sovereign individual to find and to realize his own good, to grow into whatever his unfolding desires and reason tell him to become. **Cynthia**

All this brought a response from John, the guy who'd declared before that the cosmos is silent on matters of right and wrong, and that all our notions of such things are merely our inventions. This next posting showed that he had at least the virtue of consistency, if the cosmos would consent to regard consistency as a virtue.

What a delightful combination, *John began.* Here we have these paeans to empiricism sung in the same breath as a call for us to be ruled by reason. Tell me please, just where is this "reason" to be found? If you dissect my brain, will you find it near the cerebellum? And while we are at it, how about using the scalpel to show the will and the superego? Hey, they're all fictions. Useful fictions at best, but hardly candidates for kingship.

While we're deconstructing this storytelling business, how about the mythology of science as this clear lens through which we discover "reality." Are you fellows aware of all the work that has been done in the past generation debunking this myth of objectivity, showing how science is as colored as any of our other modes of perception by the consensual realities of the culture that produces scientific thought? **John**

This last sentence elicited from Fred a one-line zinger:

Interesting, John, the way you argue your point on the basis of authority. **Fred**

Other than that, John's challenge was pretty much ignored by the group.

A Somber Empiricism

A more substantive criticism—or at least, so I regarded it—was initiated by Rev. George.

If I did not have the benefit of living in a world shaped already by two centuries of the hegemony of the Enlightenment worldview, *George wrote,* I might be tempted to get swept up in your enthusiasm for this reign of reason that you envision. But we have been there, done that, and the world I live in does not bear out your happy assumptions about the rational person and the natural unfolding of his sapient capacity.

Look around you. What do you see? Wisdom? Surely, in our society, if experience were such a great teacher and if we were such naturally good students, such great consumers of experience as we are, we should certainly see a great flowering of the reasonable and enlightened beings that you celebrate. Speaking of us as "consumers," surely the American people have had long experience of the emptiness of seeking fulfillment through the acquisition of goods. Yet analysts of consumerism have written about the cycle of yearning followed by purchase followed by disillusionment with the inefficacy of the purchase to fulfill the yearning, followed by more yearning and then the next purchase. Where is the reason in all this? Where is this vaunted ability of our consciousness to unfold, through reasoned analysis of empirical evidence, into an ever-more intimate and fulfilling embrace with reality?

Consider us also in our role as citizens. Here is where the Enlightenment most proudly proclaimed our ability to stand on our own feet and be masters of our destiny. Let us know the facts, let us deliberate together, and from our deliberations will ensue rational policy. The body politic as a self-organizing system. But here we are in America after two centuries of democracy, with a veritable glut of information, with news networks running twenty-four hours a day, with the deliberations of our representatives available on C-Span, and how do we conduct our affairs?

The citizens of the United States of America—the one remaining superpower and a country rich beyond the dreams of earlier eras—are simple and clear in their wants: they want to have their cake and eat it, too. The budget deficit must be closed. No doubt about that, we don't want to burden our grandchildren. Oh, but taxes are too high. Must get government out of our pockets, we know better how to spend our own money. But don't cut any of the programs we really want. And woe to the political leader who dares to say that these equations admit of no simultaneous solution! He won't be a leader long. So we vote for politicians who make promises that simply cannot be kept, who mirror back to us our own contradictions. And then we complain that these good-for-nothings can't be trusted, that they talk out of both sides of their mouths!

It would appear therefore that the creature endowed with reason, and given now more than three score and ten worth of experience, is still not reliably a well-ordered being. **Rev. George**

Within minutes, this brought from Larry the following message.

George has raised some very good points which I am eager to refute. Regrettably I find myself not immediately in possession of a clue about just how to go about such a refutation. But I do recall something from an earlier message posted here that might bear upon his challenge. More to the point, it might give the position I am eager to have preserved—the rationalist-evolutionary point of view, as it might be called, developed by Cynthia and me—at least a trench to slow down George's charge. And meanwhile, it will buy me time to gather my intellectual forces.

That previous message was from Keith in response to Andy's original Nintendo inquiry. Keith reported how he had not interfered with his son's obsession with video games, and how he had eventually grown tired of them on his own, relinquished his habit and gone on to other things. That sounds to me a lot like learning from experience. The child had a chance to discover where that trail led, became disenchanted with it, and proceeded to explore other areas of life. Just as I would predict.

So I would like to ask Keith to elaborate on how that worked, to share any insights he can into what made it possible for his organism-respecting approach to work. I'm hoping Keith's further testimony will help us to meet George's challenges. (For example, perhaps the natural wisdom is more intact in the child, whereas George is giving us examples of follies of people who are the products of a system that subjects them to a great variety of forces, including some—such as advertising—that work actively to subvert or circumvent the rational faculty.)

So please, Keith, tell us more. **Larry**

Reality Check

I came back in a couple of hours eager to see what Keith might have posted. But there was no word from him yet. Interestingly, there had been no other postings either. I laughed at the thought of all of us, spread out around the country, waiting for this star witness to take the stand. A few hours later, I checked again. Still nothing from Keith. There were a couple of other minor messages of little substantive content, more like the mutterings in an audience that is waiting for the real show to begin. That night someone posted a brief encouragement to Keith to respond to Larry, and then, by morning, a couple people began wondering out loud if Keith had become disenchanted with the forum, or whether his job had kept him occupied.

"Enough of this," I thought to myself. Keith and I had exchanged business cards in one of those casual moments that I expect in most instances leads to a slight increase in the nation's solid waste. But I still had his card in my wallet, I recalled, and so I decided to give Keith a telephone call. The phone is, of course, a primitive instrument of communication in these days of the World Wide Web: one gets busy signals, one is dependent on the person's being there, one has to employ one's voice box using actual breath, etc. But it does have the virtue that if you *do* get the other person on the line, you *know* that you are taking to him.

I was in luck, I reached Keith. I told him that I was calling to check why he hadn't responded to the invitations from the forum to go further into how he had handled his son's video game obsession and to tie it into the question of the human capacity to learn from experience.

"I had no idea," Keith explained, "I've been so tied up lately that I haven't even been near my computer to follow the discussion. It must be two days, now." Then he gave a strange, mirthless laugh. "This is weird. You won't believe what's been tying me up. It's my boy."

Keith's son, it turned out, was now fifteen. Long past video games, Keith explained, the young man was now into other things that made the addiction to video games look quaintly innocent.

"He's not a bad kid at all," Keith assured me, "just kind of rudderless. Just sort of innocently lets himself get blown along by whatever breeze comes along. If his friends get into horsing around with drugs, he'll give it a shot. If someone says 'Let's go cruising,' and he's got a paper due in school the next day, he'll take off. These last few weeks it's sort of come to a head—a call from the principal over some incidents at the school, some danger that he'll be held back a year if he doesn't start getting his homework in, things like that.

"Well, my wife and I have been spending hours with him these last couple of days. I've really jumped into his life with both feet. For the time being, we're taking charge of what he does and when he does it. A very short leash, until he shows he can be trusted. Seems strange to be managing a fifteen year old like that—I mean, he's bigger than I am now!

"Anyway, that's why I haven't replied to the forum. Maybe in a couple of weeks I'll be able to get back to that. I hope so. In the meanwhile, would you do me a favor? Tell the gang for me what I've told you, so they'll understand. Tell them I'm sorry not to be able to join in just now."

I assured him I would, and then we said good-bye. As we hung up, I thought to myself, Keith's situation with his child is not so different from Len's sad tale. Then I proceeded to post a message to the forum letting everyone know what was happening with Keith.

I don't know what I expected to happen when the tale of Keith's son's troubled present situation cast its backward shadow over his previous optimistic account of how years ago Keith had just let the boy work out his Nintendo addiction on his own. But I am certain that I would not have predicted the actual outcome, the way Keith's news triggered a virtual counterrevolution from the right, revealing that there were more conservatives lurking by now on our forum than had previously been evident.

These folks evidently thought that the time was ripe to set us deluded countercultural types straight about what it takes to get human beings to conform to good order.

Found Wanting
The Question of the Adequacy of the Human Being

The discussion up to this point had shown that I was far from alone in believing—and wanting to believe—that the developing human being somehow possesses an inherent wisdom and predisposition to good order. Indeed, several of my interlocutors on the forum had shown themselves considerably more doctrinaire on the question than I.

A group of more conservative people, bringing with them their skepticism about human nature, had already begun to argue with some effect against some of our more sanguine, and perhaps naive, ways of understanding how trustworthy is the natural unfolding of human development. If we are so good at learning from experience, it had just been argued, why does humanity seem to be so foolish, so prone to repeat its errors? At that juncture, Larry appealed to Keith to draw upon his experience in letting his son find his own way with his earlier video-game addiction, hoping that Keith's account would show the way that the proper self-ordering of the growing human being operates. Now, when it turned out that Keith was unable to testify because he was too preoccupied with the task of dealing with his now-teenage son's disordered life, the prosecutors of the right moved in to drive home their point.

Creatures of Habit

The first "prosecutor" was Peter, who actually was an attorney and who previously had expressed his wonderment about the culture's fear of overbearing, "totalitarian" fathers, when it is the *lack* of fathers that is the more conspicuous problem.

Peter began by saying:

I trust that Keith, if he is back to listening in on the forum, will understand that my diagnosis of his situation, although finding him in error, does not lessen my sympathy for his difficulties.

This disclaimer of Peter's made me wonder if he were operating from an image of us liberal types as being so focused on the virtue of "compassion" that we needed continually to be reassured that any critical remarks were not evidence of a lack of compassion. Then it occurred to me that perhaps in reading our subculture thus he'd not be so far off the mark.

Between the way Keith's son "learned" to handle his video-game addiction seven years ago, *Peter continued,* and the fact that Keith is now having to step in to put the young man's life into better order, there is, I would suggest, a clear connection. As I understand it, Keith reported that the boy eventually got tired of the video games and then—"wisely" it was suggested—went on to other things. But I would say that it is entirely too optimistic to believe that the most important learning in that situation had to do with the fact that video games get boring after a while. The crucial education going on, I would argue, involved the training of the boy's will, and what was being ingrained was the habit of yielding to the impulse of the moment.

Liberals tend to be great believers in the powers of human reason. This leads you folks of that ideological stripe to believe that the boy will learn some great and overarching lessons from the experience of discovering the vacuity of spending all one's hours playing Nintendo. But I would suggest that the role you give to reason reflects a very distorted—even grandiose—picture of human nature, and of how people in fact learn. The reasoning part of the neocortex is important, but it nonetheless remains largely a gloss upon other more primitive and much more powerful ordering faculties within us.

What we learn, above all, is habits. Habits of thought, habits of feeling, habits of action. And the way we learn habits is by successive repetitions of the same course of thinking, feeling, acting. Our characters form themselves the way that trails get formed in a wood. Where people or deer or squirrels walk again and again, there the trail will develop. Or like watercourses: where the rain drains off, there the gulleys will form.

And as with both of those examples, so also with the trails that we create in our character structure: every time we use the trail, we help build the trail and we increase the likelihood of the trail's being used again. The more worn the trail the more appealing it will be for the next travelers; once a trail has been blazed, the troop of deer do not reconsider how to traverse a familiar stretch of woods. Similarly, the rain wears down the stream-beds, making it all the more inevitable that the water to find its way there in the future. (Look at a hill by a construction site. The first rain seems to choose almost arbitrarily, but soon the channels formed are the obvious and necessary ways the water must run.) So also with our habits. We perform the same action yet another time, and it becomes all the more likely that the next time the situation arises, we will follow the contours of our developing habit.

Most of us, in most domains of our lives, are merely the sum of such habits.

So let us look at Keith's son. Time after time, the boy had the desire to play Nintendo. His parents refrained from entering into the decision-making process at those many junctures at which the boy either would or would not turn on the game to play. Therefore, time after time, what the boy learned was the habit of treating his desire of the moment as his governor. The trail of compliance with impulse becomes more and more clear and established, and as for other potential trails that might be formed by the intrusion of some "higher" judgment, they remain densely overgrown, impenetrable.

It is no wonder to me, then, that years later the parents will make the unhappy discovery that the boy—or young man—lacks the good judgment and powers of will to resist either his own momentary inclinations or the influences of misguided peers.
Peter

Two messages quickly arrived in response to Peter. Larry's was first:

So where is this "higher" judgment supposed to come from, by which Keith's son would have developed other, better habits?

And Peter replied:

The clear answer to your question poses the problem for you natural-man and from-the-ground-up types. The good judgment must enter the picture from above, like a *deus ex machina*. In this case, the available *deus* is the parent. The parent enters the picture and says, "You've played that enough. It's time to do something else. Hence, for the rest of today, you must obey the commandment, *'Thou shalt not play Nintendo.'* " Thus in the woods that is the boy's mind a different trail begins to form, a trail that is the habit of impulse and desire giving way to better judgment. "I hear the voice of higher authority, and I obey."

But it is vain to look to the newly forming mind itself to inaugurate this new trail. You may have heard the famous statement of Kant's, *"Aus so krumme Holze, als woraus der Mensch demacht ist, kann nichts gans gericht gezimmert werden."* ("Out of the crooked timber of humanity no straight thing can ever be made.") Within the natural creature itself, this voice of better judgment is not to be found. Good order requires the voice of the *deus*. **Peter**

Larry wrote back, in response:

I figured it would be something of the sort. Bring in the rack to straighten our naturally crooked timbers. And so the person remains perpetually under the thumb of authority, never trusted to decide for himself, right?

You speak of habit, but what habit is formed here except that of submission to the will of another? So long as the developing human creature is forced to submit to a voice that is not his own, how can we *ever* expect him to develop the habit of autonomous judgment, properly exercised? And if you place no trust in this crooked timber that is us, what difference does it make what habits we develop except for submission to some *deus* or other who happens to have the upper hand? **Larry**

Your questions are good ones, *Peter soon responded*. You have pointed to the missing step, which perhaps I should have made explicit at the outset. I share more of the value you place on our autonomy than you apparently think, and if all the learning involved were mere submission, I'd regard the outcome of the process I am advocating as pretty grim. But the other aspect of the learning is that suggested earlier by Herman: the voice of the *deus*, in this case the parent, is ***internalized.***

At the beginning of the process, the voice that says "No, you've got to do something other than, better than, what you want to do," needs to come from outside, above. But the growing child, after hearing the voice of his local god, will form a special kind of habit—that of hearing that voice in his mind at other, similar junctures. And the habit of submitting to that voice then becomes his own. Over the years, it is not the habit of submission to others that is learned so much as the habit of exercising— of submitting to—one's own good judgment. **Peter**

The other posting came from Karen, the gentle psychotherapist whose mission in life is to help people get and become what they want.

I don't think I'm likely to be capable of debating all this with you, in the fashion of point-by-point logical disputation. But I must say I am profoundly uneasy with all this talk of us as creatures of habit. Sounds rather mechanical, sort of like Pavlovian dogs who salivate when the bell rings. I think it diminishes us. It depicts us as less than not only what I'd like to think we are, but also less than what I believe us human beings in essence to be. We *do* make choices, and we *do* excerise reasoned judgments. We don't just keep on doing what we've always done. If we did, psychotherapy would be a waste of time. And I know, from experience, that it isn't. **Karen**

Peter responded to Karen:

Let me set aside your statement that my view of us as creatures of habit would render psychotherapy meaningless. Except to say that I've understood one of the functions of therapy is to give people the new experience of relating to someone, and to themselves, in different ways. And that new experience opens up new trails that make new habits possible. In other words, the talking isn't just talking, it's a kind of doing, and the repeated experience of a different kind of doing helps create a wedge that makes possible other new kinds of doing in the person's life.

But let me make a bit more tangible how the formation of good habits works in making us well-ordered creatures. If you are a parent—and unless you own the electric company—you probably have the experience of wanting your kids to turn off the lights when they leave a room. Perhaps you have noticed that you don't have to do anything to teach them to turn the lights on. They pick that one up right away, because upon walking into a dark room they immediately see that, for their own purposes, turning on the light is necessary. But when they leave the room, they experience no such direct personal need that would lead them to turn the light off.

Now, you could hope that they would exercise some rational judgment here. They might notice that the light is on and, having noticed it, they might give thought to the waste of natural resources, and of the family's money, that is a result of leaving the light on. But I expect even you will agree that is too much to expect of kids. Or, you can drum it into them—again and again—telling them to turn off the light as they leave or, if they fail, to make them go back to that room and do it, so that it gets to be an automatic action upon leaving the room. (In fact, with me, it is so automatic that it will frequently happen that, without a thought, I will turn off the light as I leave, leaving my unfortunate wife behind in that room, in the dark.)

I would suggest that making a habit of it is the only sensible way to meet the challenge. And further, that a great deal of what we want people to do in their functioning in the world is, in this respect, rather like turning off the lights behind them.
Peter

Rigged Experiments

Karen wrote back immediately asking Peter to elaborate on his assertion that a good deal of right conduct is based on inculcated habits, like turning off lights. But, before Peter could address that question, there came in the same mail a message that served to further damage our sanguine view of our natural wisdom. It launched further attack, from a different direction, on our faith in people's ability to learn from experience the wise lessons it may have to offer. The writer, Alice, introduced herself as

a practicing counseling psychologist who was also involved with a program of character education in a public schools system.

Wouldn't it be great, *Alice asked rhetorically, after her self-introduction,* if each person learned well the lessons that each experience has to teach? But we are surrounded
everywhere by evidence to the contrary. The lessons of experience are unfortunately
not self-evident to people. Peter's analysis of what is learned by a boy who gradually
grows bored with video games is quite apt; and that instance is representative of a
whole variety of ways that experience does not lead, on its own, to wisdom. Don't we
in the mental-health profession see people all the time who, if they manage to escape
an addiction at all, just move from one addiction to another?

In my practice, what I see frequently are people who "learn" from experience all
kinds of things at variance to wisdom. Consider the so-called "sadder but wiser" girl
who has learned not to trust any man, thinking he might victimize her. Has the sadder
girl truly become wiser? Sometimes learning to be less naive and careless does mean
becoming wiser. But people often learn far too much, meaning also far too little, from
their experience.

I recently saw a woman, for example, who has learned the "truth" that "all men are
bastards." She has had a string of experiences that all seem to bear out that generaliza-
tion. My marriage seems to me to contradict her general truth. She has had experience
with more men than I have. Has her experience brought her greater wisdom about the
nature of men? If experience were such a great teacher, one might assume so. But I
do not believe that it works that way. **Alice**

I had to admit that Alice and Peter were battering down an important
part of the structure of my own thought. The idea that we "learn from
experience" had always been a key part of my faith in humanity. Recollections of past conversations swelled up in my mind: before I ever became a father, I pronounced what my approach would be, declared that
my children would learn from the greatest of all teachers, experience. I
would let them make their own mistakes, I said, unless the consequences
threatened to be seriously damaging or even fatal. That way they would
form their characters around truly solid understanding, the kind that
comes from coming up against reality itself, not just up against the boundaries drawn by arbitrary-seeming authorities.

When I actually became a father, I found myself unable to practice
what I had preached. Somehow, it didn't *feel* right. I didn't want to watch
them making all those mistakes. Some people whose regard I cared about

thought me too controlling as a father, because I supplied a lot of guidance, and I worried about this, because my philosophy agreed substantially with them, even though my gut did not.

Was my "gut" just an unfortunate, "habitual" holdover from my own, more traditional upbringing? Or was it a source of a greater wisdom than my youthful beliefs in the value of learning from experience could have provided? I didn't know. But as I thought about the postings from Peter and Alice, I considered the seemingly incontrovertible proposition that in the world around us, there is a great abundance of experience, but a comparative shortage of wisdom.

I turned back to the screen and observed that Rev. George had joined in the discussion.

Alice has raised an interesting point, *George began,* about the limitations on our ability to learn from experience. If the woman—the one who has learned the "truth" that all men are bastards through many experiences that support that proposition— isn't wise, why isn't she? The answer, it seems to me, is that she—like everyone else— must learn through her own imperfect instrument. If we human beings looked out upon the world through the clear lens of Enlightenment rationality, as we would like to think of ourselves as doing, then our learning would be rather different.

This woman Alice writes about doubtless sees her data as providing a clear snapshot of the world outside herself: in this case, on the nature of men. But what about her own role in shaping the experiments she calls her life? What if she is choosing, without knowing it, a rather nonrandom sample of subjects, e.g., getting involved with men of the more abusive sort? What if her own behavior is evoking from men a particular part of the range of their possibilities, provoking them, like the people who seem to wear a sign that says "Kick me" do, to be more abusive than they might usually be? And what if, as is usually the case in these matters, she is unconscious of what she is doing and why?

To the extent that we are blind to ourselves and to our role in "rigging" the experiment of life, we become no wiser from experience. And are we not all like this woman in this significant way, that we are blind to how we fit into the picture we have created? And are we not all, therefore, inclined to mislearn the lessons that life teaches? **Rev. George**

This moved Karen to reply.

I read what Alice and George have written with mixed reactions. On the one hand, I believe they are onto something really important. This is, indeed, an important part of what we see occurring in the way people lead their lives, in how they fail to learn what experience might teach them. But on the other hand, the implication that because of this we should think less of human nature seems an unfair conclusion to draw.

On the first point, I have to mention one of my favorite movies: *Groundhog Day*. In this film, the main character finds himself compelled by unexplained forces to repeat the same day again and again—until he finally "gets it right," at which point time again starts moving. The guy is a cynical, manipulative, condescending jerk at the outset. The only way of behaving that he knows is to put other people down, to con people into giving him what he wants, and other clever and entertaining but fundamentally unappealing patterns of behavior. But the fact is, the world does not give him what he really wants so long as he keeps acting that way.

As he relives the same day over and over—with everything the same except his accumulating memory of the repetitions—we see him repeat his habitual approach to life over and over, and in various ways. And we see how the outcome always ends up frustrating his desires. His desire to "make it" with a particular woman becomes the crux of his education-through-repetition. We see his successive failures, culminating in successive slaps in the face. Finally, he bottoms out, breaking down into a suicidal depression. But even when he kills himself, the next morning there he is again at the beginning of the same day. The repetition of time forecloses the possibility of his failing to learn; it absolutely **compels** him to learn and to change.

The wonderful thing about this movie is the insight it provides into how deeply ingrained are the habits of behavior, combined with the film's creation of an artificial situation of such extraordinary power that ultimately there is no alternative for the man but finally to learn from his experience. Without the crystal clarity forced upon this character by the endless repetition—showing him that so long as he keeps coming from the same place within himself, he will keep getting back from the world the same unsatisfactory stuff—he would never be able to "learn from experience." But the universe has conspired, apparently, to make sure he learns, to rub his nose in the bankruptcy of his habits until he sees them for what they are.

At one level, it is a marvelous illustration of how a person can be redeemed by learning from experience. But at another level, I believe, it shows how resistant, how blind, how stuck the human being generally is. For having seen what it takes to bring about the redemptive education of this man, I don't see how we can escape the conclusion that without the universe conspiring to teach him, he would **never** have learned. He'd have gone to his grave believing—like the woman with her belief that "all men are bastards"—that the world is full of jerks, that life is a cheat, and so forth.

Having said all that, however, *Karen continued,* I am loath to allow this stuckness and blindness we so often see to be entered into evidence as establishing the flawed *inherent* nature of the human being. Admittedly, lots of people do things like walk around unaware of their wearing the equivalent of a "Kick me" sign. But what does this say about human nature? I see it more as neurosis. And I recall coming across, a long time ago, a definition of neurosis as "learned stupidity." The crucial word there being *learned*.

We don't come into the world twisted into unawareness of what we are really seeking. A masochistic streak is acquired, and with that streak also the unconsciousness of it. We have to be taught, by an unhealthy environment, *not* to see what we are plainly doing. The knowledge becomes forbidden because the powerful others in our social environment will punish our awareness. So, we learn to be neurotic. But this is a defect not in our nature, but in our nurture. **Karen**

At this point, I saw something quite charming, as well as inherently interesting, that seemed worth observing publicly. So I wrote:

Juxtaposing what Karen has just written with the remarks of Alice and George to which she was responding, I see a kind of isomorphism. It's kind of neat.

Alice and George were writing about the overgeneralizations to which we, as individuals, are subject because of our blindness to factors that might skew our vision. The woman who concludes from a skewed sample that all men are bastards was the example. Now Karen comes back and her defense of human nature presents a rather nifty way of turning virtually the same argument around. Her point might be restated: in using that data to speak of human nature, you too are making an overgeneralization, and in your case, too, it is because you have not factored in some forces that skew your data.

The source of the skewing is different. The woman who has "learned" from experience that all men are bastards does not see how her selection of and influence on the data make it less representative than she supposes. But in Peter and Alice's case—and I would say in the conservative tendency in general to denigrate human nature— the skewing is caused by not seeing the warping tendencies at work in the social environment, the social and interpersonal forces that can twist people into becoming something more neurotic than we human beings are, by nature, built to be. **Andy**

Pressed into the Mold

It was Peter who responded to my posting.

Andy and Karen have made a reasonable argument about not inferring too much from the ubiquity of our neurotic habits. But I would like, if I may, to return our discussion of—as I would put it—human inadequacy, to my earlier observation about habits like those learned by Keith's son.

The way that boy learned the habit of indulging desire, rather than of disciplining it, has little to do with neurosis. It is, rather, about character formation. And the key points remain, undiminished by the arguments that human beings are not inherently neurotic: first, that we become what we do; and second, that a good order to govern what we do needs to be imposed by external authority.

You liberals, in your antipathy toward authority, are prone to reject from your system—from, dare I say, your hierarchy?—of values an element that is absolutely essential to good order. Namely, the imposition of authority from above in order to shape the formation of character. **Peter**

I would like to rise to the defense of liberalism, *posted Ralph in response,* and the first step in that defense is to rescue it from definition by its opponents. You, Peter, are characterizing the liberal position as one that is opposed to all authority. But I regard myself as a liberal, and I would reaffirm the importance of a distinction we touched upon earlier: that between the proper relationship of children to authority on the one hand, and of adults to authority on the other. In other words, the question of how parents should bring up their children is different from that concerning how powers presumed to be "above" adults should respect or curtail the liberty of mature human beings.

Some people here, apparently, want the liberty of the unformed child to be respected equally with that of the fully formed adult, but I would question whether it is legitimate to equate that position with liberalism. It certainly is not my position. And the well-known liberal, Michael Walzer, has written that liberalism is not committed to the "presocial self," but rather to the liberty of the self that has developed the capacity for reflection and, in particular, for reflection "on the values that have governed its socialization."[1]

It follows from this association of liberalism with the capacity for reflection that we must divide people according to their stage of development. A young child is clearly not capable of reflecting rationally, and with a perspicacious view of her available options, upon the decisions she must make. At this stage of life, the process of character development may well be a function of the more primitive forces of habit formation, as you suggest, Peter; it certainly is not going to be reliably governed by reasoned self-reflection. Thus, your advocacy of imposing authority to help foster the formation of good character is not, as I see it, any contradiction of the liberal vision. **Ralph**

I have no especial desire to call myself a liberal, *Fred wrote back, taking up the cause of extending the realm of liberty from where Ralph had placed its boundaries,* but I do want to take my stand in defense of our humanity. After all, if we're willing to allow ourselves to be pushed and bullied by authority until we are, say, eighteen years old, how much is our later enjoyment of so-called liberty going to be worth? I'm reminded of something a Russian is reported to have said to John Maynard Keynes: "You [English] don't need the police because you all have mental straitjackets."[2] I'm not going to just sit back while those who want real straitjackets quarrel with those who regard mental straitjackets as liberation. I want humankind to be liberated to live without straitjackets at all! **Fred**

The Critique of Reason

Meanwhile, however, the gathering force of the conversation was not from the left, where Fred was making his stand, but further out from the right. Now we again heard from Carl, the man who'd introduced himself as a "biblical Christian," and who had written in criticism of the idea of the autonomous human being, declaring that we all depend upon the grace of God to find our way. Carl was evidently far from satisfied with Peter's position, finding it too accommodating of the kind of liberalism that Ralph was propounding.

Peter and Ralph apparently are happy to concur that once the light of reason has dawned in the development of the human mind, authority can retreat, *Carl's message read*. Peter wrote earlier of how the voice of the *deus* gets internalized, so that the growing individual can become his own authority. That goes with Ralph's (and his liberal authority Walzer's) paean to the powers of self-reflection in the matured individual, fully worthy of his liberty.

Surely, there is an element of truth in this. (Adults *are* a step above children.) But the question is, how much? And then, how much can we bank on that "how much" when we set up our social institutions?

A child is unformed, true. And as Peter argues, it is in profound need of being shaped and molded by wiser authorities. One might liken the child to a natural gas that simply calls out for a container to give it form. Without that container, it will be all over the room.

An adult has been through a process of formation, at least to an extent. But can the adult be allowed on his own recognizance? The adult may have brought the voice of the *deus* within, but how reliably will the adult heed its commandments? No longer a natural gas like the child, what is the adult? A liquid, a pile of sand? Adults at least do not need a lid on the container, but without the sides and bottom, they will sink to a pool, like water, or, like sand, dissipate till it's spread out on the bottom.

The evidence of this is all about us. You speak of reason and reflection. But how deep do these go? Not very, I would say. Look at the fleshpots of this, the land of liberty. Once we remove the bottom from the container, what starts to happen? Gambling spreads everywhere, for example, sanctioned even by the liberal institutions of government, happy as they are to get money without having to force it from the citizens. No need to compel through taxation what can be taken by tempting the foolish, the impulsive, those who are slave to their unrealistic fantasies. What else do we see? As the range of liberty spreads, we see Times Square transformed from the heart of a respectable country to the sewer in which every kind of vice, every kind of vicious desire, is catered to, openly, without shame. More than a million unborn babies a year are aborted, and almost a third of those who are allowed to live are born to women without husbands. Without authority blocking off the way downward, what we see is society sinking to the low level of the inherent human impulse.

I read recently a definition—from a liberal, mind you—of the "Enlightenment project" as "the experience of liberation, through reason, from externally imposed authority."[3] Enlightenment *sounds* like a good thing, but I am far from persuaded that this "Enlightenment project" is an enlightened undertaking. Even if there could be found a few people who, once liberated from the confines of authority, could use reason to hold themselves together in a good human shape—something remotely like the image of God in which we are made—I question whether they'd ever make up a large enough segment of the population that a society could ever safely entrust the management of individuals' own personal lives, **let alone the nation's affairs,** solely to "the people."

The human being, I would argue, never outgrows his need for a powerful authority, standing above, to hold human appetites and follies in check. **Carl**

Kenneth, the minister who had previously written about how the Reichian celebration of natural impulse stood the word of God on its head, wrote next.

Like Carl, I would like to challenge an idea that seems to be a rallying point for consensus in the middle, *Kenneth said*. In my case, the notion I'd like to take issue with is the one that says that "neurosis" is a product of an unhealthy environment, and that the blindness to self that interferes with learning from experience is something that has to be learned and is therefore not part of the nature of the human being.

Where I come from, the human condition is that we are born into a state of sin. Sin was once defined, by a liberal theologian I might add—Paul Tillich—as a state of **separation.** This separation, he said, is from oneself as well as from God. I would maintain that a blindness to ourselves is an inevitable—and natural—consequence of being sinful, which is to say, of being a human being. We are so caught up in our own desires and needs and interests, so inherently incapable of seeing our own proper role in the great scheme of things, that it is always "as through a glass darkly" that we apprehend the world around us. We may not all wear the sign saying "Kick me," as that woman was said to, but we all walk around projecting into the world various messages of which we have at best only the faintest idea.

Think about all the people in your lives you know best. Really think about them. Think about your brother who thinks he's quite funny, though no one finds him so humorous. Think about your aunt who thinks the world owes her so much more respect than she gets. And your cousin who thinks the reason he doesn't have good friends is because he is so much more honest, so much more capable of genuine intimacy, than the lesser beings he is surrounded by in this world. How many people can you think of who are not, in some fundamental way, blind to what they are doing in relation to the world around them? Any?

Can any of you really disagree with the notion that blindness to self is just standard equipment? And if that is so, how can you expect reason to govern in the affairs of people who have been granted freedom from the governing hand of authority?

It's not for nothing that Freud, who at one level was the vanguard of the advancing forces of reason, has also been called the gravedigger of the Enlightenment. Because he showed how shallow is our self-awareness, how paltry the powers of our reasoning faculty in relation to the irrational passions surging for fulfillment beneath the light of consciousness. **Kenneth**

Kenneth's message brought to my mind an interesting conundrum. Why was it that although the man who might be called the founder of psychotherapy—Freud—had a rather grim view of human nature, so many of the psychotherapists I knew were so sanguine about our natural dispositions and inclinations? Freud had proclaimed how man, in the grip of inner forces unknown to himself, was not master even in his own house—providing support, as we had just seen, for those carrying the traditional view of human sinfulness—while most of those I knew who worked as "mental health" practitioners believed us naturally inclined to move toward what is good and right, like a heliotropic flower. Had my friends seen a natural beauty that Freud, with his own grim inner realities, could not see? Or were they suffering from some kind of "clientitis," oversold on the point of view of those whose souls they sought to soothe?

The issues raised by Carl and Kenneth were troubling to me. It had been easier for me to dismiss their vision of human sin when I was younger. Why was that? It wasn't that I had been blind to human evils as a young man—indeed, I'd been preoccupied with them. But it seemed easier then to hold those manifest evils—the bloody trail of history, the ongoing bigotries and lies and cruelties—apart from an image I had of the natural human being, of what we *would* be if tenderly cared for, well fed with the love and support I believed we naturally craved and were unnaturally denied. Perhaps, over the years since, I'd seen too many occasions where people turned away from the good, and toward their smaller selves, and where it did not seem so easy to say with sureness: "This is because of the wounds they have suffered, the deprivations they have been subjected to. If only they had been given what they needed and wanted, they would be more loyal friends, would show more integrity in walking their talk, would sacrifice of themselves to provide for the least fortunate of their brethren."

I realized that, given the miseries of our history, there was nowhere to be found an uncontaminated specimen to gauge the nobility of our unsullied nature. But I'd also seen too many of purely private moral defects that I could not so readily connect with the forces of our flawed social environment, except by assuming the connection as an act of faith.

Thus, although I'd not "changed sides," I had lost the sureness that had once allowed me to take sides.

Following Tradition

Not long after Kenneth's posting, a response from Peter arrived. His message made me think, "This fellow doesn't like the idea of being outflanked to his right." But perhaps I was just being petulant. I know that I felt some disappointment that Peter, who seemed like a reasonable sort of fellow, did not seem moved by these strong indictments of our nature to affirm the dignity of the rational human adult that earlier he had seemed to acknowledge. That was the case I'd have liked to have seen made just now. Instead, with Carl and Kenneth waving the banner of authority aloft, Peter's move was—while using a language closer to theirs than to that of the Enlightenment—to argue for a position akin to theirs, buttressing those who would turn off the Enlightenment and take us back to what I'd always been taught to regard as the Dark Ages.

The problem with the Enlightenment is *hubris,* man's overestimation of himself. What is regarded as sovereign is the mind of the solitary individual. The Lockean view of the natural man with the inherent right of life and liberty, owing nothing, makes each individual the proprietor of his life. He is possessed of rights, and authority must not trample on them. This individual is to decide for himself what is good for him and, enjoying this autonomy, he is to be subject to no authority except that which he has voluntarily agreed to constitute—through the negotiation of a social contract—with the sole purpose of helping the aggregate of such individuals better to meet their individual goals.

But the price of *hubris,* as the Greeks showed, is the fall that cometh after pride. And so we see around us the shattering of the edifice of wisdom that the ages preceding the Enlightenment had built up to shelter us from the consequences of our ignorance, our folly, and our wickedness. The Enlightenment seeks to liberate the individual, but the result is otherwise. For the individual—given the task of finding and achieving his own good—is continually having to reinvent the wheel. The wheel in this case being an understanding of what way of living leads to good results.

What a waste! Lives are wasted, people wander aimlessly—for it is only the extraordinary individual who is capable of inventing a wheel. I would say that this reliance on reason—the foundation of this Enlightenment experiment with liberty—is itself most unreasonable. **Peter**

And what do you suggest is the alternative, Peter? *Ralph asked in a post that came quickly.* It is the reason of the Enlightenment that has put a man on the moon. It is the reason of the Enlightenment that has eliminated smallpox from the earth. Just where else do you suggest that we go to find a wheel? **Ralph**

We've talked here about learning from experience, *Peter wrote in reply.* But we should not take so narrow a view of what learning from experience can mean. The really important "learning from experience" occurs not at the level of the individual but of an entire people, accruing the wisdom of culture as they move through time of such long stretches that the individual life span is seen as the ephemera that it is.

Some of you have enshrined an evolutionary process as the Creator of good order. The argument, evidently, is that the process of selection has fashioned what is compatible with the requirements of life, and that life defines what is good. Evolution, and the accumulation of learning from experience—these are both images of good development from the bottom up. But I have another candidate for embodying these virtues. My candidate is **tradition**.

Tradition embodies the cumulative wisdom of a people, formed over generations. It is not necessary for each new cohort of individuals to reinvent the wheel of knowing, for example, which plants are poisonous and which are nutritious. Nor does each generation have to experiment to find out whether adultery should be treated as a sin, whether lying and stealing should be forbidden and punished. The wisdom that these cultural teachings represent far surpasses what any individual mind—however powerful its rational capacities are by human standards—could have discovered for itself.

Our ancestors have confronted the basic challenges of human life before us, and out of this stream of human experience have come laws and customs, commandments and prohibitions, practices and manners, that represent the fruit of a body of experience so much greater than our own that challenging them on the basis of our supposed capacities for rational judgment is folly of the highest order. **Peter**

My response to Peter's call to us to depend upon tradition was complex. On the one hand, my reflexive response to "traditionalism" was to see it as a narrowing, a confining of the human spirit to a rigid cage, a submission to the cold, dead hand of a history that James Joyce described, with good reason, as a nightmare from which we are trying to awaken.

On the other hand, Peter's argument about the accumulated wisdom of long experience also reminded me of a conversation I'd once had with Mr. Godachi. It was my first spring in the Shenandoah Valley, and all sorts of things were poking up through the earth. It's my favorite time of the year. This particular spring, however, I faced a new perplexity: I couldn't tell what was what among the new shoots. Some, I knew, were perennials and some were weeds, but which were which? I saw Mr. Godachi nimbly plucking out a few among the various shoots, and I said: "I wish I knew which ones to weed out and which to leave to grow." And he said something that was quite obvious, but still in its way profound: "When you have observed long enough, and closely enough, what grows into what, you'll know them even at this early stage."

I could imagine that the tradition Peter was speaking of might contain a similar wisdom. Societies endure for generations, long enough to witness which of our many shoots of human behaviors develop into which results, long enough to cultivate the traditions needed to weed out those with noxious fruits and to encourage those that produce beauty and nourishment. I wasn't prepared to embrace tradition, but I could imagine that it might contain something like Godachi's wisdom.

Two messages came in together, one from Ralph to put the brakes on the anti-Enlightenment roll Peter seemed to be on, and one from a new person to carry Peter's critique still further.

Of course, *Ralph retorted in his next posting*. No one is talking about each individual, or each generation, starting from scratch. The very language we speak has developed over thousands of years, and it represents in itself an accumulated treasure of conceptual insight that true children of the Enlightenment would regard as part of the necessary equipment a person must possess even to begin the process of rational reflection. When the liberal vision calls upon the rational deliberator, with his or her own life-project of finding the good life, it assumes that the reflective individual possesses a grounding in the wisdoms that have accumulated over the centuries of cultural development. Why else would that education whose purpose is to inculcate in each student a knowledge of the basic thought of our culture be called "liberal arts"?

The critics of the liberal vision often speak as if the liberal idea were for each person to make choices based on whatever of his desires seem strongest at the moment. But that's not it at all. The development of a person worthy of liberty involves a project of cultivating the self, choosing through informed rational thinking which of the various desires are worthy of being nurtured and strengthened, and which should be clipped back, so that by the time the individual comes into his liberty, the motive forces that are followed have themselves been shaped by wisdom, a wisdom built upon the accumulated experience and understanding of the wider culture.

The rational individual envisioned by liberalism, then, does not begin as if he or she just dropped in from the savannahs of five million years ago, equipped only with a variety of impulses. That individual is assumed to have been prepared by inclusion in the Great Conversation of the centuries to set upon his own voyage. The liberated individual stands on the shoulders of those who have gone before, and then, seeing from the height of that accumulated wisdom, freely and rationally chooses his way.
Ralph

Alice then responded:

When I was in college, three decades ago, I believed, as perhaps you still do, Ralph, and as Fred almost certainly still does, that we should largely be free to live our lives as we see fit, without authority overly infringing upon our right to choose. The government should not protect us from ourselves. The idea that the state should not meddle with "crimes without victims"—that it should allow consenting adults to do what they pleased with themselves and with each other—was important to me. Thus the government should have no say about people's private sexual practices, I believed, or what drugs they ingest, or whether they gamble or hire prostitutes. People should make their own choices about their own, purely personal lives.

I no longer think that way. Not only have I come to see how these supposedly private choices have ramifications that, collectively and over time, affect the whole society, but also I have come to believe that people, on the whole, are more likely to be hurt than helped by being granted such liberty. In other words, it seems that if, for example, a whole menu of drugs were freely available to all (adult) citizens, a very great many lives would be ruined by the foolish decisions those people would make.

It may well be, Ralph, as you say, that some individuals can develop their capacities sufficiently to exercise such choices wisely. But they are exceptional people, from all I can see, and it seems a rather disastrous philosophy that would sacrifice the lives of many who will abuse their liberty in order to honor the ability of a few who can use it well.

For humankind taken as a whole, the narrow confines of law and established custom is more likely to be conducive to a good life than are the free ranges of the kind of liberty a great many liberals espouse. **Alice**

You raise an important point, Alice, *Ralph replied*. I cannot say that I disagree with your point that the reflective, rational individual that the liberal vision calls for seems, in the actual world around us, more the exception than the rule. And I, too, sometimes wrestle with the question of whether people should be protected from themselves, and at what point does the price of respecting the right of individuals to find their own way, even to make bad choices, become too great. It's a question perhaps we can revisit.

But in the meantime, I wanted to raise another point *a propos* of Peter's advocating our following tradition rather than granting individuals the right to make their own choices about how they will live their lives. Contrary to what one might guess from your previous message, Peter, the "tradition" of our culture is not unitary; it does not provide the voyager with a single map about what the good life is, or should be, or how it is to be attained. Our accumulated tradition is composed of many currents, some at real variance with others. With so many alternatives laid out by tradition, what can it mean to say that the individual should surrender his liberty and submit to the authority of tradition? It would seem at the very least that the individual must exercise the right of choosing which of the maps he believes to be most valid, which of the voices of tradition to allow to mold his life.

There's another reason the Enlightenment project cannot validly be portrayed as the alternative to tradition. The very ideas of reason, of liberty, of the autonomy of the individual—these are themselves sweet fruits that ripened over the centuries on the tree of the Western tradition. It is certainly true that the liberal society's openness to new information and new ideas has loosened the grip of rigid and unchanging doctrine and thus has made tradition more capable of evolving in new ways. But the idea of liberty as a central value is itself a hard-won insight into the nature of how things work in human affairs, no less than is the way of authority. **Ralph**

This last sentence of Ralph's—calling attention to how hard-won has been the capture of Western tradition, or at least a powerful part of it, by the way of liberty—was to appear subsequently as the first blast of the rallying call of the counter-counter-revolution. But that came a bit later (see the next chapter), after the adherents of authority had still more forcefully challenged us with their vision of good order as requiring the submission of the individual to higher powers. In the meantime it seemed to be a posting that arrived simultaneously with Ralph's—one from a new person named Henry—that, by running up the flag of authority so boldly and advancing to the very capital of the liberal foe, opened the way for the charge from the right across the field of dispute.

Henry did not exactly introduce himself. He invited us to look up his Web site, which would give us access to his resume and to a variety of his position papers. I myself never bothered to check them out, but I learned later from Fred—our resident anarchist, who must have really felt that in Henry he had found a kindred soul!—that Henry's education was sterling (B.A. from St. John's College in Annapolis, Ph.D. from the University of Chicago), that his grounding was in the classics, and that he divided his time between writing polemics of a high order, tutoring the children of the rich and conservative, and working within an international network of right-wing Catholics to reinstate traditional values and institutions into the Western democracies.

It should not have taken us two hundred years, *Henry wrote,* to recognize that the path of the Enlightenment is one of folly. How near it was to the beginning of the whole misguided "project," as some of you have styled it, that the great painter Goya, observing the despoliation of his native Spain by the Napoleanic fruits of the French Revolution, penned the words, "The dream of reason produces monsters."

Reason imagines itself the lord of creation. It believes that it can think things through, come to the truth itself, devise mechanisms to make the realm of man operate as smoothly as Newton's clockwork universe. But Peter is right about the *hubris* of reason. And as with the Greeks, *hubris* leads to tragedy still. As with tragedy, each supposed strength is turned into its opposite weakness. As Oedipus's "I know" becomes transmuted, in Sophocles, into the tragedy that issued from his blind ignorance, as his "I see" changes into his self-blinding, so also does the banner of "Liberty" held aloft by the revolution in the name of Reason end up flying over the dictatorship of the Tyranny and Terror.

Reason with its blindness to its shortcomings becomes the agent not of liberation, but of totalitarianism. What else was the Marxist state but the apotheosis of the illusion that human beings can **think** themselves into a social order? Who was wiser, the revolutionary philosophes who brought us this kind of "totalitarian democracy," or the famous French "reactionary" de Maistre who, noting how "feeble" is "the guidance of reason," declared that "no nation can **give** itself a government"?[4]

The proud idea that we can know the good, and that we can manufacture the means to achieve it, stands in stark contrast with the humility of those who, with greater wisdom, understand how little it is that we can really control. The Enlightenment, like the Serpent in Eden, tells us that we can be as gods. The greater wisdom is to see how feeble are our own powers, and to submit to the authority of Him who **is** God.

Thus spake Henry.

It was over the whole idea of submission—to God, to tradition, to whatever—that we then became embattled.

Bitter Lessons

It was about this time that I got a "blast from the past," a call from an old friend. This friend was an "old friend" not in the sense that most of my friends are old friends, that is, in the sense of our having been friends continuously over a very long period of time. Rather we'd been friends a long time ago, in a very different era of our lives, and had then fallen completely out of touch for more than twenty-five years. Almost thirty. Hence I call the phone call from him a blast from the past.

"Hi, Andy, this is Mark Gold—do you remember me?" inquired the voice on the other end of the line.

"Sure I remember you, Mark," I replied, breathless from my run to the phone, as I conjured up out of my mental an image of a young man of twenty-two or three with long jet-black hair and beard, and with more of the uniform of the hippie than I was inclined to wear even back then in the late '60s, and even back there in Berkeley where we'd been friends for most of a year. He'd been especially fond of tie-dye and batik, and a necklace with an ivory skull on it, the combination of which had led me to dub him "the Thai-die kid." "How the hell are you?" I asked, "and why is this day different from all other days in the past quarter-century?"

"Man, listen to you puff," Mark jibed, "you must be even older than I am somehow."

"I'm just practicing for the role of the iceman," I joked in return. In fact, to reach the phone I'd had to sprint up our steep hill in the orchard, from the more sedentary activity of stonewall-building in which I'd been engaged when I'd heard the ring. Without those walls, all my plantings on that slope would just wash down, soil and all. And it was time for repairing some of my old walls, and for putting in a small new terrace as well for my venture into broccoli.

"Hey, I'm in Harrisonburg, and I see you're in Broadway. I'm driving through on my way to Washington, so I wondered if I could drop in and see you."

"Actually," I said, "I live off-Broadway. (That's just the town the mailman drives up out of—I don't even live in that county.) And sure, come by. I'll give you directions—if you're up for driving a bit further out of your way. But how'd you find me, anyway?"

"I've seen your byline in the San Francisco paper various times over the years—'A writer living in Virginia.' And then when I knew I'd be driving through this way, I looked you up through the Internet and found your Broadway address."

"Well, I'm glad you found me," I said. "And I'd be delighted to have you come by. Stay for dinner. Stay overnight." I knew from experience that April would always say yes if I asked her, so under the circumstances I didn't bother to ask.

"Can't stay," Mark replied. "I've got to get to Washington for an evening thing at seven. And then, day after tomorrow, I'm getting married there."

Something in his voice got my attention. What it was I couldn't say—couldn't even say if it was happy or sad. It wasn't so simple as either of those. That and the news that he was getting married—I had no idea whatever what that might mean for someone of whose life for the past maybe twenty-eight years I knew nothing. In addition to all that, I felt vaguely conscious of some old memories wafting up in my mind, and in some inarticulate way the combination of all these ingredients intensified my interest in seeing Mark.

"Well, I guess there are eight million stories in the Naked City," I said, and we both chuckled.

Soon we concluded our conversation on the phone, knowing that he'd shortly be here for a brief visit and that we'd have a chance to catch up on each other's lives. I gave him directions, we hung up, and I went back to my stone-laying.

As I mused on the abundance of rock available on our slope for the building of walls, I recalled with amusement a question my first-born son had asked when he was about seven. Observing how frequently the tops of the mountains were rocky, he inquired: "How come it's at the highest places that there are so many of the heaviest rocks?" Evidently, it seemed counterintuitive to him that big pieces should be migrating uphill. And I'd explained that it wasn't that the big rocks went up the mountains as that erosion took away from the peaks so much of the soil that was finer.

Now I lived on a ridge of an area that had been settled by Europeans for more than two centuries, that bordered on "the Breadbasket of the Confederacy," but that gave only the scantiest evidence of ever having been cultivated. On the other side of our ridge, and about a mile and a half south, I'd come upon piled lines of stones encompassing a rectangular area that must have been a farmer's field once but is now a woods in which the oldest trees are perhaps sixty years old. Someone had tried to eke out a living on the soils that can be found near the top of this ridge, but—or so I'd guessed—had given up. To subsist off this land, one probably had better be a hunter and a gatherer, and have a pretty big range of it at one's disposal—something the Native Americans perhaps had figured out from their many centuries here.

Now I, as a late-twentieth-century American who grows his daily bread from the sowing of words and not of crops, was trying to make this ridge blossom at least in a few well-chosen places that I'd liberally enriched with chicken- and pig manure obtained from friends farming in the bottom lands to our east. The soil left here by nature on this unrelenting slope—being so bereft of the fine particles and nutrients left each year by decaying vegetation—was too coarse and poor by itself. Rain and gravity continually scrubbed away the earth's efforts to generate topsoil and so, with the rocks left behind, I labored to erect enclaves of horizontal ground to arrest the downhill flow.

It was after I accidentally dropped a stone on my toe—right after, having groaned some and danced around in my pain, I thought to myself, "Over gravity there's no complete victory to be had"—that I remembered what it was about the idea that Mark was on his way to get married that had seemed strangely evocative.

When I'd known Mark, he was in a very intense loving relationship with a young woman named Alicia. She was a few years younger than we—about twenty—and came from a somewhat upper middle class

family down the peninsula near Mountain View. She was a lovely creature—long, glowing blond hair, willowy in figure, a sweet and deli-
cately featured face. And her heart was generous and kind. At the time
I was unattached, and it was more than a few times that I thought that,
if Alicia had been available and not deeply entwined with a friend of
mine, I'd have been interested.

But Alicia was far from available. In fact, of all the couples I'd known
in my life up till then, as I sometimes remarked to myself, and a couple
of times to Mark as well, the bond between the two of them seemed the
most rich and deep and beautiful I'd ever seen. "Marriage made in
heaven," was a phrase that had come, in those days, to my mind—even
though, in those days, the very idea of marriage was suspect, coming
under the cloud of the category "foolish bourgeois notions."

I had lost touch with Mark—and with Alicia—when the two of them
moved "out to the land," as people put it in those days, to establish a
commune of some sort up in Humboldt County. We'd exchanged letters
once, but I'd found Mark an unreliable correspondent, and Humboldt
County being further away from the Bay Area than I would readily drive,
and with my own life soon taking me east to resume my graduate studies,
we lost contact entirely.

But now, as I worked in the orchard, awaiting the sound of Mark's
car coming down my gravel driveway, I realized that someplace in the
back of my mind, I'd always imagined Mark and Alicia married. Always
the two of them together. Always and for life. How could it be otherwise,
so perfectly matched were they? But obviously, if Mark was on his way
to Washington to get married, it could be otherwise. I don't know if I'd
thought of them consciously during the past decade and a half, but it
now seemed to me that in the recesses of my mental pantheon, the love
of Mark and Alicia had stood as an icon of sorts for the ideal connection
between a man and a woman.

I heard the familiar sound of tires crunching on gravel, and walked up
the hill to greet my old friend.

He was still recognizably Mark. The jet-black hair of the twenty-some-
year-old had, in the fifty-some-year-old, lost its color and its luster—what
hadn't lost its moorings and dropped out altogether. The eyes had lost
some of their eager quality, some of their mirth. But it was still Mark.

And I was pleased to see that what he'd lost in mirth he'd not, like so many men our age, made up for in girth.

After I showed Mark around the place and introduced him to April, I asked him if he'd like to sit and have a cup of tea, or go for a walk, or what. "Been sitting all day," he responded, "and this looks like a great place for walking. You remember some of those all-night walks we used to take in Berkeley—full-moon nights and our hiking those jogging trails in the hills? Anyway, if you're up for a walk, I'll take it."

When we were well into our walk, I broached the topic of Mark's upcoming nuptials. "On your way to get married. Sounds like an exciting time."

"Yeah, she's really a good person. It'll be great to settle down together, live in the same place—not the long-distance connection we've been having."

There was a warmth in his voice, but also something sad, and more distant than I'd expect on the eve of such a commitment. The thought came to my mind that maybe he'd been through enough weddings of his own that this latest one could not kindle hopes too intense.

"What number marriage is this for each of you?" I asked.

"For her, this is the second marriage. She was married once before, and has two kids—one in college, one still in high school—from that first marriage, which ended about seven years ago." He paused.

"And you?" I inquired further.

"For me, Andy," Mark said, looking at me sideways, "this is my first marriage."

I was startled. He noticed.

"I bet you're thinking of me and Alicia," Mark ventured.

"Well, yeah. I guess I was. I guess I always imagined the two of you together."

"I think of Alicia, too," Mark said. "Believe me."

At this point, he walked wearily over to a large flat rock about twenty feet off the side of our dirt road and, sitting down, proceeded to tell me the story of what had happened after he and Alicia had gone up to Humboldt County to join in establishing that commune.

"You know how much I loved Alicia," he began. "Having each other, we felt we had everything. But in some ways, we didn't know what we were doing.

"The first months on the commune were difficult—building little shelters, figuring out how to do our gardens, like that—but it was an adventure, and we were glad to be there. The interpersonal scene there soon got a bit complicated.

"Several other couples were part of the scene, and with some of them there was some restlessness. Especially living so close to one another, it wasn't easy to figure out just what was OK and what wasn't OK in how people would deal with some of the sexual feelings that would arise between different men and women.

"You remember how everything was up for grabs in those days?" Mark continued. "There were no laws handed down from Sinai for our generation, nothing beyond question and experimentation?

"Especially in matters of sex. You remember? Sex was supposed to be the ultimate test of our liberation. All the restraints of the conventionally minded folks from whom we'd sprung were just so many foolish impediments to the realization of our full potential—for relationship, for pleasure, for fulfillment.

"I remember a Cobb cartoon that captured a big piece of our general outlook. Some big pigs were in this fenced area, looking disapprovingly over at some little pigs that were escaping under that fence into freedom. One big pig says to another something like: 'That younger generation—always trying to escape from reality!' And we see on the building just behind the fenced area a sign reading something like 'Acme Sausage Company.'

"We had no use for the fences of traditional morality. Marriage—who needs it? Fidelity—just more chains to bind us, to curtail life's bigger possibilities.

"That was at the level of ideology. But for Alicia and me, we really liked having that little fenced area in our lives that meant our being true to each other. And for months, in that communal situation, that's how we lived. But the others were starting to get into different kinds of exchanges, a 'go with the flow' approach to who coupled with whom.

"For a while, it didn't seem like any big deal that we weren't going along with that, but soon we found ourselves under some pressure to 'loosen up.' Some of the other guys had the hots for Alicia. And maybe there was also some discomfort with just the fact of our being different, for all the talk of 'do your own thing.' But whatever the source of the pressure, what was hardest for us to deal with was the way it expressed itself: in terms of some ideological values that we ourselves also believed in.

"It wasn't quite the schoolyard taunting of 'Are you chicken,' but it had that chicken flavor. 'What's the matter, you uptight?' Or, 'You really ought to do something about your insecurities.' And 'Possessiveness is a sign of a lack of spiritual enlightenment,' with citations of Gibran's 'If it doesn't fly back to you then it wasn't yours in the first place,' or however it goes.

"Anyway, after a while of this, Alicia and I capitulated to the pressure, and little by little started getting with this brave new experiment in freedom. We tried to tell ourselves that the ache we felt from it was just a form of growing pains. And we would come back together and cling to each other fervently. Like a kind of prayer. But something was getting damaged. I think we both felt that, but we weren't prepared to do anything to stop it.

"Maybe the important damage had already been done by the time this guy Dominick joined the commune, or maybe it's just that by the time he arrived the bond between Alicia and me had been injured enough that we were vulnerable to being destroyed by some clever guy on a power trip.

"I can't tell you how many times I've thought about all this over the years," Mark continued. "I've tried to forget it sometimes. And sometimes I've tried to remember it clearly. But I really can't do either, quite. My memory seems to get distorted in some ways—like when I try to picture this Dominick I get him confused with Charles Manson, or other evil figures I've seen in the movies. I really can't think quite straight about Dominick, I feel so much pain and rage about him.

"Anyway, let me make a long tragedy short. This guy was able somehow to use our ideology to get us men in the group to renounce all possessiveness, and then he turned around and used that same persuasive power to get the women—or at least a few of them—to renounce their freedom, to become in some way *his*, extensions of his will. I'm not sure just how he did it—the men weren't there when he worked his magic on those women—but he did it. And Alicia was one of those women.

"Alicia followed Dominick's will not with eagerness, but with a kind of resignation. The fire seemed to have gone out of her heart. The light was gone from her eyes. For a little while, she was still in some ways connected with me, but gradually that connection became only a ghostly memory of what it had been.

"I've spent a lot of years hating Dominick. But more than that, hating myself. I let it happen! How could I have been such a blind fool?

"In Alicia, I feel, the cosmos handed me the most precious treasure. My soul mate. Do you know that line in *Othello* where he decries himself for having thrown away a pearl worth all his tribe? That's me, with Alicia. Many times I've felt the rightness of Othello having slain himself—the 'base dog'—at the end of the play. I didn't do that, but sure as I'm sitting here now something in me died because of what I did, or failed to do, in that commune.

"And I'm angry also with my tribe, us young people who were willing to throw away all the rules in the belief that if we were freed of those encumbrances we somehow could readily build a better way to live. What a terribly high price some of us paid to discover that for some of those rules, there were reasons. What a bitter lesson to learn that if you get rid of some of those old structures, what you get is not the freedom of the little piggies breaking away from the sausage factory but the inexorable downhill slide toward destruction."

Mark stopped at this point, and I let the silence sit there while he crushed a couple of clods of clay in his fist.

Then I spoke up. "What about Alicia? When you realized this, was there no going back to rebuild what you'd had?"

"Ah, Alicia. That is the bitterest part.

"After a while, Dominick left the commune, and he took with him a couple of the women. One of them was Alicia. At first I felt stricken and paralyzed. But after about eight months I recovered some piece of my capacity for initiative and went out looking for her.

"I managed a couple of times to find someone who'd seen her, and to piece parts of the story together. She'd become increasingly wan and ghostlike, I heard. There's evidence that Dominick was abusive toward her. And he got her into using heroin.

"But I couldn't ever catch up with her. Every month or two I'd check with her family in Mountain View, but they'd never heard anything. So I checked with them less and less frequently.

"Finally, one day about two years after Alicia had left the commune, I called her family and her mother answered. I said hello, and asked perfunctorily into how they were doing and from the tone of her response, even before I got to my customary question about Alicia I felt this feeling of dread crawling up my spine. Her mother paused after my question, and then in a voice that sounded like it was coming from deep and explosive within her, she told me, 'Alicia—Alicia, she's dead. She died of an overdose of drugs in Eureka.'

"I was twenty-six then. I guess it was exactly half my lifetime ago. But since then, I've not had the capacity to do half my living. Part of me died with Alicia."

Silence again, and then Mark got up and suggested we start walking back.

"So, I'm getting married this weekend," he said after a couple of minutes, and as if he could read my mind went on, "and you can be happy for me. My willingness to give myself into this marriage is a sign of my coming back to life, and of my feeling entitled to some love and comfort. I've done my penance, and I'm ready to find what happiness I can."

When we got back to his car, we chatted a bit about how my life had gone over the years—the major headlines—exchanged e- and snail-mail addresses after agreeing to keep in touch henceforth, and, with April joining us for the final minutes before Mark's departure, said our good-byes.

II
Word from On High

Bow Down
Must People, to Be Good, Submit to Authority?

Gate-crashers

We had begun with a small group of people, most of whom tended to agree that the natural human being is basically a trustworthy creature. With that belief came a predisposition to hold that people should be supported in the unfolding of their inborn selves, that the well-nourished human being would manifest a natural wisdom, and that the imposition by external authority of commandments contrary to our natures was unnecessary, and perhaps even counterproductive, to the proper ordering of the human realm.

Admittedly, our shared predisposition to believe in some sort of natural goodness, and to lean toward liberty over authority, glossed over some fairly significant differences among us. Some of us objected even to the idea of proper ordering within the psyche, while others maintained that such intrapsychic governance is essential. The most extreme of us rejected the very idea of government, while most of us of a "liberal" bent, while believing it essential that government be the natural expression of the rational will of the governed, nonetheless thought it essential to have governing structures to maintain social order.

Our group then evolved into something far more heterogeneous, thanks largely to the active work of Rev. George. He had sought out some worthy opponents of what might be called our "Party of the Natural Man," and then (I later learned) some of those he recruited took the initiative to bring in new recruits of their own. As the conversation progressed, and as there came to the surface ever more difficulties with our sanguine beliefs about the "state of nature," this latter group—the "Party of Authority On High," it might be dubbed—began to make its presence felt.

As this Authority group began its ascendancy, I received from some of my friends from the California conference a few back-channel complaints about these new people. "Too aggressive," some said. "They're taking control of the conversation," my friends complained. "Authoritarian" was the epithet I remember being applied to them. After thinking some about these complaints, I sent a back-channel note to the several people who'd expressed their concern to me.

I don't think I would want to live in a world where the ideas of people like Henry held sway, *I said in that note, singling out the most reactionary voice we'd heard,* but I'm not sorry we're having to contend with him and with all the others trumpeting the horn of Authority here. If it's a problem, I'd say the problem is **our** problem. If they are taking up ever more space in our conversation, it is the holes in our own vision of things that is opening up the space they are filling.

Come to think of it, I wouldn't want to live in a world in which some of our ideas were allowed, unchallenged and unsupplemented, to order the world. And part of what bothers me about the world I see around us is the sense that just this may have been happening. I'd say, let's see what it is we can learn from these authoritarians, and see what we've got to say after we've learned it. **Andy**

Of course, with so compliant a group as ours, my message completely persuaded each and every one of them of the rightness of my approach.

Law and Order

I don't want to go as far as Henry in throwing out the political order of the Enlightenment, *began a new person, Terrence, who told us he was a professor with a joint appointment in history and law at a large private university. Terrence was referring to Henry's inaugural posting in which he represented the whole project of the Enlightenment as a tragedy of hubris.* But I would take up his theme—the need for false pride to bow down before the demands of order—by underscoring the importance of **lawfulness** in our social order.

Where the issue of pride comes in here is in many people's apparent belief that obedience to the law is an option, not a moral obligation. In this "pro-choice" party, each person is seen as entitled to be a law unto her- or himself. It is alarming to me how the modifier "law-abiding," which when I was growing up was practically equivalent to "good" or "decent," has become for a growing component of the American population the equivalent of "square" or overly conventional. The once-admired "law-abiding citizen" is now, to many, a rigid and slightly contemptible figure.

I'm not just talking about the way, when I go the speed limit on the freeways around my city, everyone on the road passes me. It shows up in much more serious forms. Think of the statistics on the use of illegal drugs. Think of how almost two-thirds of high school students today admit—they freely say so themselves!—to having cheated on some school examination or another. "Hey, if I feel like doing it, what are silly rules or laws to get in my way?" If developments like these are not a sign of moral disorder, what would be?

No social cosmos will be well ordered, or even safe or decent to live in, where the people do not look to the law above them with respect, do not willingly submit to the power of the law to mold and regulate their conduct. Individual desire cannot be held superior to the majesty of the law. Individual judgment—however reasoned—has no right to hold itself superior to law. The law is superior to any one of us, and we all must bow down to it. **Terrence**

You declare the law superior, but what makes it so? *asked Fred in response.* Are you saying more than that the brute force of law, backed as it is by the power of the armed police, is superior to that which can be mustered in resistance by any individual or group that would wish to be free of the law's yoke around their necks?

Of course that is not what I mean by superior, *Terrence replied.* Nowhere does what Peter's statement about the irreplaceable value of the accumulated wisdom of the generations apply more strongly than with the body of the law. And whereas a good deal of tradition might be considered arbitrary or irrational—does the fork go on the right or the left of the plate? does a bride wear a trailing train or not? do the guards at Buckingham Palace goosestep or march in a different fashion?—the law is codified in a conspicuously formal and rational way. Quoth the great jurist Sir Edward Coke: "The common law is nothing else but reason. . . . The law, which [is] the perfection of reason."[1]

What the law represents, then, is experience, accumulated over generations, deliberately processed through reason. It represents the rules and principles that an entire people have learned from an enormous body of cases, and which can provide the good order that society needs. If your ox breaks down my fence and eats my crops, how is it to be handled? If lies I tell about you cause you injury, how are you to be compensated? We are all better off submitting to the rule of laws made from the wisdom of long experience.

Liberty unrestrained leads, of course, to conflict: to Hobbes's anarchy, his state of nature, his war of all against all. And out of conflict—overtaken by reason—grows the body of the law: the cases are brought to court to find justice, and out of them grow the principles by which the disorder of anarchy gives way to the good order that reason desires.

That is what I meant by the superiority of law. Law is superior to the individual's beliefs and to his desires and interests, because the individual mind is inferior to the "artificial reason" of the law (again Coke), and because the desires and interests of different individuals inevitably conflict, and justice is superior to the war of all against all that would otherwise obtain. **Terrence**

Oh, wrote Fred back, drily. Then he left a space of several lines, and began writing again. Nice to have such fine laws, I guess. Nice to have such good order in a society. Then a few more blank lines, standing, I supposed, for silence, while he thought a little longer.

I can just imagine how good order would look from Pharoah's point of view. When Pharoah's in his palace and all's right with the world, it's the slave's brow that's "dew-pearled." No tomb is too great for Pharoah in this good order, and he's got lots of laws to make sure that the slaves will keep their noses to the tombstones until the pyramid has been built with their sweat and blood (and maybe here and there a crushed body-part) between the stones.

It is, of course, most important that we should recognize the wisdom of submitting to such laws, because with our feeble reason we might not understand how justice requires our obedience to the dictates of the laws our rulers hand down to govern us. We might not recognize that the government that tradition has handed down to us—with Pharoah as the living god, and slaves as beasts of burden—is far better than any order we might in our *hubris* seek to invent. **Fred**

Fred's trenchant sarcasm brought a rejoinder from Terrence seeking to clarify that it was not to a legal order like Pharoah's that he intended us to submit.

No, Fred, I'm not saying that just because some regime declares something to be the law that makes it just. You might note that my quotations were from Sir Edward Coke—a jurist from the land that brought forth the idea of the consent of the governed, and limitations upon the powers of the crown—not from Ramses. **Terrence**

Let's nail this down a bit, Terrence. If one is a slave under Ramses, does one or does one not have a moral obligation—as you see it—to submit to the laws of the land? (Or, another way of putting it, do you think that Moses could justly be prosecuted for applying coercive measures to get Pharoah to let his people go?) **Fred**

I do not regard the Egyptian slave as morally bound by the laws that held him in bondage. By what criteria do I make that judgment? By the criteria of whether the laws were justly made. I could go on and define in some detail what is required for the manner in which the laws are made to be deemed just. **Terrence**

Just tell me this, please. What if I do not believe the laws in my society to be made justly? Am I still obliged to submit to them? **Fred**

Here's where we get into the *hubris* of the sovereign individual. To put it bluntly, who the hell are **you**—or any solitary individual—to make such a judgment for yourself, placing yourself above the whole body of your society? **Terrence**

Yes, well put. Who the hell **am** I? It seems that question—in its many forms, including the question of human nature—is part of the crux of our discussion here lo these many days a-passing.

But who the hell am I supposed to entrust with that decision? Of course, I should trust the governing authorities, right? Well, ask Ramses what he thinks about how good is the order that renders my brow dew-pearled. "Yes indeed," Ramses would say, "the laws were justly made. So it shall be written, so it shall be done." Oh, and then I guess I could ask the majority of my fellow citizens, assuming that "citizenship" exists in our fine little order. "Hey, neighbors," I could ask my fellow Germans in the 1930s, "tell me, about this law that says I need to wear a yellow star of David on my coat, and this one saying you Aryans can take my property from me—were these laws justly made?" "Oh, yes, fine laws. Formulated by our duly elected Chancellor (a.k.a. Führer), and passed and stamped and everything. All most justly made by the leaders of the Master Race." "Thanks for showing me clearly my moral obligations," I'd then reply, "and by the way, do you have a needle and thread I can use?" **Fred**

Minding Our Betters

It seemed most unlikely that Fred and Terrence had finished their duel, and I actually looked forward to seeing where they might go from there. It did not seem that either was seeking a way to come to some common wisdom, but I myself thought there was enough validity in both their positions, as expressed to that point, that I had hopes that if not they, then someone else in the group, and if not the group, then maybe I on my own, would find a way to work toward a means to integrating the two positions. For as I saw it, Terrence was right that we cannot have a world in which each person feels entitled to act as a law unto her- or himself, and Fred was right that the mere fact that something is the law— made and enforced by a governing authority—by no means proves that our submission to it is the best way to achieve good order.

But at this point, the conversation took a slightly different turn. As Peter had argued earlier that people should submit to the authority of tradition, and as Terrence had just asserted that we are obliged to submit to the authority of law, now Henry weighed in again with a rather venerable proposition, although in some disrepute in a society like the United States of the past couple hundred years: namely, that among the principles of the good social order is the idea that people should defer to those who are superior to them.

The disorder of the modern world, *Henry wrote,* derives in no small measure from the extent to which the common people, in their little vanity, have lost sight of this ancient principle, that the better should command the worse. The idea of "mind your betters" used to be considered an obvious aspect of good order. But nowadays, it has the odor at best of quaintness, and at worse of a pernicious denial of the supposed fundamental equality of all mortals.

Ah, yes, equality. It says it right there in the Declaration of Independence, doesn't it: "All men are created equal." Self-evident truth, that son of the Enlightenment, Thomas Jefferson, called this proposition. If it was so self-evident, however, why is it that it escaped the notice of societies for thousands of years? Aristotle, that master of logic, must have been just too stupid to recognize what to Jefferson was so plain as to prove itself.

Now the whole world revolves around this self-evident truth, and what a mess it has made. The *vox populi* speaketh, and the world must listen. Never mind how much gibberish and folly the voice of the people has to say. If the people say, "Flatter us, indulge us, entertain us, ask nothing of us"—why, so it will be, even if in the process the nation goes bankrupt, even if the bread and circuses debase the moral level of the society, and even if the people go slack in their physical toughness as well as their moral fiber.

Now, if the mass of people would instead **listen** instead of speak, obey their betters instead of command them, then we could make progress toward restoring good order.
Henry

This time it was Larry who took up the challenge of this latest argument for submission to Authority. I thought it interesting for Larry to address this particular argument, as it had been he a while before who had proposed the idea of the "natural hierarchy." In that case, the issue was Len's having withheld the exercise of paternal authority because he felt that he should just let the development of the child proceed more or less "naturally." Larry had replied that the authority of the parent was in fact a *part* of the natural order in which the child was naturally "expecting" to develop. Now the idea of hierarchy was returning in a new form, one with which Larry evidently was in considerably less sympathy.

Submit to what the "superior people" say? Sure, why not, *Larry began*. If you want to get from here to there, follow the directions from those who know best. But there's a problem, and it is rather like the one Fred pointed out about the law: We should always obey the laws worthy of our obedience, and we should always heed the word of those who know best—but who is to decide which laws are just, and who is to decide which people in fact know best?

It occurred to me at this point that Larry was making a few somewhat sloppy assumptions here, but his point was still a good one. On the subject of laws, Fred and Terrence had discussed whether the laws were justly made, but the subject of whether the laws themselves were just had not been broached. And I could imagine that laws might be "justly made" but still be unjust. And on the subject Henry had raised of our "minding our betters," he had not really defined what he meant by "better." The idea, assumed by Larry, that "better" means "knowing best" seemed to me to give Henry much the benefit of the doubt. The image that had come to my mind when I read Henry was much more of a matter of social stratification: if you have a "von" in the middle of your name, or a "Lord" or "Duke" in front of it, you were, I suspected, one of the superior people Henry had in mind.

But careless or not on that point, in his next paragraph, I saw, Larry managed to move directly to what it was about Henry's point that had bothered me:

History shows, however, that the criteria for superiority rarely have to do with merit. Merit is, of course, claimed. But the making of an aristocracy is even more unseemly a process than the making of sausages, and it's just as bloody. Those who could look down their noses and tell their underlings to mind their betters enjoyed their high positions because they had inherited them, not because they earned them. But even worse, those ancestors from whom this "superiority" had been inherited—those who had **"*earned*"** their superior status—had risen to the top of the social hierarchy not because of merit or piety or wisdom or any of the virtues that I imagine Henry would claim for the superior, but because they had the ruthlessness and the brute might to seize the lands and terrorize the peoples whom they could henceforth count as their inferiors. The burning of villages, the massacre of men, the rape of women, the use of the rack and the dungeon—these are the virtues on which the superiority of the elites of most pre-Enlightenment societies was founded.

If this is what is at the root of so-called "superiority," what can it mean to say we should bow down to our superiors except that we should acquiesce in injustice and allow ourselves to be indoctrinated in the delusion that this constitutes good order? I'd rather take my chance with the folly of the many than with the wickedness of this "superior" few. **Larry**

At this point, there appeared one of those occasional *graffiti* postings from Victor, the Graffiti Artist.

"Quoth Francis Rous, an Englishman, in 1649: "if any man do excel in power, it is now out of doubt that he received that power of God."[2]

Henry's point seemed to me pretty well countered. But it was interesting that the next posting reopened the question—or at least a kindred question—from a somewhat different direction. This one was from Donna, the somewhat hippie-like woman who had previously assured me that my Nintendo-playing son, like the rest of the universe, was just right exactly the way he was.

I am glad that I live in a country where the idea of equality is held in very high regard. What Larry has written reminds me of all the terrible things that get done to "inferiors" by "superiors." Not that I needed all that much reminding, because it's not that long since I saw the movie *Braveheart*. If that movie doesn't make your blood boil, I don't know what will, what with the English conquerors or their commanders claiming the right to the first night with a new bride of one of the Scots, and the complete ruthlessness of the king, Edward Longshanks, and the way they butcher the brave hero at the end because he will not bow down and swear to the king the very kind of submission that Henry seems to think is such a good idea.

But there is another point that needs to be made. This idea of equality can be taken too far, and maybe we ought to look at how a lot of us do just that. Let me give you an example from my own experience. I'm part of a group that meets to discuss our spiritual growth. Recently someone in the group said that "it's essential for the spiritual seeker to find a good spiritual master and to follow his teachings."

Wow, did that statement ever kick up a firestorm! "The spiritual teacher is already inside each of us," one said. "To rely on a master is to stay in the dream state," said another. You get the picture. In my mind, this connects with Peter's talking about insisting on reinventing the wheel. But the point that's pertinent here is this: so many of us seem so attached to the idea of equality that we make no room in our thinking for the idea that there are some people who have become "masters" in a way that the rest of us have not, and that we can benefit from allowing them to guide us.

It seems as though we've reacted so strongly to all that experience—suffered throughout history—of the kind of masters who had slaves, that we are unwilling to acknowledge even the kind of masters that have disciples. **Donna**

The Anarchist Vision: A World without Coercion

Fred's reply to Donna's message finally brought out momentarily from the sidelines, where it had been lurking like some rag-tag guerilla force, into the center of our field of dispute, the political issue of the anarchistic vision.

There may be some jerks who have inflated this idea that "All men are created equal" into the foolish notion that no one can learn anything from anyone, that no one is further along the paths of knowledge than anyone else, etc. But let's not get distracted from the really vital issue contained in the idea of "Equality." That's the issue of power, of coercion.

As some of you know, in my politics I'm something of an anarchist. My vision of a healthy—"well-ordered" as some, though not I, are calling it here—human community does not obscure all differences in qualities, as some of the people in Donna's group apparently want to do. On the contrary, I see the wise elders as being treasures of any such community. But it is one thing to have people to whom one can turn for counsel. It is something very different to have people who are empowered to compel you. The disciple *chooses* his guru. He's not drafted into discipleship under threat of prison if he refuses induction. Big difference.

When "above" carries the connotations of a chain of command, meaning that one must obey, whether one is persuaded that it serves one's good or not, I hold with the great anarchist, Max Stirner, who said, "For me nothing is above me." **Fred**

Terrence wrote back,

And what kind of world do you think you'd have if everyone insisted that nothing is above them? I'll tell you what kind of world it would be: it would be precisely what Thomas Hobbes said anarchy would be, a bloody mess, a war of all against all, in which no one would be safe and no one's good would be secured.

To which Fred replied:

Notions like this are just the kind of mind-corrupting deceptions you would expect from a world which is run by our "betters," a world that is organized by structures of coercive power. Got to keep us in cages, or we'll act like wild animals. It's all propaganda, all to perpetuate the coercive regime by making us afraid of what will happen if we were to become free to find our own way, drawing upon the natural goodwill of the human being, ungoaded by the prods and whips of Henry's "superiors" and their traditional government from above. **Fred**

To which Victor the Graffiti Artist had a quick posting. (I was starting to get interested in this guy: just where did he get all these pertinent texts he seemed to have at his fingertips?)

Quoth Carl Friedrich, apostle of authority: "Anarchism, like liberalism, exaggerates the inherent good-naturedness of man. . . . Man is seen as an essentially benign creature. Man was born good, whatever that may mean, and he has been corrupted by authority and the impediments it imposes, the frustrations it causes."[3]

Ralph, who seemed to have become—by some combination of his predisposition and the circumstantial forces of the conversation—cast into the role of the defender of liberalism, then declared:

I promise to refrain from lumping anyone who thinks we should have prayer in the school together with the Grand Inquisitor. In return, I would appreciate not having the liberal vision tied together with the kind of anarchism that Fred is espousing.

The liberal order does not reject the idea of coercion. There are laws, enforced by a system of justice. The crucial thing about the liberal order is the way that it is constituted. It grows from the bottom, from the people, to the top. It is not the people who are the instruments of the state's purposes, but the state which is the instrument of the people. The people of the traditional order served the King; the President of the United States is the hired servant of the American people. That's the crucial difference.

But once duly constituted, that President is the commander-in-chief, entrusted with upholding a Constitution that binds us all—from above, once ratified from below—and enforcing the laws, by coercive force, if necessary. **Ralph**

Right, Ralph. We agree. Your liberal order and my anarchist society are on different sides of the crucial line. **Fred**

But Carl Friedrich is right, *Henry interjected,* in his central point: that both of you exaggerate the goodness of man. Fred thinks we're so good we don't even need to build a system of coercive power. Ralph—although he acknowledges that we need to be able to wield force collectively—thinks we are good enough that we can be trusted to build that system of coercive order to restrain our potential for evil, that we are wise enough and rational enough to know what we need, and to do what we know we need to do. Both of you are wrong.

Moreover, while the anarchist wants to make the domain of liberty coextensive with the entire human realm, the liberal goes at least a good part of the way down that same path with him. People like you, Ralph, think we can safely carve out a "private realm" from which the power of government is to be excluded. Marvelous how that realm just keeps on growing.

First you say people have a natural right to think as they wish. Pretty soon, the government must allow them to *say* what they wish. And it is not too long—a couple of centuries seems to do—before they are supposed to be *do* most anything they wish, engage in sodomy, abort babies they've conceived, exhibit pictures of whip-handles inserted up their private orifices. Thus does liberalism devolve into anarchism. **Henry**

Fred's interest, however, was not with the question of liberalism, which, as he had indicated, he was more inclined to lump together with the Grand Inquisitor than with anarchism. He was interested both in defending anarchism, and with it the human creature, and in prosecuting whatever stripe of statist position was to be found on the other side of that line he considered crucial.

Exaggerated sense of human goodness, eh, *Fred wrote*. That is, I say again, statist propaganda. All that Hobbesian evil they warn us against, when in fact the source of evil in history is precisely the opposite: not the human creature, but the state that claims to protect us from evil. Before there was a state, for countless millennia, little human communities got along just fine.

"Give me liberty or give me death" is the choice humankind actually faces—because the evidence of history is that we've been given a coercive regime, and it reeks of death. **Fred**

But Ralph still thought it important to put some clear distance between his position and Fred's.

A strange reading of the evidence of history. I've never been able to understand how anarchists can believe that if you get rid of the state, you'll be freed of the problems of coercion. Is it not clearly just the opposite? Look at Lebanon in the 1980s. Look at Somalia in the early 1990s. (And there are countless other cases.) Is it not clear? Whenever the state is fractured, destroyed, swept aside, it is **precisely** the Hobbesian war of all against all that breaks out. Instead of less coercion, less injustice, what anarchy brings with it is unbridled coercion, the unadulterated injustice of "might makes right." **Ralph**

That's not anarchy, *Fred maintained*. That's chaos. Read the literature of anarchism: no one advocates what you are describing. The anarchistic vision is of a very different sort of community—not chaotic, not embroiled in the combat of warlords, but working together without whips to drive them in their labor, cooperating because that is what is in their hearts. At least do us anarchists the justice of critiquing **our** vision, and don't just pin on us some easy target that has nothing to do with our philosophy. **Fred**

I was somewhat taken aback by the next message. From John, it brought me into the discussion in a way I'd not anticipated.

This conversation reminds me of a fascinating bit of polemical debate I followed closely while it was going on in the mid-1980s. It was in the pages of a journal called *Earth First!* published by the famous radical environmental organization of the same name. The first thing was, there was this review of a book by a newly published author named Andrew Bard Schmookler. The book was called *The Parable of the Tribes* and it was a theory of why civilization had developed in as destructive and tormented a way as it has.

The review was favorable, but it also chided the author for identifying anarchy— which he saw as prevailing in the system of sovereign societies—as the source of the destructive tendencies of civilization's development. The author then responded to defend his analysis of anarchy, and his response drew fire from a handful of anarchists, to whom the author responded, and so on for the better part of two years. One of the articles published in the journal had the title, I believe, of "Schmookler Replies to the Anarchists' Reply to Schmookler's Reply to the Anarchists." As I recall Schmookler's arguments, I would say that we have in our figurative midst someone quite suited to the task of addressing Fred's most recent complaint. So I invite him to do so. **John**

Thanks a lot, John, *I wrote sarcastically to John back-channel.* I would much rather have had you encourage me privately than put me on the spot like this. I prefer to choose my battles, and this particular battle is, as you have said, one I have fought before. These days the interesting questions are the ones about which I myself feel most unsettled. But I am also flattered to learn that you read—and even remember— that old exchange in *Earth First!* Which reminds me, there's a bit of a story about how that exchange came back across my screen recently. I'd be glad to tell you that story if you'll promise me that you won't bring it into the public forum. But that'll have to be a bit later: I have an assignment to do, some message to compose for our forum, lest I embarrass both myself and some creep who, uninvited, just shone the spotlight on me. **Andy**

Then I wrote to the forum.

John is correct that in that published exchange with the good people of *Earth First!* I was confronted with an argument much like yours, Fred. To my essentially Hobbesian view of anarchy, one of my interlocutors (or is it interscribners—and sons) argued as you have that the chaos then ravaging Lebanon was hardly what they were advocating. Of course it wasn't. Who would advocate that? But their complaint, and yours, misses the point.

The case against anarchism is not that the wonderful portrait you paint of "how it's gonna be" is undesirable. The lion lying down with the lamb in the Peaceable Kingdom is a wonderful vision. The question, rather, is whether the consequences of the arrangement you advocate would correspond to that utopian portrait. And the answer, I think, quite clearly is no. Just putting words on paper that say, "We'll get rid of coercion and everything will be peachy" doesn't make it so. And all the weight of history argues to the contrary.

The challenge I posed those anarchists then, and would put to you now, Fred, is this: What arrangement are you going to make in this anarchistic society to deal with the threat that would be posed to your happy little order when some folks arise who are not so nice, who are eager for dominion, and who are able to put together the raw power to seize control over a society lacking an effective governing structure to coordinate a defensive response? Unless you have developed the apparatus of organized coercive force to handle these rogues, the future of your system will be shaped not by your vision but by the vision of those who love power and know how to wield it. **Andy**

May the anarchist reply to Schmookler? *Fred soon posted.* Your reasoning appears to me to be circular. You look at what people have become under the boot of coercive systems, and you draw the inference that we need coercive systems to make provision for people behaving like wounded, twisted animals. It reminds me of gangsters collecting protection money: "Wouldn't want some terrible accident to happen to you'se."

I say that human nature is good and that, to quote my buddy Carl Friedrich, we have been "corrupted by authority and the impediments it imposes." After a transitional time of healing, when the evils stemming from the statist system have had a chance to dry up and blow away, I say we'd not have to worry about those rogues you want us to mobilize against. **Fred**

What I would say, Fred, is that it's *you* who have a logical problem here, *I answered.* The trap closes on you in three moves. First, you say that the state is evil. Second, you say that all the evils around us are the result of the rise of the state to tyrannize over us. And you look back nostalgically to a time before there was any state. Which leads, thirdly, to this insoluble problem: If the state is the source of all evil, how did the evil of the state ever arise in the first place? **Andy**

A Story of a Delayed Splash

Then I heard from John, back-channel.

Now, tell me the truth, wasn't that fun? And while you're at it, I would indeed like to hear that story you alluded to. And I won't go public with it. **John**

Here's the story, John. I've always felt good about that exchange in *Earth First!* At one point, it even occurred to me to see if it might be published as a little booklet. But I never thought it meant anything to anyone but me—until very recently.

It's been almost ten years since the exchange occurred, and I'd never heard a word about it. Then, just a couple months ago, I was at my local library, which serves a mostly rural county in Virginia. While they were checking out my stuff, I looked over a short shelf of new books. There was one called *Earth First!* written by someone named Martha F. Lee, and because of my small history with that organization I picked it up and started looking through it.

In a modest way, I've had a bit of a public life since I emerged, when *The Parable of the Tribes* was published, from a long trek in the figurative wilderness. But for the most part, I spend my life as a private and obscure man. The public world is this place **out there** where I occasionally make a brief appearance on some wing of the stage. Suddenly, however, at this moment in the library, I had an almost uncanny experience when the two worlds unexpectedly converged. For there, on the page before my eyes, I saw the name "Schmookler." It wasn't on my library card, it was on the book. To a Schmookler, this doesn't happen regularly. It's not like being named Johnson. It was **me** being talked about. And it wasn't just that one mention. It went on for four pages: the author was telling the story of this exchange between Schmookler and the Anarchists.

I read the account and discovered that this exchange had been a powerful event in the history of the organization. It turns out that this dispute had brought to the surface some long-simmering differences between two factions within the movement. And once they had been brought to the surface, they could not be buried again. Nor could they be resolved, however, and the ultimate effect was that the movement that was Earth First! split in two, each faction going its own way.

I can't convey how unreal it felt to learn this while I was just standing there as the private me going about my business. It was as though I were a character in some Borges story, where the line between reality and fantasy dissolves—or as if a character in a movie started talking directly to me. No longer just an observer and commentator on the world, I was suddenly one of the actors. **Andy**

John wrote back to me:

Congratulations! That is really far out. You really **did** something. I must confess your story makes me envious. If I could look at my own efforts, and see that I'd had an impact like that, I'd feel satisfied I'd amounted to something. You must really feel proud. **John**

Not really, John. That's not the way it feels. Having an impact, I figure, isn't necessarily something I should congratulate myself for. It's not clear to me that my impact on this small part of the picture—precipitating a schism in an organization trying to stop humankind's reckless assault on the biosphere—was a positive one.

I was being true to my own vision in that exchange, and acting on a more or less permanent article of faith: that my being true in this way, bearing witness as best I can, will help things move in a good direction. Maybe that's true. But I have to confront the possibility that maybe this article of faith is something that is simply convenient for me to hold, giving me as it does a *carte blanche* to follow my own *daemon* and let the chimps fall where they may (as the primatologists would put it). Where, after all, is it written that speaking the truth—even if it **is** the truth—will automatically help move the world where it ought to go? **Andy**

Overarching Order

Meanwhile, that discussion of anarchy and its relation to my book on the evolution of civilization had prompted some further comment on the forum.

Peter wrote a public message to ask me to explain something he thought odd.

It was my impression, Andy, that you were among those whose habitual leaning was toward the natural-is-good, order-from-the-bottom-up side of the ledger. And now here you are attacking anarchy for not being prepared to deal with evil people, and talking about the dangers of anarchy obtaining among sovereign societies. These positions would seem to suggest that you do not have so much faith in human nature, and moreover that you are contemplating not just **some** kind of order but an all-encompassing order of the kind espoused by the World Federalists or other such elite, top-down social thinkers. Please clarify what seems to be a contradiction. **Peter**

I don't know that there is a contradiction, *I replied.* There are two aspects of my view that make me opposed to an anarchistic approach to order. My belief in the goodness of human nature stops short of Fred's sanguine assumption that the natural man will always and necessarily be good. I believe that evil is one of the human potentialities, and that any way of arranging the world must make provision for its occurrence. Thus I am with Ralph in thinking that even though good order must be built up from the people, we need a strong order to deal with potentially disordering forces.

But more important is a dimension of the theory of social evolution I developed (that *Parable of the Tribes* idea), according to which certain kinds of evil—having to do with the quest for power—tend to spread across a fragmented or anarchic human system until it characterizes the whole. This tendency of power to act as a contaminant, in other words, means that it is not enough for a majority, or even a very great majority, of people to be good and to love peace and justice. If they are not organized in a way that can contain the evils of power-seeking that may arise, their world will come to be dominated by what might have begun as a very tiny evil exception to a not quite universal benign rule.

In the anarchic system of interacting societies, as I put it in that book, ***"No one is free to choose peace, but anyone can impose upon all the necessity for power."***[4]

So, yes, I do think that the human realm will be fundamentally in bad order until we manage to construct a good order that is overarching. It need not be so centralized and powerful as a One World Government. But it does need to be strong enough to keep those within it from struggling for power in an unrestrained way. As I see it, that is the only way that humankind can escape from the anarchy that has obtained in the human system—taken as a whole—since our kind took that step ten thousand years ago, unprecedented in the history of life on earth, of extricating ourselves from the niche in which we had evolved biologically and we thus ceased to be held in check by a natural order.

According to my understanding, it is the fact that human beings—since the dawn of civilization—have been unrestrained by *any* power above them to govern how our societies would interact with each other—neither a biologically evolved order, nor one of human creation—that accounts for how painful and unjust and just plain evil so much of civilized history has been. **Andy**

I can contain myself no longer, *Carl interjected at this point.* This discussion demonstrates how much people need to contort themselves if they leave out of the picture the one element that is ***most essential,*** the one that makes everything else fall into place.

Submission to the Will of God

Carl then supplied what he'd called the most essential, but missing, element.

Without God, you imagine that if human beings are not constrained by natural controls, they are ruled by nothing and thus are condemned to anarchy. When one fails to acknowledge the sovereignty of God, one can entertain such delusions as that expressed by that fellow Stirner, quoted by Fred, who declared that "Nothing is above me." Without God, you can get into a dispute about who can reliably be certified as "superior" so that we can know that we should submit to the order they would impose on us.

But with God, these problems dissolve. We see ourselves not as so many creatures crawled up from the slime, but as God's children, always dwelling under His overarching divine order, and owing our Father obedience. We are cured of the arrogance and disorder of imagining that we are the pinnacle, with nothing above us to govern our steps. And we know that we have before us commandments derived not from fallible mortals like ourselves, whose superiority to the rest of us can be disputed, but from the one Almighty Creator whose superiority to us is infinite.

To align ourselves with "good order," we need but submit to the Will of God. **Carl**

A pair of responses came back. A nice combination, I thought, as if by some invisible hand it had been arranged that they would come together.

One came from Ralph.

Of course, Carl, you must realize that this idea of God is not exactly new to us. We've been around this civilization for a while, and so too has been that idea. The notion that mortals had better bow down before the divine doesn't exactly come as a—pardon the expression—revelation. So I don't know just what you expect we will be able to do with your assertions.

But neither, I expect, will it surprise you to learn that even if we all decided you were right that we must obey what the Divine commands, and turned to discover just what it is that the Divine expects of us, it would leave a lot of problems unsolved. To which God, pray tell, do we owe our obedience? Is it the one who tells the Jews that it is an abomination to eat pork, and that—as presently interpreted—no lights should be turned on after the sun goes down on Friday? The one who tells the Sikhs not to cut their hair or beards? The one who tells you that Jesus is the Way? Or others of the countless religious concepts of the divine to which human beings have bowed down?

How do we tell which of the competing religious dogmas is the right one? **Ralph**

The posting that arrived with Ralph's was from a man named Shefik of whom I had never heard.

I am writing to convey how absolutely completely my tradition—which is Islam— would agree with Carl on the necessity for any person who would be good to indeed

submit to the will of God. As you may not know, the very word "Islam" means surrender—and it is precisely to the will of God that we must surrender. Those who follow
the prophet Muhammad are called "Muslims," and the meaning of the word "muslim"
is "that which submits."⁵

Allah—or God, if you will—has created a magnificent Order. It is not for us to
create good order but, by submitting to the will of God, to simply align ourselves with
the good order that God has provided us. We find that good order set down with
meticulousness and clarity in the Koran. By submitting to the laws Allah has given
us, we find peace and fulfillment. **Shefik**

Back-channel, I checked with Rev. George to see whether Shefik was
one of his recruits, and he confirmed that he was. His brief message—
"Yup"—provided no elaboration, but I felt that I discerned in his machinations the same trouble-making playfulness at work as in his original
move to bring the likes of Carl and Henry into our circle. He seemed to
be an equal-opportunity discomfiter.

The idea that by submitting to God we would find peace and fulfillment
was reinforced by a posting at this moment from Kenneth, who had earlier written to suggest that the space within us that Herman thought was
reserved for the superego as parental introject was, in fact, a place for
our Heavenly Father to dwell within us.

In this modern world, with its emphasis on individual autonomy, the idea of obedience is in disfavor. We don't want to be pushed around. Like in those old ads for a
headache remedy, we want to shout out "Mother, please! I'd rather do it myself." But
in the difficult task of navigating our way through life, the reality is we cannot do it
ourselves.

Some weeks ago, I was on a whitewater rafting trip as part of my pastoral duties.
The rapids were dangerous, and only our guide *really* knew the river and the art of
navigating the rapids. Believe me, in that situation, we were happy to obey the instruc-
tions he called out. When he yelled "right-forward," that's precisely what we did, and
without a question. The experience brought home a lesson that more pious generations
before us understood much better than we: that obedience can be a way of saving
your life instead of losing it.

That's how I think God's commandments should be understood: not as a way of
controlling us, but as a way of making us safe, even of setting us free. **Kenneth**⁶

Carl had also posted again. His response seemed to be to Ralph, who
had questioned how meaningful it could be to say "Submit to God" when
there are so many different claims, made by different mortals, about pre-

cisely to which God to submit, and just what it is that He commands of us. To Shefik's posting about Islam, Carl paid no evident attention.

Reason has always been adept at ways of undermining faith. This is one of the snares by which the souls of the unwary are captured by the forces of Evil. But make no mistake, the Creator of the Universe has indeed placed us into that moral order of which I spoke. Whether or not you are prepared for it, there *is* a Judge before whom you will stand when your days have come to an end. This Judge will reward those who have come to Him and lived by His ways, and He will mete out harsh punishment to the wicked and those who have refused—because of whatever rationalizations— to submit to His will. **Carl**

It was Fred who, at this point, launched what I thought was an effective salvo to challenge our more orthodox forum-mates. Fred's own (bottom-up) solutions to the problems of order had flaws that seemed to me pretty glaring. But Fred also often seemed able, with the precision and economy of movement of a graceful picador, to penetrate to some painful node of confusion in the body of his adversary's thinking. (He was good, that is, at showing how the other guy's position was just so much bull.) I wondered how come, with such incisive skill, his own position had not become more complex and nuanced. And the question brought to my mind that phrase of Jesus' about seeing the mote in our neighbor's eye but paying no mind to the beam in our own.

Whatever the reasons for Fred's mixtures of strengths and weaknesses, his posting at this point initiated a turn of sorts in our discussion, from a thrust by which the advocates of Authority advanced their positions to a new one driven more by our awareness of the dangers of orders imposed by such authority.

Built upon Sand
Can a Good Order Be Based on Hierarchy?

Our conversation had brought forth arguments for several kinds of order premised on the assertion that a good order—placed above us—can be identified and that this order warrants our obedience. If the human being cannot, by nature, be trusted to be good on her own recognizance, the solution to the problem was for us all to submit to the indicated authority, accepting its imposition upon us of those rules and structures necessary to build something as straight and true as it is possible to fashion out of the crooked timber of our humanity.

In the last of these arguments, Carl made appeal to what would seem to be the highest conceivable authority, God. After Ralph had questioned how this could resolve the question, in view of the diversity of religious understandings of the Divine and of the commandments issuing therefrom, Fred came back to challenge Carl from a different angle.

Issues of Might and Right

OK, Carl, *Fred began,* you don't think reason is the be-all and end-all of our thinking. Still, we have to make sense, right? Our words have to mean something, because if they don't, there's no way you can preach to us and try to get us to see the light. So when you say that we **should** obey God because God is good and has, with His commandments, provided us a way of achieving good order, the word "good" as you use it must have some real meaning. Right?

I assume, then, that you are saying more than that there's an Almighty out there whom we'd better obey because otherwise we'll be in Big Trouble. Yes? You're making assertions about the moral qualities of His nature and about the rightness of His commandments. And when you argue that there's a Judge who will reward or punish us according to whether we've been properly subordinate to His will, I understand you also to be claiming that this Big Guy in the Sky is not just throwing His weight around, but is dispensing Justice. Right?

Or is that a misunderstanding? Are you perhaps simply saying that because He is so powerful, and so meddlesome, that the only way we're going to get any peace is to knuckle under to Him? Or perhaps you're saying that simply because He created us, we owe Him obedience regardless of the inherent wisdom of His commandments?

Well, with that second argument, I would certainly disagree. If our Creator were an erratic Fool, whose commandments were actually contrary to our own best interests, I would not think us morally obligated to do His bidding. And as for the first point— that as creatures of a Creator who will otherwise do terrible things to us, we ought to keep our heads down and slog away like smart slaves for whom no better fate is conceivable than to avoid being noticed and punished—although I'll concede that obedience to a God with the character of a Pol Pot or a Hitler might be prudent, such obedience would have little to do with morality or "good order."

I don't know you, Carl, except for your few postings here, but given the strong moral overtones of your messages, I cannot believe that you are arguing either for blind obedience to a Fool or for prudent acquiescence in the dictatorship of a Cosmic Tyrant. That leaves, I believe, the other argument: that we should obey God not because He is Almighty but because His commandments are right and good in some meaningful way. Right?

He's like that whitewater captain in Kenneth's posting who, when he says, "right forward" says so because that's really what we need to do to stay afloat, not because he likes to see us crack up and go under, not because he likes acting wise even though he hasn't got a clue about the river, and not because he's just on a control trip.

The problem is, Carl, it is not at all clear that you've identified such a God. Even if it were the case that everyone knew your God, and knew that He was the One and Only True God—the Almighty Creator of the Universe—the record of this particular Almighty does not inspire moral confidence. I mean, look at what this God has done according to your very texts.

Fred seemed to be warming to his iconoclastic task.

This God of yours, *Fred continued,* smites all kinds of people for reasons that seem dubious to me. He commands His people to do acts that, today, would have them up for crimes against humanity. He imposes punishments—like death for violations of the Sabbath—that would have Amnesty International put His regime high up on the list for tyrannies that routinely violate human rights.

And consider His description of Himself as a "jealous" God. Such a phrase would certainly seem to indicate that He does not just have our well-being in mind. Think of it. If His commandment about having no other gods before Him were for our sake,

He'd express himself differently, saying something like, "because otherwise you'll get confused, or you'll lose your way, or your raft won't make it through the next rapids." But no, He says that He is a jealous God, showing that He is bending us to His will in order to meet some need of His. And if He does so here, at this central juncture on Sinai, what guarantee is there that He's not doing the same thing—creating a Self-serving order in which we are means to His ends—at many other places in the whole set-up to which you say we should submit?

So in other words, Carl, it does not seem that you've freed us, as you seemed to believe you had, from the confusions of the other Authoritarians whose top-down orders are morally questionable. Simply making assumptions—this is the one God, and everything He says is true and wise and just—doesn't make it so. Unfounded claims can just as easily be asserted about any other authority—as, they indeed have been throughout history—but mere assertions do nothing to take from us the burden of having to sift through what is true and good and what is not.

Just as traditions might be good or not, just as laws might be just or unjust, and people in superior positions might be 'noble' in character as well as title, or might just be scoundrels with better swords, so also with your Deity. With your God, too, as with an unreliable map, we are **still** left having to find our own way.
Fred

While I doubt I'd have been as blunt as Fred in making that argument, I nonetheless appreciated what Fred was saying. For years, I've simultaneously envied and resented those Bible-quoters who seemed to think that morality is such an open-and-shut case. Too often, the supposed foundation of their certainty seemed to be an unconscious and unquestioned equation of might and right: "If the Almighty says it, it must be good," despite such disturbing evidence to the contrary in their own texts. To me, that was always good evidence to think that those texts were not faxes direct from the Creator. But in any event, it seemed to me that Fred was right in challenging Carl's assumption that our possessing the commandments issued by the Creator automatically answered our basic moral questions.

Carl was not persuaded. That was a surprise. He wrote back, tersely:

Who do you think you are—or any of us could be—to question God's goodness and the rightness of His commandments? **Carl**

Sounds to me, Carl, *Fred responded,* as though maybe I was wrong about the nature of your argument about God. Maybe you **are** claiming that we ought to obey Him even if God is some Saddam-Who-Art-in-Heaven. After all, to say that our obedience should be independent of any judgment we make of His character and the rightness of His commandments is to say that by virtue simply of His position and power, we must obey His *diktats.* You seem to have excluded our coming to any other basis for choosing to obey God.

Out goes right, in comes might. So much for morality. Order *si,* good order no. **Fred**

Hungry for the Undeniable

The fact that the next message was written by Rev. George made it especially interesting to me. I suppose I should not have been shocked that George would express the position that he did. Perhaps I was surprised because in the context of our original group at the conference, he had always held aloft the image of timeless truths, and because his main role in our forum to this point had been to bring into the discussion people like Carl and Henry, whose views seemed immutable, like words carved into ancient monuments. But of course, I should have remembered that George's relationship with orthodoxy was a good deal more complex than theirs.

It is a terrible human dilemma that we see in this exchange between Carl and Fred, *George said.* In the form they are conducting this discussion, I doubt they will arrive at any acceptable way of resolving it. But I must confess, it is not clear just what **would** be an acceptable way.

Carl's God is no Saddam, of course, *George continued,* and I expect Fred knows it. But the texts that have been handed down do contain more than enough within them to make this God a troubling figure. A whole book could be written about these problems, and of course many have. But even if somehow the process by which those biblical texts had been produced—however we conceive those processes—had yielded us a picture of something we could easily recognize as displaying unadulterated goodness and fairness and admirability, problems like those Ralph pointed out would remain. How do we **know** that some particular set of beliefs—written down in texts claimed to be divinely revealed, or passed along orally from generation to generation—gives us **The Truth** about the ultimate order of the universe?

I could hear in this George's own impassioned search, his lifelong effort to bring together his modern, reasoning mind with his heart's love of his own religious tradition.

Yet the **need** to know is so great, *George continued,* that for many of us the solution is simply to **declare** about some body of belief or other, "This is it." Like Jesus saying

"On this rock I will found my church," whole peoples will make of some beliefs the rock on which they will found the certainty they crave.

The dilemma is this: On the one hand, simply banishing doubt by fiat is intellectually indefensible (and lauding this act by calling it the "leap of faith" seems like just another magic trick). But on the other hand, it may well be that allowing doubt to persist interminably will in time turn everything into sand. So it seems that we face a choice between building a life upon a foundation whose solidity is an illusion, or building a life upon no secure foundation whatever, a life in danger of crumbling like a sandcastle in the waves. This I would call a significant dilemma. **George**

Larry joined in this meditative line of thinking.

It is not alone with God, *Larry suggested,* that we find this "myth of the great Authority," this declaration by fiat of some unassailable rock on which to found our certainty. People's need for incontrovertible order also expresses itself in the form of the imputation of infallibility to mere mortals.

One instance that readily comes to mind is the doctrine of papal infallibility in the Roman Catholic Church. It's not enough, apparently, that we possess a text that can reveal to us the essential and timeless truths; we need to have ongoing and timely access to undeniable truth. If God will not call some contemporary Moses up to the mountain for regular installments of tablets, we will simply declare that our intermediary, though human, speaks God's infallible truth when he pronounces on the big questions. (You might be interested to know that the fellow de Maistre, whom Henry quoted a while back about no nation being able to "give itself a government"—insisting instead on the immutable forms received from some historical tradition whose rightness is claimed to be beyond questioning—also advanced a case for papal infallibility practically a century before the Church declared it official doctrine.)[1]

But even outside the religious realm, there are the cults of personality that make of Mao's thoughts, or Stalin's great ideas, a kind of infallible guide to the Truth. It is not coincidence, of course—and it is consistent with what George said about the **need** for certainty—that it is precisely those social orders that swept aside the rock of traditional religion which then erected their mortal leaders as gods themselves. **Larry**

Plant Hierarchy, Harvest Injustice

Next came Jeff, from whom we'd last heard promoting the rule of reason.

George and Larry have brought our attention to the tendency for Authority to be presented and perceived as infallible. They explain this tendency in terms of the need people feel for certainty: we need to believe we are building upon rock, and we will declare sand to be rock if we need to. That may be a part of what's going on, but it's not all of it, and may well not be the heart of it. The supposed "needs" of the people may be less pertinent here than the interests of those who rule them.

Let us remember that these Authorities—with the possible exception of God about whom, at least most of us seem to agree, we just don't know—are generally in positions maintained, and often seized, through the exercise of raw power. Submit to tradition; submit to law; submit to our betters; submit to God. All these equate, to a greater or lesser extent, to submitting to power.

Tradition and law were presented to us, as they have been to countless generations in traditional societies, as the fruit of accumulated wisdom. But what of the tradition in India by which the upper castes—who arrived as conquerors millennia ago—retain dominance and privilege over the lower castes? And what of laws that "detain both man and woman/who steal the goose from off the common/but leave the greater felon loose/who steals the common from the goose"?[2] Fred and others have already uncloaked the pretense of these supposedly solid authorities.

The truth, of course, is complex. Tradition and the law are simultaneously collective wisdom and partisan interest. It would be great if we could find something purely good, but unfortunately that is not how human things work.

And that, I think, is the ultimate point. All we have are human things. All the orders available to us are the fruits of the labor of mortal beings, with their follies and their moral corruptions. For this reason, we are forced to admit what we've been calling "top-down" is really just founded on the same stuff as "bottom-up." The only difference between them is that with those orders based on "higher" authority, we have some of the stuff of the bottom—mortal, fallible humans—pretending that they and/or their principles are something more than they are. **Jeff**

That statement of Jeff's I found most striking and disturbing. Wherever we look for a reliable basis for order, he seemed to be saying, we find the same thing: our own flawed selves. It seemed to be a counsel of despair, suggesting that there is no basis on which we might make any kind of progress, no source of guidance any more reliable than any other. Intuitively I felt that there was a fallacy in that reasoning, if I understood it correctly, but it was not immediately apparent to me just what it might be.

Meanwhile, Ralph was continuing the work of chipping away at the supposedly solid structures of order based on good authority.

Yes, let's talk more about justice, *Ralph wrote soon after Jeff's message had appeared.* Andy once declared his interest to be in the question, "What is the source of good

order?" What characterizes "good order" in the human realm is, above all, **_justice._**
Each should get what he or she deserves, not more nor less. The opposite of justice
is what happens when it is power, rather than right, that decides who gets what.
Hierarchical systems are about unequal distributions of power, and because of this
inequality the resultant order will be—unless the mighty voluntarily restrain themselves, and do what they should instead of what they can—an unjust order. History
suggests that such restraint is rare at best.

Thus it is that top-down systems of ordering are practically inevitably plagued with
the vice of injustice. **Ralph**

I will not deny that there may be injustices embedded in some traditional structures,
such as the caste system in India that you mention, *Peter responded in a tactical retreat
the better to defend the essence of his previous arguments in defense of the sanctity of
tradition.* But I would still maintain that tradition has a basically humanizing and
ameliatory effect. Consider that Indian caste system: even if it began as a relation
between conqueror and vanquished, it nonetheless evolved into a way of life that
provided the essential necessities for all strata of society. That's the virtue of tradition:
it crafts what is viable, it lubricates the movement of the social parts. Without such
a tradition developing to create "a way of life," the people would have been left with
only the naked relations of power. **Peter**

Tradition in that portrait, *Ralph replied,* appears as the moss that grows upon the
cold iron fist of brutal rule: it is softer to the casual touch, which is a virtue, but
nonetheless whenever the fist has occasion to land a blow, it is the iron and not the
moss that is relevant. And in the meanwhile, the moss also serves to obscure—from
the victims of injustice—the hard and harsh underlying realities.

For the Untouchables, it might be better to see the unvarnished—or unmossed—
truth rather than to be sold the idea that they are the feet of Brahma while
the Brahmins are the god's head, and that their exploitation is divinely ordained.
Ralph

Next came Eleanor, the militant defender of the abused. As it had been
so long since we'd heard from her, I had felt some concern that perhaps
she'd left in a huff after discovering the limits to our sympathies with her
preoccupations. But, like a patient triangle player in an orchestra, she
turned out simply to be waiting for her cue. This, evidently, was it, and
so she sounded her distinctive clear note.

A good while back, I referred to original sin as a calumny against human nature.
Of course, that doctrine is well established in religious tradition, a tradition that developed and thrived in a world hierarchically arranged. No coincidence there, I would

suggest. Original sin devalues the human material on the bottom, justifying the descent of all goodness from above—with whatever fury is deemed necessary or desirable. (I would suggest, by the way, that the top-down approach to moral order is most pronounced in those societies—such as the caste society of India, to return to that example, and in the American context, in the South—where the divisions between the ruling groups and the lower orders are most deeply drawn.)

Now, as some of you know, my own specialty concerns the treatment of children. On this subject, I may seem "extreme." I'd say that my being regarded that way is itself a reflection of how widespread is the denial in our society of just what has gone on—and in large measure still goes on—in the treatment of defenseless children. But whether I am extreme or not, I'd like to cite Rudolf Dreikurs, the expert on child discipline who is considered, by most, pretty mainstream. In his overview of the thought and practice in the area of childrearing through history, Dreikurs explicitly draws a connection between the belief in original sin and centuries of treatment of children as "little more than slaves."[3]

Hierarchy always justifies itself by declaring that which is above to be superior to that which is below. Such a declaration always seems to serve as cover for the abuse of the supposedly "lower" by the "superior" element. That's why hierarchy is very dangerous. Those below get the shaft. **Eleanor**

Victor the Graffiti Artist attempted, using words, to post a cartoon:

In this cartoon, there is an outhouse belonging to a fraternity. The outhouse has two doors, one marked "Actives" the other marked "Pledges." The outhouse is a narrow, two-story structure. The "Actives" door is directly over the "Pledges." **Victor**

Terrence wrote next.

The problem is, there is nothing better to propose than, say, an authoritative framework—*as best it can be worked out*—to which all consent, and/or are required to submit. My fear, listening to you liberals make your reasonable (and sometimes unreasonable) cases against the framework of authority, is that this will simply open the door to all kinds of illusions, some of which I thought had already been exposed here in our discussion, and to the destructive chaos to which those illusions lead. Yes, a legal system can have injustice embedded in it. But as several of you argued effectively against Fred's anarchism, in the absence of systemic controls operating *from above* to constrain all, there would be even more injustice.

Let me quote from another great English thinker, of my general political stripe, who saw deeply into the meaning of the law. This is how Edmund Burke described a constitution: "an elaborate fabric fitted to unite private and public liberty with public force, with order, with peace, with justice, and above all, with the institutions formed by bestowing permanance and stability, through the ages, upon this invaluable whole."[4] If you ask me, when it comes to good order for human beings, you can't beat that. **Terrence**

Terrence's argument resonated with me, and gave me a glimmer of what might have been the flaw in Jeff's previous argument—or at least how I heard his argument—about everything reducing to the same flawed stuff of us mortals. A constitution—such as the Constitution of the United States, of which I'd long been an enthusiastic fan—may be the creation of human beings, but it can nonetheless embody not the whole of our humanity but the best and wisest of our judgments. A purely human-made constitution, if it is constructed carefully and well, can help us elevate the order in which we live well above the level of, say, an anarchic system. So not everything that derives from us, I thought, leaves us at the same level.

Was this the way out from the pit that I had thought Jeff's earlier re-marks had seemed to consign us? So I was wondering, when Jeff himself posted the next message.

Jeff responded:

Yes, it does sound very nice, that constitution of your man Burke. And if we could be sure that the "justice" to which he refers was indeed justice, that whole would indeed be "invaluable." But if I imagine myself one of the common folk of the England where Burke was writing in the eighteenth century, I find myself wanting to say to him, "Yes, Ed, if only it were as good for me as it is for you." Because in fact, those common people were being screwed.

In the same land where Burke was writing about justice in an order that would be stable and permanent, there were other well-born Englishmen who were articulating various arguments about why the rich and the poor were equal in happiness. To the wealthy, said one, "riches were often a burden, and to the poor their poverty was often a blessing." Never mind that the rich always had the option to give away their wealth in order to enjoy the blessings of poverty, while if the poor tried to give away the blessing of their deprivation by seizing the wealth of the rich, they'd be hanged for their good deeds. How was poverty a blessing? Well, another Englishman—not blessed with poverty, we may safely assume—argued that enduring hardship gave the poor those "opportunities for contentment and a patient submission to providence, as a low and penurious condition affords." Thanks a lot. And then there is the myth of the hardy peasant: "if the rich had more meat, the poor had better stomachs for digesting it."[5]

I've seen poor people and rich people in our country, and all over the world. There's no question which group looks the healthier, the hardier, the stronger, the better—or which has the longer life expectancy. What I can't figure out is: how is it that over the past two hundred years, the poor managed to lose their advantage, in terms of health, over the wealthy?

Seriously, if we are dealing with a species that is so adept at rationalizations and denials of the most patently unjust realities, how can we ever trust any of their talk of "justice" except in those circumstances where equality of power—from-the-ground-up democracy—compels justice on all regardless of their fervent desire for an injustice that is favorable to themselves? **Jeff**

Eleanor returned briefly.

Don't we see this kind of unredeemably unjust perception all the time? The rich are continually decrying the vices of the welfare recipients, while never mentioning all the welfare for the rich that is built into our system. The middle class loves to think of the poor as lazy, but their image of the poor makes little allowance for all those people who work much harder than they, under much worse conditions, and barely earn enough to survive with considerably fewer comforts.

This always seems to happen when power flows downward. Oh, and by the way, a century and a half ago, Herbert Spencer—no radical, in my book—wrote that our various regimes of disciplining children always focus on the faults of the children, and never attend to those of parents.[6] **Eleanor**

At this point, Peter joined in.

Granted that people are often unjust, that we can easily find instances of double standards being wielded. But I think that this bandwagon of discourse decrying hierarchical systems may be yet another instance of finding fault with the other side and ignoring the faults on one's own. Because it is not only the powerful and privileged who do this.

Consider this passage I read a few weeks ago in an article discussing the black leader, Jesse Jackson. The author of the article, Eugene Genovese, is expressing his appreciation for the "great merit" of Jackson's "restoring sin to Protestant discourse, from which it has been disappearing. . . ." He then goes on to say, "But the sins in question usually turn out to be racism, sexism and social oppression—a tiresome left-wing gambit that makes sin a monopoly of white heterosexual males. When poor people, blacks, women, or homosexuals slip into antisocial behavior of an incontrovertibly sinful sort, they are allegedly only manifesting their victimization by an oppressive society."[7]

It is not only the poweful who practice injustice. **Peter**

This drew a response from Ralph:

Truly, you are right. There are no good guys and bad guys when it comes to whole categories of people. The proletarians are no more noble, it turns out, than the capital-ist barons. Which is one more reason, I would argue, that we ought to operate in an essentially Madisonian—which is to say, liberal—framework, in which power is disseminated throughout the body politic and the moral defects of one faction will be more or less neutralized in the political arena by the moral defects of the many others. **Ralph**

And then Fred reentered the conversation.

I fear, Ralph, that you are too eager to be agreeable. Perhaps your own appetite for contending factions is not up to Madisonian snuff. Was it not you who said that the opposite of justice is simply that the more powerful party gets its way? (Recall the famous passage in Plato's *Republic* where the character Thrasymachus defines jus-tice as the advantage of the stronger party.) So that points out how although it may be true, it is also completely irrelevant that the weak have the same unjust tendencies as the mighty.

To say that "You **would** do the same to us if you could" may be true, but it in no way counterbalances the weight of "You **are** in fact doing it to us." The unjust heart matters only when it is armed with the power to work its will. Justice does not prose-cute people for homicidal urges, but only for doing actual violence. Likewise, if our concern is with justice, we must reject hierarchy because it is always a means by which those on top do violence to those on the bottom. **Fred**

Doing Violence

This brought Henry back to our inboxes. (I thought to myself, what would it be like if Fred and Henry were marooned together on some small island?)

You may decry the evils of hierarchy all you want, *Henry began,* but it is all so much foolishness, because there is no real alternative. You might as well complain about gravity, and wish to live on a planet where you'd not have to be pulled downward on account of your mass. You may decry violence as an evil, but if you want to have order you must have violence—if not as a continual fact then at least as a continual threat.

For without hierarchy, there will be no viable structure for order. And without vio-lence, there will be no obedience to that order. De Maistre, whom I quoted earlier, captured this grim but inescapable truth well when he wrote: "All grandeur, all power, all subordination depend upon the executioner: he is the horror and thereby the bond of human society. Remove from the world this incomprehensible agent: that very mo-ment order is replaced by chaos, thrones fall and societies disappear." **Henry**

And why, please explain, Henry, is that? *Jeff wrote to inquire.* Why should all order depend upon violence?

For the simple reason, *Henry replied,* that the human creature is fundamentally a disorderly creature, the demands of social order go against the grain, and thus whips and goads are needed to keep him moving along the lines that society requires. Get rid of the hangman, de Maistre was saying, and the rabble will burst out of all confines, heading every which way, laying waste in their path. Only fear can hold a social order together. **Henry**

These terrible words provoked me to write to the forum.

Here we are once again, at the very root of the issue with which we began: the question of the relation of human nature with the requirements of good order. Just what is the "grain" of our natures, and how does this correspond to the requirements of order?

What Henry says seems true enough of many of the orders that people *have* been compelled to obey. Throughout history, orders have been constructed that have made war against our humanity. If the hangman has been necessary to maintain those or-ders, it is no wonder. But to admit that some kinds of order would be impossible without fear and coercion is not to concede that only such orders are possible for humankind.

We in the liberal world are embarked on a noble experiment to see how much the liberation of the human creature can be reconciled with the maintenance of good social order. The evidence on this question, I would say, is not yet all in. But I for one am far from willing to consider the experiment a failure. I have some concerns, but I am still fundamentally hopeful. I still believe that an order based on love and freedom, with fear and coercion available only at the margins to deal with aberrant cases, is possible.

But I will concede that achieving such an order is a greater challenge than most— or at least many—in liberal society today are willing to acknowledge, much less meet. **Andy**

In speaking of such an order as a great challenge, *Peter replied,* are you not in effect conceding that the order does not come naturally, that it must in some fundamental way "go against the grain"? If such an order does not come easily to us, in other words, does that not mean that we must be pushed (perhaps whipped and goaded) and that therefore such an order as is envisioned in your "noble experiment"—one based on liberty, on going with the grain—does not really exist? **Peter**

You pose an interesting challenge to me, Peter, *I replied.* And it hinges on how we understand our relationship with challenge: does "challenge" imply going against the grain? This question was the very nub of the challenge to my own beliefs that I raised with the Nintendo Dilemma. As I showed then, I myself am uncertain whether there is a satisfactory answer to your question. But I believe, and I hope, that *some* kinds of difficulty do not go against the grain.

If my belief is correct, then there is a difference between a regime that commands us to acquiesce to our being injured and violated, and one that requires that we stretch to develop our capabilities and resources as human beings. De Maistre's hangman is an instrument of that first kind of order: he stands over the peasant to intimidate him into accepting his being turned into a beast of burden, into knuckling under to an unjust system of status and privilege, into conforming his mind to a system of teachings that call injustice justice.

The second kind of order puts in the place of the hangman the teacher of self-actualization, a figure that calls upon us to become, I suggest, *who we really are,* fulfilling our potential to expand our minds, to develop inner resources, to achieve a wisdom and a moral stature that take work but are not against the grain. The idea is that it is *with* our true grain to become the responsible, knowledgeable, caring citizens that liberal society requires. The idea is that with enough sun and water and Miracle Gro, we will grow into the kind of person who will take the time to understand what's really at stake in the issues, who will open his heart to care about other people and future generations, who will not simply entitle himself to make self-interest his god.

But that vision makes assumptions about "who we really are," assumptions that may be erroneous. Rev. George, for example, wrote earlier that we are by nature lazy creatures, inclined toward sloth and taking the spiritually shallow way out. And we've had plenty of discussion that imputes to us a tendency toward the kind of selfishness that makes us unjust. If these grim assertions about our natures are true, then meeting the challenges of the liberal society would require us to be pushed and goaded, as you suggest, Peter, and thus would seem to be against our "grain."

But even that kind of compelling would seem to be fundamentally different in kind from the kind of violation that Henry, and de Maistre, see as essential to order. Somehow, I can't believe that Carl Rogers is the moral equivalent of de Maistre's hangman. **Andy**

But you acknowledge, *Peter then wrote,* it hasn't been established that Carl Rogers suffices to make good citizens.

I don't know how we are going to resolve disputes, like these, over human nature in general, *Eleanor wrote.* But there is one place where it does seem to me rather clear that our cultural order wantonly and needlessly violates our humanity. And that, as followers of my messages might readily guess, involves our treatment of children.

One can quarrel about what we need to do with people as they grow up—whether nurturing our natures instead of violating them would undermine the basis of order. But I simply cannot imagine a justification for many of our widespread teachings on how to deal with newborns.

Consider schedule-feeding of infants, just to take one example. Why should newborn humans, of all the mammals, be compelled to eat by the clock rather than being allowed to suckle when their own need and desire arise? Even today, I have heard pediatricians talk about imposing a schedule on babies just born. "So they'll learn to discipline their wants" or some such thing. Absurd! I hold with La Leche League that in the first year of life, there is no such thing as spoiling a child. They say that the best thing you can do for the first year is simply give it all the love and care you possibly can. After a year, the issue of disciplining may arise. But newborns?

This schedule-feeding business just seems emblematic of the mainstream culture's insistence on imposing order where there is no disorder—violation for the sake of violation. And if it is entirely superfluous here, I can readily suppose that most other instances where we see people being forced into molds contrary to their natural shape are likewise superfluous, violence for its own sake. Pathologies of order! **Eleanor**

Henry then posted an interesting thought.

You say that you cannot imagine a justification for such violative impositions. Try your imagination on this one.

What if I conceded to you that feeding-on-demand for newborns would not be disorder, that it would serve mother and child perfectly well for that first year? You seem to think that it necessarily follows that there can be no good reason for thus violating the inherent order of the organism by imposing another order opposed to it. But that is not so.

Consider the possibility that, in order to develop an adult who is prepared to fit into the existing social order, it is useful—perhaps even more kind—to begin bending the creature to another's will from the outset, rather than to allow that will to get the false impression that it will be much heeded in the world. It may ultimately be more humane to discipline in this way from the outset, than to wait until the need for the discipline has become more visibly manifest. One does not wait until the battle is joined before imposing discipline on military recruits. Rather, one constructs a boot camp with artificial and apparently—but only apparently—superfluous disciplines. **Henry**

And then I wrote in:

I was schedule-fed, fed not only by the clock but also in amounts regulated by the book rather than by my appetites. All this was on advice from supposedly "wise" pediatricians, and from all the stories I have heard these regimens were very much contrary to my needs and nature. But, Henry, the only result that I attribute to this feeding regime is that my favorite places to eat are all-you-can-eat buffets. **Andy**

Maria spoke up next. She had espoused, a while back, a Taoist way of looking at the question of hierarchy versus the unfolding of the natural process. At this point, she appeared in the forum again to share another bit of Taoist mythology.

The story has it, in the Taoist tradition, that Hun-Tun—who was this very amorphous and wonderful being—had benefacted Hu and Shu. Wanting to reciprocate in some way, Hu and Shu set to work on Hun-Tun to try to change his amorphous countenance into a human face. To do this, they began boring holes in his head. The outcome, regrettably, was that rather than turning Hun-Tun into that human form they hoped would be the result, they only succeeded in killing him.[8] **Maria**

Back with a Pitchfork

Herman picked up on the conversation we'd just been having about whether or not it is necessary for society to violate our natures to achieve order, and he proceeded to turn the discussion in an interesting direction. We hadn't heard from Herman since he'd spoken up about the superego as an example of "natural hierarchy."

We've heard a good deal here about the question of the justice or injustice of the order that comes with hierarchy, *Herman began*. And appropriately so, because it is a most important question. But our conversation has just brought us, I believe, to the point where we can see that injustice is not the only possible difficulty with an order that violates our natures in some way.

Let us imagine that we have a hierarchical order that really is just, that imposes no burdens that aren't truly necessary. Perhaps this order is imposed by God, and God is really as good as they say He is. Perhaps it is governed from above by paragons of virtue, Plato's philosopher kings or whatever. But in any event, the order is one that is free of corruption, that demands from those below only what is required for the good of the whole, including themselves (needing as they do to live in a well-ordered world).

Let us further grant Henry that a well-ordered world must necessarily be one that violates our natures. Whether or not the hangman is as indispensable as claimed to this order, it would follow from that supposition that there is an inescapable coercive dimension to the regime. People uncoerced would not fulfill what the order requires of them, would not obey, would not play the roles. We concede, that is, that whatever it takes to achieve social order is in some measure "against the grain."

What I would like to point out is that this war against our natures will be productive not only of order, but of disorder as well. This is a fundamental psychological truth, I believe: that the natural impulse, forbidden its free expression, does not disappear but is driven underground to reappear again as it gains some kind of expression. No, it is more than that. By being driven underground, it not only does not disappear, but it will return in a new, and quite likely more virulent form.

Andy's hunger did not disappear because it was "disciplined." His appetite for a limitless bounty on the table sounds pretty benign, but I wouldn't be surprised if society has reaped from its attempt to break his appetitive will some magnification of that very appetite and will. You do have, Andy, *Herman continued, evidently drawing upon his recollection of our time together at the California conference,* some of what was ascribed in *Julius Caesar* to Cassius: that "lean and hungry look." (Just kidding. Sort of.)

More seriously, though, the coerced renunciation of natural inclination—of pleasure, of spontaneous impulse, of whatever seeks to express itself through us from within—inevitably creates a destructive and aggressive tendency. I think for example of a book by a Scandinavian author—Ranulf, I believe was his name[9]—who wrote a book called *Moral Indignation and Middle Class Psychology.* His thesis was that the burdens of taking on the severe moral disciplines of bourgeois life engendered a psychological structure that was geared toward meddling, toward a kind of free-floating punitive impulse, toward a desire to stamp out in everyone else the capacities for enjoyment that had been injured in oneself. One thinks also of those antipornography crusaders who seem positively pornographic, though unleavened with the capacity for direct and unfettered enjoyment, in their pursuit of anyone with a "dirty mind." The tormentors of the Inquisition and their ilk throughout history appear to be externalizing a destructive war that coercive moral orders have engendered within them.

In ways like these, a top-down system of morality based on coercion seems to entail some fundamental kinds of disorder even in the name of creating order. In other words, if we were to accept it to be true that a hierarchical and coercive order were necessary, because the nature below—that is, within us—is inherently at odds with the requirements of order, then it might well follow that no very good order for human beings is possible. **Herman**

Victor the Graffiti Artist then posted this:

"Naturam expellas furca, tamen usque recurret." (If you drive nature out with a pitchfork, she will soon find a way back.) **Horace**[10]

Immediately on the heels of Victor's graffito came a message from Alice. We'd not heard from Alice, a counselor involved in character education, since she'd argued rather forcefully about the limits of people's ability to learn from experience.

What Herman has said about how the parts of us that are driven underground do not disappear, and Victor's quote from Horace about nature finding a way back, reminds me of something I heard not too long ago, on the radio I think. A nun, or former nun, was telling about her long experience of living in a convent. The nuns were forbidden to form close friendships, she said, in order to discipline their affections for more purely religious purposes; but instead a nun would take on a cat, and lavish affection on it, and then be jealous if she found some other nun even petting it. The nuns were forbidden to own valuables, in order to prevent their becoming covetous of property; so they took to collecting—and coveting—worthless items like pins. A lesson in there somewhere, I'm sure. **Alice**

Coming to Grips Together

Peter closed out this line of discussion with his next and, ultimately, surprising posting:

I must confess that I have noticed, when the presidential season is upon us in America, and the two main parties field their troop of competing candidates, that the meanness quotient is not evenly distributed between the two groups. When I look at the candidates for the Democratic nomination, I certainly find them wanting in many ways—I especially don't like their tendency to indulge the voters in their dependency and in their refusal to take responsibility for their own lives. But they seem overall like a nice bunch of people. By contrast, I find the Republicans considerably more solid and upright; they seem better constructed to uphold the order that I think the country relies upon for its long-term viability. But in purely human terms, they seem a dour, sour, and mean group. Among those most concerned about order, it seems, meanness seems at best an incidental by-product of taking on the burden of holding the structure together, and at worst is regarded as a positive virtue in itself.

Then Peter proceeded to conclude his message in a way I'd never have predicted of him. And with this surprising gesture, Peter took us off into a new whirlwind of an exchange to assess just what our exploration had revealed thus far, and where we might go from here.

Handling Wild Creatures

"I think it's dumb! And I can't wait to get to Middle School!" Nathaniel was obviously angry, though it wasn't obvious why it was this particular occasion that had triggered this anger.

By now in the fourth grade, Nathaniel was indeed in his last year at the elementary school that he'd been attending since kindergarten. In those almost five years, the same set of rules had been in effect all along, including the rule that today he'd been chastised for violating. He had lived without complaint with the stricture that no student be allowed to drink from the drinking fountain for more than five seconds.

Today, however, coming in from one of the rare recesses the school allows the children anymore, Nathaniel had a wonderfully intense thirst that he wanted to honor properly. After drinking the cool water from the fountain for a few seconds, Nathaniel had stood up and savored the slaking of his thirst, before bending again to partake of the clear stream. There had been one of his fellow students behind him, waiting patiently, saying nothing. But a teacher had seen Nathaniel's forbidden intermission and resumption and had immediately chastised him and reported him to his teacher. As a consequence, Nat was forced to do some additional, make-work assignment.

For a kid like Nathaniel, who was almost invariably cooperative and on the good side of the authorities, this reprimand had filled him with indignation. And the anger was still ready to well up when he got off the bus a few hours later and came into the house declaring the school and its rules dumb.

It had been different a few years earlier. Then it had been I who'd thought the school unnecessarily regimented, while Nathaniel regarded it all as a matter of course. Perhaps he was a first-grader at the time, when little by little he'd report to us some of the regime of regulations by which the school authorities kept order: classfuls of students moving to and from such appointments as gym and lunch only in strictly maintained single-file lines; each child allowed to sit at lunch only in places assigned by the teacher, without regard to who might be friends with whom; students who were being picked up after school being compelled to wait in the school library but forbidden to read anything from the library's shelves; etc.

When I learned about these things, I chafed inwardly at Nathaniel's having to conform to such a strait-jacketed order, but when I saw that Nat wasn't feeling bothered by it all, I said nothing to him about it. I didn't want to fan discontent where it needn't be, and so I confined my expressions of concern to conversations with April about it. And we gave some thought to possibly asking the school authorities if, perhaps, they might loosen up somewhat in their handling of these young children.

Meanwhile, back then, we were also hearing from some of our friends, in more liberal environments back in suburbs of the metropolitan area, about how disorderly some of the schools there were: chaos in the classrooms, noisy hallways, disrespect for authority. When we contrasted with this disorder the calm atmosphere and well-mannered students in Nathaniel's school, we thought that maybe these conservative imposers of elementary-school strait-jackets were giving us the best of the available bargains. Besides, in a great many respects the school provided a genuinely caring environment for the kids.

Now, with Nathaniel old enough to feel affronted at the inhospitability of the cage in which the school authorities were confining him and the other students, the issue was once again before us. Did the school really need to run so tight a ship? Couldn't they give the students a fair amount more room for self-regulation without surrendering to chaos?

But again, I held back from dealing directly with the school authorities. We'd had a good relationship with these people for more than four years, had found them very dedicated to the children under their tutelage. True, there was room for them to reconsider their somewhat authoritarian approach to order in the schools. But with Nat due—as he happily remarked more than once in these days—to graduate from the elementary school to the proto-adolescent environment of the middle school, it seemed somehow untimely to confront them now with our misgivings.

Neither did I drop the matter altogether, though. At this point I had recently become a weekly commentator on the local TV station, which served a market in which our county was but a somewhat minor backwater. From this little perch, it seemed to me, I had a chance to give voice to some of my concerns in a constructive but general and indirect—and thus less directly confrontational—way than the one that April and I had considered and rejected.

After doing some research with people knowledgeable about the schools in the region generally, I crafted a commentary that gently challenged the rigidity of the approach to discipline in many of the region's elementary schools. I played around with some of the proverbial wisdom according to which many of the region's cultural traditionalists oriented their child-rearing strategies, like "Spare the rod and spoil the child" and "As the twig is bent, so grows the tree." I'd noticed from my radio shows that many people seem to assume that youthful criminals have been "spoiled" and indulged, apparently oblivious to the evidence that a good many of them have been struck aplenty. And while bending the twig may incline it in the right direction, I argued that exerting a small force in the right direction was probably a better initial strategy than trying to overpower it at the outset.

What I left on the figurative cutting room floor—commentaries must be spare—was any mention of the impetus to "break the will" in order to domesticate, an approach with which I was familiar both from studying Alice Miller's work on the "poisonous pedagogy" of child-rearing "experts" in Germanic culture in the centuries leading up to the Nazis, as well as from the "breaking" of horses in the rodeo culture of the American southwest. But I sensed that even after this material was excised, it left a vibration remaining in the text in something like a homeopathic fashion.

As I left the taping session at the TV studio, I thought of a passage quoted by Alice Miller where some wise soul named Sultzer was advising parents to break the will of their children when they were very young, administering blows to them early. "Over the years children forget everything that happened to them in early childhood," Sultzer wrote. "If their will can be broken at this time, they will never remember afterwards that they had a will, and for this very reason the severity that is required will not have any serious consequences."[1] And in my mind, I made a connection between this idea and the way that Nathaniel did not take offense in the first grade the way he did subsequently at how controlling was the school's regime of rules.

That day, as it would happen, there were two disorders in the news, one regional and one rather local. At the regional level—though I later learned that it did make some of the national media—there was a scandal at one of the area's famous military institutes where some hazing of the freshmen by the upperclassmen had gotten out of hand and resulted in serious injury to two of those college-age youths. It seemed that criminal charges were not out of the question, and private lawsuits were already being mentioned by the parents of one of the victims.

The local incident took place on a schoolbus in our county, and Nathaniel was a witness to it. It did not, however, occur on Nat's own regular bus, but rather on the bus of one of his friends, for on this particular day, by prior arrangement, Nat was going home with that friend for an afternoon and early evening of companionship, a bit of homework, and dinner at the friend's house.

The bus rides had always been a regrettable part of Nathaniel's overall school experience. In a rural area like ours, there was no practical way for the different age groups to have their own separate buses—one for the elementary, one for the middle, and one for the high school. Each bus therefore contained the whole spectrum of ages, from five to eighteen, which meant that younger children were daily exposed to the behavior of the older children.

And that behavior chronically left a great deal to be desired. Crude language, rowdy conduct and, occasionally, downright meanness were common on the various buses. I could not recall my own adolescent cohort in the suburbs of the Twin Cities in Minnesota being as wild and unruly as these youth apparently were, but perhaps I recalled my past through distorted lenses. I did wonder, however, why it was that the same rural subculture that was producing such sweet children in the early grades was also generating such wild teenagers. Over the years, we heard a lot of parents of the young ones complain about their having to spend time on these buses, going to and from school, with these older students.

Some bus drivers were better than others at commanding the respect of their passengers and thus of maintaining a modicum of discipline. Nathaniel's bus was not one of the worst, we came to understand, but it was bad enough. Occasionally we considered chauffering Nat to and from school each day, but with the school being fifteen miles from our place, such a remedy would have consumed too much of both time and fossil fuels for parents, like us, who had a lot to do as well as a strong commitment to the environment. And, besides, Nathaniel's basic sturdiness reassured us that he could handle the toxicity of the bus rides, a belief that was soon strengthened by his getting into a routine of using the time on the bus to do homework, to read books he found of interest, and to explore music with the Walkperson we provided him.

On this particular day, however, Nathaniel was riding on one of the notoriously rowdier routes.

The problem began when the driver either forgot or refused to let out a new transfer student at his grandmother's store in a little town not far from the school. Whatever the cause, the youngster—like Nat, a fourth-grader—began pleading with the driver to turn around and take him back or, at the very least, to let him out right there so he could walk the half mile back to where he was expected. The driver mantained that he did not have explicit authorization to let him out at the grandmother's store, but only at his own house which was located further along the route. The boy maintained that, as his parents were working, no one would be there to take care of him at his own house. But the driver remained adamant—"The rules are the rules!" he shouted, as if to end the matter—adamant, that is, at least until a group of several adolescent boys rose up and walked down the aisle assailing the driver verbally.

"You let that kid off this f***ing bus or we'll drop you off the bus," one of them shouted into the face the driver.

The driver then stopped the bus, and told the new fourth-grader to get the hell off the bus, and added a few other choice words. And then as the boy got off, he turned and dressed down the three youths who were now backed off about four or five feet from him, and advanced on the one who'd threatened him. "And you, sit down, punk!" he shouted at the youth, and gave him a shove on the shoulder.

At this, according to the witnesses, including Nathaniel, the youth in question pushed back and the driver fell over backward. Then these three young men, joined by several other students of both high-school and middle-school ages, began kicking out a few windows.

Well, this little mutiny on the bus didn't make the newspapers, but it spread quickly through the grapevine, and was regarded somewhat as our area's wake-up call about youth violence. Some made connections with the recent schoolyard shooting in Jonesboro, Arkansas, in which a couple of students—ages 13 and 11—had gunned down their school-mates, killing four of them plus a teacher. Suddenly there was a sense of alarm.

For April and me, the nature of the adolescent subculture in our area—with the high rates of drunken driving and of teenage pregnancy—had been a source of concern as we looked to a future when Nathaniel would be coming of age in this area. This disturbance on the school bus seemed to us just one more piece of a larger pattern. But for many others, apparently, this mutiny stood out as a sudden blotch on an otherwise unblemished picture.

It was only a couple of nights later that I had occasion to pick up Nathaniel at the school, about a half hour before school let out, so that he and I could run some errands together. After the office sent word for Nathaniel through the intercom, and as I stood in the school office waiting for him to leave his classroom to join me, the school principal—Mrs. Reynolds—spotted me as she came out of her office to give a document to her secretary.

"Mr. Schmookler, how are you?" she said, in a tone that suggested that this was just a means of measuring me for distance.

"Not bad, Mrs. Reynolds, and you?" Despite some of my reservations about some aspects of the school, I really appreciated the job that Mrs. Reynolds did. Her caring for the children was palpable, and she managed either to recruit teachers with similar dedication or to imbue that caring in her staff, because all of Nathaniel's teachers were basically good with the children and responsible in their work. So, when I sensed the edge in Mrs. Reynold's voice, I felt inclined to prepare more for peacemaking than for combat.

"I heard your commentary the other night on TV," she said. "The one about strict discipline and what you thought might be the value of giving young children somewhat freer rein. Well, now, I supposed you've heard about that incident on the bus the other day."

"Yes, Nathaniel actually was on the bus."

"Well, I'm glad that I work with the elementary school kids. Really, between you and me, it's not all that seldom that these high school students act really wild. I've spent time over there in classes at the high school, and I tell you—they're a disrespectful, unruly lot.

"Anyway, maybe this incident has got you reconsidering what you said the other day on TV?" she concluded, with a question in her voice.

"Reconsidering? Why would that be?"

"Well think of it. If you recognize how much impulse toward disorder there is in those young people, how much native wildness there is at that age. . . . Well, think of it! If we didn't train them as tightly at the young ages like we do where we've got them from five years to ten, if we didn't get them used to discipline at the outset—just think of how wild they'd be then!"

I didn't quarrel, but only indicated that I wasn't sure that was necessarily the only way to look at the connection, making some reference to how pressure cookers can explode only because of how tight the lid is. And we were talking pleasantly with each other when Nathaniel showed up in the office with a happy, "Hi Dad!" and we took off to do our errands together.

III
Under Construction

In What We Trust?
Do We Have the Moorings We Need?

Where Are We?

At the end of that long discussion of the shortcomings of order imposed by Authority from above, Peter had concluded his message (containing his observation about the tendency toward meanness of conservative politicians) by going on to say:

> If the overall thrust of this conversation is something like "Humankind, we've got a problem here regarding this pursuit of good order," I must say that I feel compelled to agree. And, more than I would have expected, it has been the experience of following the twists and turns of this challenging conversation that has made that difficulty much clearer to me than it was.
>
> I'm far from clear precisely about all the lineaments of the problem, much less about what kind of solution to the problem might be possible, but I have become more open to recognizing that hidden in the tresses of my well-brushed belief system, there are some big and hitherto unrecognized tangles. **Peter**

Coming from Peter, this surprised me, because I had thought him somewhat doctrinaire in his conservatism and more inclined to protect himself from being considered wishy-washy by those still more orthodox than to seek some common ground in the middle. But just as unexpected, to me, as Peter's new openness to confront the tangles hidden in the tresses of his well-brushed belief system was the way that several others immediately chimed in with similar confessions of newfound dissatisfaction with their own beliefs and a growing sense of there being here some deeper, more complex problem than they'd previously recognized. Larry, Karen, and Alice were those who wrote to reinforce what Peter had said. I felt rather encouraged by this development, interpreting it to mean that the process of inquiry was proving a powerful goad, driving us toward a more complete understanding.

It immediately became clear, however, that this sense of newly discovered problems in old positions was not universally shared. After the flurry from Peter and the others, Ralph wrote in to ask:

> Maybe I'm missing something here. Could one of you please explain just what it is that you think has been established here that calls so much into question?

To which Larry replied, with similar brevity:

> It seems to me that the discussion has shown that both bottom-up and top-down approaches to building a good order are fundamentally flawed. That seems to leave us floating in a sea without a mooring.

And Peter added, right on Larry's heels:

> Precisely. It seems we have shown that human nature is not something we can rely on to just "naturally" unfold in good ways, but also that any "higher authority" we might imagine to whip us flawed creatures into shape or to keep us on the right path might be as defective as we are. So it becomes unclear where those forces might come from that would create good order.

Ralph was not persuaded.

> My understanding of what we've done so far is different. To me it seems that it is just some extreme, somewhat simple-minded positions that have been explored and proved wanting. Among the bottom-ups, it's just those who have some naive view of our innate wisdom and goodness whose positions were revealed to be insupportable. And among the top-downs, it is just the doctrinaire views founded on some notion of infallible authority that we just got through demolishing.
>
> My position isn't founded on either of those simple-minded extremes and, frankly, I don't see any more problem with my position than I did at the start. In fact, most of the people I know are so far from those simple-minded positions that I'm not sure how much bearing these arguments would have on their positions either. **Ralph**

Again it was Larry who answered.

> I must confess, Ralph, that my sense of what we've done here so far is more intuitive than mathematically tight. A couple of reasons for this. One is that our discussions have moved pretty quickly, sometimes leaving a position wounded but not necessarily mortally so, and then with the next message we've rushed on before the question of

that previous position's viability has been wholly resolved. Another reason I feel I'm having to fly on intuition is that, frankly, this question of good order gets too deep and too complex for me to be able to hold it still and tight enough in my puny little mind to be able to say, "Yeah, here's the void that none of us here has filled." Yet, my intuition tells me that unless one of those "simple-minded" positions can get firmed up, nothing else can be built with a reliable structure.

But hey, I could be wrong, and I'd like to check it out together. (This all reminds me of the story I heard as an undergraduate about some professor—of mathematics or physics, or something like that—who, while lecturing to a class, said of an equation he'd written on the blackboard, "And the rest, of course, is obvious." Then he paused and contemplated it, silently, for twenty minutes while the students waited. Finally he broke the silence, declaring, "Yes, it's obvious.") **Larry**

At this point, the conversation became quite intense, and more than usually difficult to follow. The predominant thrust of the newly arriving messages was to declare that "No, we don't have a problem." While sharing this denial of there being any great problem to be solved, however, the messages differed in what each thought the already-clear solution to the problem to be.

To make it somewhat clearer than it was for me, as all these messages appeared in my inbox, I might say in summary that the "no problem" assertions came basically from three directions. In quick summary, these were: (1) a Taoist version of "no problem," in which "trust the spontaneous unfolding" was asserted to be sufficient to meet our needs; (2) a liberal version, in which "whatever we're doing is working" was said to demonstrate the needlessness of philosophical struggles such as Larry and Peter were now engaged in; and (3) a "put your faith in the Lord" version, in which the sufficiency of the Word from on High was reasserted.

Left, center, and right, in other words, all reannounced the adequacy of their original positions.

Go with the Flow: Taoism Revisited

I'll relate first what I'm calling the Taoist version of "no problem," because it is the quickest in the telling. Though I have a love of the Taoist vision, for the most part what got posted seemed like warmed-over leftovers from our previous discussions of the bottom-up vision. We heard again that we should make ourselves like water, which moves on its course without having to decide, or to be controlled, or to control anything. We heard a passage from the classical Taoists decrying the Confucians: in pursuing the illusion of ruling, the Taoists evidently declared, the Confucians had brought ruin. We were exhorted to follow the *tzu-jan*, that which unfolds spontaneously of itself. This prompted the part of the exchange that I, at least, found the most interesting.

Maria quoted from the Taoist *Chung Yung*: "The Tao is that from which one cannot deviate; that from which one can deviate is not the Tao."[1]

That prompted Larry to write:

If the Tao is that from which one cannot deviate, then how can the Taoists complain about the Confucians ruining things? After all, they must have been following the Tao. They couldn't deviate from it if they wanted to, right? I mean, if we can trust that which unfolds spontaneously, doesn't that—at some fundamental level—include everything? Even if some new things arise—the making of distinctions, the passing of judgments—must it not be said of them that these new things also unfolded spontaneously? **Larry**

Larry was referring here to another of the Taoist classics that had been quoted, the passage in the *Chuang Tzu* complained about the progression of the ancients from a time when they "knew there were things, but did not yet make distinctions between them. Next, they made distinctions between them, but they did not yet pass judgments upon them. When judgments were passed, Tao was destroyed."[2]

This led John to write in and make what seemed to me an interesting and telling parallel.

Good point, Larry, *John wrote.* Yes, it seems to me that the Achilles' heel of this "trust the natural" position is that, while it complains about the unnatural, it seems to have no way—consistent with its celebration of the initial state—of explaining how that unnatural could have come along to ruin things. This reminds me of that theodicy problem—by which I mean here not anything to do with God, per se, but more generally with how to solve the riddle of the origin of evil—in the anarchists' position. Remember? It's the move that Andy made about the anarchists and the state: if all the evil comes from the state, and if the state itself is both evil and something that was not present in some golden original condition, then how did the state arise? This Taoist argument seems beset by the same fundamental flaw. And I, for one, cannot see, therefore, how anyone can continue to hold to this "In the Tao we trust" position as a way of getting out of the problem that Larry and Peter were posing about a lack of reliable moorings.

A brief interchange about this brought a consensus—well, at least among several of us—that while Taoism itself might have a sensible rejoinder to a challenge along these lines, it did not seem as though any of us on the forum were able to provide one.

I've mentioned that some of the Taoist ideas that were posted seemed like warmed-up leftovers from earlier in our discussion. These weren't the only leftovers being served up. Although I'd noticed this repetition, and had been subliminally aware of some feelings of disheartenment in the face of it, it was a back-channel message from Larry that really brought my attention to focus on it.

You'd think that none of that earlier discussion had even happened, *wrote Larry after ticking off a few of the instances of people reasserting the very same positions they'd put forward weeks ago.* To my mind, the original presentations of those ideas had elicited some pretty telling critiques. But it seems they were like the proverbial water off the duck's back, so unchanged are the positions in their present reappearance. I'm wondering what this persistence of people's original views says about the value of our conducting a discussion of this kind.

I appreciate, Larry, *I replied,* your bringing up this issue, even though it makes me somewhat uncomfortable. I had believed that when some of these arguments were rendered silent in the face of some stiff challenges, it meant that their proponents were back at the drawing boards, either redesigning their ideas to meet those challenges or coming up with new positions altogether using the new things they'd been compelled to see. But it seems that at least some minds were not so readily changed.

What bothers me, *Larry wrote back,* is when it seems that people hold beliefs as if in some intellectual vaccuum. "Don't confuse me with facts," as the old joke has it, "my mind is made up." If beliefs aren't subject to being tested by evidence, and by reason, then on what basis are they being held?

Perhaps we should be content, *I suggested to Larry, and perhaps was speaking equally to my own disappointment,* that at least **some** among us take the argumentation process sufficiently to heart—or to head, as the case may be—to allow their—or our—initial complacency to be disturbed enough for them to reconsider, or even to revise, their beliefs when they no longer seem rationally tenable. For me, the way that you and Peter have pronounced yourselves disturbed and mystified must weigh at least as strongly as the way some others run off their intellectual cliffs confident, evidently, that if they only don't notice their predicament, like the cartoon characters who do not fall until they look down and see there's nothing there to stand on, they can continue running as before. **Andy**

Zeno's Paradox

Meanwhile, another line of discussion was unfolding. In response to Larry's exchange with Ralph—in which Larry was taking the position that our discussion had shown that, there being a profound problem in both the top-down and bottom-up visions, we lacked any reliable place to moor our moral craftings—Jeff launched the second kind of "no problem" argument.

I get somewhat impatient with this philosophical stuff, *Jeff protested*. With all due respect, it seems like something of a game to me, cut off from the real world I live in. I am a practical sort of a guy, I'm interested in what works. And you folks with philosophical underpinnings and all that tightly connected logical framework may claim that the Emperor has no clothes but, logic or not, I know the clothes are there.

I'm out there in the world where people *do* maintain pretty good order. They say "Excuse me" when they bump into you. They don't steal your silverware when they come to your house. They obey the law and take care of their sick kids and all that sort of thing. I don't know how all these people or anybody else are thinking about goodness that makes it possible for them to be decent folks. But it's not clear to me that it much matters. Who needs that kind of philosophical "foundation" when we can just wing it? So long as we can stay afloat in your "void," how important can that void be? **Jeff**

This reminds me, *wrote Fred*, of the old paradox by which that ancient Greek Zeno "proved" that in a race with a tortoise, if the tortoise started out in front, Achilles could never catch up with it. Before he could catch up, he'd have to catch up halfway, Zeno proposed, and before he could do that, he'd have to catch up a quarter of the way, and so on in infinite regress. And so—by gosh!—with an infinite number of things he'd have to do first, he'd never be able to get around to pulling even. But of course it was all so much baloney, since what he'd "proved" was impossible was something that we see happening all the time. **Fred**

To which Herman then posted:

That's a nice analogy, Fred. But let's extend it a little more. It took the mathematicians and logicians a couple of thousand years to figure out how, cleanly, to deal with Zeno's paradox. Of course, it wasn't necessary to do this in order for runners to overtake other runners. But the exercise of figuring out how to escape from the paradox taught people something about how to think about such problems, what kinds of defects in our logic we may be encumbered by. Likewise, perhaps, even though we might agree that, like Achilles overtaking the tortoise, the achievement of good order is, manifestly, not a complete impossibility, even so we might learn something important from working through whatever it is in our way of thinking that *seems,* at this point, to make it hard for us—or at least some of us—to envision how it can be possible, given the apparent impossibility of finding anything reliable to build order up from or hang order down from. **Herman**

Ralph then reentered the conversation, to respond to Larry's sense of the difficulty our discussions had demonstrated.

Your intuitive sense, Larry, that the undermining of both of the extreme positions— all for liberty, or all for authority—might pose some genuine problems for all the points in between is a proposition that I'm willing to explore. But overall, I hold with Jeff's sense that the proof is in the pudding.

We do manage to create good order, I think, in our liberal society. We don't rely either altogether on liberty, as if authority is unnecessary, but we tend to be very careful about how authority is constructed, for all the reasons we've explored in the past several days. Good elements from one side combined with good elements from the other and—voila!—the good liberal order. Add two parts liberty and one part well-constructed authority and you've got a recipe for a decent society.

And if we don't have the certainty that comes from having a simple-minded dogma, well, that is part of what the tradition of liberalism has long embraced: no questions (and, one wishes, no minds) ever get closed, no authority is above question, the search for the right and reasonable path is never-ending.

So, rather than saying that we are floating in a void between two crumbling foundations—one above, one below—I would rotate the image ninety degrees and say that we liberals are swimming, rather contentedly, in the middle without attaching ourselves to the immutable moorings either on our right or our left. **Ralph**

If that previous reassertion of the Taoist position (of the cultural left) led us to what was essentially a rehashing of old positions, this reassertion of the ostensibly practical workability of the liberal position (of our cultural center) led us into some more exciting terrain. We're doing basically OK, it was being argued. And therefore we have no real need for a philosophically satisfactory accounting of how we *could* be doing OK, of what kind of secure hitching post our moral vision might have.

The challenge to this sanguine view got started with a posting from Alice, which followed immediately upon Ralph's description of swimming happily between two unnecessary extremes.

You know the joke about the guy falling from a 100-story building? *Alice asked*. Someone asks him how's he's doing as he streaks past a window on the twentieth floor, and he calls out "So far, so good."

Well, in my view, the liberal order has pushed society off that 100-story building, and we're heading down. The 100 stories are the edifice of authority that earlier, non-liberal phases of our history built up. These have to do with culturally inculcated character-structure and child-rearing practices and such, with traditional systems of ethics and morality, with old-fashioned virtues like patriotism and sacrifice, and the old dogmas of established religion. The liberal order when it emerged could take the existence of these for granted, but then that order knocks away the supports for those old dimensions of the moral order.

So we're heading downward toward a crash that's only hinted at by some of the winds rushing around us and the bruises we get as we hit flag poles and awnings on the way. **Alice**

In support of what Alice says, *Terrence added at this point,* I'd like to cite Adam Smith's manifesto for capitalism. *The Wealth of Nations* was written by a guy who had also written *The Theory of Moral Sentiments*. He could assume that in the world around him the people carried in their hearts some basic moral commitments and involvements that, two centuries and more later, we discover are being eroded by that liberal order he helped to establish. **Terrence**

Yes, *Ralph rejoined*. I'm familiar with this point of view. (A good book on all this is Bell's *The Cultural Contradictions of Capitalism*.) But I'm not persuaded that there's really a problem here. The moral level of the world is something that has always had its ups and downs. I'm not convinced that there is any overall trajectory to the liberal order—from the 100th floor downward, for example—that warrants our concern. **Ralph**

I'm wondering, *Alice posted next,* just what kind of evidence would persuade you that we are in the process of plunging from some height toward a crash below. Are you familiar with that list of what were the greatest disciplinary problems facing schools a couple of generations ago, and what they are now? After years of liberalism be-coming increasingly ascendant over our cultural life, we've gone from bubble-gum chewing and passing notes in class to rape in the hallways and assault with a deadly weapon in the lavatories. If that is not evidence of some kind of plunge, what would be? **Alice**

Have you ever heard, Alice, *wrote Fred,* of the fallacy of *post hoc ergo propter hoc?* It means that just because something comes after something else, it doesn't mean that the earlier was the *cause* of the latter. **Fred**

God's Place

At this point, there was the posting from Kenneth.

I am sorry to interrupt your present discussion about whether liberalism is living off the moral capital of traditional belief systems that it itself has corroded—sorry not just because of the bad manners of interrupting, but also because I think the question an important one. But there is a still earlier line of discussion that I think was skipped over altogether too hastily.

I'm talking about the issue of God and of received (traditional) religious belief—an issue raised not long ago by Carl, and then brushed aside as if it were some small thing. For most of you, evidently, it was sufficient to call attention to the disagree-ments among religions and to the fact that, in the Bible, God didn't always act the way you thought He should. So much for God.

I don't know what Carl's silence since then might mean, but I doubt very much that it means that he has learned the "error of his ways" that you were trying to teach him. And now that the conversation is proceeding along as if the rule of God had been disposed of with finality, I feel moved to end my own silence and say to you: Stop! It is not our ways that are in error, but your own. There is more in heaven and earth than is dreamt of in your rationalist philososphy. **Kenneth**

With all due respect for the sensibilities of the religious people who have chosen to join in this conversation, *Jeff answered,* I, for one, would rather we not get bogged down in this God issue. The people who believe, believe. And in my experi-ence there is nothing any of us is going to be able to say that will persuade them otherwise. As for any of them persuading us of their beliefs, forget it. We've all heard it before. And other than the fact that they happened to be born into families that taught them what to believe before they were able to think clearly about the evidence on their own, I've never heard any good reason why they believe it either. **Jeff**

And Kenneth responded:

Do you really think that your reason and your empiricism are so obviously superior to the system of belief that has provided the beacon for millions upon millions of souls across a hundred generations? Are you really so certain that you can live without God, that your vision of life with no God, with nothing above you, can really carry you and your seed forward in this world (let alone to the next)? Do you really think we who believe in God are so foolish that we hold our faith simply because we imbibed our silly superstitions with our mother's milk?

If that is what you think, here is a little empirical puzzle for you. How do you account for the millions of people these days who grow up without these silly superstitions and false certainties and then proceed in adulthood to come to God and to make Him the center of their lives? **Kenneth**

Then Herman came in:

This does seem a big divide, perhaps unbridgeable. A terribly important one, but I am at a loss to know what to do with it. Two big groups of people, one of which cannot understand how anyone *can* believe in God and the other of which cannot understand how anyone *cannot* believe in Him. Other than good manners, I don't know what to recommend. **Herman**

I agree with Kenneth, *wrote Rev.George*, about the unacceptability of dismissing religious belief so facilely. At the very least, to do so is to cut oneself off from the heart and guts of our history and from a great many of one's fellow human beings. And these are not just the benighted eras of history, nor the foolish and ignorant among humankind. At the most, it may be missing something absolutely key about the truth of our existence in this mysterious cosmos.

But I share with others a degree of perplexity about the epistemological question: on what basis can we legitimately feel that we *know* anything about God, or even that there *is* a God? Indeed, I expect the tension between those two points of view is a more central part of my life than of anyone else's here. (If I can hardly bridge those two in my own life, I will certainly make no pretense to being able to create a bridge over this space for anyone else!)

Truly a vital question, but it's not clear, *George concluded*, just where we can go with it now, unless Kenneth (or Carl) has some particular idea or challenge he wants to present. So for now, I suggest that we hold open a place for God to reenter our conversation as the occasion warrants, and resume that line of inquiry about the limits to the liberal vision in creating a good moral order. I have a feeling that the two questions are not entirely separate. **George**

And, as I describe shortly, in the next chapter, we did indeed, as George suggested, pursue the inquiry into the limits of the liberal vision in creating a good moral order. But most immediately, the energy remained bound up with the question of God. Henry reappeared, declaring:

As for that supposed great problem some of you declare you have discovered—how to find a reliable, fixed point for your moral orientation—no such problem exists, *Henry propounded*. There is one true God, who has given us all the Word we need to find our way, and we have no need for any moral moorings beyond God and His Word.

Nothing you have said remotely proves otherwise. Nor even cast a shadow on that central and eternal truth. **Henry**

Immediately, his declaration was answered with challenges. He was attacked for his dogmatism, for acting as if he could, by divine fiat, establish as True something that he held either "for no good reason," as some styled it derogatorily, or as "a matter of faith," as he characterized it as a badge of merit.

More interesting, however, was the line of challenge that took Henry more on his own terms, that is, that posited the validity of his text as the Word of God, and then went on to challenge the moral acceptability of the cosmic vision that went with it.

So what we had, ensuing from these latter two versions of the "no problem" response—the liberal "whatever we're doing works, so we don't need to figure out how to resolve the paradox," and the religious "God above is the fixed point by which we can guide our souls and our world"—were two very challenging discussions. On one thread, we had the critique of the moral order of liberalism from the perspective of traditional (and religious) morality. I'll recount that thread in the next chapter, "A Passion for the Whole." Meanwhile, along another thread, we watched unfold a critique of the traditional religious moral vision from the liberal and rationalist point of view. This will be presented in the subsequent chapter (chap. 10), "The Idiocy and Theodicy."

It was out of the struggles of those two controversies that a rather different approach to Peter's and Larry's problem eventually arose. From the unfolding inquiry, a different way of thinking started to arise, one that offered—or at least so some of us believed—a way out of that "Zeno's paradox" of finding neither bottom-up nor top-down satisfactory as a source of good order.

It was interesting how this new, fourth approach to getting past—or in this case, through—our problem brought together elements of all that had gone before. With the watercourse lovers, it shared a sense of how it is all an unfolding. With the bow-down advocates, it shared a sense of the indispensability of good order coming from above. And it was like the liberal swimmers-in-the-middle position that Ralph had proposed in its sense of a recipe combining the various elements. Yet it also confirmed Herman's sense that there is indeed a pay-off for not just saying that the Achilles must overcome Zeno somehow—because, after all, there we see him overtaking the tortoise—but rather working through our paradoxes to some greater philosophical clarity.

And oh yes, it also confirmed the sense that Peter and Larry had there we human beings really do have a problem here, one that must disturb an honest mind desirous of ease and certainty.

But before we get to this integrative approach to the bottom-up/top-down controversy—in chapter 11, "Under Construction"—let me tell you about the disputes and struggles that somehow seemed to lead us there.

A Passion for the Whole
When Bad Things Happen Because of Good People

The issue had been likened to that famous paradox of Zeno's in which it had apparently been "proved" that Achilles could never overtake the tortoise. With both bottom-up and top-down arguments discredited, as some saw it, how could we possibly find any reliable source of good order? Are we not condemned to float at sea with no secure moorings?

Don't worry, others—of a liberal bent—had said assuringly: just as Achilles' ability to win the race is indisputable, whether we can handle Zeno's argument or not, so also is our ability to establish good order. After all, this argument went, we're doing it well enough as it is, so why worry about explaining *how* we possibly could be doing it.

The idea that the liberal moral order of contemporary society was doing well enough had then been disputed, with our circumstance being likened to the man falling from the hundredth floor saying that he's feeling fine as he passes the twentieth.

It was at this point that Kenneth had reentered the conversation, diverting some of the flow of argument toward his attempt to reassert the unquestionable top-down authority of God. At the same time as Kenneth's message on God's place had arrived, there also came a message from Cynthia, reinforcing the earlier arguments of Jeff and Ralph that the proof is in the pudding. It is from this posting from Cynthia that we can follow what became a rather interesting challenge to the liberal worldview from a more traditionalist and, ultimately, religious standpoint.

The Moral Culture of Liberalism

Like Ralph, I don't see that our basically liberal vision of things creates any basic problems for the moral order, *Cynthia wrote.* I am middle-aged and a middle-class professional, and a liberal. Over the course of three decades of being an adult, I've known a lot of people like me. Basically liberal. We vote Democratic in presidential elections almost always, though we're not always happy with the candidate; at least he's not likely to wrap himself in the flag, like Bush did in 1988, or use "family values" as a club to beat up people different from himself. Almost none of my friends goes to church or, if they do go to something, at least it doesn't have any hard-and-fast dogmas they push on people. That kind of thing.

But my point is, these are **good people.** They're not part of any one-hundred-story plunge. They are kind and decent folks, they love their kids. They support civil rights and the protection of the environment. They have compassion for people on welfare, and they don't complain about having to pay some taxes so that people less fortunate than themselves get enough to get by on. I am willing to bet a hundred dollars that not one of fifty of the men I include in this circle beats his wife or climbs into bed with his daughter. I think I really know I'm right on this.

Now, when you talk about problems with people like the Christian Coalition, I can see what you're talking about. The idea that their way is the only way makes for so much conflict and difficulty. So much of their righteousness seems to lead to coercive and punitive ways of relating to other people's difficulties. But when it comes to the liberal perspective of decent people like my friends, I just don't see the problem. If anything, having **more** people just like them seems like the solution. And for that, I think we just need to have better education, more humane and child-centered child-rearing, and more opportunities for people to develop themselves. **Cynthia**

Next came Larry.

Do you believe in synchronicity? I don't: I mean, how **could** it be true? It's one of those mystical beliefs that, if I were to recognize them as valid, I'd have to change my whole picture of the world. And why should a few coincidences call for such drastic measures? But anyway, one of those occasional striking coincidences just happened.

Strangely ("Twilight Zone" music to be heard in the background), just when I was about to read Cynthia's message, I got a call from a dear friend in another part of the country. Although I'll conceal his identity, I'll tell you about the conversation.

My friend's daughter is in her early twenties. She's been going with a young man, about her age, for the better part of a year, and they were planning, in a loose sort of a way, to get married sometime. Three months ago she gets pregnant. They talk about abortion, but the young woman has strong convictions against it. They talk about marriage—before the baby comes, after it comes, never? The girl wants very much to get married. The young man is noncommittal: he's not sure what he wants to do. All that's pretty familiar terrain. Here's the interesting part.

My friend is a wonderful man, a concerned and dedicated citizen, a true friend, and a person of great insight. His professional training includes a good deal of background in counseling. He arranges for the two young people to meet with him to discuss the situation. The young fellow comes in, petrified. But he needn't have worried.

My friend described to me how he conducted the meeting. His goal, he said, was to help both people get in touch with **what they really wanted.** And the outcome was this: the meeting served to help the young man become clear that he does not want to make so big a commitment at this time. The possibility was left open for reconsideration at some undefined future point.

I asked my friend, "What would you have said to the guy if he had been your son?" And he replied, "I'd have pointed out to him that there are other aspects of his behavior that suggest that a part of him really does want to commit to this relationship, and I'd have encouraged him to look closer to see what this might say about what he really wants."

We joked a bit about the contrast between how it was for the young man in that meeting and the traditional image, in song and story, of such an interaction: the image of the shotgun wedding with the girl's father providing the shotgun. Then I wished him and his daughter all the best, and said good-bye, and came to the screen to read Cynthia's message. That's when it really hit me.

I called my friend up and asked him if it would be OK for me to share with him my second thoughts about how he'd handled the situation with the young couple. After getting his encouragement, I went ahead and I told him that I thought the emphasis in his meeting with them was wrong. The issue with which the young man should be confronted is not just what he **wants** to do, it is also most emphatically about what he **should** do, what his responsibility in the situation is. A few months ago, as the pregnancy demonstrates, this young fellow went for what he wanted, and now there are two people besides himself—a young woman he has loved, and a new life that he has helped bring into being—whose fates are substantially in his hands. Where, I asked, does the question of what a person owes to more-than-himself enter into the picture? If not in this situation, when **would** a person be obliged to think about the good of something bigger than himself?

I wasn't recommending that the grandfather-to-be should bring a shotgun into the picture. The coercive mode of the shotgun wedding completely bypasses the moral appeal: it stays on the level of what the young father wants, but rearranges the options by making the irresponsible option even less pleasant than the responsible one. But, I said, just helping a person to clarify his own desires also effectively eliminates the moral dimension entirely: in an interdependent world, each following his wants doesn't make the world a very healthy place.

He said I'd given him some food for thought and thanked me, and soon we said good-bye again. **Larry**

Yes, precisely! *Peter wrote in the next message.* This captures what I've tried to convey to some of my liberal friends, usually without success I might add. I don't question that your friend is a wonderful person, possessing a host of good character traits, just like those Cynthia attributes to her circle of good people. But could it be clearer how the ethos of liberalism, even when emanating from good people, greases the skids toward human catastrophes of moral disorder?

I expect your friend is fully aware of the tragedy of fatherless children that has beset this country, and I expect he mourns the suffering and deprivation that a great many of these children are subjected to. If he's like a lot of my liberal friends, he blames the economy for not creating enough opportunities, or the absence of some government program or other. Meanwhile, the conservatives are saying no, it's a moral issue. "It's the culture, stupid," as some say these days. Here, Larry, in the story you've just told, is the answer. This fine liberal gentleman sits down with the father of someone who will soon be his grandchild, in the presence of his own pregnant and heartsick child, and he follows his liberal moral vision to help the young man become clearer about what he desires for himself.

Like life's some big store, and the customer is always right! **Peter**

Interrupted by Business

Just then I started receiving a fax. I ran over to the machine and saw from the letterhead that it was from my agent, Lila. I knew it had been several weeks since she'd put my book proposal into the hands of some editors, and I was apprehensive about the fax. If the news had been great, she'd have phoned me to give me the news herself. The tea kettle started steaming and screaming up in the kitchen, so I bolted up the stairs to take care of that, and ran back down just in time to discover that the fax machine had jammed, and that, after the first paragraph, the whole message was being printed on one line till it was black. I tried to get someone on the other end of the fax to pick up, but to no avail. I called her office, but got a machine. I noticed it was just after five, and whoever had sent it for Lila had apparently assumed her mission had been accomplished and had left for the day. So I was left with the partial message, which I sat down to read.

"Dear Andy," it read, "I believe I warned you that this would be a hard sell—a book about how to think about moral order. Now I've got a handful of responses back, and I wanted to share the gist of them with you. We've still got a few more to hear from, but I thought you might want to think about the reaction we're getting.

"Three of these editors said that they are intrigued with your ideas, but they all say that it is very hard for a 'self-help' book like this to find its niche in the market. Two other editors, including that very bright fellow I was talking about who had enjoyed your critique of the market economy (I forgot to ask him if it was *The Illusion of Choice* he was talking about or *Fool's Gold*), said that . . ." That's where the damned fax had jammed, and the rest was unintelligible.

So, at least until the morrow, I was left with that truncated message. But food for thought it was, nonetheless. *"Self-help"* book!? What self-help book? Hadn't they read the proposal? The book is about how to think about how the world can be made into the world as it should be. It's not about how to improve your sex life, or get rich, or lose weight. I wondered, was it the device of the Nintendo Dilemma at the beginning that had led them astray? Did they think somehow it was another book on how to discipline your kids? "Just say 'no' to video games." Parent effectiveness training for the nineties. No, that couldn't be it: even the Nintendo Dilemma is posed as a question about human nature and its inherent trustworthiness and not as a how-to.

Then it struck me. Maybe in the cultural framework within which these editors are operating, the issue of what kind of moral philosophy to employ registers as an issue of self-help, self-improvement. Making choices about what lifestyle you want to adopt. That in itself, it seemed to me— that way of comprehending the fundamental issue I was raising as the heart of the book—was already knee-deep in a moral philosophy. And while it was not a philosophy that I thought adequate to our challenge, it was one that I hoped this book would address.

The Self at Sea

Larry's account of his friend's facilitating his non-son-in-law's getting in touch with his desires brought Kenneth back into the conversation.

Yes, here is where liberalism, with its person-centered rather than God-centered worldview, falls short. Larry's liberal friend inhabits a world that consists of individuals with rights, among which are life, liberty, and the pursuit of happiness. It is a world of autonomous beings, each entitled to give himself permission to find his own way, to serve his own purposes.

So Larry's friend, believing the world to be properly thus ordered, sits down with this young couple, a threesome actually, including two who are flesh of his flesh, and works to be a channel of good order in the situation. Given his beliefs, it makes sense that he would think that if he just helps clear the channels for each to become more enlightened searchers for their own happiness, good order will arise. And so he unwittingly becomes an accomplice in what previous ages would have regarded as a great moral wrong: a child has been conceived, a woman has been given the weight of maternal responsibilities, and this young man is helped to follow his own energy out of the situation, out from under the weight of his own moral responsibilities as a man.

The problem is that the energy whose flow is thus facilitated is not a moral energy. What flows spontaneously out of the springs of our sinful natures is the passion for self-gratification. This selfishness is precisely what a true moral order must work to overcome. And unless it is overcome, the human world falls apart.

To know God, and to keep Him ever before one's eyes is the key to living as a moral being. "Thy will, Oh Lord, not mine." **Kenneth**

Ralph responded quickly to that.

I know that it is often reflexively assumed in various culturally conservative circles that liberalism is somehow equated to a lack of moral concern, a lack of real values. But no matter how many times that gets said here—including in such iterations as yours, Kenneth, according to which putting some God at the center of one's worldview is a requirement for being a moral person—I am willing to stand up and simply bear witness that it just ain't so. Liberalism, as I see it, is grounded on some very substantial and deep values, values having to do with the dignity and autonomy of the free human being. **Ralph**

Here's where I think you are both right and wrong, Ralph, *Peter wrote next,* and the two exist at different levels so that the task of seeing both parts of the truth can be unusually difficult. The thing is, ideas can have a dynamic within them, so that over time they evolve from one thing more or less naturally and inevitably into something else. It seems to me this has happened with liberalism.

Let me illustrate with something I've read about recently in my studying some matters of American constitutional law. Take the matter of *the right to privacy*. It came to the fore in a decision about contraception (*Griswald v. Connecticut* I think it was). At the outset, this right had to do with protecting people from the kind of government intrusion that would be entailed in enforcing any such law as Connecticut had against contraception: the idea wasn't that the state had no right to impose a moral judgment of that sort, as I understand this reading of the history,[1] but rather that what it would take in this instance to impose such a judgment—putting government in the bedroom—would do more damage to the fabric of a moral society than would restraining government from involving itself in such moral issues. But—and here's the point— the concept evolved into a moral right of individual autonomy, an enthronement of the individual as the decider of moral issues however he or she sees fit, unaccountable to any higher standard.

I know that we touched upon this idea of liberalism having some kind of inherent moral half-life before—your recent mention, Ralph, of *The Cultural Contradictions of Capitalism* was part of that—and that you are not much persuaded by it. You are evidently seeing the liberal individual as one who can be trusted to define and fulfill his own moral responsibilities. But I do think that there is something that pulls the understanding of the individual from what you are enthroning to another, lower image: the person who not only enjoys the right to be free of the imposition of some morality that is not his or her own, but also refuses to take on any yoke of moral concern whatever. **Peter**

This elicited from Cynthia a rebuttal of this characterization of liberalism.

Really, Peter, I think that's unfair. I don't want to repeat myself, but the liberals I know are not amoral people. They don't think that absolutely anything goes, and they don't live their lives that way either. **Cynthia**

Cynthia, I don't doubt the decency of your friends, *Peter responded*. But ideas do have a life of their own, and as they evolve and effect their ramifications on the society in which they flourish, even decency can help foster indecency.

Let me bring in here another piece from my work these days on constitutional law, one which, in fact, touches rather directly upon the idea of "indecency." In a Supreme Court decision overturning an antiobscenity law, the Court expressed disapproval of the law's imposing a moral judgment on how individuals choose to express themselves. Such moral policing, it said, does not "comport with the premise of individual dignity and choice upon which our political system rests." But the Court went beyond saying that individuals have a right to their own path to the Good, and—at least as I see it—called into question the whole idea of the Good. Legalized moral judgments, the Court said, lack any "objective or rational basis." After all, "one man's vulgarity is another's lyric."[2]

So it seems that from the idea of the right of each individual, with her inherent dignity, to be in charge of her own morality, we seem to move—devolve, I would say—into a view that morality is not really real—having no objective or rational basis—and thus that questions of the Good are beyond the legitimate scope of the law. Which leaves each individual more or less alone, without much guidance or encouragement from the surrounding environment to live in the service of anything higher than her own wants and impulses.

Sounds a lot like the young man in the nonshotgun nonwedding story Larry told us, doesn't it? **Peter**

Beyond the Small Self

This image of liberalism as tending to devolve into a moral universe of individuals acting as a law unto themselves, and being led—or perhaps just allowed—by their environment to become the kind of people who obey only their own appetites and desires, elicited a dramatic message from Kenneth.

In a sense, he was picking up just where he left off a little while before. In another sense, it seemed that he was now bringing in a new dimension.

A while ago I alluded to the importance of taking the Will of God, rather than one's own small and sinful will, as one's guide. I know that I'm not about to persuade anyone who is not on that path to turn his or her life around and take that path. But I believe perhaps, if I tell you something of my own experience, I can at least correct what I think is a misconception about the spirit of what is at stake here in such a choice. For my own life has taught me that the life of "autonomy" is not necessarily one of freedom, and that the life of subordination of one's heart to something greater is nothing at all like allowing intrusive, "jackbooted" agents of the State into one's bedroom.

So let me get beyond the mere assertion of the centrality of God in the moral life, and tell you something of my own story. Because I did not always live my life with the Lord. I was not so different from the young man in Larry's story. I should correct that: by myself, I am still not so different from him, but something changed at a critical point in my life.

I was in my early twenties, and was married to a very sweet woman to whom I was giving not much but grief. My idea of an evening well-spent was to go out with my buddies to a local tavern and have a few beers, talk about work and football and women, and then go home around one in the morning, when my wife was or wanted to be already in bed asleep. She was suffering from my immaturity and selfishness. I could see that, but I did not feel prepared to give up anything to help soothe her pain.

Then, one night, I felt restless in our house and walked out onto the front stoop. It was a fall night, and I remember the sky was exceedingly clear because I was dazzled by the number and the brilliance of the stars. Still, nothing special seemed to be going on in me. I strolled up a grassy hill that was near our place, and stood a minute leaning against the tall stump that remained of an ancient oak that had lived atop that knoll. All of a sudden, I felt something stirring in my chest, and it was as if some hands not of flesh were moving around my heart. I can't put it adequately into words. In a few seconds, a great sob rose in me and I shook with tears of both pain and joy. I found myself on my knees next to that great dead oak, and I felt the presence of the Holy Spirit in me, all around me.

Somehow in that moment—from that moment—I saw myself and my place in the great scheme of things quite differently. I saw how small and humble a being I am, and how great is the Lord, and I felt a great heart-filling love of the Lord. I understood that it was folly to live for my own selfish wants, that we are on this earth to serve the Lord, to help bring about God's good order on this earth. I understood that my wife was a piece of God's wonderful creation that was mine to cherish, to hold dear and serve well.

Well, to make a somewhat longer story short, I returned to our little house a changed man. I became, from then on, a good husband. From that night on, I have seen my life as a smaller piece of some very great picture that the Lord seeks to create through us. Within a few years, I felt that I was called to become a minister of the Lord and went to seminary, and now, for the past thirty-five years, have served my God to the best of my very limited ability, with all my heart and all my soul.

Having experienced God's love for me, and having opened my own heart to the love of the Lord, I was able to put behind me my sinful way of living just from the natural and immoral love of myself. I don't see how those who do not have the Lord in their hearts, who do not see themselves as creatures in His great Order, can transcend that little picture that so well fosters our selfishness. **Kenneth**

Ralph wrote back quickly to answer Kenneth.

That is a lovely story, Kenneth, and I do appreciate your giving some more flesh— or is it soul?—to the nature and sources of your religious belief. Truly, something happened to you up there on that hill beneath the stars, and I would not pretend to know what it was, or presume to challenge your interpretation of it.

But I would like to challenge your image of the moral universe of the liberal mind, and your apparent assertion that without God a person's concerns will inevitably be small and selfish. Really, all it takes to make my point is to put into evidence those remarkable people of liberal and nonreligious worldviews who work tirelessly and dedicatedly for justice and compassion and goodness in the world. A Ralph (no relation) Nader comes to mind. A person does not need to see the Good Order of the World as God's to care deeply about it. **Ralph**

To Ralph's message, Rev. George posted the following:

To you, Ralph, I would say yes and no. Yes, you are right that the willingness to override one's own selfish desires in the service of some vision of a larger good is by no means the monopoly of the believers in God. But at the same time, it seems to me that there is a power that is missing—not always, but generally—in the absence of some very palpable, identifiable Image of the Whole in relation to which a person sees himself or herself. Without God as an emblem of that Whole, it becomes much more difficult for the commitment to the Order of the Whole to go very deep. **George**

Ralph wrote back:

I would venture to go further than I have in my defense of liberal morality. Not only do I see my liberal associates as moral people, not selfish, but when I compare them with people who are more from a conservative religious background, I see the liberals as **_more_** willing, not less, to sacrifice for the public good. It is not the liberals who are constantly complaining about taxes being too high. It is not the liberals who begrudge having to give up some of their hard-earned cash to keep people who depend on welfare from being thrown onto the street. **Ralph**

Alice addressed Ralph's last point.

Yes, I will concede, Ralph, that liberals are more willing to be taxed. And that is not nothing. But neither is it everything. The liberal is willing to give up some claim to material wealth to serve the public good. But such a sacrifice is not a gut-level sacrifice, and that's because with the larger Whole there is no gut-level relationship. After throwing money at a problem—like poverty—the next thing the liberal throws at it is reason, congealed in the form of a bureaucratic institution.

It took us half a century, but I think we are coming to understand that money and reason lack something when it comes to addressing our truly human—which is to say, moral and spiritual—problems. What bureaucracy—interfacing with humanity—lacks is Spirit. After decades of money and effort, we're still stuck with the problems which, indeed, may have only deepened. And why? Because without Spirit, nothing moves.

Kenneth has told us how the Holy Spirit entered into his life and **moved** him from one way of life to a better one. That's what the Spirit is about—it's about movement. It is what animates us. (The words for spirit, breath, and movement are all connected: *anima, animate, animation.* To animate is to give life, to inspire; to inspire is to instill spirit, to breathe in. God breathed into the dead dust to animate Adam, the earth.) For the human animal, no reality without real Spirit can move him deeply.

Not always, but too often, the liberal's sense of the Whole is purely a headtrip, an abstract idea, something removed from the heavy-breathing of life that really animates him. **Alice**

Terrence wrote:

It seems to me that what liberalism has infused into our society over the generations—with its emphasis on the sovereignty of the small, purely individual ego unsubordinated to any larger whole—is a feeling of entitlement. And liberalism is so pervasive that what I'm saying here is not confined just to political liberals; in this land of the free, the preoccupation with rights and entitlements is more widespread than that.

Paramount among those entitlements is this notion: "I've got a right to be comfortable." I've got goodwill toward the world, as I peer out from this liberal outlook, and I'm glad to give a wave and smile and a variety of other gestures to show that I wish the rest of the world well. But when the chips are down, when some piece of the world beyond me calls out in pain for attention, will I be willing to give up my comfort to help set things right? Or will I say, "Gee, it's really a shame," as I put aside my newspaper and settle into my easy chair.

But take those people who actually get up out of their easy chairs and go visit prisoners, and go ladle out the soup to kids with distended bellies in East Africa, and I think you'll find that a disproportionate number of them are animated by a sense that they are called upon to do God's work. **Terrence**

Reminds me of something a Unitarian minister once said to me, *Karen then posted.* If you need some piece of legislation passed, call the Unitarians. If you've got a family whose house just washed away in the flood, call the Baptists.

And then George spoke up again.

Yes, I think we're on to something here. For a few exceptional souls, it is possible to extend their hearts and souls and imaginations out beyond their own boundaries without giving some clearly defined **Form** to the larger whole that they envision in their service. But most of us operate on a much simpler, more primitive level. For God and Country—those are the ways most people can practice personal sacrifice, because these are the kinds of Forms of a Larger Whole that people can relate to. You may point out the flaws in their concepts, how the Country has lousy policies or how God misbehaves or fails to provide sufficient evidence of His existence. But a life of sacrificial devotion is hard to practice without enshrining some kind of personalized higher Order as sacred.

Even if these images must be constructed out of distortions, or even fabrications, such ideals of a higher order worthy of subordinating the self must be—for most people—embodied in definable ways for their hearts to attach to them, for the force of attachment to pull them out of their petty and selfish desires, for them to be able to make themselves into instruments of some greater Good than their own comfort and pleasure.

What's realistic to hope for among us humans? I don't know. One might say that we have made progress in the development of our capacities. For millennia, the gods had to be visible for most people to be able to relate to them. (The tangible flag—Old Glory—is still something many Americans are readier to die for than the intangibles of the Constitution.) It was a breakthrough to get to be able to say "no graven images." God then becomes an idea, a ubiquitous but invisible presence. But if there is Nothing standing for the Whole, just an amorphous "out there," an incoherent mass of billions of people, a planet with countless species and ecosystems—then we lack what is basicaly hardwired into our natures to be the lever of power in motivating us: Relationship.

What are we willing to die for (or give our lives for)? For many, there is nothing. For many others, it is our children, or maybe others we love. For others it is God and Country. But how many can get passionate enough about Justice, or about a healthy environment? In the absence of the Fatherhood of God, how many people can find the Brotherhood of Man meaningful enough that they are inspired to consecrate their lives to it?

Liberalism—by which I mean the whole wonderful clear-minded rationalism of the Enlightenment, and all those political and economic and social institutions that have grown out of it—this liberalism lacks, I fear, the animating core, the overarching Power, the vision of the whole to pull us out of our small selves. **George**

Tired Questions

I finally reached someone at Lila's office and had them fax me her letter again. I read down to where the previous transmission had become bollixed up.

"Two other editors, including that very bright fellow I was talking about who had enjoyed your critique of the market economy (I forgot to ask him if it was *The Illusion of Choice* he was talking about or *Fool's Gold*), said that they found all these moral questions somewhat old hat. One said, 'People have been talking about such questions since Aristotle, if not before. Where does it all get us? The readership is going to ask, "Does Schmookler have some new answer that might settle these questions?" and if he doesn't they'll just yawn. Been there, done that.' The second fellow wrote: 'There's no denying Schmookler's passion and, as one who was a philosophy major as an undergraduate, I certainly enjoy going through some of these paces. But I just don't think we will find a big enough readership of people who will share his deep involvement with these questions.' One last editor, a fellow about our age, wrote: 'It seems Schmookler wants to challenge everybody and comfort no one. He is saying that none of us has worked these issues out satisfactorily. Then, from this proposal, although he does a good job of putting the problem in front of us—he even managed to make me feel discontent with my own wisdom on these matters (which I don't really appreciate)—it seems he's going to leave us to do a lot of the work. I'm not up for wrestling with an assignment like this and neither, I suspect, are our readers. Upsetting our apple-carts is doing us no favor.'

"So, Andy," Lila's message continued, "I really think you need to give some thought to the implications of these responses. As I feared, in the sophisticated world of publishing in New York nowadays these questions just seem kind of tired, they don't really grab people. I know you've got a lot to say, but if you want to reach an audience in today's market, perhaps you'll need to come up with a different subject area than this search for goodness and its sources. It just doesn't have enough sex appeal. Yours, Lila."

So Lila wants me to think about the implications, I mused unhappily. Well, one quick implication is that paying the bills this year might get tough. But of course that's not the kind of thinking Lila had in mind. Or is it? No audience, no income. To grab an audience in this market system, you give people what they want. And what do they want? Not to be asked to take these moral questions too seriously, apparently. Certainly not so seriously as to be challenged to do the hard work of rethinking their worldviews about these matters that are so core, so central. But I guess they don't seem so central to them. What was it Lila had said earlier? Oh yes, that my thoughts on mortality really spoke to her, but the subject of morality was remote. (Funny, just take out the first "t" and the subject ceases to be close to home.)

But wait a minute! I had good reason for thinking that this topic was vibrant and alive for other people besides me. I've experienced it. In my talk-radio shows, I'm constantly raising questions of this sort—and the phones ring off the hook. The conversations are animated, impassioned. Why do the editors say there isn't a readership to explore issues for which I *know* there's a listenership?

Maybe the groups are of a different nature. The place where I can see the phones ringing off the hook is out here in the Shenandoah Valley. Conservative, traditional, religious people: not the kind of folks I would have thought would be interested in a guy like me. But the questions I raise—about right and wrong, about the gap between how we do live and how we *should,* about our role in making the world a better or worse place—these questions are absolutely central to their way of looking at the world, as they are to mine. We come at these questions from very different directions, but we share a passion for addressing them. Most of my callers seem to think that they've already been given good answers to these questions, but they're happy and eager to have their say and to contend with me about the adequacy of their positions.

Are the editors in New York inhabiting so different a world, in moral terms, or acting as gatekeepers for readers whose world is so different, that the questions are just not alive enough to enlist their passion? Does the task of pouring one's heart and mind into becoming as clear as one possibly can about what one is called upon to do, and then doing it, seem too remote from the core of their lives?

Great. Seems like I'm caught addressing two different audiences. On the religious conservative side are the people who agree with me that the questions are important but who believe they already possess The Answer, and thus have no use for the challenge I offer. With the liberals, by contrast, while at least they make no claim about possessing The Answer, the questions I regard as vital don't seem important enough to be worth discomfiting themselves about.

Old Virtues

My mind was still embroiled with the publishers' responses—with the way they saw my book about good order as a "self-help" book, and with how they regarded the old questions about morality as lacking sex appeal. But I was still eager to see how the group would respond to Rev. George's last posting about the liberal culture's lack of connection with anything beyond themselves worth sacrificing themselves for. Come to think of it, maybe those two sets of issues were not completely separate.

I went back to the screen to see how the discussion was going. A message had been posted by Frank, the Reichian-style therapist who'd argued the value of liberating the natural sexual creature.

This talk about what are we willing to die for gives me the creeps. "Dying for God and Country." That old propaganda of the power systems that leads people willingly to the slaughterhouse. It's the old oppressor's trick of turning abuse and exploitation into a standard of virtue. As if it were not enough that people are treated as mere means to others' ends, they must be deluded into seeing themselves that way as well. **Frank**

Frank evidently roused Carl from his silence.

Yes, and you think that each person should think of himself as an end in himself. "For me! What's in it for me?"

Don't trouble yourself to argue that terrible wrongs can be committed in the name of asking people to sacrifice. I know that. But none of these abuses of the idea of sacrifice negates the imperative moral importance of the willingness to place something higher than one's own good. This, as has been said here, is the essence of morality, and without sacrifice the human realm is unredeemable. Christ allowed himself to be sacrificed for our sins, and in countless ways, trivial and important, we who would do God's work are called upon to sacrifice ourselves. That young father-to-be in Larry's story, for example, must sacrifice his footloose liberty, if that is what he values, to make sure that the life he has helped to create comes into a well-ordered little corner of the world, so that this child will grow up as sound and healthy a soul as can be. There are good reasons why sacrifice—whether in the colloquial sense of what we do for our children, or in the ancient sense of rendering up something of value to the divine—has long been integral to our notions of morality and good order.

Speaking of sacrifice—an aside on a current political matter. A lot of people on the liberal side don't seem to understand why people like me, on the conservative end, have such a visceral reaction against our current president—Bill Clinton—for his machinations to avoid serving his country in wartime. It's not that we (or at least I) hold against him his views about that war. He's entitled to his views. It is rather the suspicion that in that situation he showed himself to be a person who was unwilling to subordinate his own good for the sake of the larger whole, in this case, America. Would he have sacrificed himself for his views about the war? I doubt it.

Now Dole, you can say what you want about his limitations, *Carl continued—this was in the fall of 1996, when a presidential election race was ongoing,* —but you only have to look at him to remember that this is a man who, when the country called, was willing to put his country first. **Carl**

This really slays me, *Fred posting shortly thereafter.* A Christian minister—a bearer of the Gospel of him who said "resist not evil"—extolling the virtues of military service. For me, if there is one thing that gets in the way of my taking the morality— and moralizing—of the traditionalists seriously it is that they are so often hip-deep in hypocrisy. **Fred**

The question of a Christian's relationship to war is a complex one, Fred, *Carl replied,* "and in itself worthy of an exploration that would be too extensive for the present discussion. But for the present, suffice it to say that for me, as a conservative Christian, the issue I was raising here has to do with whether the person puts other, higher goods before his own selfish good. "I have a right to be comfortable" doesn't cut it as a maxim for good character. In an age like ours—self-indulgent, self-centered, making a god of one's own desires—the willingness to show respect to something above one's self is in itself an important indicator of character. The military holds a place in this moral world not only because of such palpable aspects of sacrifice like Bob Dole's useless right arm, or Sen. Kerry's missing right leg, but also because it is a place where one must display a willingness to obey a command that does not come from within. I am not so deluded as to equate the commands of a sergeant with those of the Lord God Himself. But a person who is unwilling to submit to the one, I figure, is probably unwilling to submit to the other. And when I choose which leader to vote for, I am looking for someone who has a respectful ear cocked in the direction of Higher Authority. I'm looking for someone who has in mind some good beyond taking care of himself. As Jesus said, "The greatest among you will be a servant." **Carl**

Fred's charge that traditionalists tend to be hypocrites is something I feel moved to address, *George wrote.* Once again, I am compelled to deliver the clear and definitive answer: yes and no.

Yes, there is a lot of hypocrisy among the moralists of the right, although I am not sure that they are any more guilty of the sin of hypocrisy than anyone else who holds up ideals and ethical values. After all, for us human beings, the only sure prophylactic against hypocrisy is to uphold no principles at all; then one cannot contravene them.

(And this is one prophylactic that, I fear, is being widely distributed to our youth.) Maybe it's a matter of the burden of hypocrisy being greatest among those who measure themselves by the highest standard. People in general have limited tolerance for acknowledging their own moral failure, and the more stringent the moral standard the further short one is likely to fall.

Yes, also, in that all too frequently, the standard of virtue is something that is applied as something for ***other*** people to measure up to. If we're talking about sacrifice, for example, the image that comes to mind quite readily is one of the blood of someone or something else being shed on the altar. "Hey, let's you sacrifice." To appease the gods, we've always been good at finding substitutes for ourselves as sacrificial objects, only sometimes being willing to deal with the sacrifice of "the foreskin of our hearts," or that other foreskin.

But there are some other aspects on the other side of this business that bear comment. The first is that I notice that many liberals seem quite determined to reduce all claims of righteousness to sheer hypocrisy. A Jimmy Swaggart, or a Jim and Tammy Bakker, are such welcome emblems for the liberals. As if the image of Elmer Gantry can serve to dismiss the very possibility of true righteousness. "See, it is all a sham. They pretend to care more about the righteousness of the world than I do, but it is a fraud. Underneath, they are as full of vice—just as self-centered and bent upon their own gratification—as anyone. And seeing them this way, I relieve myself of the burden of having to worry about whether there is a higher standard to measure myself against, a deeper passion for righteousness, than the half-hearted one I already embody."

Then there's the charge that the traditionalists commit that terrible evil of laying their moral trips on other people. When the religious moralists aren't being condemned for being hypocrites, they are taken to task for being meddlers. "What business is it of theirs to go involving themselves in evaluating other people's family values? If Larry's friend's daughter ends up raising her child alone, who are they to intrude with their values and say that anything's wrong with that?"

In this context, the concern and the involvement of the moralists looks like "meddling" only in that limited perspective that lacks any sense of the Whole that calls for our attention, in that narrow moral viewpoint in which we are not called to take responsibility for the larger picture beyond ourselves. The people who take the Whole seriously cannot help but care about what is happening to God's children, even those on the other side of town. We know from bitter experience by now that not every arrangement works as well as every other, that there are millions of children being raised in America without getting anything like what a child needs for a healthy and happy childhood. And situations like that of the young woman in Larry's story are correlated strongly with all that pain and difficulty. If our brother is deaf to the call of his higher duties, is it not incumbent upon us to make that call louder?

The last point I'd like to make is that many liberals seem unwilling to recognize that conservative religious moralists—for all the moral shortcomings of many of them (they have by no means escaped the net of sin)—by and large *do* work harder than most of us on the culturally more liberal side at being what they believe they *should* be. If there is some cost in harshness, and in self-righteousness, to pay for this impassioned striving for righteousness, we might at least acknowledge that something important nonetheless might be purchased with it. **George**

I find something quaint and comforting in hearing talk once again of old-time virtues, like sacrifice, *Terrence wrote in*. And I'd like to extend that discussion to another venerable quality that harkens back to an earlier age—loyalty. That's another one of those notions, like sacrifice, that calls upon one to set something up higher than one's own convenience or even well-being. Consider the marriage vows: "in sickness and in health, for better or for worse . . ." That means you stick with it even if the going gets tough.

Yet we've developed a culture in which each person feels so entitled to look to what will serve *him* (or her) best, that if better turns to worse you can feel free to sever the bond. Divorce rates, as we all know, are way up. The vows mean little, because there is no imminent sense of that Power above us in whose presence the vow is made, and because the sovereign individual is supposed to remain so free that the purely lateral connections aren't strong enough to impede the search for individual fulfillment. "My word is my bond" rings pretty quaint these days. Junk bonds. **Terrence**

If you want to talk about "loyalty," *Larry wrote back,* let's not just talk about divorce. Look at the corporate world. Look at these lay-offs, just pushing out the door people who have given some company the best years of their lives. And how about these sports teams, teams like the Cleveland Browns who enjoyed the loyalty of generations of fans in the Cleveland area. A chance comes to maybe get a better deal and make some more money somewhere else and the owner plucks the team up and moves off to Baltimore. Loyalty between these owners and the cities that hosts the teams, I guess, is supposed to be a one-way street.

I get a little tired of the way some conservatives focus on divorce rates, and blame liberal values, but ignore the disloyalty of these big private powers. I bet the executives throwing out their workers and these owners scrambling over their fans' feelings for a few extra bucks are mostly "good Republicans." **Larry**

To which Peter replied:

You are entirely right about the erosion of the value of loyalty going way beyond divorce rates. And you're right also about the issue transcending political parties. But I would say that the forces at work *do* have to do with "liberalism" understood in its full historical meaning. Our politics obscure this, because business interests make alliance with traditionalists to form the political right. But the business interests are really the embodiment of one of the main roots of liberalism: the whole notion of the right of owners of private property to seek gain in unfettered markets. Never in history has there been so potent an engine of dissolving the old bonds among people as this 'liberal' institution of the market. The economic system operates through the liberation of atomistic actors, who owe one another only what they contract to give them, and owe the social whole little or nothing. This great economic revolution did as much as anything to create the liberal order that allows us to think in terms of the pursuit of happiness, the possession of rights, and the sanctity of unfettered individual choice. **Peter**

Once again I'm not satisfied with the depiction of liberalism that's being put forward here, *Ralph responded*. From this discussion, one would think that liberalism can be reduced to some amoral vision of society, like the atomistic market where nobody owes anyone else anything. But that leaves out a vital dimension of liberalism that gives expression to real substantive values.

Contrary to the impression given here about liberals, in fact it is among liberals that the image of our political society as a vital whole, a kind of family entailing mutual responsibility, is most strongly articulated. **Ralph**

There's truth in what you are saying, *Terrence interjected*. Which is why, I believe, those who are working to pull liberalism back from the abyss of radical individualism are issuing their call in the name of "community." I mean, of course, the communitarian movement that has been seeking to redefine liberalism to bring back into it a measure of responsibility to the larger world, and a corresponding limitation on the free range of individual pursuit. The fact that the liberal world has provided for the idea of community has made that notion a kind of anchor in the realm of interconnectedness to try to restore to liberalism at least some dim recollection of the idea of a larger Whole. **Terrence**

As we make our way through the old-fashioned virtues, *Alice wrote*, —can chastity and prudence and honor (and all those other antique names for girls) be far behind?—I'd like to expand the conversation to include the concept of "challenge." I note that the idea of challenge has recurred occasionally in our discussions. It's one that recent experience brought to my mind.

Let me first put "challenge" into the context of what we've been talking about. "I've got a right to be comfortable" is a doctrine that runs counter to the idea of challenge. Of course, one can always challenge oneself, saying I have a right to choose not to be comfortable. But the idea of a right to comfort can rather easily devolve into an insistence on comfort. And then you end up with a society of people who will not expect anything of themselves that is so difficult it brings strain or pain.

In the past few years, I have had the enjoyable opportunity to give sermons to several different Unitarian churches. And my theme has in fact been about challenge. I speak of the way, during the past century, the culture of this country has changed so that people are less receptive to their leaders' communicating to them in challenging ways. (I cite, by the way, how it is practically a running joke these days that no political leader running for office dares use the s-word: sacrifice.) Our political leaders pander to our wants, and ask little of us. Our children's teachers are not really allowed to make our children feel that they haven't measured up to some standard; the teachers are expected to make the kids feel successful whatever they do. And in my sermon itself, I adduce some evidence that sermons have also changed over the past century, with it having become considerably less likely that the person giving the sermon will deliver to those in the congregation any message that implies that they should be doing better, and that challenges them to reach down into themselves and summon up the will to meet some higher moral standard. The fire-and-brimstone of yesteryear have given way to the "feel-good" sermon of today.

One interesting wrinkle in this. A few months ago, I went to an old Unitarian church in New England. The church itself had been constructed in the second half of the nineteenth century, and had always been a Unitarian church. The old stained-glass windows remain, and I found myself surprised to see that they depicted Jesus in a variety of settings. Today's Unitarian churches, as you may know, are unlikely to have even a cross. The original pews are also still in place, and as I sat there I became aware of how "challenging" it is for the modern body to sit in one of those pews for more than a few minutes. Unyielding, these wooden structures compel one into an upright posture that is not easily held. No sense there of a universal right to be comfortable.

One more word about challenge, in terms of their being a larger picture. It seems to me that wherever there is a welcoming of challenge, it implies a sense of their being **something** that stands above, some authority or some ideal that is held worthy of sacrificing one's comfort for. **Alice**

This put me in mind of that story from my own experience, that had been part of my thinking at the beginning of this exchange when I was coming back from Mr. Godachi's place, about the soccer coach and the girl who stooped to pluck the dandelion. It had been my thought that the coach, rather than indulging the girl's surrender to her impulse, or her evasion of her moment of truth, or whatever it was, should have challenged the girl to see herself as being called upon to subordinate

herself to the team of which she was a part. That instead the coach operated from the assumption that what she did was what she should be doing
(at that point in her growth) seemed connected with an era in which
our politicians never ask us to sacrifice, and our clergymen do not issue
challenges from the pulpit.

While I was thinking this way, I saw another message had arrived. This
one was from Peter.

I like that last point you make, Alice, *Peter said*. It seems that a great many of
those old virtues have to do with recognizing that something that is above should
take precedence over something that is below. That came out with respect to self-
sacrifice, with its ethic of subordinating one's own welfare and will to some higher
cause. As you say, it applies to the idea of meeting a challenge, where some higher
standard, some ideal, some goal is employed to stretch one upwards, to rise above
what would come easily and with comfort. And it fits also with the virtue of loyalty,
which again has to do with the subordination of one's own insatiable and wandering
appetitive will to a discipline of commitment to bonds that are held superior to one's
purely selfish concerns. **Peter**

Let me throw in another old-fashioned notion which, like challenge, has already
been a minor theme here, *Terrence wrote in next*. I'm referring to "judgment." The idea
of Judgment, of course, has a profound connection with the idea of God—the One
who will judge us all come Judgment Day. But even without God's judgment, the idea
of being judged is an important one, and one that seems to be in great disrepute
these days.

Once again the controversy over the old virtue in question relates to the issue of
whether one element in the order will be entitled to stand above other parts of the
system. And again it bears upon the question of whether the individual is or is not
seen as having to fit himself into a larger whole.

If the individual's desires are paramount, then desire is everything and there is no
need to ask whether the desire is a worthy one. Hence, no judgment. If the individual
is a universe unto himself, then there is no higher good to which the good of the
individual should be subordinated. Hence no judgment. And if each individual is entitled to legislate for himself what is important and good, then there is no basis on
which one person can legitimately pronounce judgment on any other. To do so would
be "judgmental." Hence, no judgment.

The liberal—or countercultural—antipathy to anything hierarchical is demonstrated by the fact that there's hardly anything of which one can be accused these
days that's worse than being "judgmental." **Terrence**

To Jeff, this attempt to resurrect judgment was of uncertain value.

Before we get all enthusiastic about the virtues of judgment, let's remember there's a good reason why judgmentalism is in ill repute. Judgment seems more often than not the vehicle by which one group of people can impose their narrow concept of the good upon others, or can punish them for not living up to it.

Not long ago, for example, I read an article by Elshtain, critical of Hillary Rodham Clinton's book *It Takes a Village*. The author tells a bit about her experience growing up in a small town in Colorado. She praises the solidity of the community, the virtues of the way kids were brought up there. And in the context of this adulation of your basic traditional American town, she tells about how the women of the town looked askance at one particular woman because she hung her colored clothes interspersed with the whites, a practice that was interpreted as indicative of a slightly unhinged mind.[3]

Now, Elshtain seemed to be conjuring up this image to indicate the charms of this small-town life, but to me it served as a useful reminder of how foolishly "judgmental" the exercise of judgment so often is in the maintenance of a social order. "This is how a decent woman hangs her clothes, any deviation reveals defects of character." What a straitjacket! The newer, more liberal ethic of live and let live, and refrain from judging, seems to me an improvement over that more ordered, more hierarchical, and more judgmental community of yesteryear. **Jeff**

Of course, judgment can be exercised in a stupid way. But to say that is not to say that it is smart to do without judgment, as many nowadays seem to want to do, *replied Terrence.*

This prompted me to write in:

As a few of you know, I do talk radio as a regular guest here and there. One of the "heres" is on Wisconsin Public Radio where, last May, I did a show where I raised this very question. WPR has an intelligent and liberal audience, and a number of the callers raised just the concern that Jeff has, seeing judgment as being "judgmental" in the pejorative sense. I tried to salvage the idea of judgment as a positive and necessary capability by suggesting that by "judgmental" we mean a particular kind of judgment that is characterized by narrow-mindedness and foolishness leading to inappropriate conclusions. When people who do not understand the larger human picture make judgments as if they did possess such understanding, then what results is the kind of judgments to which these listeners seemed to be allergic—the kinds of judgments that condemn a woman for how she hangs her clothes, or that assume there is only one decent way for a family to be.

Toward the end of the show, a young woman called from Black River Falls, and explained how uneasy she felt even hearing the word judgment. As a child she had always felt judged, and she wanted to be free of that baggage. I asked whether she thought it inappropriate for her to make judgments on the behavior of other people whose conduct was cruel or injurious of others. I used the example of a man who batters his wife. She said that she dealt with difficult people without making judgments. If there was something going on that she felt uncomfortable with, she'd try to work it out, and if that did not work, she'd just avoid having anything to do with that person. At that point, the host thanked her for her call, said good-bye to her, and turned to me for my thoughts.

I said: "Just turning away from someone with whom you can't get satisfaction seems like a feasible solution only within the individualistic framework in which one's world consists of one's own circle, voluntarily chosen. But the larger reality is that we share a planet, a society, sometimes a neighborhood with a great many other people, whether we choose to be with them or not. A man who batters his wife may not be a problem to us, but we may still have some moral obligation to make some judgment about his conduct—to say 'This is unacceptable'—in order to protect his victim. And then there's the fact that, as a society, we cannot simply choose, as an individual can, to have nothing to do with everyone we don't like. If large numbers of young men are fathering young children whom they then abandon to an inadequate upbringing, and that results in a whole class of problem kids—illiterate or unemployable or criminal—growing up to be a drag on society or to prey upon society, a failure to pass judgment and enforce suitable consequences can lead to a disaster for the society as a whole."

So this seems to me another dimension in which the "freedom froms" of liberalism, if carried too far, bring about a false freedom. Our lives are inevitably grounded in a larger Whole, and if we fail to bring to that whole the means to maintain a good moral order, we all end up not free but impoverished and diminished. **Andy**

I can certainly affirm the spreading plague of anti-judgmentalism, *Kenneth wrote.* I've got a little story to tell. A woman in my congregation came to me to see if she could teach in our Sunday school program. She probably would be a good teacher, but I had a problem with the idea. This woman is married to one man, but is living with another. I won't go into the details, but I will concede that, if any circumstances would be extenuating, this woman's situation would qualify. But it is still adultery, and our tradition is quite unambiguous about it. I have commiserated with the woman about her circumstance, and she knows that if she were to divorce and remarry, I would certainly approve. So long as she is living adulterously, however, I told her, as pastor of our church—who has taken an oath to uphold its core teachings—I cannot assign her to teach in the Sunday school. She didn't appreciate my decision at all. Getting somewhat huffy, she pronounced, "Who are you to judge me?"

You know, since that happened, I've heard from several other pastors that they are hearing the same thing from their own congregants: even when they speak from the clear teachings of the church—a church these people have freely chosen to join—people are saying, "Who are you to judge me?"

If not a minister of a church they have chosen, applying the clear word of God, then who will they grant standing to make a judgment? I'll tell you: I dread the thought of living in a world where everyone feels immune from any judgment that issues not from themselves. **Kenneth**

Would We Have to Invent Him?

OK, what if Carl and Kenneth were right when they say, without God, we can have no good order? *Larry asked in his next message.* What if they are right that out of flawed humanity left to itself nothing adequate to the task can possibly be constructed? And that the liberty-oriented order of liberalism tends to erode our ability to connect with the Divine Whole?

But what then? Just because we might need some kind of good order-supplying God that doesn't mean there's one out there. What is a person like me to do, committed to an intellectually honest pursuit of the truth? Am I supposed to just wish myself into believing in such a great Moral Leaning Post? More generally, is the modern civilization of the Enlightenment supposed to just throw out all the clear-thinking epistemology that humankind worked so hard to achieve, just because it makes it impossible to believe that we possess God's Great Truth? **Larry**

Let me get in here quickly, before Kenneth and Carl get a chance to take offense out loud, *George answered.* Larry, I understand your dilemma, because as I indicated before it is one with which I struggle mightily: ***How can we know?*** I can't see how, either. And yet, I also feel that it would be untenable to live with nothing where that knowledge would be.

There's a mathematical riddle I sometimes think of when I contemplate the role of God in my life. A man dies and leaves to his heirs a herd of 17 horses. To one of his heirs, he leaves half his herd; to another, he leaves a third, to another, one ninth. Of course, 17 horses cannot be so divided, and so the heirs start fighting over who gets how many horses. A wise man, passing by on horseback, overhears all the disputation and offers his help in bringing peace. They explain the situation, and the wise man gets off his horse, leads the animal to the disputed herd, and says to the heirs, "Now, divide them." With eighteen horses now in the herd, the first heir takes nine, the second takes six, and the third takes two, which leaves a single horse. The remaining horse is the one belonging to the wise man, of course, who proceeds to mount it and ride away.

Sometimes it seems to me that God is the horse that has to be added to the pack so that it can become clear how all the other pieces fall into place, and then it can safely disappear. **George**

Believe and not believe. Think and suspend thought, *Larry then posted.* As I said some time back: yes, this conversation has persuaded me that we have a problem.

Wait a minute, *Jeff exclaimed.* I'm still far from persuaded that we need to worry about this God business.

I will grant that a lot of people have been able to use belief in God to help them be better people and act better in the world. But it isn't so clear how well such belief, in general, feeds the creation of good order. There have been plenty of ages where people believed in God something fierce. And I mean fierce. Burnings at the stake, racks of the Inquisition. This is no cure-all, remember. Just as often, it has appeared to be a big part of the disease.

I say we can do fine without God, or some other highly charged "sacred" image of the Whole, or whatever. Let's build our good order in a more commonsensical fashion. Let's keep our eyes open for problems, and bring sensible solutions to bear on those we find. What we've got now—this social order whose defects we seem so preoccupied with—is pretty good by historical standards. I'd say that we in this practically minded and largely secular society, are doing pretty well. **Jeff**

To which Alice said:

As the falling man passed the fifteenth story. . . .

Your way of looking at the meaning of religion in history is one way, Jeff, *George then posted,* and I won't deny there's something to it. But I would suggest that another way captures a more important piece of the truth.

In all the millennia of human life that we know about, across cultures and throughout history, societies have organized themselves around numinous cores of meaning that brought them in relationship to some Sacred Whole. Carl and Kenneth have been speaking from just one of those numinous traditions, albeit one of great historical importance, at the least. But many other religious visions and traditions, large and small, have been at the core of various cultures. Wherever a people has flourished, that numinous core of their vision has been alive.

Ours is an age where the vitality of that core may be dying out. I think it would be a very dangerous experiment for us to suppose that we can flourish if we allow that spiritual space to go dead. **George**

Which led us into a rather energetic investigation of what it means to the concept of "good order" to fill that "spiritual space" the way it has traditionally been filled in our civilization—by a God who, as it became evident at least to some of us, seemed nearly as bound up in the problem of good order as in its solution.

Interlude

A Colonel of Truth

Just as I saw the group start to take off on some of the God-and-good-order questions, I turned off my computer. For me, the previous discussion of the moral order of liberalism, and of the ostensible need for a passion for the whole, had been rather intense, and I felt the need for a break. I welcomed, therefore, the call to attend to a social obligation April and I had that evening, giving me an excuse to abandon for a while my task of monitoring the conversation. It'll all be there when I get back, I said to myself happily. And off we went to a garden party six miles away, down on the northern hump of Supinlick Ridge, at a nice house on the fringes of the Bryce Resort.

Immediately upon entering the place, April and I were introduced to an older couple—the Morrisons. When they heard my name, their faces showed a flash of recognition. This, for me, is one of the pleasures of my present life, one which I did not get to enjoy during my first almost fifty years. "Don't we hear you on the radio?" Mrs. Morrison asked. I tried to think of something clever but not smart-assed to say in response, something good-naturedly calling attention to the fact that the question, as asked, was clearly beyond my knowledge to answer. But failing in that brief search, I simply said, "Yes, I'm on 'The Mid-Day Show' a couple times a month." "Oh, we like listening to you," Mrs. Morrison said, "when we're in the car. Don't listen to the radio much, otherwise, except when Andre is on." Andre is Andre Viette, world famous gardener who is also a regular guest on the program where I appear, dealing with questions of a rather different sort. A few minutes of chit-chat later, upon learning how extremely serious a gardener Mrs. Morrison was, I pronounced myself mollified that my shows do not elicit the same devoted attention from her as do Andre's.

"Oh yes," Mrs. Morrison said to another woman who had just joined the conversation, "you can just call in and tell him your problem and he has the answer." At which I chimed in, "I assume that you *must* be talking about Andre there and not about me." And there was laughter among us, since the one thing that certainly does not characterize my programs is my having the answer to all the problems. My specialty could be described as the opposite: posing the problems and disclosing, in a polite and respectful process of inquiry, the inadequacy of other people's glib solutions to them. My refusal to light upon Answers and to declare the inquiry complete and closed is the main complaint of my critics. "Can't this guy make up his mind?" the complaint goes, inspiring me at one point to do a two-hour show—and a lively one it proved to be, too—on the question "Just how wishy-washy is Andy Schmookler?" In the context of responding to such a charge, I allowed myself to wax very assertive in developing my point that keeping the big questions open is not wishy-washiness, but is in fact—as several centuries of the development of science demonstrates—really the key to coming truly to know very much at all.

After Mrs. Morrison moved on into conversation with the other woman—about zinnias, I believe—Mr. Morrison began a conversation with me. He too had moved to the Shenandoah Valley from the outside, he indicated. "A great place for a radio show like yours," he said. "This area's fertile soil for what you're doing," he said. "What is it that makes it fertile?" I inquired. "The people out here have strong opinions on the kinds of questions you're raising." "Do you think," I asked in a playful tone, "that strong opinions make the ground fertile?" His answer was a bit vague so, changing subjects, I asked Mr. Morrison about what he does out here.

"I'm retired," Morrison said, "and I do whatever I can to be of most service to this area. You'd be surprised how much need there is here in the Valley." I asked him what kinds of needs he was referring to. "There's a lot of really deep poverty that you don't see very readily. People living in trailers tucked away in the woods . . . off the beaten track. Anyway, I get involved with the Salvation Army, and I work with a group of foster parents, trying to get good things like food and care and love to places where it's sorely needed."

I looked at Morrison, and I liked what I saw. He was a guy who, when he looked at you, seemed to know what he was seeing, who came at things without fear or pretense, and who not only meant what he said but wouldn't really entertain the idea of saying anything he didn't mean. "I like what you said about doing what you could to be of service," I said. In my mind, I was thinking about the little culture on the edge of which we were having this social gathering, a resort populated largely by retired military and intelligence officers for whom the country club was the hub of the universe, and the game of golf the closest thing to a raison d'être they had. When I had moved to the Valley five years earlier, I'd felt doubtful I'd be able to connect with the locals—rural Virginian people, many of them uneducated, deeply enmeshed in a very conservative tradition—and so I had arrived with my hopes for fellowship centered on the more cosmopolitan people—outsiders like myself—at the resort nearby. But it only took a few months before I discovered that it was the locals whose soil-weathered hands I was more eager to shake than those of the fellows at the resort whose calluses came from the daily round of golf.

"Yes, I'm retired," Morrison said, "but being sixty-nine these days isn't like in my father's time. I don't feel used up at all, and I have my pension to take care of me, so I'm free to make myself of use however I can." When he said "sixty-nine," my eyebrows shot up, because the man in front of me seemed younger than that. Of course, since I still tend to think of myself as being in my thirties instead of my fifties, almost everyone looks younger to me than they are. But with Morrison's tall and erect figure, the discrepancy was even larger than that generally caused by my customary failure to integrate time into my understanding of human life. "But for my whole life, even when I was a youngster, the idea of *service* was pretty much what I was devoted to. I was in the Air Force, you know, and I didn't regard the 'service' part of 'military service' as just a word without meaning."

A sixty-nine-year-old career military man, then. He was of the age that would have commanded me if I'd gone to Vietnam, I figured. I thought I'd steer clear of that thicket, at least for now. "So, your years in the Air

Force felt like a life of service then?" "Yes they did. I love my country, and when I joined up in 1949 it was clear the world was a pretty dangerous place. I'm talking about the Cold War. I feel pretty good to have contributed to that having come to the successful conclusion that it has." "Yes, it was no small thing," I said, thinking about the world as it had appeared to me as I was growing up in the fifties, as well as my enduring sense in my adulthood that *on balance* it was a good thing for humankind that there had been a United States to defend democratic values against the Stalinist regime that Morrison—now Colonel Morrison, USAF, retired—had joined to defend us against. "Not that I'm all for violence and killing," Morrison resumed, "but I'm willing to fight to defend what's right. I was proud to devote my life to serving a force in the world that was on God's side." Again, I thought about that terrible war we fought— we as a country, that is, not including me as a soldier, thank whatever—in Vietnam, and again, I did not inject that old difficulty into our conversation.

Morrison returned to talking about the kind of service he's involved in now, talking about children in need, and families under stress. And again I felt appreciation of this man living under very privileged circumstances whose devotion spreads so far beyond his own gratification, and who feels called to attend to the needs of those he sees struggling far below him on the scale of privilege and power.

"How widespread in the military you knew is that sense of being there in the spirit of *service?*" I asked Col. Morrison. His answer was a bit noncommittal, or perhaps I didn't understand precisely what he was saying. But in about his second or third sentence, he somehow shifted the conversation to recent disappointment he felt in some military leadership. "These sex scandals," he said, referring to the sexual harassment cases in the Army that had been in the news, "as far as I'm concerned they show a lack of leadership." "You're not just referring, I gather, to the level of the drill sergeants we see at trials like this one at Aberdeen?" I inquired. "No. There was something seriously wrong, going on up the line." "Do you see the Army itself as, in some sense, complicitous in this sexual abuse of power?" "No, it's not like that. What I mean is that this whole problem could so easily have been foreseen, and having been foreseen could have been prevented. I mean, you don't have to be a rocket scientist to be able to figure out that if you have a lot of young women under the complete control of a young man of higher rank, something has to be done to protect against such sexual exploitation." Col. Morrison's cheeks looked especially taut as he was saying this; his distress at such failures, and at the discrediting of the institutions in which he had given a lifetime of service, was quite palpable.

"So you think that the Army could have taken preventive measures, and should have known they were needed?" "Indeed I do." "What happened, or what failed to happen? I mean, how do you understand this failure to institute the kinds of protections that would have prevented this abuse?" "Asleep at the switch," Morrison said. "Meaning?" I prodded. "I think they just weren't paying attention." "So 'Asleep at the switch' is not a matter of a moral failing, any kind of defect of moral values, just a kind of carelessness? Or does your 'asleep at the switch' contain that Socratic idea that evil is just a matter of ignorance?" "Well, in my book, being inattentive to one's responsibilities is no small shortcoming. But still, if I get your drift, no I don't see a moral defect here, but more a kind of innocent oversight." Then, Col. Morrison, witnessing my dubious expression, asked, "What else would it be?"

"My gut feeling is that such oversights don't just happen by accident. They're not random. Let me say, this is just my hunch. I've never been in the military. But I did grow up an American boy and an athlete, being socialized—often by former military men—in that symbolically military environment of the athletic team. Our mission was moving the line of scrimmage down the field, against resistance, rather than firing rifles from trenches. And my experience in sports tells me that there's something in the culture of the male fighters in our society that inculcates a demeaning and devaluing image of what's female. Nothing worse that a coach could say to us in the locker room at halftime than we're playing like a bunch of girls. Nothing worse than being called a sissy, or a pussy. It seems as though to produce 'a few good men'—to fashion young men into something tough enough and hardened enough to go about the business of combat—you've got to cleave the world sharply between the male, which is good, and the female, which is contemptible."

Morrison seemed like he recognized something in what I was saying, and then he asked, "How does that connect with what happened at

Aberdeen?" "As I sense it," I resumed, "if the brass were, as you say, 'asleep at the switch,' the inattentiveness was not random, but rather a function of something—how shall I put it?—less than fully devoted to honoring the female vulnerability in the Army's midst, the females trying to succeed in what used to be a quintessentially male preserve. In other words, maybe the sergeant who raped his recruits was acting out in a powerful and destructive way some feelings—feelings with a dangerous moral valence—that went further on up the line, and that led to that 'inattentiveness' you were talking about."

We mulled this over a bit, and then Col. Morrison returned to what I'd said earlier about my not having served in the military. I saw him appraising me with what seemed a mirror image of my earlier sense of him as of the age to have commanded me if I'd gone to Vietnam. "You come from a generation—I mean a part of a generation—I'm guessing, that didn't have much use for the military." I heard this as a question, and I tried to answer. "No, I didn't serve in the military, and given the family I came from, it was never in the cards that I'd have made a career of it. But I grew up having it in me to be a soldier. Being born just after World War II, and brought up an American boy, the image of being a warrior, fighting for what's right, protecting the innocent—that image went deep in my heart. I'd go to see movies about such men, and I was ready to be one, myself. But I came of age at a different time from you. When the time came for me to answer my country's call, what it was saying was not 'Go stop Hitler,' but 'Go to Vietnam.' And I couldn't in good conscience do that, so I made sure the Army took some X-rays of my back and then I didn't have to."

I was not looking forward to having Morrison tell me that we don't have the right to decide according to our own supposed conscience whether Uncle Sam is right or wrong when we get the call, but whether or not he was thinking that, that wasn't where he went with the conversation. "It was a tough war to fight," Col. Morrison said, looking into the distance as if he were peering back in time rather than space. He'd been a commander of a squadron of fighter-bombers, I then learned, most of whose missions had involved flying north of the DMZ and demolishing the infrastructure of North Vietnamese society.

As we talked about the war, and turned to the question of what was wrong with it, I did hear some of what previous conversations with military men had led me to expect from Col. Morrison. The ultimate problem with the war, in that view, was that we had lost it, and the reasons for that were two: that the politicians in Washington had been unwilling to fight to win, but rather had, out of fear of bringing the Soviets or Chinese into the war, tied the hands of the military with various restricting 'rules of engagement'; and later, that Congress had refused, after the disengagement of American forces, to authorize the sending of the necessary equipment to allow the South Vietnamese to defend themselves.

Thinking of what it would take to hash through those arguments brought me into what felt a bit like a time warp. Old issues, old frustrations. They led, however, especially that question of the fear of widening the war, into a very empathetic discussion of just how hard it was to know how to conduct so dangerous and vital a challenge as the Cold War, a struggle between profoundly antagonistic countries in possession of unprecedented weapons that, at all events, must never come into play. How to protect one's interests against an enemy, yet assure that it not come to all-out war! No small challenge, and so it was no wonder that people like Col. Morrison and I—people with mostly decent moral passions—had found ourselves, thirty years before, on different sides of one blood-soaked issue that arose from that terribly complex gameboard. Being a human being is never easy, as I see it, and that particular passage in history was unusually difficult for a society to navigate morally.

"I'm gratified," I said, "that we can see in each other now that love of what is right that we share. If we'd met on some airplane in 1968 or 1970 or thereabouts, I wonder, would we have been able to see it then?" Morrison seemed to think so, of himself, but I expressed my doubts about whether I'd have been able to then. Perhaps some things would have seemed so clear to me that I'd not have been able to understand how a good person could have seen them differently.

"If you don't think the problem with that war was with the politicians," Col. Morrison began, returning to that previous line of discussion, "just what do you think it was?" "Oh, I didn't say it wasn't with the politicians," I replied. "After all, it was the civilian leadership that got us into the war. I just don't see the problem with the political judgments the way you warriors—with your preoccupation with victory—see it." "Victory matters," the colonel said. "We were engaged in a worldwide struggle. I don't think you'd have liked the outcome if we'd lost it." "Ah, yes. Dominoes. Appeasement. But we're talking about Vietnam, not the whole Cold War. But in any event," I declared, warming to the topic, "one can be too fixated on seeing everything in terms of victory versus defeat, perceiving as the only acceptable outcome the triumph of the 'good' guys over the 'bad' guys." I hesitated, groping for something, then ventured: "Actually, I think there's more to it than that."

I sort of shrugged myself into a question-mark for a moment to think. "Let me venture to put it this way. I believe we fought a war we shouldn't have fought, and we did so—ultimately—because we are predisposed toward too simple-minded a view of good and evil. The world was cloven into just two sides, corresponding—not coincidentally—to the great cosmological drama of our main religious drama. In this struggle of good against evil, everyone who was not for us was against us, and everyone against us was aligned with the great Adversary on the other side.

"We couldn't even see, for years, that the Chinese and the Soviets were far from allies with one another. So, in Indochina, this group of communist Vietnamese nationalists beat the French, and they were getting support from our enemies. So, with our predisposition to see the world in terms of the side of the light against the monolithic side of darkness, we never imagined how a fierce and proud people like the Vietnamese were not about to play the role simply of pawns for some other, larger chess player. And so we fought them instead of doing what we're doing now, decades later, after losing the war, which is come to terms with them and find common interests. Oh, and incidentally, that same Manichean kind of moral thinking also helped lead us astray in reasoning that if we're on the side of the right, then anything we do must be justified. Which helped enable us to do some pretty terrible things."

"But those guys on the other side—I mean both the Viet Cong and the North Vietnamese—they weren't such nice guys," Morrison said. "And from what I can tell, when the North Vietnamese took over, they were pretty oppressive." "Oh, please don't take anything I said as suggesting otherwise," I replied. "There are lots of bad guys. But it's not as if we haven't been able to accept bad guys running countries elsewhere, and in some instances we have even played a pretty powerful role in setting them up. The Vietnamese communists may have been oppressive, but what about the Guatemalan regime we've been so involved with—just to name one—that murdered a couple hundred thousand of the Guatamalan Indians who dared to refuse to acquiesce in the oppressed state to which they'd been forcibly consigned?"

"Yeah, I can see your argument," the Colonel said. "I really don't know. All I can say is that it was a pretty full job for me just to fulfill the duties I was given, trying to complete our missions, and maintain morale, and keep my men alive." "I'm sure it was," I responded. "I really want you to know that I was never one of those who blamed the soldiers. You know, those stories of the guys being spat upon by the antiwar types when they got home in uniform. I figured it might be me in their position, you know, there but for the grace of an X-ray go I. . . . And as for my thesis about the war, I don't claim any certain wisdom. What I said may not be the real 'lesson of Vietnam' either. It's just my best guess. Whoever said that '20/20 hindsight is easy' probably hasn't studied much history."

Colonel Morrison's wife was by now pretty eager to go. It was at this point that I learned that when April and I had met the Morrisons on our way in, they had been on their way out. That was now forty minutes ago. We all laughed about how the Colonel hadn't left and I hadn't made it to the table with all the wonderful food. It was a conversation about which both of us felt very good, worth the sacrifice in his departure time and my arrival at the salmon. We shook hands warmly, agreed it would be good if we could find some other occasion to resume our exchange, and then he and his wife headed out.

The Idiocy and Theodicy
What Does This Creation Say about the Creator?

When I got home from the party, I debated whether to postpone till morning my checking in with the forum. I decided to do so and went to bed within an hour of our return, only to find myself not getting to sleep. My mind was on fast idle, recalling aspects of my conversation with Colonel Morrison, the good man who had fought for God's side in his years of service with the U.S. Air Force, and that recollection led to my growing increasingly curious about what my buddies on the forum were up to. I've lived with myself long enough to know that when my curiosity has been seriously engaged, and when the satisfaction it seeks is available, trying to go to sleep is a waste of time. So I got out of bed and went down to see what was in my inbox.

God's Moral Accounting

Rev. George's assertion—that it would be most dangerous for our culture to allow to die that spiritual space that has been filled by previous human societies with images of sacred order—had elicited an extraordinary posting from Carl. What Carl had brought forth was an extended paean to the Almighty God, Ruler of the Universe. Carl wove a variety of biblical quotes and pronouncements from important Protestant theologians into what may have been the longest single statement in the course of our discussions. He went into how God pronounced "good" what lay before Him at various stages of the process of creation as told in the Book of Genesis. He spoke of how Eve (under the influence of the Serpent) and Adam (under the influence of Eve) had disobeyed the single "shalt not" that the Lord had imposed upon them, with distastrous punitive consequences for themselves and for all the rest of us of Adam's seed. And then he went on to the great Flood in the time of Noah, brought about by the Lord to cleanse the world of its wickedness, and how God had made a promise in conjunction with the famous rainbow that he would not deal in that way with any recurrence of that problem of human sinfulness. And then he was on to God's thunderously putting Job in his place when Job dared to question the rightness of such terrible sufferings being inflicted on a righteous man: where were you when I made the whirlwind, and such.

And I was still less than halfway through Carl's description of God's wonderful role in the ordering of the world when I discovered that my sleepiness was at last starting to overtake my curiosity. So I did something—I never could figure out just what it was—to set Carl's message aside for more reading later and, lo and behold, somehow it had vanished altogether from my system. That startling mishap woke me back up. Even doing a "Find" availed nothing. It was gone!

I realize I could have written to someone on the forum to get another copy, and doubtless I should have. But I didn't. I saw, still unopened in my Inbox, such a flurry of other messages from various members—including Carl—that, reinvigorated by my mysterious encounter with cyberdemons, I put off bed a little while longer to get some sense of where the discussion was going.

Larry's was the first sally in what proved to be the interrogation of Carl.

If I understand you correctly, you are saying that we live in a world that, thanks to God Almighty, is sharply tilted to create a good order. And the tilt that He has provided is that the good are rewarded and the evil are punished. From this reading, it appears to me that you are saying that God has arranged the world so that, in a sense, it is in each person's enlightened self-interest to do what the moral commandments require of him. Am I right? **Larry**

I don't know about the aptness of the phrase "enlightened self-interest" to describe the righteous path. I'd prefer to think of it as something that one does out of a love of God and of righteousness. But yes, God rewards the righteous and punishes the wicked. **Carl**

It seems to me that the history of the world shows **anything but** such a pattern of rewards and punishments. Even in the Bible, are there not a number of passages where one prophet or another laments that the wicked prosper and the good suffer? **Larry**

Victor the Graffiti Artist quickly interjected:

"For if injustice is to get the better of justice we must no longer believe the gods exist." Aeschylus, *Orestes*.[1]

And on his heels, Carl was back to respond:

God's order is not fully displayed in this, the visible world. In this world, sin and Satan hold considerable sway. But in the hereafter—in the fires of hell and in the heavenly bliss of the saved—accounts are balanced. It is there that the consequences of good and evil are meted out. **Carl**

The problem with heaven and hell, *Ralph posited,* is that it appears to be a hypothesis created merely to save a theory rather than one growing out of the evidence. The theory is that God has created a moral order, and that therefore we are wise to be good even if we are not good out of goodness. Then, if observation shows that the world is not a place where good is rewarded and evil punished, in order to preserve the theory, instead of regarding it as refuted, one postulates an invisible world that undoes the contrary evidence all around us.

But that seems, if you'll pardon the expression, a hell of a way to come to one's beliefs. It seems, that is, to assert as a given—the moral order of the cosmos—what should logically be taken **as the question:** is there a moral order in the cosmos? And—using the evidence of what we see, rather than concocting hypotheses of realms we do not see—the answer seems clearly to be that if there is, it is at best a very imperfect one.

By that I mean that yes, in some ways evil does often bring upon the evil-doer some kind of negative results—what some child-rearing authorities call "natural consequences"—and yes, the good who cast their bread upon the waters do often reap rewards, but it is at best a quite unreliable dynamic. The way the evils of the Nazi regime helped bring about its utter destruction is a case for there being some such ordering process in our world. But the way millions of innocent people were marched by the Nazis into the murderous showers of Auschwitz is evidence of how terribly limited is the reliability of that ordering. **Ralph**

Well, one part of the nature of things seems to be that it is part of our nature as human beings to interpret events as having a moral meaning.

This voice was Herman's.

Maybe it is the way we were wired as we evolved to be cultural animals, that is, to be creatures who are able to learn right and wrong through the rewards and punishments that our environment doles out to us. For primates like us, the family situation into which we are socialized at the beginning of our lives can generally be relied upon to provide such an environment: parents smile and cuddle us for doing what they think good, and they yell at us or give us a knock when we misbehave. And by crafting our natures to interpret our sufferings and joys as a kind of *post hoc ergo propter hoc* moral judgment on the behaviors that preceded them, nature has fitted us to live as creatures capable of the kind of learning needed for social life in a system in which culture, and not just instinct, defines the rules of life.

But I agree with Ralph: that same interpretive tendency that serves us well as we grow up in the family or clan will lead—when we leave that clearly teleological universe of the human family, and try to interpret the meanings of our experience in the less governed environment of the wider world—to distorted thinking in our cosmological beliefs. So the poor Israelites—a tiny nation sandwiched between greater powers—when they suffered the predictable fate of such minor powers, interpreted it as a reflection of God's moral judgment upon them. "We did not keep the commandments well enough! This is punishment for our iniquities!" And when the Lisbon earthquake struck a couple centuries ago, this calamity too was of course interpreted as divine wrath, punishment for the sins of the afflicted people.

What I am suggesting is that there is probably an evolutionary reason that we seem so inclined to interpret our happiness and misery in terms of a cosmic moral judgment upon us. In a sense, the idea of heaven and hell represents an improvement in our contact with reality: it reflects the realization, at least, that the world around us does not confirm our congenital interpretation. An order where virtue is rewarded and wrong-doing punished may be the order that we yearn for, but we come to recognize that it isn't the one we've got, and the invention of heaven and hell reflects our realization of this discrepancy. Likewise with the ancient Greeks: in the face of the obvious injustice of the world—thank you for the quote from *Orestes*, Victor—they tried to sustain the belief in a cosmic order from the top-down by positing that, even if the **immediate** actors do not get their just desserts, the rewards and punishments wash up downstream upon their lineal descendents. The House of Atreus, of which Orestes represented one more afflicted generation reaping the harvest of ancestral sins, comes to mind. And then, in India, we have the idea of **karma** which, when combined with the notion of reincarnation, allows for the belief in the moral order of the cosmos to be sustained, with consequences being meted out to the same souls in subsequent embodiments.

In other words, this belief that we are embedded in an order that makes moral sense runs very deep. **Herman**

There's something in this whole approach, *Alice wrote next,* that bothers me. I think it is contained in that idea of 'enlightened self-interest' that Larry raised a little while ago. The idea seems to be that when we do the right thing, it is to serve ourselves. What I want to call attention to is how this way of understanding our choices robs us of something important. And that important thing is the moral dimension itself.

If the choice we face is between serving our own needs in a foolish, shortsighted way, or serving our own needs in an enlightened way, what happens to morality itself? No room is left here for the love of something beyond oneself. It becomes just a matter of foolish strategies for self-gratification versus wise strategies. Being good is reduced to being smart. **Alice**

Yes, Alice, you've put your finger on an important point, *Herman responded.* It comes up with the ancient Greeks, in the later generations of their civilization. When the traditional beliefs in the gods, and the system of rewards and punishments for mortals imputed to those gods, came into question, a cultural crisis occurred: could any alternative basis for a moral order for their society be found?[2] According to the Greeks' understanding, an individual would always choose to act in whatever way he believed would contribute best to his own ultimate well-being. In their thought, that is, an appeal like yours, Alice, to someone to act contrary to self-interest for the sake of morality would have made no sense. It is in the context of that ongoing cultural crisis, therefore, that it became meaningful to argue, as Plato did through the voice of his Socrates, that evil is ignorance and goodness is wisdom. For if morality required only more complete knowledge of one's own good, then the cultural order could survive the loss of faith in divine sanctions.

But it hasn't only been the Greeks who have wrestled with this issue in the same way. We've talked about the whole Christian idea of heaven and hell as a way of rewarding and punishing, and especially in some cultural contexts—like the theology of nineteenth-century Britain—the idea that virtue and happiness had to be ultimately in harmony has seemed essential.[3] I'm not sure, but perhaps it was in the context of the same cultural forces that gave rise to utilitarianism that achieving such harmony was especially seen as necessary. If it is assumed that human beings must necessarily act from a motive of self-interest, then virtue must ultimately be the route to happiness or it makes no sense to summon people to it. **Herman**

Yes, I guess if one's understanding of human possibilities is that people in some sense always and inevitably seek their own good, *Alice replied,* then the only way of talking about morality and virtue is either to prove that one's own good (in the sense of welfare) and goodness itself (in the sense of morality) are always pointing in the same direction, or to concede that people will be immoral and lacking in virtue wherever self-interest and morality point differently.

But as for me, I'm not ready to concede that this is the way to understand our psychological and motivational possibilities. It seems to me at the heart of the whole issue of morality is that sometimes we are called upon to act in ways that, in some sense, go against our self-interest. In other words, that morality goes against our natural grain. And then the interesting question becomes, what is it, how is it, that we can freely and knowledgeably choose to serve the Good even at some cost to our own good? **Alice**

The thing that gets me about heaven and hell, *Jeff began in the next message posted,* is that it seems to reflect such a terrible view of what kind of beasts we human beings are. Set aside what kind of God it would be—hardly All-Good I would say most emphatically—who would inflict on sinners the kinds of torments that are depicted in, say, medieval art. Consider what kind of creature would require the threat of having to suffer such incredible torments for an eternity in order to be kept in line. Any regime that needs that kind of torture to maintain order must be, I would argue, in itself an evil. Good order would not require such cruel and coercive devices. **Jeff**

There once again is that sanguine *liberal* view of human nature, here presented not as an assertion but merely as an assumption,

Henry said in reply, reminding me of that awesome and awful quote he'd posted a while back from de Maistre about the indispensability of the hangman to human society. At least he had the virtue of consistency, I thought—if such a consistency can be considered a virtue.

But what if the impulses within the human heart are themselves so evil that great force must be applied against them to maintain any kind of good order at all? **Henry**

Precisely, *Kenneth concurred.* God knows how base and sinful is the human creature, and He has established His order with that understanding. The human heart with its base sexual passions, its utter selfishness, cannot be the basis of any good order. By the Grace of God we can be lifted out of our lowly impulses into a love of the light, but left to our own devices, we are terribly flawed creatures. And as so many people never do open themselves up to the saving grace of the Lord, the fires of hell rightly loom before us as a threat, and a reality, to help keep unredeemed humanity in line, and to redeem order by bringing justice. **Kenneth**

Once again, I'm with Jeff, *Ralph said*. Not only does the invention of heaven and hell serve, as I suggested earlier, like some kind of 'dark matter'—invisible, but required to make our calculations come out according to theory—but there is also something quite repugnant about the image. The punitive fires of hell seem not like a component of some elevated Good Order, but rather a reflection of the kinds of cruel and barbaric order represented in most of the civilized societies that have shaped our religious tradition. And from these barbarous orders, with their dungeons and tools of torture, it is the liberal idea, so much maligned here, that has given human history a most-welcomed redemption. **Ralph**

The Scene of the Crime

Carl, let's leave these guys to pick apart why you believe in this Godly Order of heaven and hell, and let's take a different tack. Let's assume everything you say about God is true. All-Powerful, All-Seeing, All-Good, meting out rewards and punishments. OK Carl?

It was Fred, that sly fellow. As I read this, I thought that if I were Carl, I'd be grabbing the theological equivalent of my wallet to make sure it was still there.

What I'd like to explore with you is whether—given all you say—the order you depict is really a moral order. Are you up for that? **Fred**

After Carl assented, Fred continued in his next posting.

If God is so good and so capable, why is the world He created so filled with people who do terrible things? Why isn't there a more perfect Creation down here to mirror the wonderfulness of its Creator? **Fred**

God created man in His own image, but He also gave to man free will. He gave to man the ability to choose between the path of righteousness and the path of evil. Fundamentally sinful creatures that we human beings are, this free will all too often is used to choose evil. Hence the world of sin that we see around us. **Carl**

Now, let me get this straight, *Fred replied*. God—omnipotent and omniscient Being that He is—created us to be free, and we chose badly. Let's leave aside the question of why He'd prefer us free to make a mess of things rather than to have things be perfect, like Him. Assuming that you are right, if He's perfect, why is it that we chose badly? Or, if He's so good, why is it that we, His creatures, are (in your words) so sinful? **Fred**

Our sinful nature has been established since the beginning, since the first human beings disobeyed God in the Garden of Eden. This is that idea of "original sin," which someone here sometime back called a calumny against human nature, but which in reality is our own calumny against our Creator in whose image we were created. **Carl**

Oh yes, Adam and Eve in the Garden. A pivotal story in the account of how the world got screwed up. But let's take a closer look at that story. Let us return, imaginatively of course, in a philosophic vein, to the scene of the crime. OK?

Now, if God is all-seeing, would it not be correct to say that, when God made Adam and Eve, He already *knew* that these people were going to disobey Him about not eating of the fruit of that one tree? **Fred**

Yes, of course, in the mind of God the future is visible just as clearly as is the present. So God of course knew all that was to come. **Carl**

Yes, I thought so, *Fred replied.*

I could picture Fred pacing back and forth in front of the witness box, hands loosely clasped behind his back, lulling the witness into unwittingly aiding in the construction of the trap that would shortly slam shut, with the unsuspecting witness snared within.

Now, Carl, this omnipotent and omniscient God that has completed the first five days of Creation and is, on the sixth, about to create the first human, endowing him with the free will that He can foresee will be abused by this first human, does this God have at this point another option? Specifically, does this God have the power to create—instead of Adam who with his helpmate will freely choose to disobey God and get himself infected with original sin—a different human being? Could he have created another first man, and out of his rib, another first woman, who—fully endowed with free will—would have used that free will to choose to obey, to choose the path of righteousness? **Fred**

God has it in His power to create anything that He wishes. **Carl**

Let me pin this down a bit. I am supposing that the implications of what you have said include: that the free will with which God endowed human beings *could* have been used to choose right, and not just wrong; that God *could* have created a different first human who would have used his free will rightly; and that He knowingly chose rather to create Adam and Eve whom He knew even before hand were going to use their freedom to take the wrong road and subject all their descendants to the ravages of a world ruled by sin. Is that correct? **Fred**

For some reason, Carl did not write back. And after a pause of some time, Fred wrote again.

Yes, it is hard to see how it cannot be correct. Not if you posit that God is omnipotent and omniscient. If you have a God who has that range of powers, and who knows what the consequences of His actions will be, and whose creatures turn out to be sinful—such a God seems inescapably to bear responsibility for the defects of His creation.

It will not do at all to blame the problems of the world on original sin. For God had the option of giving us a progenitor who would have employed his free will differently and endowed us with original virtue. The real crime, therefore, occurs at the moment God chooses to create Adam, and thence Eve. And the real criminal is not the creature, whom God chose in preference to a better option, but the Creator Himself. **Fred**

Free to Be You and Me

It was Kenneth, rather than the still-silent Carl, who chose to respond to Fred's nifty bit of philosophical Perry Masoning.

A cheap debater's trick, Fred, that's all it is, *Kenneth wrote.* You've just found a way to make a mockery of the idea of free will. The point is, that Adam was free to choose. And so is each of us. Thus sayeth the Lord: "I have set before you life and death, blessing and cursing: therefore choose life, that both thou and thy seed may live" (Deuteronomy 19:30). We are the seed of Adam, and he disobeyed the Lord. Adam brought death into the picture with his disobedience. The wages of sin is death. (Romans, 6.23) Your blaming the Lord for the sinfulness of Adam's seed—for our sinfulness—is just a way of evading moral responsibility. **Kenneth**

Actually, Kenneth, I'm not sure that Fred hasn't shown something more profound than you give him credit for, *Len wrote in response. It had been a while since we'd heard from Len.* Fred has posed his argument in terms of the story of the Fall in Genesis. But it has a larger ramification, it seems to me, one that calls into question not only the meaning of a concept of "free will," but of the whole notion of "moral responsibility," and whether it makes any sense to blame anybody for anything.

What I am saying is that a permutation of Fred's reasoning leads, I believe, to the conclusion that the whole idea of free will—although appealing in some ways—just doesn't make sense. **Len**

Peter quickly posted a brief message encouraging Len to elaborate on his point, and so, shortly, Len resumed.

At the core of Fred's argument is this paradox: the idea of free will implies that the choice is somehow yet to be made, and could go either way; but the idea of God's being able to know the future implies that the future is already visible—at least to God—and therefore cannot go either way. If Adam is truly free, God cannot know how Adam will choose. But if God can know how Adam will choose, Adam's freedom can have no meaning. Am I right, Fred? **Len**

You're right as far as you go. But that doesn't take into account that other piece of my particular prosecutory argument: the possibility of God's having created a different man who would have chosen differently. After all, if Adam somehow were really free, then God is off the hook—at least for His botch job having been premeditated. But if He simply, unwittingly made the wrong guy, when He could have made a better one, then the problems of the creation—of human sinfulness, specifically—are still laid at His door, the only difference being that it isn't a crime anymore, just a blunder. **Fred**

Yes, I see your point, even if I am having trouble holding this all together for my philosophical purpose here, *Len responded*. Admitting that my mind is not necessarily wrapped around this whole complex matter, let me try to proceed.

Let's set aside this particular "In the beginning" story. There is always some kind of "in the beginning." And as your argument, Fred, suggests, the present always grows out of the past, and the future grows out of the present. In this perspective, I want to argue, the whole notion of free will is simply incomprehensible, and therefore should be jettisoned.

For something to unfold that's **different** from what actually happens, something would have had to be different in the time before it. Whether it is a first man named Adam, or a better one named Fred, a different outcome cannot come out of an identical situation. Can it? Therefore, since everything unfolds through time, and since each one of us—as well as humankind as a whole, and the world itself—has a beginning, there is no place in the picture for any of us, or anything about us, or anything we do, to be other than the fruit of the world, a result of things that lie outside of ourselves. **Len**

Larry wrote:

I think I follow you, but explain it more thoroughly.

I'll give it a try, *Len responded*. OK. Let's say we do have free will. What do we mean by that? It seems to mean that a person makes choices, and that the explanation for how he chooses lies **ultimately within his own being.** What I want to ask is: where can this being, or this part of himself that is making the free choice, have come from that is **not** the product of forces outside itself? What we seem to have with this doctrine is a creature that is somehow his own Creator, *ex nihilo*.

How could free will work? Let's imagine a person who is about to make his first choice. There must be a first choice at some point, whether it be regarded as occurring at age one year, or one day, or *in utero*. Before this first choice, the person cannot have chosen how he has developed. (Otherwise there will have been a previous choice, which would then be that first choice we are investigating.) Therefore, at this crucial juncture, the person as we find him is **necessarily** the fruit of forces outside of himself—the forces which led to his heredity plus his subsequent environmental influences.

He makes his choice, whatever it is—to smile, to put a pebble in his mouth, to bite the nipple. What does it mean to say that the way he chose is ultimately not wholly a function of external forces? For what he is until that instant derives wholly from the world in which he has grown. What can there be within him that he has made for himself, of which he is the ultimate cause? Nothing. If our choices are a function of what and who we are, then this first choice is caused ultimately by those external forces that shaped what and who our chooser is. At its birth, therefore, our freedom is discovered to be the child of our necessities.

The logic of this seems to me inescapable. Ultimately, we must be the products of the world from which we emerge; we cannot be self-creators *ex nihilo*. **Len**

You say, Len, that our freedom is the child of our necessities **at its birth**. *This was Peter.* But what about the unfolding of that life after this birth? What about the way we all make choices during our lives that subsequently help to mold the people we become? Surely you do not deny that—even if we do not create ourselves *ex nihilo*—we do create ourselves through the choices we make in the course of our lives, do you? **Peter**

No, I acknowledge both that we do make choices, and that the choices we make will mold us into one kind of person rather than another. The issue, specifically, is whether these choices are "free," which I understand to mean that they are not ultimately traceable to causes that lie outside ourselves. And that's why the logical analysis of this hypothetical first choice is so crucial. If—as I argue we must necessarily conclude—our presumed first "free" choice is the function of a will that we ourselves could have done nothing to create or shape, then it follows that all subsequent choices must likewise be the fruit of what we are, which—inescapably—derives from the determinative influence of forces lying outside ourselves. It is like that proof in mathematics where, once it is established that if a proposition is true for "p," it is also true for "$p + 1$," then all that is necessary is to show that it is true for $p = 1$ and it follows that it is true for all integers above 1.

Or, to put it another way, if logic can show that there can be no **first** free choice, then it follows that there can be no subsequent "free" choice either. **Len**

I am not a physicist, *Terrence began by conceding,* but it seems to me that there is something antiquated about your Newtonian causal assumptions. Here's what I mean. A few messages ago, you argued that for something **different** to emerge at a subsequent time, there had to be something **different** about the previous time. This kind of rigid determinism, however, has been undercut—if I understand correctly—by the physics of the twentieth century, specifically by quantum mechanics. Is it not the case that quantum mechanics declares that which atom—among a bunch of atoms—breaks down radioactively and which does not is purely random, that is, that completely identical situations can and do produce different outcomes? And if that is so, does not the deterministic causal framework that you are relying upon break down? **Terrence**

I confess to still operating in a Newtonian kind of world, in terms of cause and effect, which makes this kind of quantum mechanical randomness hard for me to comprehend. But at the same time, in terms of the question of free will, I fail to see how this little piece of randomness at the level of atomic quanta helps to resurrect a self-determining will, one that is not the fruit of the world. It's hardly clear how microrandomness is relevant to the macrolevel on which we and our choices happen.

But beyond this issue of scale, I can't see how randomness at *any* scale would confer upon us anything like "free will." After all, simply escaping the confines of rigid causality—through random firings or swerves—hardly provides us a basis for being able to be masters of ourselves. (Earlier, when I wrote that for choices to be "free" meant that "they are not ultimately traceable to causes that lie outside ourselves," perhaps I should have added that whatever allowed them to be free of such causality nonetheless allowed them also to be controlled by ourselves.) **Len**

How does this argument you've made connect with Fred's prosecution of the God of Genesis? *Ralph asked Len in the next message.* As I recall, your refutation of the idea of free will came up in the context of your suggesting to Kenneth that Fred's case made some important, larger point. **Ralph**

In a sense we are all Adam. Each of us coming into the world with a beginning, each of us making imperfect choices, *Len responded.* Just as Fred showed, pretty persuasively to me, that the roots of Adam's sin must lie ultimately outside himself, so also does the sin of each one of us lie in the forces which created us.

Now, unlike with Fred's rather creative prosecution, I am not trying to place the blame for the defects of human beings on any other Being. That blaming is predicated on a Creator who knew what He was doing and chose to create something flawed. In my analysis, which posits no such conscious decision-maker in the creative process, the point is to prosecute the idea of **blame** itself. Blame is based on a logical fallacy, which is that people are the source of their own defects. Certainly, at any rate, that's true of the kind of blame on which the notion of eternal torment in hell is predicated.

The consequence of this insight into the fundamental unfreedom of the human will—that it's ultimately the fruit of the world—is a compassion for one's fellow creatures, an understanding that, no matter what evil we may encounter in another person, we should hold onto the knowledge that "There but for the Grace of Circumstance go I." We are all caught up in a process which is simply unfolding. **Len**

I do think, *Larry wrote,* that this discussion of free will has served to bring into clear focus one of the most important defects in traditional Western religion's moral image of the cosmos.

This top-down cosmos—with the Almighty God standing apart from and above Creation—runs into trouble as soon as it encounters the reality that the world is a troubled place. Perhaps it wouldn't have to be a problem if this Creator were conceived to be, like us, less than perfect. You know, He makes mistakes. Maybe He has His moral deficiencies. Perhaps the whole universe is a work-in-progress, with God trying to figure things out as He goes along. But as soon as you insist on His perfection, it seems inescapable that somebody has to take the rap for the realities that are all around us. In other words, the way this God is conceived makes inevitable a whole moral regime founded on **blame**.

That's what I like about what Len's argument does. It breaks open that terrible prison in which so much of Western consciousness has been confined. "Sinner in the hands of an Angry God," and all that. **Larry**

I appreciate your calling attention to that aspect of it, Larry, *Herman wrote.* Indeed, a most striking aspect of specifically Western religiosity is tied in there: namely that, in our tradition, the source of Goodness and the source of Evil are conceived as so radically distinct. That which is above is seen as All-Good, above reproach. That which is below must, as you put it, take the rap for all the evils and suffering. God gets all the credit: "Praise God from whom all blessings flow." Humankind gets all the blame. Heavy load.

But if we end that dichotomy—between the eternal and wonderful Creator and the fallen and blameworthy creation and creatures—then we are freed to build an image of the unfolding cosmic order that provides room for a more integrated, less split understanding of good and evil, of what bottom-up means and what top-down means. These don't have to be so split apart, I don't think, if we look at them from the right perspective. I have in mind here a more evolutionary view of the unfolding of our world through time—in both its wonders and its catastrophes, in the flows not only of the blessings but also of the curses. **Herman**

This message pointed—as will be shown in the next chapter—toward a perspective on the unfolding human drama that I found to be the most clarifying of any we'd found in our quest. But before we got to that, there were more disagreements to be resolved around the matter of free will and compassion, and one more journey, led by the more traditionally religious among us, into the top-down cosmos ruled by an all-powerful and good God.

The Question of Compassion

I like what Len's shown, *Donna said,* that blame is misguided, and that compassion is always called for. I've always felt that, at some fundamental level, everyone is doing the best that he or she can. **Donna**

I'm not sure if that conclusion is warranted, *Ralph interjected, almost parenthetically.* According to Len's logic, it is equally true that everyone is doing the worst that he or she can—since we're all doing the only thing we can, since we are all shaped, ultimately, by forces lying outside of ourselves. **Ralph**

I certainly cannot join in this celebration of Len's acquittal of all of us for everything, *Terrence wrote.* For a while, I thought that maybe some of you bleeding-heart liberals were getting somewhere from being in this discussion. When we were talking about those "old virtues," it seemed to me that you were getting it that a world in which we abandoned venerable moral categories like *responsibility* and *judgment* was a world that doesn't work well, a world that disintegrates. Now here we are back in the swamp of **compassion.**

You've apparently got it all figured out how we are not really responsible for anything that we do. We are just the fruit of the world, you say, and so it cannot mean anything to say that we have free will. And from there it is just a hop, skip and a jump to the disastrous kind of worldview and policies that encourage the worst in people. I'm talking about "compassionate" policies that demand nothing and make excuses for anything. Just as the Fall isn't Adam's and Eve's fault, but God's, so also are the muggers and rapists not at fault for their evildoing, but are rather innocent products of the world that shaped them.

If you get rid of free will, you end up in the compassion trap in which the evildoer becomes the pitiable victim. The abuse excuse. Dissolve the idea of moral responsibility and you get—unsurprisingly—more irresponsibility. Make excuses for criminals and you get—again, not surprisingly—more crime and more criminals rather than less. (Same, by the way, is true of poverty: treat the poor as victims of circumstances rather than as moral agents with the capacity to make better choices to better themselves and their circumstances, and you end up with this miserable "culture of poverty" we have seen emerge in America.)

All because of rationalizing away the central moral fact of human existence: *we are responsible* for what we do, and we need to treat each other that way. **Terrence**

Well said, Terrence, *Henry added*. This attack on the idea of free will is indeed just that: an attack on the idea of responsibility. And I think it notable that the argument is being made by Len. Are you not, Len, the same person who earlier was compelled to confess that you'd abdicated your responsibility as a father, thinking that paternal authority was superfluous and everything in your child's moral development would just unfold naturally on its own? **Henry**

I thought this something of a low blow, and was considering posting something to suggest that we avoid anything like personal attacks in the process of discussing these issues. By now, I was pretty well current with the discussion, and so such a message from me would not have been belated. But when Len responded quite promptly himself, and without seeming to be any the worse for Henry's *ad hominem* comment, I decided to keep my peace.

Touché. I say, touché, Henry, because I do believe that there is a flaw in my position, and that this flaw has some organic connection with my mistakes as a father.

It occurred to me that perhaps Len was able to respond in this undefensive way because he was able to be compassionate with himself in his own imperfections and mistakes.

What seems deficient in my position is—I agree with you—that somehow it is important that we be held morally accountable for our actions. At the same time, I still emphatically do stand behind my critique of free will. Free will, I still maintain, is an illusory and ultimately nonsensical concept. So the challenge I feel I have not met is that I do not know how to reconcile those two positions: the lack of free will and the need for moral accountability. **Len**

A message then arrived from Fred, taking the position that Len had conceded too much in granting the idea of moral responsibility.

I was so pleased, Len, when I thought perhaps you had cleaned the traditional moral stables of that ubiquitous and foul-smelling dropping: blame, *Fred wrote.* And now it seems you are ready to sweep the stuff back into the barn. Too bad. But I am willing to take on Henry where you have fallen down on the liberationist job.

To hell, say I, with this pernicious holding of the wrong-doers' feet to the fires of moral accountability. What it usually represents is somebody who has had all of life's advantages—comfortable home, decent treatment, etc.—coming in to punish some-one else who had the terrible moral defect of choosing to be born in a deprived and abusive environment. The reality is, if the Inquisitor had been born into the other fellow's position, he'd be the one on the rack instead of the one turning the screws. **Fred**

Oh come now, Fred, are we supposed to take you seriously? *Rev. George was making his first appearance here for a while.* It's not clear to me just what position you are arguing for. How about we strip away the punitive spirit from the issue and engage simply the matter of moral responsibility? **Rev. George**

Take away the punitiveness, and what do you have left of the idea of moral responsibility that Henry defends, or rather, with which Henry attacks? **Fred**

I'll speak here for myself, rather than for Henry, whose position I don't necessarily know well enough to represent. I would say that whether Len is right about free will or not, we have to press one another to do the right thing, and to provide incentives—both positive and negative—to induce one another to take the moral path. **Rev. George**

And how, pray tell, RG, are your "negative incentives" any different from the puni-tiveness of God's holy hell? **Fred**

One of the main points of hell, if I understand the idea, is that the wrongdoer **deserves** to suffer. And so his experience of suffering is considered a good thing in itself. But my negative incentives are intended solely to help make the world better, with the suffering of the wrongdoer regarded not as a good in and of itself but rather as a cost toward that larger end. **RG**

Donna entered here, with her gentle spirit if not always clear thinking.

I do think everyone is always doing the best that they can. And I do not think it makes the world a better place if we have someone—God or a judge or whoever—standing above them to punish them if they make mistakes. That's not how people learn best. We see from prisons that if you abuse people, it only makes their spirits more twisted rather than helping them to find a more loving and caring way to deal with the world.

It seems to me that sometimes the arguments about the "insanity defense" are kind of foolish. They'll be trying the case of someone who has done some really terrible thing—like torture and rape and kill some child—and there will be this quarrel about whether the person who did this terrible thing is sane or not. I mean, all you have to do is look at the misdeed and you **know** that no one who wasn't crazy would have done it. How could anyone in his right mind do such a thing? They couldn't, so I don't understand why they have to quarrel about whether to be compassionate or not. **Donna**

I'd go further with that, Donna, *Fred contributed*. If it is true that "there but for the grace of Whatever go I" then it would seem to follow that whatever the **reasons** were for the person to do what they did, the reasons were necessarily adequate. So why quarrel about whether their abuse or poverty or mental state was sufficient to excuse their actions? Obviously, **something** must have been sufficient to drive them to it. The only difference is that in some cases—like people whose histories show quite obviously how tortured their lives have been—the reasons are clear to us, while in other cases the reasons are not so visible to us. But of course, they must be there. **Fred**

You speak of people making mistakes, Donna, *Terrence came in, with a lawyerly tone*. But let us consider some cases to see whether your words serve us well.

Not long ago, there was a case in Utah where some high-school students—popular kids, athletes, from prosperous, supposedly good middle-class families—were caught for having done a number of armed robberies of local stores. (They were caught because they'd bragged about it publicly enough that it was no secret.) The network TV news-people went to Salt Lake and interviewed the fellow students of these young criminals in this suburban school, and what was striking to me about the interviews was the language the students used. "Everybody makes mistakes," one said. "I hope everyone doesn't hold it against all the rest of us because a few of us made mistakes," said another.

Now my question is, does "mistake" capture the essence of what these fellows did?

To my mind, it does not. If the shortstop takes his eye off the ground-ball because he's looking to see if the second baseman is coming to the bag to help start the double play, and the wayward glance allows the ball to go between his legs into left field, **that** I'd call a mistake. If I'm trying to hang a picture by driving a nail into the wall and I hit my thumb instead, that too I'd call a mistake. But these are fundamentally different from the young men deciding to go rob a store.

And what is that difference? The answer seems clear: it is all a matter of **intention**. The shortstop did not intend to miss the grounder, nor I to hit my thumb. But the young men did exactly what they intended to do, and it was their intention, rather than their execution, that was wrong. **Terrence**

Nicely done, counselor, *Ralph applauded*. And I believe that piece you have provided helps me see how Len can accomplish that reconciliation he was seeking. That is, the reconciliation between treating people as morally responsible while at the same time recognizing that "there but for the grace of Whatever go I," that is, that they are in some ultimate sense not responsible for being who they are, and thus for doing what they do. (And I do concur with Len's basic analysis.)

Len's argument, it should be recalled, was **not** that we do not make choices, but rather that we—and all the choices we make, therefore, as well—are ultimately the fruit of the world. We are not, that is, self-creating. But we do make choices. We make them differently depending upon the forces that have borne upon us up until that moment.

Among those forces are the moral pressures that are brought to bear upon us, including what other people expect of us, how they treat us when we fulfill their expectations and when we disappoint them, and how much of all that gets internalized into our own inner emotional lives. And whatever the internalization, our choices continue to be influenced by the world around us, including what kinds of positive and negative consequences will ensue from different courses of action.

Whether or not we have free will, our choices will thus be shaped by whether or not other people treat us as morally responsible actors. If they continually make excuses for us—talking about how we were abused, and how we deserve compassion—we might be more likely to continue to do the things for which the excuses must be made than if they continually treat us as if they expect us to do right, and will be angry and unhappy with us if we do wrong.

So it could well be a mistake to convey too completely the compassion we might feel for the evildoer because we realize that this person might have been us, had forces beyond our control operated differently. The person might deserve our compassion, yet it is possible that compassion could be counterproductive from the point of view of the moral order of the whole society. Conversely, even if punitiveness of the crude and repugnant sort such as we see from the salivating lovers of capital punishment may be morally indefensible in philosophic terms—the rage failing to take into account the way in which each person is but the fruit of a world he or she did not create—it might nonetheless be valuable in terms of helping to maintain moral and legal order within society. I am not saying that these *are in fact* the case—this problem with compassion and value of punitiveness—but only that it could be.

So, we **need** to hold each other morally accountable in order to help induce one another to act morally. **Ralph**

That is helpful, Ralph, *Len wrote*. We treat each other as responsible for what we do because our decision to do right or wrong—however "unfree," ultimately, that choice may be—might be swayed by the pressures of being held morally accountable. Neat solution. Thanks. **Len**

From a legal point of view, *Terrence wrote,* I also find that analysis helpful, Ralph. Like Donna—though from a rather different set of concerns—I've also found the debates over the insanity defense problematic. "The ability to know right from wrong" sometimes seemed a pertinent standard, but sometimes it did not. ("Knew what he was doing" also seems an insufficient guide.) But perhaps—I can't be sure without giving this matter further thought—Ralph's argument indicates a useful approach.

We might ask, in a given case, "Would a person in this situation and mental condition be less likely to commit this presumably criminal act in a society that holds such people morally responsible than in a society that does not?" Such a standard would differentiate between people who believe, say, that God has commanded them to kill their child because it is possessed of demons, and those who have no illusions about the forbiddenness of their action. It would differentiate between those who are so possessed of their impulses that no conceivable awareness of consequences could have deterred them from those who were able to weigh possible courses of action and their results.

I think it also provides a rebuttal for Fred's sophistry about the reasons for misconduct always being sufficient because, lo, they did what they did. Wherever the bringing to bear the force of holding people morally responsible for their actions might weigh against those "reasons," and make the crime less likely, that is justification enough for treating them as culpable and responsible, whatever those reasons might be. Compassion is not a sufficient reason to coddle. The need to hate the sin can outweigh the call to love the sinner. **Terrence**

It strikes me that there may be a variety of ways of combining the compassion that Len's argument implies with the imposition of moral accountability that Ralph's argument justifies, and that, as they say, reasonable humanoids can differ on just which combinations are wisest. *This message was from Larry.* But that's not the issue that prompts me to write at this point.

What strikes me about beliefs is that there are two important values, and that they are not necessarily always in harmony. There is the value of truth, in that we—at least it is certainly true of me—want to arrive at beliefs that are true, that correspond with how things really are. And then there is the value of consequences—we want to believe things that help us lead good and fulfilling lives.

Truth or consequences! I'm alarmed to think that we may have to choose between these two important sets of values in deciding what we should believe. I've always proceeded as if it were somehow self-evident that we are best served by the truth. "The truth shall set you free" and all that. But I'm no longer at all sure that's so. That's why what Len declared a "neat solution" also represents a real problem for me.

It's the same sort of problem I felt with the idea that perhaps we need to believe in a personal God—to be the object of our passion for the Whole—even if He does not exist. In this instance, we're told we have to treat one another as morally responsible, even if we understand that ultimately we are not, that logically we cannot be. And come to think of it, although I regard the idea of heaven and hell as wholly implausible, I do think it is entirely conceivable that it would be better to live in a world where people generally believe in such hereafters, rather than a world where more reasonable and presumably more valid beliefs predominate.

I have this commitment to the idea of living with the truth, and I'm disturbed by the notion that some illusions—or fictions—are necessary. I'm not proposing any solution to this problem. Just wanted to share that it's coming up as a recurrent issue for me in our discussion. **Larry**

Providence

I feel sorry for you folks, *Kenneth had posted in the meantime, in a message appearing not long after Herman's suggestion that the traditional cosmology might better be replaced by an evolutionary perspective,* who reason yourselves out of the greatest experience that human life can offer, which is the knowledge of, and relationship with, the Living God.

I can imagine it might be a relief to persuade yourself that there is no Eternal Judge to Whom you will have to answer. And I can see how the idea might be appealing that no matter what you do you will not deserve, nor be made to endure, the fires of damnation. But there is another part of the order that comes from God's wisdom and goodness that you are also missing, and for that deprivation I do feel, as you say, compassion.

You make fun—or at least you are dismissive of—the idea of praising God from whom all blessings flow. But what joy there is in the realization of our relationship with God, and of our place in his great Plan for the world! You have spoken so often of the defects of this world, of all the terrible wrongs and suffering that human beings through history have seen all around them. How narrow a point of view that is! There are indeed evils, but they are not the work of God. They are, rather, a function of how fallen and sinful we, His creatures, have allowed ourselves to become. (And then, of course, there is God's great Adversary, Satan.) Take away the sinful actions of us humans (out of our own sinful hearts, as well as from being led astray by Satan), and what is left is a Creation that is truly awesome to behold.

Are you truly so ungrateful for the gift of life in this beautiful world? Can you not look out upon this world and see how beneficently God has provided for us? When you look upon the magnificence of the design of every little bit of this creation that sustains us, can you really believe that it all happened just through chance and mechanics, the way the evolutionists claim? When you look upon the many prophecies that have come true, and the unfolding of all our lives, can you really doubt that there is a loving God that looks out for us all and is moving history according to His Plan and Purpose? **Kenneth**

Sorry Kenneth, but in a word, "Yes." Yes to all those questions. Except maybe the first, the one about ingratitude—I do think life is a trip. *This was Larry responding.* But as for those other questions. . . . I am at a loss to know just how you reached your so-firm conclusions from the evidence of the world around us. What, for example, leads you to believe that God has provided so wonderfully for us? **Larry**

Look about you, *Kenneth replied*. Look at the marvels that make life itself possible— the atmosphere, the temperatures neither so hot as to burn us up nor so cold as to freeze us to death. Imagine how terrible it would be if the things that we need— such as water to drink, or our daily bread to eat—were as scarce as the superfluities like diamonds and gold. God made the fruit that we eat to taste sweet; if He were so cruel as many of you make Him out to be, He certainly could have made them bitter. It is so easy to take all this for granted, but our existence depends moment by moment on a great many of God's benefactions. **Kenneth**

Kenneth, I have a fond feeling for you, especially after the way you shared that lovely account of your transformative experience under the stars that night when you were a young man, *Larry began*. But I somehow despair of our ever achieving any kind of meeting of minds on such an issue as this. So often it seems to be—as Ralph said earlier about the belief in heaven and hell—that what's supposed to be the conclusion of your inquiry is really contained in the original premises. You seem to be reasoning in a different direction from what I have learned to do.

Take this blessing of the abundance of necessities. From my point of view, that proves nothing about the benevolence of a Creator. Reason back in the other direction: what if it were *otherwise?* what would happen then? The answer is, that we would not be here to talk about it. Or, to put it another way, any creatures that came to live in any environment would necessarily have for their necessities only those things that were available in adequate quantities.

I enjoy a delicious ripe apple probably as much as you do, and I am grateful to be alive to have the pleasure of savoring it. But as for what that proves, I ask you: how else would a creature develop but to find tasty those pieces of its environment that nourish its body? **Larry**

I know nothing about your life, Larry, *Kenneth answered,* so I can say nothing about how the hand of God may or may not have guided your course, or how you may or may not be working as part of His greater plan for things. But in my own life, I have felt the hand of the Lord upon me, and not only that night under the stars that I've told about. There have been times when what I wanted to happen was not given to me, and then some time later I saw that the course things had taken was really all for the better. There was one night when the brakes gave out on our car when we were driving on a windy mountain road, the car overturned, and it was a miracle that we were able to escape from that mishap alive. I know that God was watching over us.

I know that, if your mind is set upon not believing, nothing I will say to you will bring you to see this precious light. But take it from me, I have had many experiences that have shown me how that light is leading the way in my life. **Kenneth**

I'm glad that you and your family escaped from that car accident unscathed, Kenneth, or at least alive, *Cynthia wrote.* But I am wondering, what about the people whose cars spin out of control and are killed? Wasn't God looking out for them? **Cynthia**

God has His reasons for taking people to Him when he does. His reasons are not always for us to fathom, *Kenneth replied.* Sometimes He chooses to spare us, sometimes to test us. Whatever He sends our way, my faith tells me, ultimately it is for the best. **Kenneth**

I've never been particularly enthusiastic about the logical positivists' ideas about **falsifiability,** according to which no proposition that is not falsifiable is meaningful, *Cynthia posted next.* But there does seem to be an obstreperous epistemological barrier here, Kenneth. And again it seems a matter of evidence being bent to fit a preconceived conclusion.

Sometimes on the news I'll see someone who was one of, say, two people who survived the crash of an airliner. Or perhaps the survivor was someone who was supposed to be on the plane but, at the last minute, could not make the flight and thus was spared the fatal crash that snuffed out everyone on board. And then we're shown this survivor in front of the camera, shaken but feeling blessed to be alive, and declaring, "God was looking out for me." And I want to scream at the TV set: "But what about the other 140 people who are dead? What makes you think that somehow your being alive is a sign of God's special favor when the only reason you're the one in front of the camera is that the others are dead?"

I interrupted my reading of Cynthia's message to note with wonderment that it was that very evening on the news that I'd heard a woman, who'd survived an unusually violent tornado that had practically obliterated her hometown of Jarrell, Texas, and had killed dozens of people, declare to a newsman: "I don't know how we survived, when so many around us didn't. I do know that there's a reason, and that some day we'll find out what it is." I turned back to the end of Cynthia's message.

How would the world look any different, Kenneth, if God were not involving himself in doing favors for some, tempering the souls of others with suffering, submitting others to tests? Would not such a world look precisely like the one we see around us now, one in which a certain percentage of people get cancer while others do not, in which some are struck by lightning while the great majority escape that fate, where a few people win the lottery while most lose money by playing, where you survived the overturning of your car but others die by the side of the road, and where for every plane crash that kills many there will be a few who feel that they've had a close brush with mortality but have been somehow favored by fate, or chance, or the hand of the Lord? **Cynthia**

It's like taking candy from a baby, Cynthia, your making this argument against Kenneth's providential God. And I fear it may be just as disreputable a thing to do, *Larry wrote,* though I confess I was engaged in the same attempted theft. I've had the same thoughts.

I remember watching the Olympics a while back in Atlanta, and this American runner—Gail Devers was her name, I think—had a disappointing race and did not win as expected. And in the inevitable post-race interview, up close and personal, a tranquil Devers was telling the sportscaster "It wasn't my time. Everything happens for a reason." And she is at peace because she has faith that—in the context of some larger, benign plan—the outcome was what it should be.

The other day, I went to pick up my daughter at the home of a friend, and got into a conversation with the friend's parents. A propos of something, I forget what, I told them about a big disappointment I'd had—something that I'd wanted for a long time, that seemed on the verge of happening, and that had fallen through at the last minute for reasons outside my control. They responded by saying they knew just what that felt like, because they were going through something much the same. The mother had applied for a job to teach in the same school that the father taught at, a job that would have spared her two hours a day of commuting to her present teaching job. There seemed to be *no good reason* why the school wouldn't have picked her for the job, and plenty why they would. But, without explanation, the job was given to someone else. They were very disappointed. So we talked and commiserated.

But here's the point. Their experience was not the same as mine actually, because it turned out that they had something I don't: faith—faith in the kind of divine providence that Kenneth is talking about. They were saying that it was probably for the best, even though they didn't see just *how* that would be, that there will probably prove to be some reason why this course of events will serve better than the one that they, in their human fallibility, had thought the more desirable. And with that faith, they enjoyed a kind of peace and comfort that someone like me—for whom every disappointment or catastrophe can be a learning opportunity, but is nonetheless never redeemed from being essentially *bad news*—does not enjoy.

When I was younger, I worked in a hospital, and I saw plenty of evidence that for people with that kind of faith, life's trials and torments are more bearable than for the faithless if more clearsighted likes of me.

So is it not a kind of theft to try to pry loose such beliefs? **Larry**

I must confess to one of my own occasional, rather heretical thoughts, *Rev. George wrote to the forum*. Some weeks ago I was watching the unfolding saga of these terrible floods in North Dakota. What an ordeal those people were going through. And then— *mirabile dictu*—out of nowhere comes this anonymous California woman giving to every victimized family in Grand Forks a check for $2,000. Now that's a good order, I thought: these people working so heroically to save their homes from the flood, but overwhelmed by destiny, and here comes this guardian angel to help lift them out of the pit. And the idea popped into my head: now wouldn't it be great if God operated like that! **Rev. George**

How do you know that this was not God operating like that? **Kenneth**

No one addressed that question from Kenneth. Instead, the next posting was a musing from Herman about some of the emotional needs that may color people's concepts of the surrounding cosmos.

It seems that human beings need to see the universe in some way that *makes sense, Herman wrote*. But what does "make sense" mean? It seems to mean, for one thing, at least for most people, that somebody is in charge, that there is a reason for what happens. Not just a cause-and-effect type of reason, but one that makes sense emotionally. And that kind of reason, it seems, has to have a moral dimension.

We want neither to be the playthings of chance, nor of completely capricious and impersonal forces. That so much of our fate *appears* capricious poses a serious challenge to our getting that need met. And so there have been a number of cosmologies that do posit deities that act on whim, rather than on any kind of consistent principle. But it seems to me that the direction of the pull, as religious ideas evolve, is generally toward an image of moral forces governing the unfolding of events. I suppose— if my observation is correct—this could be explained, by believers, as a growing understanding of the true nature of the cosmos, and I'm willing to concede that at some level that may be true. But to me this belief appears to me above all to be a reflection of our own emotional predispositions.

We want our cosmos not only to dispense justice, but to radiate benevolence as well. At times I have wondered how believers in the biblical religious tradition have been able simultaneously to ponder the stories in their sacred text *and* maintain a belief in the God Jehovah's complete and pure goodness. His behavior in those stories does not seem to me the image of such wonderful goodness. I wonder if the stories come from an era in which the **power** of God—as seen by a people caught up in the capricious and painful forces of history—was the central truth, and that His benevolence became a major focus only later, when they were, awkwardly, already stuck with the God who smites and rages as we see this one do.

And then, of course, there is the story of Job: the infliction by God of terrible suffering upon a good and upright man, and for what? To win a bet with His Adversary, Satan, who teases and challenges Him. For all His thundering back at Job to silence him, it is not clear that the story really justifies God. Satan's challenge to God has been met by Job, but Job's challenge to God remains unanswered—or unsatisfactorily answered—by the ruler of the universe who created the whirlwind.

In more modern times, coincident with the rise of scientific thinking, the written texts have been more and more explicitly supplemented by the text of the world itself as a source of evidentiary clues about the nature of its Creator. It is in this context that notions such as those Kenneth was raising have been brought forth: the sweetness of the apple, the plenitude of our necessities, and so forth. Creation regarded as text to be used to praise God from whom all blessings flow.

But as several people have observed here, the conclusions about the nature of this Creator seem to have been given before the text of the world was closely consulted. Confirmation of belief seems to be the purpose, not really the testing of them. This idea that this is the "best of all possible worlds," for example, has been around for a while, but I'm not sure just how rigorous the intellectual process ever was that gave rise to it, *Herman continued*. What is the method by which one assesses the limits of possibility in the "possible worlds"? How does the idea of "possibility" come to limit what the Omnipotent Creator of the Universe might have crafted?

As for me, I stand in awe of this Creation. But I am uncertain how much of the kind of sense that we humans seem generally to need—or at least to want—can be derived from this cosmos, taken as a text. **Herman**

Your discussion crystallizes in my awareness some ideas that had been lingering in the shadows of my mind since the earlier exchange about heaven and hell and all that, *Larry posted next*. It was Carl, I believe, who maintained that the defects of the world are all the result of fallen and sinful humankind. But if we take human beings and their defects out of the picture, and go back to the time prior to human existence, and look then at the world, it is not clear that what we see there is so ideal. Think of all that eating of flesh, of parasites in the gut, of diseases of all kinds. Think of all the eons of time of lifeless matter swirling in space.

An incredible panorama. Absolutely awesome in scale and complexity. But there's a thought experiment I've done on occasion with results that have been, for me, pretty unsettling. Here's the experiment. I open my mind to everything I know about the cosmos and how it works: from the microscopic to the astronomical. Then I posit that there is, indeed, a Creator behind it all. And then I ask: what can we infer about the nature of such a Creator, and what Its purposes or goals or values or feelings or needs or whatever might be? And the result, when that experiment is performed in *my* head, is a strange and ineffable mixture of thoughts and feelings—but whatever else it may be, the amorphous image is not a warm or cozy, or particularly benign, or even moral one. **Larry**

This is all so terribly bleak and unsettling, *wrote Alice*. How could one possibly live in a universe that had no morality to it? A cruel joke is what it would be, to have creatures like us—with the awareness that comes with being *homo sapiens,* with the kinds of needs you've described, Herman—living in a creation that stands before us not as a **good creation,** but as cold and indifferent. Part of that cruel joke seems to be that this unsettling perception seems to be the fruit of all that marvelous intellectual progress we've made over the centuries—the kind of progress that allows us to know that the universe did not just spring into existence five thousand years ago, but has been churning and swirling for many billions of years, that tells us that whatever the nature of any Creator there might be, He (or She, or It) was in absolutely no hurry to move the cosmic drama ahead to the scene where we humans appear. Not the sixth day, not even the six-billionth year.

But, of course, it seems pretty clear that at least some of you are bent upon depicting the Creation without a Creator. And that feels quite desolate, too. Alone in the universe, without the caring—even if sometime punitive—presence of someone for Whom what we do and how we fare really matters. A universe just of accident, right? That's what you have in mind? No "good order" as the source from which we spring, just accident. Nothing above us to guide us, to order us, with which we should align ourselves. Just chaos and chance. It makes me shiver. **Alice**

The image of the universe that we come to—if we employ our reason to an openminded viewing of the evidence displayed by the cosmos—lacks some of the comforting amenities of the top-down cosmology of our religious traditions, *Herman answered*

Alice. But—to my mind—it is not so cold or barren, nor so chaotic and senseless, as you seem to imagine. I think there is a way of comprehending our situation that can integrate and harmonize some of what our religious traditions tend to leave dichotomized and polarized. We do lose something, but something is gained, too. If we take out of the picture the kind of God that Carl and Kenneth hold before us, we have a chance to see the world no longer as fallen but, in some important and wonderful way, as rising. **Herman**

I take it this is that "evolutionary perspective" you mentioned earlier, *Ralph wrote.* Well, I'm receptive enough to the idea of evolution. The Garden of Eden has always seemed to me just a myth from an earlier phase of civilization, and I just assume that whatever is true has to be consistent with an evolutionary history of life on earth. I know that not **all** of us on this forum are of that mind, but I expect a good number of us are. So if you think that perspective has something to offer in the context of the kinds of issues of morality and good order we've been wrestling with, I'd like to hear about it. **Ralph**

As several other people then posted messages in concurrence with Ralph, Herman commenced this exploration of an evolutionary approach to the question of good order.

Interlude

A Hand in the Miracle

The Creature in the Creation

There's more to my life, of course, than the forum. More even to my work. My next radio show on WSVA was coming in a week, and I was groping around for a good topic. It had not been very long since "Dolly," the cloned sheep, had been in the headlines, and a 63-year-old woman had recently given birth to a baby conceived using someone else's ovum. It occurred to me that it might make for a worthwhile show to raise the overarching question that these developments, and a great many others, bring to my mind: what limits, if any, should there be in what human beings allow themselves to do in remaking the natural order?

That's an important question for humankind in general in our era, but I thought it might be especially provocative for my audience in the Shenandoah Valley. On the one hand, many of these are people who by and large adhere closely to traditional morality, with its associated skepticism about human wisdom and goodness. The idea of people "playing God" is anathema to them, as I learned in a previous show several years before where the question was about the appropriateness of people committing suicide, or even getting assistance in doing so, when they are suffering from illness and great distress from which no relief would ever come except through death. On the other hand, these same people are gung ho for capitalism, and for "getting government off the back of the American people," and they are forever bemoaning the regulatory state that sets limits on what can and cannot be done in the pursuit of profit.

I have often tried to point out that there could be, in an unregulated economy, profits without honor. But many of the people who would call it a sin for human beings to play God would also speak derisively about the Endangered Species Act. A caller might speak of "free enterprise" as if waving that phrase proved it was OK for some developer, in the pursuit of profit, to remove from the earth some unique life-form with an ancestry reaching back as far into the primordial ooze as our own. Of course, the tracing of ancestry back to the primordial ooze was not a perspective about whose validity all these Virginia conservatives concur with me. But some people unalterably opposed to the idea that a Darwinian process of self-organization could possibly have brought about anything so well-ordered as ourselves will nevertheless accept unquestioningly the idea that the Adam-Smithian process of self-organization through the market economy will yield ideal outcomes on which no intervening authority could improve.

With these competing systems of thought both active in my audience, sometimes in the very same minds, I thought it quite possible that my raising the question of "the role of the creature in the creation" might help to focus thought on some important but neglected nodes of contradiction.

The more I thought about this question, however, the more blurry it got before my eyes. It seemed to me that the business of remaking the natural order was as old as civilization. The forebears of these Shenandoah farmers had, themselves, come into a wooded valley and stripped it of trees in order to make room for the growing of crops, creating what was to become the "breadbasket of the Confederacy." Was that playing God? And the crops they grew had been the outgrowth of a process, stretching across millennia, of domestication and selective breeding by which people had taken the wild forms of plants (as well as animals) and rendered them into new kinds of plants more productive of what humans wanted, or more docile to human control. Was this playing God? Is the breeding of big-eared corn to increase bushels of harvested grain per acre, or of big-uddered cows to increase gallons of milk per animal, different—in some fundamental way that bears upon the moral and ethical issues involved—from the alteration of animals through recombinant DNA? Or is the only significant difference that the first set of changes was effected over many generations by people who barely knew they were making important decisions, whereas today people can effect changes virtually overnight, and with full awareness that they are tinkering with the design of life? Or is the difference that we take for granted what was established before our own time, but feel unease about the next steps along the same trail?

Coming to the conclusion that I was not prepared to launch the conversation without first getting clearer in my own thinking about some of these issues, without being readier to respond—on my virtual feet, and in a very public setting—to the kinds of ideas and examples my listeners were likely to present, I decided that I'd better do some consultation with some of my friends around the country. So I sent out an e-mail to about a dozen people I knew whose insight I thought might help advance my thinking.

After introducing the issue—talking, as above, about genetic engineering, and the history of farming, and a few other ripples of the expanding topic—I concluded in this way:

One might take the position that we have a right to do anything we have the ability to do. If one rejects this position, then the challenge is to enunciate the principles that differentiate what is going too far and what is not.

The idea that there are things beyond the appropriate reach of mere mortals is an ancient one—Icarus, Frankenstein, a million sci-fi flicks—and I expect that it is well represented in my listening area. But the forces working to push past all bounds seem also quite powerful. Where would wisdom come down in this conflict, and how should that boundary be defined?

At present, I do not feel prepared to pose these issues, or play Socrates in relation to the likely points, well enough to do the topic justice. Any suggestions about how to go about it? about examples that will help elicit good discussion? about points that should be anticipated? about useful probes or challenges to those anticipated points?

Your suggestions are welcome, if you want to play. **Andy**

A number of them did, indeed, want to play. One of my friends wrote back:

In raising this question, are you suggesting that we might embrace once again that antiquated notion that there should be limits to human understanding? Or perhaps only limits to what human beings should permit themselves to *do* with the power that comes from increased knowledge?

It occurred to me that I had never, with my Enlightenment upbringing, even considered the possibility of shutting the door to human knowledge or thought. It was only regarding the actions that might be taken on the basis of the knowledge that I had concern. But my friend's question did prompt me to wonder how realistic it was to think that humankind might possess powers and yet voluntarily refrain from exercising them. As I thought about this, the image came to my mind of the commandment in Eden, "Don't eat of the fruit of this particular tree."

Another correspondent, Frederick Turner, poet and philosopher and evolutionary thinker at the University of Texas, replied to my query by e-mailing me a copy of a talk that, by coincidence, he'd just been delivering in Indiana at the time my inquiry arrived in his inbox. In the paper he'd delivered there, Turner had written:

Bioengineering, even including the altering of human genes, is ethically defensible, since nature has already been engaged in the activity for billions of years, and the ability to perform it ourselves was given to us by nature. In Spielberg's and Crichton's *Jurassic Park,* and in a great many other politically correct popular entertainments, there is an implicit argument that God made living organisms, and that they should not be tampered with or claimed as intellectual property. This idea leads immediately to absurdities. It would, for instance, make it illegal to sell thoroughbred horses and cattle or put them out to stud. . . . To be absolutely literalistic, such logic would even forbid marriage, since marriage connects economic obligations with selective reproductive planning.

This is not to say that any proposed genetic intervention is permissible. Genetics is a fantastically complex subject, and it is extremely difficult to predict the consequences of actions in this area. The ethics governing any weighty, far-reaching decision apply more strongly to biogenetic intervention than anywhere else. The work should be fail-safe, and every possible consequence should be examined. But on the other hand, all human decisions are subject to unpredictable consequences. This is the tragic field of action.[1]

When I had composed my e-mail message of inquiry, I had feared that my friends would think me absurd to lump Dolly the clone with the likes of thoroughbreds (connecting modern genetic engineering with the ancient practice of selective breeding), but not only had that fear proved groundless, but now here I was, on the other side of that issue, feeling that Fred Turner was lumping too much together in describing marriage in terms of "selective reproductive planning."

Marriage a form of tampering with nature? To me, marriage upset no natural order, but rather was just a way of putting a cultural stamp on a process of genetic transmission that had been there since long before we humans, with our newfound powers to reshape our lives into forms in no way given in our genes, had arisen. But to Turner, *all* our powers were, at the most fundamental level, to be understood as having been endowed within us by nature, and thus they and their effects were continuous with the natural. To me the distinction between natural and unnatural was an important one, whereas to Turner that dinstinction clearly was—pardon the expression—an artificial one.

But at least as pertinent as that issue, for my present purposes, was this question of consequences. Certainly, Turner was right: our powers so often outstrip our wisdom that our exercise of them can make us a bull in a biospheric china shop. "Forgive us, Father, we know not what we do." ("So, why don't you stop doing it, then?" is how I imagine Father responding.) But there was more to the problem than *unintended* consequences. What about consequences that we might intend, but that are not legitimate, that are somehow unjust?

As I was considering this question, my brother Ed wrote me a response that helped bring that issue into focus:

> One way of putting it to your religiously conservative people is:
> In the Bible it talks about us being on top of creation, and being the ones to rule over it. But it also talks about selfishness being sinful. How do these relate to the issue of dominating over the environment, exploiting it to the point of destroying species?
> I think an important question here is the "for whom?" Is it for all creatures that we engineer or just for us?

Yes, that was what was most troubling about this issue. It is here that the distinction between the natural and the unnatural becomes meaningful. Ideally, one could see humanity as the best tool that life possesses for extending and elaborating and elevating the domain of living nature. We humans might act as the agent's of life's empire in a lifeless universe. But there is also a problematic dimension that emerges when one part of an interdependent system gains power over the whole. How are we to police ourselves? And from where get the wisdom to pass the laws such policing would enforce? Is the species that turns chickens into egg-laying machines confined within a cubic foot of space, that strips tropical forests—squandering eternal biological treasures for temporary riches—is such a species to be entrusted with the job of delving into the blueprints for all of life's designs?

Even after contemplating the responses that my query had elicited, I still felt unsure about how effectively I'd do such a show. In that state of uncertainty, I went out to do some physical work, hoping that things would become clearer in the process. It was still fairly early in the spring—not so early by the calendar, but with the unusually cold spells we'd had through April, it was still early by the look of the land—and I was still putting seed into the ground, as well as transplanting a few of the seedlings I'd begun indoors. And now there were lilacs to pick for the table, as well as a few remaining daffodils. And the tomatoes indoors I'd begun from seed were showing signs of readiness to start their blooming.

The Magic of It

It was almost magical how the work of gardening unknit the tensions I had been feeling. Not so much from the actual physical labor, or the caking of the hands with the soil. More from the joy of the little discoveries I would come upon: the asparagus that weren't there the last time I looked—was it just yesterday, or the day before?—now shooting their spears out of the trench I'd dug for them a year before; the sprigs of thyme that I now found were coming out of the soil within a five-foot radius of that great bush of thyme that the howling wind of one April night had blown clear away. (I'd joked about it not being possible to make up for lost thyme, but now here was the earth showing me that it had found a way to do just that.)

It was then and there that I decided that I'd put off the show about the limits to human powers, and do a program instead on "What makes gardening meaningful?" I knew from poll data that an extraordinary proportion of Americans consider gardening an important hobby of theirs, and it seemed that every home around here, however modest, had its little garden plot, at least gestures of gardening. Perhaps it would be a successful show like one I'd done before about "The Land and People of the Shenandoah Valley." On that occasion, I'd invited listeners to call in and share whatever meaningful experiences they'd had with this land that affected how it felt for them to live in the area, and I was delighted how many presumably simple people were able to find a place of poetry within themselves and were willing to call in to share it publicly. The experience of gardening, I thought, might likewise bring out such poetry.

This decision brought me immediate delight. It felt right, at this point, to do a program about sharing experience rather than arguing issues. The most recent show I'd done had been about whether government should use its legal powers to protect people from themselves. Dealing with such issues as sexual morality, the "war on drugs," gambling, etc., this program had engaged that point of tension between two strains of conservatives—the libertarians and the moral conservatives. It was an stimulating show, but it seemed to me, upon reflection, that the question of the proper limits to the human empire was too similar to be the right show to do immediately afterward. Better to convene a more embracing, less contentious, forum—one that simply allows experience to speak its voice, telling stories of the kind that bring us together, free of the need to reach the kinds of judgments that divide us. Let's just witness one another's humanity this time, I felt. And the topic of gardening was one that was close to my own heart, especially this time of the year.

Now, I wondered, how can I launch the conversation? Have I myself ever been eloquent about gardening? Not really. And it could be dangerous if I invite such calls without having much to say, myself, that could serve to get the pump primed. Ah yes, I did write a piece last summer, it occurred to me. "On the Rationality of Gardening" it was called, and it was published in the *Christian Science Monitor*. I could begin the show by reading that.

For this purpose, however, it was not an ideal piece. As I recalled the article, my attempt was less to speak eloquently about the experience of gardening than to critique the kind of "rationality" that underlies the cost-benefit analysis of conventional economics. The piece began with my contemplating the damage to my pumpkin crop inflicted by hedgehogs, and wondering—as I set up fortifications around the surviving plants—whether it made sense to expend so much of my labor just for a few pumpkins when, come fall, I could purchase from local farmers pumpkins as good as mine for less money than I'd be paid, at minimum wage, for my pumpkin-growing labors. Then I summoned up a recollection of a friend who, reckoning up the costs of growing his modest cucumber crop at five dollars apiece, vowed never to garden again. And from there I proceeded to speak of a different way of calculating the costs and benefits: the costs reduced by taking into account the pleasure of the activity in itself, and the benefits magnified by including something of the spiritual yield of being part of this living process.

It was regarding this latter, spiritual dimension that I had written a little about the meaning of gardening. For example, in the passage: "For the part-time gardener, the means is part of the end, and it enriches beyond the production of a mere commodity that can be purchased in stores. I become connected with the organic processes of the earth in a way that pulling some produce off the counter could never do. I participate in a miracle. . . . Tonight, when I combine the berries [I'd gathered by hand from our hillside] with yogurt and cinnamon, the result may taste no different than if the berries had been store-bought. But for my family and me, it will not be the same bowlful of food. We will be savoring also our place on the earth, the ground on which we live."[2]

Was that bit of evocative prose enough to encourage the kinds of calls I'd hoped would come? Pretty meager and sketchy, I thought. Doesn't begin to capture the way art and magic combine in the gardening experience. "Art" in the way that the land becomes my canvas—a space in which I can mix form and color and texture in the attempt to create a beautiful order. And "magic" in the way that, though my hand places the elements into their pattern, the most profound unfolding is not at all of my doing.

It may be I who drops the seed, but what the seed does then in its given domain comes from a source of design way beyond me. It may be I who says "Sunflower, grow here," but the way the small seed—even as I sleep, and eat, and tend to my business—turns earth and water and light into this bulbous golden lamp of gleaming seeds—that draws upon a power not under my command. It's as though a composer had only to place a few notes upon the paper, and they turned themselves into a symphony.

At best, my hand in the miracle is like the conductor bringing the music and the musicians together and with his baton helps them play ensemble. Or perhaps it is more like the waving of the magic wand. Or maybe my role should be seen as still more humble, like that of the magician's assistant who, with a gesture toward the wonder that the performer of stupendous tricks has accomplished, says with her hand, "Behold!"

It's important to the spiritual dimension of my experience that I have a role. I love to visit fabulous gardens that put my comparatively feeble efforts to shame, but it is my own duet with the earth that best lets my spirit sing. I do not forget, however, that my role is not so much to create as to make possible the creation—to open the space for special seeds and the earth to work their wonders, clearing out the unwanted competition, providing food and water. When the earth is turned into the fragrance of the basil leaf, or the crimson rose petal, I will say, "Look what I grew," but really I know otherwise. Even when Nathaniel was born, so perfectly formed, April and I knew that we'd not really grown him.

With such thoughts, combined with the previously written piece from the *Monitor,* I felt I had enough to be able to launch and to lead a good conversation on the subject. I came in from the gardening to hear that my phone was ringing. Racing to get to it before the fourth ring, when my machine would come in, I picked it up and was greeted by my mother's voice. She was just checking in, wanting to know what was new. I answered by telling her of the decision I'd just made about the topic for my next WSVA program. My mother by no means shares my enthusiasm for gardening, but she is always there to encourage me in my creative endeavors, and so she was quite happy to make my radio plans a topic for conversation.

"How will you pose the subject for the listeners?" she asked. I told her I'd use the *Monitor* piece, and then reminded her of what that piece had been about. "Ah, maybe you'll find," she suggested, "that by doing this show you'll come up with another idea for a piece for the *Monitor.*"

I discerned a couple of elements behind this suggestion. In the first place, my mother is partial to my work in print, and I'm always proud to send her copies of whatever I get published. And then there was her ongoing awareness of the financial aspect of my situation. She knows that, in my radio shows, I am giving myself away. All this work I do, she observes, and I don't get paid a cent for it. On the one hand, she's proud that I do what I love and I believe in, not allowing the apportionment of rewards by the market place to channel my life. On the other hand, she wants for me to succeed, or at least survive—and since her generosity is one part of the reason that I do manage to keep body and soul together, despite my economically irrational lifecourse, I figure she's entitled to nudge me in various ways, subtle and not, toward making my work pay. And even though writing a piece for publication in the *Monitor* is hardly something one would do for the small remuneration it entails, still, as the economists say, something is decidedly better than nothing. And such considerations fed into my mother's suggestion that I might look to generate another gardening op-ed out of my upcoming radio show.

"Yeah, I suppose it could," I concurred, "but it ain't likely."

"Why not?"

"Mom, I'm surprised at you. You know how creativity works." Indeed, it had been my mother who had taught me most to orient my life around the creative endeavor. She was the playwright, the poet, the one who modeled how becoming the channel of some creative process could bring a special kind of fulfillment. "I'd love to get some nifty insight worth crafting into an op-ed. But that kind of creativity is not something that I can get on command. If it comes to me, it comes to me."

We talked a few minutes about how in the classical world this recognition of the way creativity came from someplace beyond our power to control was expressed in the image of the Muses. They were sacred beings who might visit a person with the gift of the creative insight. "Genius," as the word's derivation showed, was not understood as the property of an individual, but rather as a sign of the presence of some special spirit.

And indeed, this has been my own experience. Even aside from one life-changing moment of vision in which I felt that I had—somehow—actually been *shown* something, my own creative insights have felt like something that happened through me, not from the exercise of my own conscious design. All that I feel I can do by my own intention and decision—I was now telling my mother—is to prepare myself by various disciplines of opening and preparation, such as doing yoga as a way of loosening the soil of my spirit, and engaging in a process of reading and talking with the rich minds of others, as a kind of fertilization.

As soon as I'd said that, I laughed out an audible "Ah hah!" I realized that perhaps my mother's suggestion had already borne the fruit she'd expressed the hope for: in that metaphor in which the process of gardening and the process of creative writing had come together, I felt something essential had been captured about what I believe to be an ideal for the whole process of human creation. That it happens at our hands, but also happens through and beyond us. That we have a hand in the miracle, but that it is also not only a matter of our own purposes. That there is a partnership involved here between the intentions of the human sphere, and the mysterious powers of living nature with its mysterious unfolding.

"Thanks, Mom," I said. "I'll see what I can come up with."

Under Construction
An Evolutionary View of Order

The Darwinian Ban on Skyhooks

Was there ever an idea at once so elegant and so significant? A number of us on the forum shared a great enthusiasm for the basic Darwinian idea. It was not Darwin's alone, of course. Indeed it had been in the air, wafting on the reverberations of Newton's clockwork universe, of Adam Smith's self-regulating market, of Malthus's dismal vision of reproduction outstripping subsistence. But Darwin's achievement had been considerable nonetheless, and when Herman brought the discussion, with some encouragement from others, to focus on the evolutionary vision of our origins, we spent a bit of time simply admiring it.

Here was a vision of how order could come into existence from the ground up. Start with the simplest life and just add time enough and, presto! the tree of life unfolds with incredible inventiveness and grandeur. More even than that, the origin of life, too, can emerge without being directed by purpose: start with a cosmos with stuff and time enough and there will emerge enough different scenes with enough different conditions that someplace it is possible and perhaps inevitable that the drama of life itself will unfold on its own out of the lifeless universe.

No need for a watchmaker on the scene to assemble the watch—to refer to that old image employed by those to whom it had been obvious that the presence of Design must necessarily prove the existence of a Designer. No need for the miraculous, no need for any One to be in charge. No need, in other words, for what Daniel Dennett, in a book to which Herman made reference,[1] for a *skyhook*.

A "skyhook" in this image is something that does not rest on any ground. It is something that does not emerge from below. It is the quintessence of the top-down kind of ordering. It is an ordering agency that exists prior to any of the material below that it proceeds to order. God is the Ultimate Skyhook.

The kind of ordering to be contrasted with the skyhook, the kind revealed by Darwin's insight, Dennett dubbed the "crane." The "crane" may reach down from above, but it itself rests on the ground.

The genius of Darwin's insight was that it showed—with such elegant simplicity—how mere mechanism plus chance would inevitably, over time, create order. What works and can perpetuate itself tends to spread; what doesn't work and cannot perpetuate itself will disappear. Over time, therefore, the world is permeated by those forms, arising by chance, that can maintain and reproduce themselves. The name of this key idea is "natural selection," and natural selection is a crane.

Predictably, there were several people on the forum—those most invested in the the received skyhooks of our religious traditions—who challenged the Darwinian position. "Just a theory," was one claim. "Questioned even by biologists," was another. But the critiques really amounted to nothing of substance, and a couple of people—including Herman and Cynthia—were so steeped in those scientific findings (from several different fields) bearing upon evolutionary theory that it was established to my satisfaction, and I would say to that of any really open-minded and rational person, that the evolution of life on earth is as established a fact as virtually anything in science.

Science may not understand absolutely everything about electricity or about gravity, either. But we do not dismiss these ideas as "mere theory." The only reason, it seems evident, that some people are eager to belittle evolution as "just a theory," or to seize upon controversies in the field as evidence of how insubstantial is the scientific edifice of evolutionary understanding, is that the theory of evolution—unlike those of electricity or of gravity—poses a serious threat to their world view. Their dilemma is one for which I feel some compassion, but I also had to concur with a line from Dennett that Herman quoted, however harsh it may be— something to the effect that there is no intellectually defensible basis for not believing in the basic truth of the evolutionary perspective.

Evolution happened. There is room for a variety of uncertainties about some of the whats and whens and hows of it. But the basic validity of evolutionary theory is as well established as virtually anything else we understand about our world. That was the framework within which at least most of us conducted our discussion of Herman's assertion that an evolutionary perspective could give us some help with our quest to understand the sources of good order.

A Crane Is Not a Pyramid

When we turned from that general discussion of evolutionary theory to the more immediate purposes of our particular forum, Larry posed what I found to be a clarifying question.

I'm still stuck with that Zeno's paradox of a problem, guys, *Larry wrote*. You remember: it seemed to me, and not only to me, that we'd pretty much demolished the chances of finding a reliable source of good order. Both the bottom-up and the top-down approaches had been somehow discredited. And though Ralph and I disagreed about how serious the resulting challenge was, and though Jeff was content with the fact that we **do** get some good order, even if we can't explain how—just as Achilles **does** overtake the tortoise, Zeno's paradoxical argument notwithstanding—the question remains unanswered in my mind: do we have an insoluble problem or not, and if not, then what's the solution?

Now, I can see, Herman, how your evolutionary view undercuts the skyhook worldview of the God-centered among us. (Although how can you undercut a skyhook?) But for all I can tell from what you've said to this point, evolution is just another way of packaging the old bottom-up approach. And, starting with Andy's posing of the Nintendo Dilemma, and at several junctures since, we've been there and found that approach wanting. Most recently, we revisited what was called a Taoistic view and once again seemed to see defects in that purely bottom-up approach. So what I want to ask you, Herman, is this: How is the evolutionary view you're proposing to be distinguished from the bottom-up ideas we already discussed? In other words, if Taoist ideas don't fill the bill for me, will I find in yours a satisfactory solution to that Zeno-paradoxical problem I bewailed a while back? **Larry**

I don't want to over-promise here, Larry, *Herman responded*. If by "satisfactory solution" you mean a way of understanding good order that makes everything easy and straightforward, let me hasten to confess that I've got nothing of the sort up my sleeve. Carl's Skyhook of a God, who hands down unquestionable command-ments on Sinai, gives him a kind of clarity about what is required of him that noth-ing in my perspective will offer. (I'll leave aside the kinds of problems—logical as well as evidentiary—with Carl's position that some of us have pointed out along the way.)

But I do believe that this perspective may afford us a way of broadening our under-standing of the bottom-up approach beyond what's been offered, for example, by what was called here the Taoist position. And the key here is that while evolution builds from below, what it builds includes structures that order from above. Let me see if I can explain.

Do you remember the idea that surfaced very early in our conversations, the idea that nature does not build only one-story buildings? That, it seems to me, points to an important piece that sometimes gets left out of some—I would say, simplistic—bottom-up perspectives. What is simplistic is to say, "Hey, there's nothing above me. Let's just do what comes naturally. Go with the flow." But nature is often putting dams in the way of the flow. Every living thing, and every piece of every living thing, is embedded in orders that circumscribe its freedom of operation. Evolution creates a stratified system. And that goes for the system in which we—as individual human actors—are embedded, too.

Do you see what I mean? Or should I elaborate? **Herman**

Elaborate, by all means, *Larry replied*. I mean, is it not the essence of the Darwinian idea that everything just unfolded, with no direction? Isn't it all a matter of things "going with the flow?" **Larry**

Yes and no, *Herman answered*. Yes, it all simply unfolds. But what unfolds is a many-leveled structure. What works is not "anything goes" but an ordered system. Over time, what we see is that elements that used to "do their own thing"—as it were—start being impelled by the order in which they are embedded to keep their 'thing' aligned with some larger order.

We could probably start at the level of inanimate matter, but let's look instead at our own bodies. Not only does it turn out that each cell in our bodies is the fruit of historical mergers between previously separate lines of living organisms. (I'm thinking here of the way the mitochondria in our cells give evidence of being symbiants that joined at some point with the ancestors of the rest of those cells.)[2] But also as multicel-lular creatures, we keep our individual cells—whose ancient ancestors were autono-mous one-celled animals—very strictly in line.

Why should we assume that this process of stratification of ordered systems neces-sarily must stop with the human individual sitting on top of the edifice with nothing but the clear sky of untrammeled freedom above us? **Herman**

Cynthia came in swiftly after this to buttress Herman's remark with some conceptual framework.

What I think is key to what Herman's driving at here, *Cynthia wrote,* is the concept of **emergence**. Emergence is what gives the bottom-up theory of evolution a way out of the kind of collapsing view of the world contained in reductionism. Reductionism is the kind of thinking that says that *A,* which is made up of *B,* is "nothing but" *B.* But emergence says that when a lot of *B* gets organized into the level of *A,* the ordering principles that govern *B* are not sufficient to explain *A.*

Maybe that's way too abstract. This level of thought is always somewhat abstract, but I can get more specifc. We're made up of atoms, which is physics; and the atoms get organized into molecules, which gets to be chemistry; and the chemistry becomes the substratum for biological processes, and so on. At each level, the elements continue to obey the laws that govern that level, but they also are ordered into another level that is governed by other principles. The atoms in our bodies do not violate the laws of physics, but neither are the laws of physics, or even the laws of chemistry, with which everything that happens is also **consistent,** adequate to explain what's happening at the new level.

Here, let me quote something I read in an article recently by a couple of German scientists. It appears in a book *Self-Organization: Portrait of a Scientific Revolution.* These fellows write about "emergentism": "Emergentism . . . accepts that organisms consist of nothing but physiochemical components. However, for emergentism the knowledge of the properties of these components is not sufficient to deduce the properties of the system. These result from the organization of the system, including the existence of 'hierarchical levels.' "[3]

These "hierarchical levels" comprise, I believe, what we've been calling—following Dennett—the cranes. In other words, in the evolutionary process various levels emerge out of the levels that preceded them: with the emergence of each new level, a higher level of ordering principles is established that holds everything in a sense "from above"; yet those higher-ordered systems themselves developed in a bottom-up fashion, growing up naturally from the earlier and simpler elements. **Cynthia**

Yes that's helpful, *Herman resumed.* The cosmic evolutionary process has been a long process of emergence of new, more highly ordered systems out of the previous, simpler levels. I used the example of the cells within our own bodies—behaving like cells, but also embedded in our larger bodies. But, as Cynthia's concept of emergence as a central dimension of the cosmic evolutionary process suggests, analogous kinds of emergent orderings could be found further back, and—more to the point of our ongoing discussion—further forward in this unfolding process of emergence.

For starters, we could apply this kind of stratified ordering even to the inanimate world. After the original Big Bang, even atoms took some time to form, bringing together particles that had been separate. And at the other (macro-) end of the evolutionary scheme, there has been order created all the way up to the planetary level. The biosphere is more than just the sum of a huge variety of parts, each doing its own thing; it's an extremely ordered system. Not as closely ordered as a single cell, perhaps, in which each molecule is kept in a particular place, but ordered nonetheless. **Herman**

Pretty interesting stuff, Herman and Cynthia, *wrote Larry,* but even if I am a bit clearer from it about the meaning of the "crane," I'm still pretty much in the dark about what this has to do with the bottom-up, countercultural or liberal view of good order. Can you bring these "levels" together? **Larry**

Oh yes, sorry, *Herman responded.* It is something of a leap, since we've not really examined here together just what kinds of orderings may have emerged—or be emerging—with us human beings and our eruption into dominance in the biosphere. Because humankind does represent some new departures in this evolutionary unfolding, at least in the context of life on **this** planet.

But making that leap, here's what I'd say. What I think I discern in some of the countercultural bottom-up thinking is what appears to be an assumption that the ordering process somehow **stops** at the level of the "I" who is doing the talking. "Nothing above me to which I am obliged to conform." But why should it be that an evolutionary process that ordered particles into atoms, and atoms into molecules, and molecules then into living cells, and cells into bodies like ours, would necessarily just screech to a halt and say to us, creatures, "Hey, just do whatever you feel the impulse to do!"?

"Doing what comes naturally" may be fine for a beaver. But since mammalian life came along, there has begun another main event in the history of emergence, and we're it. We're the creatures who bit of the fruit of the tree of the knowledge of good and evil. I'd say, we're the creatures who **had** to bite of it, because of our emergence into an unprecedented kind of freedom. No longer so well regulated by instinct or closely governed by the genetic pattern: hence the emergence of choice, and with it the distinction between those choices that work and those that don't, between good and evil.

With that freedom comes some new burdens, having to do with good order. In a sense, our challenge to create that new order is just the latest stage of emergence, and it's thus a kind of "doing what comes naturally" at a new level of unfolding. But it means we're compelled—unless we're to create disorder—to leave behind at least that straightforward sort of "doing what comes naturally" that the beaver and the other critters are free to enjoy. **Herman**

This evolutionary perspective gives me knots in my stomach, *Rev. George posted next,* since it brings into sharp relief some of the ambiguities and ambivalences I have never managed to resolve. But I think I see what you're saying here, Herman, and it is helpful.

It seems that you are saying that evolution may have created us, fashioned us into the beautiful order that has made pre-Darwinian thinkers marvel at what the hand of the Creator has wrought. But that does not necessarily mean that we have emerged out of this process, to this point, as wholly finished creatures, just fine the way we are, needing nothing further to improve upon the given order we inherit biologically.

Here we are, acting like the Lords of Creation, and some of us have taken to believing that there can be nothing higher than we and our desires. A total rejection of any notion of verticality. Everything on a plane, which of course means that whatever has the most force behind it will inevitably prevail. A kind of Hobbesian psychology ensues, a "state of nature" in which mere power rules in the psyche. Which means that the strongest impulse is the one to be obeyed.

There's a line in Marlowe's *Faustus* that describes such a psyche: "The God thou serv'st is thine own appetite, Wherein is fixed the love of Beelzebub."[4]

In the absence of the proper verticality of psychic organization, what prevails is sin. **Rev. George**

I like that notion of verticality, *Peter chimed in.* It does seem a central issue of our cultural struggles: the question of whether anything is to be conceded to be above something else. And Herman's bringing together this notion of stratification with the evolutionary perspective seems promising. Evolution has always seemed to me so bottom-up, so devoid of any kind of moral principle, that I'm quite excited to discover that there might be some top-down potentialities not only compatible with an evolutionary worldview, but even implied by it (or contained within it). **Peter**

Getting rid of skyhooks in favor of cranes does not mean everything gets leveled, *wrote Ralph.* Cranes are, it should be noted, means of supporting things from above, even if all the weight ultimately does rest on the ground. **Ralph**

Alice wrote next: Like Rev. George, I'm trying to connect this line of discussion with how we've been talking about human nature, and moral order. Last night a conversation with a friend put me in mind of that line that appeared here a while back—from Kant I believe—that nothing straight can ever be made from the crooked timber of humanity.

My friend described himself as a terrible skinflint, one whose urge is to hoard his resources and who finds within himself little spontaneous generosity. But he believes strongly that a person should act very differently from the way his own stingy inclinations pull him. He believes that a good man will give of his resources to make the world a better place, not just look out for himself.

So my friend, feeling a commitment—from someplace within him—to be a good man, comes in from above and declares to his base self, as if from some internal Mt. Sinai, "Thou shalt tithe." And thus, disciplining himself to follow that commandment, he overrules his nature, and takes a dime of every dollar he earns and dedicates it to good causes he thinks serve the world well.

I am trying to translate my friend's work on himself into the language of this conversation we are having here. I'm imagining that if we could look at how his organism evolved, and how subsequently his personality evolved, we would perceive that this voice within him, issuing the commandment to tithe, *is a kind of crane.* Am I right? In other words, if we could see how his "should" developed we would understand it as part of some top-down ordering of human conduct that itself grew out of a bottom-up evolutionary process of individual development embedded in some emergent process of cultural evolution.

To straighten the crooked timber of our humanity, that is, we erect these cranes we call moral structures—from the inner voice to social laws—to command from above in order to correct what is deficient in the natural structure below. Am I right? **Alice**

Before anyone could address Alice's inquiry about whether she was understanding correctly the idea of cranes in relation to moral structures, we had several others jump in to express their reservations about the thrust of this discussion. And these reservations brought to the fore a subject that had been lingering for some time in the background. That subject was the whole question of order, and whether this emphasis on order was healthy or perverse, whether order is something we should welcome or dread.

A Call to Order

I'm getting nervous with this stress upon—and celebration of—verticality, *Jeff wrote.* What I sense is coming here is some kind of notion that the next great phase of evolution is the construction of some big oppressive order that will trample on our liberties. If this "breakthrough" is the solution to our so-called problem, I'll take the problem. **Jeff**

The word "nervous" doesn't do justice to my squeamish feeling, *Fred wrote.* I'm not certain where you are heading, but I think I catch a whiff of that old justifier of the unjustifiable, Social Darwinism.

But what I'd really like to blow the whistle on here, though, is this blithe assumption that order—whether it is top-down or bottom-up—is a god we should be eager to worship. Think of the reverberations of that word, ***order***. *Alles in Ordnung* is not a banner that I will march behind. "Law and order" has never been associated, in my experience, with anything but repression and domination.

We've been talking about "good order" for a long time here, but let me propose that this phrase is an oxymoron. **Fred**

This challenge from Fred to the premise of our discussion was, in fact, both new and not new. Off and on this issue—the question of the value of order—would surface, and then it would disappear. In reporting our discussion, I had been tempted on various occasions to bring that thread to the fore, but somehow I could never find a really suitable place to put it. I'd considered putting it in after chapter 5, when the bottom-ups had received their comeuppance, and before chapter 6, where the top-downs were about to receive their godownance. But I feared that such a digression would interfere with the flow of that dimension of the discussion, obscuring a certain musical rise and fall in the flow of ideas. (Not to mention that I didn't want to leave the field too long apparently in the possession of the top-downers.) So I put it off, hoping that a more suitable moment would appear.

Now, as Fred made his challenge in the context of this attempt to see how the evolutionary perspective might illuminate the issue of good order, it seemed as good a moment as any I was likely to get to weave together some of those order-related themes.

Fred, your irreverence is as always refreshing, *Ralph wrote,* but I am, as always, relieved that you are not in charge of the cosmos. *It occurred to me that our anarchist friend, Fred, was probably not aspiring to such a position.* The fact is, as Herman has shown, order is not just a right-wing buzz word. It is an essential characteristic of everything that makes our existence possible. Not only is the universe itself an orderly one—an orderliness without which science would not be possible in the first place—but order is especially necessary for all the systems of life. The amount of order contained even in the tiniest organism is breathtaking.

And, for life, the breakdown of order is almost invariably disastrous. The intrusion of disordering elements—whether it is the genetic damage inflicted by radioactive particles, causing cancers in exposed organisms or damage to the biological inheritance of their offspring, or the chaos brought on by huge asteroids crashing into the earth (a disruption that apparently led to the extinction of dinosaurs and others at the famous K-T boundary)—such disordering is almost always the cause of death and destruction.

At the social level, too, as much as you, Fred, in your fondness for some anarchistic ideal, might not like to acknowledge it, disorder is the enemy of viability. Whether it is the disorder of family structure breaking down—as in America's inner cities— or the disorder of governing structures collapsing—as in Somalia a few years back, or in Liberia, or any of those other places where "law and order" give way to murderous disorder—a society that fails to maintain the various systems of order in which individual lives are embedded is not one where life is good or, sometimes, even possible.

"Good order," therefore, is hardly an oxymoron. If life is good then good order is a concept that makes a lot of sense. **Ralph**

That remark of Ralph's put us right on the edge of confronting yet another question that had been occasionally bobbing up through the surface of our conversation from the very beginning: namely, the question of what is meant by *goodness* anyway. This issue had come up rather quickly when I'd first posed the Nintendo Dilemma, and then had become one of those loose threads I'd never known how to weave into the discussion without getting too sidetracked. But again, it seemed that an opportune moment to present that line of discussion might now be at hand. And when the discussion of the value of order unfolded a bit more, it was clear that indeed, it was going to be as good a place as any to weave in that thread, too. That's because the next posting, from John, focused attention on a central issue about order that applied also to the question of goodness.

It seems to me, *John wrote,* that you have elided too glibly from the order of, say, an organism's DNA to the order of some social system that dictates, say, that a "family" is supposed to consist of a mommy and a daddy who are bound together in a legal relationship called marriage. The one kind of order is natural, and I guess I would say objectively given. But the other is really just a social construct. Order at that level is just something that we make up, and it has no real objective standing. And it is this sociocultural level of order, I would suggest, not the molecular level, that has a bearing upon the issues of morality and goodness (or "shouldness") that we've been discussing.

It seems to me that this is the essence of the bottom-up view of morality—that it's all a matter of what we each may choose to prefer or to believe. **John**

Yes, that is where this evolution business will lead, *Kenneth pronounced.* If you are not willing to acknowledge the sovereignty of God, if everything is seen as simply so much machinery that has managed through chance and over time to pull itself out from the muck, what can there be by way of principles of order except what we may choose to make up? Instead of divine principles that warrant our allegiance and obedience, we are stuck with man-made fictions that we can entertain or reject as we choose.

"Thou shalt not kill." "Thou shalt not steal." In our religious framework, such commandments are not **options** for people to pick and choose among. Or to make up alternatives to. They are God-given requirements for living in accordance with what is good and right. But if all we are is glorified animals, with no Creator to govern us or to whom we have to answer, no divine order that we are required to obey, what can such moral principles be except fabrications that people have dreamed up, little constructs that waft out of brain tissue that traces its ancestry to the primeval slime?
Kenneth

Fast on the heels of this, we heard once again from Henry.

Kenneth, you have put your finger on the void at the core of the whole modern enterprise. And this spiritual vacuum goes beyond, even, the rise of this evolutionary form of the modern denial of God-given order.

Even before the descent of man into the depths of evolutionary thinking, the modern way of thinking was already well embarked upon this path away from the recognition of Order and toward the creation of disorder in the name of order. The turning point downward in this, as in so much else, was Hobbes.

In the classical worldview, order was taken as natural and as a given. The great threat to the natural order was understood to be change, and it was understood, too, that the source of this disorder was human initiative. It was Hobbes who turned this on its head, regarding flux as natural and order as something that human beings had to create in order to contain the natural movement of things.[5] So Order, to which people had in the past reverently understood themselves to be obliged to submit themselves, was now understood to be something that *Homo not-so-sapiens* was free in his supposed wisdom to create for himself.

Hobbes at least had the sense to argue for an order in which a great power would be set above men, *Henry continued*, to hold in check the natural war of all against all that would otherwise obtain. But the authority of that power no longer derived from anything transcendent or essential to natural order, but was rather understood to be an artifice created by those to be governed.

Human beings—in the brave new world of this modern philosophy—were now supposed to have become masters of their own fates, subject to nothing outside themselves, to nothing, that is, except that to which they had voluntarily subjected themselves by entering into a **social contract**.

Despite the realism of the hierarchic order—the Leviathan—that Hobbes declared that people, in their reason, would set up, this manner of thinking only opened the way to all those other, more liberal social-contract theorists. In the hands of Locke, the supposed liberty of humankind to invent such arrangements as might suit them was put to different uses, resulting in the preservation of that area of presumed individual freedom and autonomy subject to the reach of no authority whatever.

Even without evolution, then, this modern way of thinking freed people to entertain the illusion that they are free to live howsoever they wish. **Henry**

My sense of order, in the evolutionary perspective, contains no such illusion, *Herman responded,* for our wishes must yield to some larger realities. Let's go back to that notion of order as mere construct.

I believe there is an alternative point of view, *wrote Herman then,* one that lies between John's view that any ordering principles are mere constructs and Kenneth's maintaining that some great Skyhook has inscribed them for us and handed them down to govern our conduct. (Although the two of them are on opposite sides, they agree with each other about there being **only** these two options, and it is on this point that I take issue with them both.)

Evolution does not bring us out of that slime in a random fashion, but rather in a form that fits us to be successful in the business of survival in a particular environment. That environment has an objective existence, and our organismic structure represents, in a sense, a kind of projection of the world in which we evolved. Had there been no air through which vibrations could be transmitted, we'd not have developed ears to pick up those transmissions and experience them as sounds. Had gravity been much stronger on our planet, or much weaker, our bodies would have evolved correspondingly different shapes. And so forth. . . . Animals emerge out of evolution structured so that they will behave in a manner that facilitates their survival and the survival of their kind. Not just **any** principles governing their behavior will be OK, but only those that correspond with the demands—the opportunities and the dangers—of their environment.

The situation with us human beings is both the same as and different from that of other species. But in the truly relevant dimension, it is the same. What's different is that we have taken the evolution of life into a different phase, where the biologically inherited blueprint is no longer nearly sufficient to regulate our conduct. We enjoy— or suffer from, or more accurately, both—an unprecedented degree of indeterminacy: instinct, which is given to us, must be supplemented by culture, which we create. But to say that we create it is not to say that it is "just something we make up." That is, although human societies are free to invent their cultural rules, **the same necessities that have always impinged upon living things still constrain us**. Our relative freedom from the regime of instinct and biologically evolved nature does **not** free us from the need to order our conduct in a way that corresponds to the requirements of our objectively existent environment.

If one way of looking at our situation, then, is to say that we are the creatures who are free to create our way of life—which is true in some sense—then another, and perhaps more meaningful way of putting it is to say that we are the creatures who need to **work** to **discover** the ordering principles that will achieve for us what other creatures get, pretty much, as a birthright.

Our survival and our well-being are still at stake in whether or not we manage to order our behavior in accordance with the objective realities into which we are born. We create culture, but it is not just an arbitrary creation. Not just anything goes.

So yes, there is a sense in which the commandments, or other ordering principles, by which we order our societies **are made up** by human beings. But there is also a fundamental sense in which what we devise must be objectively validated. Commandments like "Thou shalt not kill or steal or covet" are validated in Kenneth's system by their having been pronounced by the Creator of the Universe. In my evolutionary perspective, those same precepts can also be validated by being found to correspond to **the way things work** (or don't work) when human beings in their cultural world try to survive.

Our cultural creations, in other words, are not fictions, if by fictions we mean something that can be created however we might choose. But they *are* like theories, by which I mean notions that are to be tried and evaluated by objective criteria of performance having to do with how well they serve the values embedded in human life. Our constructs must pass an objective test: how well do people following such constructs survive, flourish, find life fulfilling? **Herman**

I do have a glimmering, Herman, *Terrence wrote,* of a difference that might exist between your point of view about how human beings might "construct" their cultural principles of order (moralities, institutions, and the like) and the kinds of arguments one hears from the social constructivists and other cells of the cultural left, so eager to free us—or at least themselves—of all constraints. It reminds me of a line I read: "A conservative is a realist, who believes that there is a structure of reality independent of his own will and desire . . . a creation that was here before him, which exists now not just by his sufferance, and which will be here after he is gone."[6] (So I welcome you aboard the conservative ship!)

In your thought, this preexistent order is apparently that of biologically evolved nature. You seem to be enshrining nature as having some sort of judicial review over the fabrications of human culture. But I wonder if you are aware of how much of the cultural left is ready to make no such concession to nature. Nowhere is this more visible than on some of the radical fringes of feminism. The feminists, of course, are striving to liberate themselves not only from supposed male domination, but also from whatever constraints nature may have imposed upon their sex. (So abortion, for example, simply becomes an issue of "choice," with no regard to whether there are any obligations that the woman may have entered into with respect to her unborn fetus.)

Not long ago, for example, I ran across a review article in the *National Review*. The writer of the piece is trying to show how ideologically tainted is the most recent edition of the *Oxford Dictionary of Sociology*.[7] For that purpose, he cites the discussion of the idea of "maternal deprivation," quoting the Oxford book as saying that "maternal care is **considered** necessary for later mental health." (The reviewer added the emphasis.) This "reference" work then went on to report that "Feminists denounce the idea [of maternal deprivation] for its role in subordinating women to motherhood." To which the reviewer responds—rightly, I would say—that, "From a naturalistic perspective, however, motherhood is not in the first instance something to which women are **subordinated**." Meaning, I take it, that motherhood—rather like eating and breathing and alternating cycles of waking and sleeping—is for an adult female human not something imposed from some alien source but something built into the very nature of the female.

Am I correct in believing, Herman, that your view of the status of our ordering principles is more in sympathy with that naturalistic perspective to which that *National Review* writer refers than with the Oxford types who, between the lines, are promoting this feminist notion that inborn nature has no role to play in circumscribing what would be the right way for a woman to conduct her life? **Terrence**

If you don't mind, Terrence, I will not try to pin myself precisely on the spectrum you laid out, *Herman responded*. (And as for your so generously admitting me into the club of conservatives, as defined by your quote, I prefer the designation of the *sadiq*, a term from the Islamic tradition, which I've read defined as "the individual who . . . acknowledges his place in the scheme of creation" and who is "characterized by the intention to be true to reality."[8]

But, with respect to your inquiry about these tendencies of some on the cultural left, I will say that I am basically in concurrence with you on several key points. First, I do see that there is a danger from the cultural left that people will regard themselves as entitled to invent their own moralities without having to respect anything but their own wants. And I concur that the realities of the constraints of nature—nature within as well as without—are part of what needs to be respected.

Second, and here I also tip at least a piece of my hat in Henry's direction, I do see a problem with the social contract approach to our understanding of our relationship to order. In a sense, I see social constructivism as a form of social contract theory gone wild: the existence of reality itself is denied, and replaced with a notion that nothing is real except that we choose to agree together to so regard it.

I believe that reality is out there—or, more accurately, that it is both "out there" and "in here," meaning that human nature also exists, even if less rigidly than in other creatures. And I believe that this reality—with which we must deal whether we want to or not—embodies a kind of order—whether we like it or not—with which it behooves us to align ourselves. For our own good. And for goodness's sake. **Herman**

For goodness's sake, *John intoned,* would you please tell us on what basis you can so facilely refer to the good? The "good," I maintain, is nothing more than what any person chooses to place a value on—and thus our evaluative statements merely express our subjective preferences. **John**

What's So Good about It?

John had raised this same challenge with me at the very outset, when I was struggling with why Nathaniel did not seem to do, on his own, all that I felt he should to realize his best potential. On the questions of right and wrong, good and evil, John had said, the cosmos is silent. Similar objections had arisen from time to time from different quarters—mostly from the cultural left—during our discussion. Sometimes these objections had been addressed briefly by someone in the group and sometimes just disregarded, as those people who, however much they disagreed on other matters, agreed that "the good" was a real and meaningful category pursued issues they felt to be more pressing. Now, at last, the time had come for this issue to come more to the fore.

I hope you liberals realize that this kind of relativism, *Terrence interjected, referring to John's challenge,* is the natural fruit of the ideology underpinning the liberal state. I have in mind that liberal idea according to which it is not the business of the state to impose any idea of the good on its citizens. The state, rather, is to be neutral among the competing concepts, according to this liberal ideology, and individuals are to be free to choose their own values and ends. And of course, the citizens receive from this neutral stance the perniciously relativistic message: "There is no authority higher than you, values are whatever you want to choose, there is no basis on which any values can be declared any more valid than any other." **Terrence**

I hope your realize, Terrence, *Ralph responded,* that this is *not* the liberal idea. One can believe that there are good choices and bad choices without thinking that it is advisable for the state to take on the powers to enforce those good choices and to forbid those bad choices. **Ralph**

How about, rather than fighting over who is responsible for reprobates like me, you guys deal with me and my challenge? *John interjected.* On what basis—other than your own arbitrary, subjective preference—can you say that one thing is good, and another thing is not good?

Recalling my earlier interaction with John on precisely this subject, I decided to plunge in.

Truth be told, John, I'd hoped that I'd made some dent in that position earlier, *I wrote.* Do you remember, that point at which I said that if I were a gentleman I'd let you take your move back? You'd used the arbitrariness of whether one should drive on the right (as in the U.S.) or drive on the left (as in Britain), and I said that yes, the choice of the side of the road was arbitrary, but not the choice to manage traffic so that people could get where they wanted to go without getting killed in car crashes.

In line with what Herman was just saying about order, I would say that the bottom line about "good" is that we as creatures—individually, collectively in our societies, and as a biosphere—have genuine needs. The meeting of these needs is **what our good is.** Since what we need is not wholly arbitrary, and since not everything meets our needs, therefore what is good for us is not arbitrary. The good is at least in large measure given in the nature of things, which is objective, and not just something for us to make up howsoever we might choose. **Andy**

Human beings are malleable. Cultures can be very different. So what's "good" to an American is very different from what's good for a Chinese. **John**

Again let me harken back to Herman's account of how evolution has left us straddling a couple of realms—the biologically given and the culturally created, *I replied.* Listening to you, one would think that we were completely free to take **nothing** as given. But there's plenty that's given. There's a good reason one would want to be what Herman called a *sadiq.*

Do you have any children, John? They come to us as "givens" from nature, and they carry with them into the delivery room a whole satchel full of givens that are their inheritance as human beings. A baby who's not fed suffers—and lets you know it— and a baby who's not held suffers, too. We are still animals, and we still have a substantive inborn nature.

We emerged out of evolution with this capacity to create, but that capacity was something added on to a structure that had been there long before. Just as the neocortex is an overlay upon our older brains that still endure, so also, I would argue, is the range of our indeterminacy something added onto, rather than displacing, the ancient **given** nature that we came equipped with as mammals, as vertebrates, and on back in time.

So when I say that "the good" is, for us, not something arbitrary that we can just "make up," as you, John, seem to be suggesting, it is on these **givens** that I claim it **must** be founded. And when you suggest that our choice of the good is somehow just a "subjective" preference, you neglect the fact that we make this choice on the basis of an inborn nature that—just like our anatomy—we share with others of our species. Therefore this "good" that we naturally choose is not "merely subjective," if by that you mean "idiosyncratic." One baby's sense that it is good to be held reflects an objectively wired-in, species-wide need.

The good inescapably grows out of the interface between the needs of our nature (which are, at least to a degree, given) and the structure of the environment in which these needs will or will not be met (which again is not wholly ours to make up). **Andy**

I'm not sure I ever really mastered the concept of "the naturalistic fallacy," *Terrence wrote next,* but I have the suspicion that you, Andy, may be committing it.

As some of the philosophers might put the issue, how do you get from **is** to **ought?** Or to put it another way, how do you make the leap from talking about what human beings **need** (even if we could agree about that) to the question of what is **good?** **Terrence**

Before I got a chance to formulate a reply to Terrence's challenge to me, another message arrived from Kenneth that seemed at first a distraction from the kind of argument in which I thought we were now engaged. But it soon seemed to me that Kenneth's challenge was not so bad a way into the issue.

Here we are once again at what seems to me the morally perilous core difficulty with you bottom-up thinkers, with your denial of God and your enshrinement of the creature as the *summum bonum* of the universe, *Kenneth wrote.* How convenient to declare the foundation of morality to be the meeting of your needs. "What's good is for me to get what I want!" Is that not, instead, what a **real** morality seeks to combat? If the creature is inherently sinful, how can the meeting of its sinful needs constitute the essence of the good? How many people, in our society, have made a god of their lusts, calling them good because they experience themselves as filled with desire?

No, that is not what the good is. The good is obedience to God's will (not ours). It is for things to be God's way. **Kenneth**

Is this déjà vu all over again? *This was Fred, back on the job.* Hey, Kenneth, is it good because God says so, or does God say so because it's good?

Put another way, if God were some monster like Saddam—an image I employed previously for this purpose—would obedience to His will be the essence of the good? "I don't phink so." And if that's agreed, then it must be something else besides God's being Almighty and the Creator that makes His Way so way good. And if there is such a "something else," pray tell, what is it? **Fred**

Fred's mention of "déjà vu all over again," combined with my revisiting with John that question about the arbitrariness of our ordering and evaluative principles, brought me again to ponder the question of how much such discussions can serve to help move people's understanding in some meaningful sense *forward*. Isn't that the whole purpose of the process of inquiry?

It seems to me that, living as we do in a cosmos that does seem to be orderly, we—the creatures with the capacity to reason, to make our various beliefs and the bits of evidence that reality presents us with consistent with one another—can be rewarded for the application of reasonable thought processes by the uncovering of at least parts of the truth. As a believer in the quest for the truth, I find it disturbing when people continue untroubled with their original way of thinking even after serious problems with that thinking have been pointed out. This obliviousness challenges my faith in the capacity of good argumentation to move people away from less valid positions to more valid ones as they discover which ones make good sense in the face of all the evidence and logic that can be mustered.

Should I abandon my faith in the capacity of reason to move people? I thought of Larry's dilemma about the "truth or consequences" of our beliefs, and wondered whether the perseveration of people's beliefs— even when checkmated in one or another well-played argument—indicated that they had some enduring *need* to cling to those beliefs, whether or not they were true, valid, defensible, sensible, in accord with reason and evidence.

Well, for me a central need continued to be to live up to the standard of integrity that my father had set down, in which acknowledgment of reality trumps other needs. So, at this point, the value of reasoned argument was itself open to real question.

I agree with Fred, *Larry wrote next*, that, even if we absolutely **knew** who God is and what He wants of us, this would not translate at all automatically into an answer about what is good. (Call that the divinist fallacy.) It could be that, as Fred argued a long while ago, in a cosmos where God punished us severely for disobedience, our obeying even a cruel and tyrannical God would be the best available course for us, under those circumstances. But "under those circumstances" is the key here, because I would also argue that it is clear that it would be *better* to live in a cosmos ruled by a different kind of God and not by that tyrant. And my standard of "better" would be like Andy's notion that what's good for us is what best meets our needs. **Larry**

The modern disorder, *the next message, from Henry, began,* is indeed this reverence for our petty little needs. If you set about to meet everyone's needs, what ensues is not the Good, but just Disorder and Anarchy. **Henry**

So what is your idea of what makes something good, if you will be so kind as to enlighten us? (Oh! Sorry about using the e-word on you like that.) **Fred**

What is good, *Henry responded, ignoring Fred's little jibe,* is stability. And what makes for stability is an intact hierarchical ordering of society. **Henry**

Before anyone takes on Henry's politics, *I jumped in,* I'd like to take this occasion to respond more fully to Terrence's challenge to me about the naturalistic fallacy, about how I am able to get from the "isness" of some supposed set of needs in our inherent nature into that dimension of "oughtness" that has to do with the good.

What I mean by "this occasion" is Henry's enthronement of "stability" as the essence of the good. As an aside, though, I do wonder if Henry would stick by such a definition if pressed. I mean, I can see that stability can be a virtue, but is it really an end in itself? The Thousand Year Reich did not make it for the duration, but if it *had* been successful in being stable for that entire intended millennium, would that stability have been a good thing? I doubt if even Henry would argue that it would have been, though with his last posting he's left himself no basis on which to argue otherwise. But Henry's point about stability does provide a way into talking about what is meant by meeting human needs.

Yes, it is conceivably true that attempting to meet *all* human needs—one by one, as soon as they arise—would result in anarchy. (Which would in turn likely result in many of people's quite fundamental needs going unmet.) What would make that so is there being such fundamental inconsistencies among our needs that blindly attempting to meet them all would lead to a breakdown of the order on which meeting our needs ultimately depends; it could well be true that we would be better served by a strategy that places a high priority on the preservation of stability.

But my point is this: what would make that stability a good thing worth working for would not be that the stability was a good in and of itself, but that it was a necessary means to the more fundamental end of meeting—as much as possible— the needs of the human beings dependent upon that system.

And here I get to the nub of my point to Terrence. It is all a matter of means and ends. And the question of what is good has to do with the question of what it is *that*

is worthy of being called an end in itself. I say it is good to hold a baby because this is what the baby needs, as it shows by its crying when abandoned and babbling happily when held. But then the question can be asked, why is it better for the baby to be happy than to be miserable and afraid?

Whenever we say of something that it is good, the question can always be asked, what makes it good? And for this not to continue *ad infinitum* we have to be able to come to the point where we can say, "It just is, it is good in itself." But what can that thing that is good in itself be except something that lies in the dimension of the experience of creatures for whom some things feel good and other things feel bad? In the absence of that, what else can possibly matter?

In a wholly lifeless universe, it doesn't matter what happens because there is nothing around for it to matter to. Only because of the existence of creatures for whom some things matter is any scenario any better or worse than any other. Why is it better that a kitten not be in excruciating torment, even if it is all alone and no one knows about it? Because that kitten, if tormented, is compelled to have an experience that it would desperately seek to avoid, or to escape. The same is **not** true of, say, the disintegration of a lifeless stone. It just doesn't matter, because the stone is itself indifferent. But for the kitten, and for all sentient beings, the quality of experience has a built-in evaluative dimension.

It is the emergence of creatures for whom some things are desirable and valuable and other things are repugnant and painful that brings value into the universe.
Andy

So does God have no place at all in your definition of what is good? **Rev. George**

The question might also be asked, "What place **could** God have in our effort to define the Good?" *I replied.* Fred rightly challenges the notion that simply God's wanting things to be a certain way automatically means that way is good. God could conceivably be a monster. If God's wants have any inherent claim on the definition of the good, it would seem to me, it would be through "His" status as a fellow sentient Being. One would hope that, if there is a God, Its sense of well-being would not be opposed to ours, Its creatures. But if there were such a conflict, I would say that such a God's desires or preferences would enter into the definition of the Good only to the extent that Its experience should be weighed in relation to ours. I would not concede that it would be just if God were to claim, that "Because I made this game, I insist on winning, even if all you, my sentient creatures, must suffer."

And as for the guidance that any Word of God might provide, I would argue that such a Word can reasonably be said to define our good only to the extent that it provides us with genuine wisdom about what, overall, is actually the best way to meet our own experiential needs. **Andy**

This is helpful, *Herman added soon after my message,* in highlighting some of the aspects of this evolutionary vision of order. To start with the last piece first, Andy's remark about "the Word of God"—that it can be said to define the good for us only to the extent that it actually gives wise guidance to how our real needs can best be met—is congruent with what I was saying about our ordering principles being, in a sense, **theories** about how things work, or how they will work best. The evolutionary approach leads to a grounded view of morality because, like evolution itself, it maintains a pragmatic focus on efficacy.

If we say that it is wrong, for example, for young men to go around fathering children for whose upbringing they are not going to take any responsibility, what we mean—or what I am suggesting we should mean—is that in a world where men act contrary to such an ordering principle the results are that a lot of children grow up without some of their fundamental needs being met. And we also, perhaps, mean that a society peopled by such neglected children is one that will be afflicted with such disorders—like crime, unemployability, dissoluteness, etc.—that the quality of experience for everyone else in society at large will also be degraded and diminished.

Conversely, if we say that "free love should be the rule, let people seek pleasures unrestrained," we are saying—or should be saying—that this is a strategy that will do the best to lead to human fulfillment.

As theories, they are subject to confirmation or refutation by the evidence. The evidence may be complex and not easily sorted out. But in this pragmatic view of value—where needs getting met (or not) and quality of experience being enhanced (or degraded) provide the criteria—disputes about morality are not inherently futile or empty, like one person saying "I like the taste of chocolate" and the other saying "No, vanilla tastes better."

In the instance of some of our competing sexual moralities, I would say that in America since the 1960s some experiments have been conducted and that at least some of the propositions of the sexual liberationists have been disconfirmed. The costs of some forms of freedom have proven too great to justify their benefits. It turns out that—for the sake of meeting as well as possible the wide spectrum of human needs—sexual behavior does seem to need to be regulated by more than merely the gratification of immediate impulse and the pursuit of personal pleasure.

But let us be clear about the justificatory basis for any sexual—or other—morality we may decide to be valid and appropriate. The principles should be understood as attempts to codify the pattern of cause and effect that is observable in the world that we are **given,** and they are valid to the extent that they provide a good strategy for the maximization of the meeting of human needs.

What are the reproductive consequences, or the effects on people's emotional and spiritual lives, or the impact on their physical health, of following one set of rules of conduct versus another?

We should follow "good" moral rules not because those rules **define** the good but because they help to guide us toward it. For a **good** morality is one that serves best to meet the needs—immediate and long-term—of human beings and other sentient creatures.

And here's my last point. This is an understanding of goodness as unfolding with the evolutionary process. Evolution always chooses what works, which with living things means what survives. Carl quoted a biblical line, a while back, where God says something like "I have set before you both life and death; therefore choose life." What I am saying is that this is precisely the choice that evolution has always made. And it has crafted us to do the same, and crafted us moreover with an inborn tendency to experience what is life-enhancing and life-preserving as pleasurable, as a good that we will seek, and conversely to experience what is life-degrading and life-destroying as unpleasant and to be avoided.

In other words, what we are designed to want has tended to be aligned with the good. **Herman**

The Direction of Our Grain

You are confusing me somewhat, Herman, *Terrence wrote next.* On the one hand, your discussion of free love and of the need for responsible fathering sounds like you acknowledge something akin to what Kenneth dubbed the sinful nature of our lusts. On the other hand, you just finished saying that what we are designed to want has tended to be aligned with the good. How are these to be reconciled? **Terrence**

Talk about déjà vu all over again. As soon as I read Terrence's message I immediately felt propelled out of that somewhat confident place from which I'd happily been posting my understandings of how the basis of goodness had emerged with evolution back into that more bewildered place from which I'd launched this whole discussion when I originally posed the Nintendo Dilemma. Yes, our needs and desires are directly tied in with any meaningful concept of the good. And yes, the challenge of good order seems somehow to entail our having to regulate our pursuit of our desires. But rabbi, how can they both be right, they contradict each other!

Needless to say, I was eager to see how well Terrence's challenge could be met.

That's a good question, Terrence, *Herman wrote.*

As soon as I saw that, my hopes for complete deliverance from my own perplexity sank. I have long noticed how, whenever people say "That's a good question," what they really mean is "Your question is one I can't answer." So I sensed that Herman was not in possession of any magic key to open this conundrum. But as I read on, I saw that Herman was at least struggling manfully (or does one say, now, personfully?) toward getting a handle on how the two sides of this reality can in fact both be right.

Part of the answer, it seems to me, is that while evolution has done an incredible job of producing good order, it does not produce any **perfect** order, *Herman continued.* Take our body's responses to threats from disease. Anyone who has studied the body's immune system will tell you what a truly fantastic piece of work it is. And yet—there are occasions when it is the body's own efforts to protect itself from some kind of assault that end up doing the most damage, sometimes even bringing on death. So there's no reason to suppose our evolved natures would not have problemmatic dimensions. Evolution provides no guarantee against defects. Life is and has always been a work in progress.

And then there is the phenomenon of changing circumstances. Evolution is not forward-looking, and it is always having to deal in the present with what has emerged from the past. Evolution does not have the luxury that a vehicle manufacturer might have in moving from the stage of horse-and-buggy to that of the automobile. The manufacturer can just throw out reins and harnesses. He doesn't need to design his cars with a tail on the back. But evolution can't just start over, it has to build on what's there. So we end up with glands that are the descendents—as one can see from embryology—of the gills of our fishy vertebrate ancestors. And this need to make our progress on a trail of atavisms causes us some problems.

Our spine comes to mind here. As a large proportion of the adult human population can attest, our spines are not a complete joy to own. The spine is a marvelous construction, but we are beset by backaches.

Talk about being an "upright man." It is not all that long, in the great scheme of our evolution, since we were like other quadrupeds, locomoting on all fours. And then, for a variety of reasons, the use of the forelimbs changed—allowing us to grab branches, as many other primates do, and then the growing importance of tool-use and voila, here we are on two feet. And now the suspension bridge that our spine originally evolved to be in the era of our ancestral quadrupedal locomotion, has had to become the pillar of our upright posture. If the god of evolution had the luxury of just going back to the drawing boards to create an upright creature, we humans would have a lot fewer backaches.

Similarly, I would suggest, some of our impulses might be leftovers from earlier circumstances and thus not fit so well the changed situation of later stages of our evolution. **Herman**

OK, Herman, *Larry wrote.* Circumstances change. So how does that connect with the question of sexual morality, which was the immediate occasion of Terrence's question? We need something more here than that the notion of "Keep it in your pants" doesn't arise until we acquire pants. **Larry**

You're right, *Herman replied.* A really fleshed-out answer, as it were, would have to be very complex, and steeped in a degree of anthropological knowledge that I do not claim to have. I'm trying to sketch what might be some of the dimensions of an answer but I make no claim to have anything complete to offer. But I'll speculate a little further.

A line that has recently made the rounds in our culture just popped into my mind, so maybe it's relevant. I mean the saying, "It takes a village to raise a child." My knowledge of its history is that it has undergone three incarnations in our society in recent years. First, it appeared as an African proverb. Next, the president's wife used it as the title of a book. And then the conservatives have attacked what they took to be her collectivist notions of responsibility and came back with "No, it takes a *family* to raise a child."

In the African context, this proverb made a kind of sense that perhaps harkens back to the earlier eras of cultural evolution: a village is more or less of the size of family-based clans or bands that people lived in for countless millennia, from even before we emerged from our primate past. Responsibility in such a society might readily be spread around. Hillary Clinton was speaking in a rather more complex society, one in which neighborhoods and communities have been breaking down and in which the power of the state in society—in a bureaucratic form—has increased in recent generations. The conservatives are attached to the more modern—though in the contemporary perspective, *"traditional"*—structure of the nuclear family. This family is a comparatively small unit, highly bounded-off from the surrounding community and from public institutions, and functioning as the basic arena of interpersonal responsibility. I would say that it is "no coincidence" that the people who are stressing the responsibility of the nuclear family for raising children—the ones who respond with conservative rhetoric against Hillary Clinton's book title—are the same ones, by and large, for whom sexual morality is at the top of their list of moral priorities.

Here's what I'm driving at: as social structures change, the requirements for the morality also change, and the fit between natural impulse and social demand can become less harmonious.

To return to the particular example: the raising of children is **always** going to be an important task in a society, and thus all societies must create a moral structure that leads to providing their young with a solid foundation for life. Different social arrangements will make different kinds of sexual morality necessary for the achievement of that task. (To that extent John may be right about how different societies can—legitimately—construct different moralities. But that doesn't make them arbitrary, or place moralities beyond the reach of meaningful evaluation.) Anyway, if you have a society like ours in which contact among a great many people occurs all the time—unlike in the tiny bands of our origins—so that men can readily have sexual encounters and then have no proximity to the consequences, and in which the responsibility for the upbringing of the young is placed on a family defined by marriage between a man and a woman, then it will become very important for that society to create a moral order in which sexual impulses are regulated, in which, that is, they are subordinated to various systems of responsibility and obligation.

But at the same time, our sexual nature did not begin its evolution in this kind of a world. Hence there can emerge a mismatch between the inherited tendencies of desire and the more recently developed cultural context in which we must decide whether or not to act on those desires. **Herman**

Of course, this matter of sexual impulses being mismatched with civilized circumstances, *Ralph wrote,* is just the proverbial tit of the iceberg. So much of human life has been altered by the recent millennia of our history that our stone-age natures are far from an accurate guide to the requirements of contemporary civilized life. I think of that much-reported flight-or-fight response to threats, and how the inapplicability of such physical responses to most of the threats we actually experience feeds into various psychosomatic forms of distress (such as chronically elevated blood-pressure).

And then there is anger, which brings the impulse to strike what hurts us, an ancient response enduring in a creature now possessed of new destructive powers. It's one thing for a creature whose weapons are hands and feet to have violent impulses, but quite another when half the homes in America have firearms stashed in them. Not to mention the problem posed by having mere human animals in charge of nations armed with nuclear weapons. Arms used to be only parts of our bodies. Now—unless our aggressive impulses are ordered by some structures that judge reliably when and how those impulses will be blocked, and when allowed to flow—"arms" could become the means of species-wide self-destruction. **Ralph**

These remarks from Ralph and Herman reminded me of a part of my own previous work in *The Parable of the Tribes* that was pertinent to the problem of the mismatch, so I wrote in to amplify the thrust of their comments.

That book of mine that John mentioned some weeks back argues that this incompatibility between our inborn nature and our contemporary circumstance is an even greater problem than would be implied by merely the magnitude of the transformation of human life.

In *The Parable of the Tribes,* I tried to show how about ten thousand years ago, humankind's crossing a crucial social evolutionary threshold—from social life in a form more or less continuous with our primate past into a new kind of society called civilization—unleashed forces that were not a function of human nature and that have remained beyond human control. These forces, I argued, have played a powerful role in shaping the evolution of civilized society, from the beginnings of the domestication of plants and animals all the way up to the present time. As a result of having our societies so powerfully molded by forces not derived from our nature and largely indifferent to our needs, the conflict between our natural inclinations and the requirements of our societies has been tremendously exacerbated. **Andy**

Is it your contention, then, that if we could only devise our societies more benignly, *Terrence inquired,* that our natural inclinations would adequately guide us toward good order? **Terrence**

At first I wasn't sure whether Terrence was addressing me, or the fellows who'd written before, but then I saw that his question could apply only to what I'd written, and so I responded.

I confess to having a degree of confusion on this point, Terrence, that is, on the extent to which it would be possible to have a human society that would be in harmony with our natural impulses and desires, one in which we would both have our cake of a well-ordered world and the pleasure of eating it (getting our needs met), too. All I'll say is that I do not believe the world as it is organized around us now gets very close to the limit of what harmony is possible. **Andy**

Your challenge remains a most important one, Terrence, *Herman came in next.* I would like to make an additional effort to meet it. I claim that we are crafted to align ourselves with what is good. (That makes sense, since I also am in accord with the notion that there is no other sensible way of defining what is good except to say that it is the meeting of the needs of sentient beings, most especially including us humans.) But I also am aware, as I said, that the same evolutionary crafting process does not create perfection. And one aspect of this falling short of paradise is that in any given system there are a great many goods to be considered, and it is not realistically possible to think that all of them can be achieved at once. There are too many equations for any simultaneous solution to fit them all.

Just look at that "red in tooth and claw" aspect of nature: evolution may have created a biosphere in which all the components *tend* to act synergistically to preserve the system as a whole, but it is also one in which some creatures eat others, some are parasites on others, etc.

In the large picture of the human system in which all of us operate, there are likewise a lot of goods, not all of them compatible all the time with all the others. Since different human goods inevitably will frequently come into conflict, something—call it a moral system of some kind—has to provide a means for deciding which will be sacrificed for the sake of which.

Natural inclination will only go so far toward achieving the best ordering of competing needs—partly because evolution doesn't automatically achieve what we might regard as ideal, and partly because of that matter of changing circumstances creating changing requirements.

Take self-sacrifice. The dimension of self-sacrifice can be found in biologically governed living systems. Mother animals often risk or sacrifice for their offspring; social insects also lay down their lives for their gene-mates. As J. B. S. Haldane said famously, "I would willingly lay down my life for more than two brothers, four nephews or eight cousins."[9] But among human beings, this challenge goes well beyond the "interests" of what Richard Dawkins has called, equally famously—have you noticed this new intrusion of "famously" into our language?—the "selfish gene." For we humans have envisioned the possibility of more ideal orders in which still larger aggregations of "goods" can be taken into account—beyond the scope of our genetic bonds—with the result that still greater good might be achieved.

So we find ourselves called upon to attend not just to ourselves, not just even to our kin or our kind, but to a larger sense of the good. My fundamental desire to remain alive, and with all my limbs attached, may at times be in conflict with the good of the larger world so that I might risk or even outright sacrifice all that in order, say, that the Nazi regime be prevented from the realization of its plans for world domination.

Socializing people to be ready to make such sacrifices is doubtless fraught with dangers. But in a world such as we have created, depending solely on the selfishness of our genes would also be a most perilous course. **Herman**

I have heard it quoted, *Fred wrote,* —'twas the philosopher, Hume—that 'Tis not contrary to reason to prefer the destruction of the whole world to the scratching of my finger. **Fred**

Perhaps, *Herman responded.* But this brings us to a dimension of that greater moral order that we, as cultural animals with understanding, can reasonably seek to establish. Imagine that we had a whole society consisting solely of such sociopaths, those given to such "reasonable" preferences. Even with such creatures, it would be even more reasonable for them—if they were capable of it—to band together and to transform themselves into different kinds of beings.

Think of morality as a treaty. It's an agreement that is in everyone's interest—though it conflicts with some of our own immediate desires—if we agree together to abide by it. Without such a treaty, a society of your "reasonable" sociopaths might have the freedom to pursue all their impulses untrammeled, but they have a much better chance of getting many more of their needs met if they all abide by a treaty of morality—by which conflicting needs and desires are ordered—than if none do. **Herman**

This reminds me, *Peter posted quickly after Herman's message,* of something I read recently about Shakespearean tragedy. The tragedy is created, this piece said, by individuals who are trying to be true only to themselves—in some respects an admirable, a heroic trait—disregarding the need to adapt that self to the needs of their social context.[10] **Peter**

Your point, Herman, about how not all the equations can be solved simultaneously is worthy of expansion, *Cynthia posted next.* You've framed it mostly in this large societal picture, where we make a treaty with other people that we will all order ourselves morally so that we can increase the probability that our needs will be met. But the same phenomenon of competing needs also occurs at a smaller level, that is, within any human individual.

In any person's life, choices need to be made. We want to enjoy ourselves, and we want to get things accomplished. We appreciate the pleasures of being a grasshopper, but we also want the benefits of having done the toils of the ant. As that Aesopic fable makes clear, an important dimension of our ongoing choices involves the competition between the short term and the long term, between getting immediate gratification and receiving the future dividends that investment pays. While the rise of civilization may have accentuated some of these kinds of choices—providing greater pressures and rewards for future-orientation at the cost of the experience of ongoing enjoyment—I believe we can assume that competing desires and needs of this sort must have been the human lot since way before history, as far back as the species goes, if not further.

So, even without the changing circumstances that may have required people to develop more powerful and demanding ordering structures to regulate our natural inclinations, the human being needed to develop an internal order to mediate among the competing considerations in life.

In other words, what I am arguing is that it is **natural** for us to develop some kind of **character structure**. Without *some* kind of structure, there would be only impulse, which would mean a great deal of chaotic behavior, which would be disadvantageous in any conceivable human life. Successful living has always entailed, I suggest, some reflective capacity from above to hold in check those impulses and desires that need to be sacrificed on behalf of a strategy for one's greater good.

The idea of a greater good to which lesser goods must be sacrificed is, then, important for the individual psyche, as well as for the human society, and so the disciplining of some wants in favor of others would be a naturally evolved tendency of the human being. But by calling it natural, I do not mean to deny that in the process of individual development some people would achieve a better ordering than others.
Cynthia

All this seems interesting enough, *said Terrence,* and in some measure it does seem to answer that challenge I put to Herman a while ago. But I'm not sure that you've clarified how your account of the impulses and desires that will be denied their fulfillment differs—other than in tone and terminology—from Kenneth's characterization of our natures as sinful. You do, after all, agree that some of our desires need to be rejected as forbidden. What's the difference between your saying to some young man, "Don't be a grasshopper in the pursuit of your momentary pleasures, or else you might well do damage to various lives, perhaps even your own," and Kenneth's saying "Your lust is sinful, and it must therefore be denied"? **Terrence**

Yes, let's stick with the instance of sexual desire, though many others of our wants that need to be regulated might also be suitable for my answer to your question, *Herman began.*

Although not all of our religious traditions have characterized human sexual desires as intrinsically sinful, this rejection of a fundamental part of our nature has been a powerful current in our civilization. My evolutionary view differs from that rejection in an essential way. In the evolutionary perspective, these desires are full of life, in the service of life, and are therefore worthy of being affirmed as fundamentally valuable.

Whether or not it was necessary, in order to maintain good order in the much earlier social groups of our distant ancestors (of, say, a hundred thousand years ago or, for that matter, four million), to regulate human sexuality, it appears that sexuality, at least in the circumstances in which we now live, needs to be channeled in some ways in order to reap its life-giving fruits while minimizing its disruptive and disordering potentialities. But even if this need for channeling and regulation is granted, that in no way makes the desires themselves bad or sinful.

Our desires and needs are expressions of the life force. Their messages to us are important clues to the nature of our good. That is true even of the impulses that we may decide must be forbidden expression. Sexual desires that we decide cannot be allowed fulfillment (or rages that we realize must be held in check)—even these, sometimes especially these, must be heeded and respected, even though their meaning for the pursuit of our good may require some work to understand. **Herman**

The Unfinished

Your perspective, Herman, has a lot that's intriguing in it, *Larry posted,* and I appreciate your work in presenting it. But I have to say, as a solution to that Zeno's paradox problem, it leaves a lot to be desired. Your use of the word "theory" to describe any attempt we might make to create good order captures the difficulty: I'm still left saying, "We've got a problem."

The question at the heart of my dilemma was: Is there anything reliable on which we can found a good order? If the bottom is unreliable, for all the reasons we've seen, and if the top is always contaminated with various kinds of corruption, in the ways we've explored, then how are we to find anything reliable? Even the second time around, it seemed clear at least to me, the Taoist-left and the Godly-right both failed to escape those initial pitfalls uncovered earlier.

Now you have spoken to us of "theories." Our moral orders sound, in your account, like mere stabs in the dark, attempts that might hit or miss. This hardly sounds like the kind of reliable basis for good order I was looking for. **Larry**

I told you earlier, Larry, *Herman replied,* that my perspective would not solve your problem altogether. What it ***does*** do, I would maintain, is give us a way of getting past the bottom-up and top-down dichotomy. With the concept of emergence, providing for the erection of "cranes," we can have an understanding of order that is grounded in scientific knowledge, that shows simultaneously how order unfolds from below ***and*** at the same time reaches down from above.

This seems to me no small improvement over the kind of arguments—both bottom-up and top-down—we heard before.

The advocates of the old bottom-up approach seemed unwilling to countenance anything being placed above the individual and her choosing according to her desires. For, if we have real regard for human nature, the argument was, how can anything be placed above it to rule it?

And the top-down arguments we heard always enshrined some kind of "skyhook"—whether it was God or tradition or the law or state power—that was represented to us as somehow wholly other than—superior to—the human beings whom they were to keep in line, beyond the reach of question or challenge from below. (Sort of like King James of England defending absolutism by declaring that the king "is ordained by God to judge and not be judged by his subjects.")[11]

The evolutionary perspective takes important pieces of each and integrates them in a way that eliminates some crucial defects of each. Like the bottom-ups, we do indeed enshrine human needs as the source of the standard of goodness. We look to human fulfillment as the telos of any justifiable morality. But, unlike the bottom-ups, we can understand how it is that good order doesn't "just happen" automatically through the spontaneous impulses of human nature. The evolutionary perspective also reveals how there can be a need for there to be an ordering from above to make the world safe for humanity. In that way we are like the top-downs. Yet that ordering from above is not seen as a skyhook that stands apart from us who are to be ordered, but rather as a creation from within us, something that is the fruit of our groping for that good order that is the object of this forum's quest as well.

Is that not something? **Herman**

Then Larry wrote in response.

Yes it is something, but I was hoping for that something to end with us in a more solid posture than the "groping" you just mentioned. **Larry**

Ah, yes, that is indeed where my "answer" does not answer your problem, *Herman acknowledged.* That want of yours for an Answer seems to be rather fundamental to people, as I said before. But I do not think that there is any intellectually respectable way of getting one. Evolution has never given final and complete answers. Perhaps that reality has been just as painful for other creatures, but in an entirely different way. I think of all those creatures coming up against the various cul de sacs in evolution, struggling to adapt to changing environments, possibly starving or being eaten as selection takes its picks among the given options. But for us humans this unfinishedness of all of evolution's answers imposes intellectual and spiritual burdens that, I'm sure, no creature before us humans has had to bear.

Our species is now at the cutting edge of that evolutionary process, and our every step is—as it were—into *terra incognita*. For us, "good order" is inescapably an enterprise that is **under construction**. We may seek to escape our confrontation with that reality, by declaring certainties—commandments carved into stone by Skyhooks—where none exists. But there is no true escape from the reality of our uncertainty. **Herman**

Yes, in our stay in the universe, we have to get by without an instruction manual from the manufacturer, *added Cynthia.*

It's even more than that, *I chimed in.* If as Herman says—and I think correctly—the whole thing is under construction, we **are** in part also the manufacturers.

This is not comforting, *Peter complained.* If we are as flawed as we seem to have established that we are, what business do we have manufacturing the good order we need?

Comfort may be something that is not in adequate supply, Larry, *Herman wrote.* But this manufacture of good order **is** precisely the business that our species is engaged in. For other creatures, it's possible to take, more or less, what is given and live out the preordained design. But for us, the design is inevitably one that, at least in large measure, grows out of our own thoughts and beliefs and values. **Herman**

I think you are missing a piece of the picture, *Terrence wrote.* For most people, for most of history, it has been possible to live in accordance with an order that they received as a given. I am referring here to tradition, which most people experienced as a moral order received as if from time immemorial, as if given in the very nature of things. **Terrence**

Yes, you are certainly right about that, *Herman responded.* A tradition might be described as a theory that corresponds well enough to reality to be able, at least, to persist. And that is a possible "minimax" strategy for human culture: take what's at least "good enough" and stick with it. But how good is good enough? And at what cost does one arrest the process of unfolding by trying to freeze human life into some particular more-or-less functional form? It's as if in astronomy we stopped with Ptolemy, and closed our eyes to Copernicus and Galileo (with his telescope that the churchmen refused to peer through) and Newton and Einstein. You know when the seasons are coming, even if you're stuck in an archaic astronomy, but you miss out on so much of the cosmic drama of which we are part. **Herman**

I can really see and appreciate this integration you have been laying out. Intellectually, it is quite appealing, *Larry wrote next.* But I can't get over how little this provides in the way of answers to the many questions we've been struggling with. It doesn't tell Andy whether he should challenge his son to develop himself into "all that he can be," or let him unfold according to his own naturally occurring inclinations. It doesn't tell us whether the best government we should set up should be direct democracy or representative democracy or a hereditary monarchy. It doesn't tell us whether we should outlaw pornography, or legalize the use of marijuana. This list could be elaborated at great length, but I trust you get the picture. **Larry**

You're entirely right that none of the answers to those questions can just be cranked out from this evolutionary framework, *responded Herman*. But I wouldn't want you to conclude that therefore this perspective gets us nowhere in our search for answers to all those questions.

Haven't you ever observed how often in our cultural controversies the conversation never really gets engaged because the starting sets of assumptions and criteria wielded by the disputants are so completely at odds? These starting places are often left unstated and unacknowledged, so that the people are really just talking past each other. If the parties to the conversation could begin with some agreement about the nature of the question, their conversation—about pornography, or about child-rearing, or whatever—would be far more likely to bear fruit.

It seems to me that this evolutionary perspective offers a way to move toward that more fruitful starting place. If we understand the good as somehow inevitably founded upon the meeting of the needs of sentient creatures, if we see that we are challenged both to discover and to invent an order that best serves that good, if we understand our moralities as being therefore theories about how things do and will work, if we understand ourselves to be at the cutting edge of the evolution of life on earth—I think we are more likely to find our way to good answers to all those important questions. **Herman**

To me, the quest has always been the essential dimension of life, *Ralph wrote in the wake of this*. Exploring is my idea of a good time, and I am not all that well equipped for stasis. So the image that you paint of our condition is not so disturbing to me as, apparently, Larry finds it to be.

I, for one, like the combination of elements that come with this evolutionary perspective. On the one hand, all our moralities and our laws and traditions and other ways of ordering-from-above can no longer be mistaken for God-given absolutes. Once we recognize that all of it grows out of the "crooked timber of our humanity," we are freed of the blinders that so often lead the right to fail to note the contaminations by power and lust and greed that beset almost everything we touch. The hunger for something absolute, certain, beyond question—however understandable that hunger may be—has resulted in so much rigidity, so much justification of injustice, so much entrenched refusal to see the fingerprints of flawed humanity all over the scene of so many crimes committed from above.

At the same time, and on the other hand, this open-ended vision of how things are continually unfolding, and must continue to find good ways to unfold if the human project is to succeed, helps to sweep away some of the glib claptrap of unreflective liberty and unrestrained gratification that seems to endanger our present, rather loosened social order.

An interesting dialectic emerges. On the one hand, the fulfillment of that which is below—the needs of human nature—is enshrined as the **purpose** of the whole enterprise. On the other hand, as we travel forward into that *terra incognita* of the human future—a future for which our origins give us no adequate preparation—we are compelled to recognize that what is below does not afford adequate guidance for the crafting of the order.

So, on the one hand, we must work to create higher-order levels that will provide for the meeting of the needs of a flawed and inadequate human nature. Yet on the other hand the structures we create—these sociocultural cranes—are all inescapably the fruits of that same flawed and inadequate creature. **Ralph**

I think you have captured nicely, Ralph, the irreducible difficulty of finding the wise course, navigating between the bottom and the top. **Herman**

This evolutionary "breakthrough" of yours does not impress me. If it's a breakthrough, it's the kind of breakthrough a person might experience trying to walk across a floor whose boards are all rotted out. *This was Henry again.* It's just another version of that disastrous breakthrough that Hobbes gave the modern world—a denial of the God-given order that is our duty to know and obey, the granting of a pernicious freedom to change whatever we want to suit our own base purposes. **Henry**

Thank you, Henry, for reminding me: you've called attention to another kind of integration of vision that this perspective offers us. *This was Herman responding.* A while back, you explained to us a crucial dividing line in the history of Western thought: we had moved, with Hobbes as the pivot, you said, from a classical view where order was taken as given in the nature of things and where change was something that human beings created, often dangerously, to a modern view where the world is seen as a place naturally in flux with human beings compelled, in order to contain that flux, to invent and create a order. It was an illuminating dichotomy you provided, I thought.

But the evolutionary perspective offers one of those "But rabbi, how can they both be right" kinds of opportunities for synthesis. We see that the classical world was right in asserting that a magnificent order is provided us in the nature of things, an order that we disregard at our peril. But we also see that this same natural order is founded upon, that it emerged through, a process of natural flux. Change is just as essential a part of what nature is about as is order, for without change matter would never have become life, and from life consciousness would never have emerged. It is nature's intrinsic drive to unfold that made possible the emergence of a creature that could look around and behold, with awe, the cosmos that gave him life.

On the other side of this new integration, we see that Hobbes and company were right—that they did provide a breakthrough, and not just like falling through rotted boards—in discerning the kind of *terra incognita* we had washed up onto, and the great challenges that imposes upon us. This challenge includes the need for us to create a good order to regulate ourselves in our unprecedented freedom. But it is not just **any** order that we have to invent, but rather one that is aligned well with the order that is given. And the creature at the cutting edge of evolution must also understand that, as the classical world recognized, it is the human system that, more than anything else, has now become the principal source of change. Humankind has thus become a dangerous addition to the natural order, capable in our freedom of wreaking havoc on ourselves and all the rest of life around us. This realization thus adds to the moral pressure on us to create an adequate order to govern the exercise of our powers.

That, the rabbi said, is how they can both be right. **Herman**

At this point, a striking message came in from Fred. Had you asked me to assess the probability of our seeing such a communication from him, I'd have given you extremely long odds. But as the poster on the wall of a friend of mine says—and this poster is quite reliably on his wall, year after year, now going on past thirty years—"Expect the Unexpected."

Bingo! Herman, old buddy, somehow you just broke the bank, *Fred wrote*. I'm not sure just how it happened, but something just shifted inside. A glimpse—no, more than a glimpse, more like a flash of lightning—of how my anarchistic perspective needed some additional dimension, something crucial added to it. Perhaps I should wait until the dust settles to write in here about it, but one piece of it leaps out for telling now.

There's a story from the Hindu tradition that I've always liked. It hasn't really played any evident role in my philosophy, so far as I can tell, but I always found it immensely amusing, and so it's become part of my raconteur's repertoire. In this moment of breaking the bank, this story came vividly to my mind, and I think it is a metaphor for whatever it is that just broke through for me, and that I expect I'll be working through for a while.

In the story, this guy goes through the jungle to meet with his guru, and on this particular day the guru teaches the fellow "You are God." He takes in this important truth and, all excited, he departs for home back along the jungle path. As he's walking along, telling himself "I am God, I am God," a voice calls out to him from a not-great distance, "Out of the way, the *mahut* is coming through." (The voice is from a man perched on an elephant, riding the beast along the same trail.) But our guy isn't listening, so absorbed is he in absorbing the exciting truth that he is God. The call then comes again, "Out of the way, the *mahut* is coming through." This time our student hears the voice, but he tells himself, "Hey, I'm God, so why should I have to get out of the way?" By this time, the elephant and rider have reached him, and while our student is thinking about the dignities of his newly discovered status, the elephant reaches down with his trunk without even breaking stride and grabs our fellow and throws him aside into the underbrush.

Completely amazed, as well as somewhat scratched and bruised, the young man picks himself up and, when he gets reoriented, takes the trail back to the guru's place. There he tells his teacher what happened, and ends his account with the challenge, "But I thought you told me I was God." And the guru replies to him, "So you are. But why didn't you listen to the voice of the *mahut*, who is also God, telling you to get out of the way?"

I think I just got it how the *mahut* is also God. **Fred**

The Creature and the Creation, Revisited

The Spell of the Ideal

The radio show about gardening went well. Not as much poetry as I might have hoped for—gardening seemed more practical to my callers than I'd expected, more a matter of feeling secure about being able to get food—but worthwhile nonetheless.

The day after the show, as I was working at home, I was startled to find, as I answered a knock at my door, my friend Mr. Godachi. It wasn't the first time he'd come to my house—we'd had him to dinner a couple of times—but it was the first time he'd just shown up. It turned out that the pump in his well had died, and it was apparently going to be at least a few days before it could be repaired. In the meantime, he needed some water and had come by with some five-gallon jugs to request some of ours. While I filled his containers, I suggested that he stay with us at our place until the new parts for his pump arrived. He smiled a wonderful smile at my invitation, but declined. "All my green children are still back at my place," he explained. "I can't abandon them." Of course, I understood.

When we'd loaded the containers into the back of his little truck, Mr. Godachi asked me how my green children were doing, and in response I invited him to come out with me to the garden to check them out. After we'd taken a bit of a tour, we sat down on the bench I'd placed where the view across the valley was most open. Then I saw a big snakeroot coming up next to the little persimmon tree that every spring I believe has died, but which nonetheless survives, and I leaped up to pull out the snakeroot. This year I'd been struck by how ubiquitous those snakeroots were, springing up virtually everywhere there wasn't something else going on. I commented about how successful this unappealing little plant was, and told Mr. Godachi what I'd heard from one of my weekender neighbors (a toxicologist with the FDA) about that plant—that Abraham Lincoln's mother had died from drinking milk from cows that had eaten snakeroot, which has toxins in it. "If I had a dime for every snakeroot I've plucked out of the ground this spring, I'd be rich," I said.

On my way back to the bench, I was struck suddenly by how old Mr. Godachi was looking. Had he lost sleep over the breakdown of the pump? Was he in his early seventies, I wondered? Somehow I always thought of him as virtually ageless, but at that moment his age was showing. The thought that he might not always be there made me sad, and I sat silently next to him in my sadness.

Mr. Godachi broke the silence. "You've made something quite lovely on this piece of earth," he said to me. "It is not highly polished, not all under control, the way that some really accomplished gardeners can make their places seem. But still, there is a sense that the earth is happy here, like a home where the kids are growing up well, even if they don't always hang up all their clothes." His words gratified me immensely.

For a moment I said nothing, and then I shared a vision with my friend: "Sometimes I like to imagine the whole world turned into a garden. Nature everywhere allowed to flourish, yet also embellished by all the care that a good gardener can provide. Fragrance and color, everything brought together in beautiful patterns. Many diverse spaces, each with its own kind of loveliness. Paths for walking. Areas for people to graze, picking fruits and herbs and eating them as they walk along. An ideal fusion of the natural with the human."

"You know, I have had a similar fantasy," he replied. "And then I wonder, who is going to decide just what kinds of gardens to have? Would there be a place for everything, or only for the things that are appealing to people? Like that snakeroot: would your planet-wide garden afford that little plant its proper niche? I still like the idea, but it does get complicated."

Soon, he stood up to leave. I tried to persuade him to stay a bit longer, but he seemed clear that he wanted to get back to his place, and after a warm farewell, he drove off.

I went back to my computer to do some more writing, and decided first to check my e-mail. There I discovered a message from Barbara Marx Hubbard. I'd had a friendly acquaintance with Barbara some years ago, but we had not maintained contact. But our mutual friend Layne Longfellow had forwarded to her my inquiry about the "creature and the creation," and this new message was evidently her reply.

Dear Andy:

Layne sent me your interesting question. I am glad to be back in touch with you. Here is a response.

The real question is: What is the "natural order"? If you take the evolutionary perspective, it is clear that the nature of nature is to transform. It seems to me that the design of nature has been to create beings ever more capable of knowing the design, and thereby ever more able to co-design, or co-evolve with nature. From a theological point of view, we were created in the image of God, and godlike we are becoming.

I believe we are going through an evolutionary transformation comparable to the jump from the most intelligent animal to the earliest human. God is reproducing gods. Our task is to learn to be good gods. By "gods" I only mean what we used to call gods. Actually, it is to become fully human humans.

And she continued for a bit with some eloquent envisioning of a future with our kind as "godlings," using our knowledge and power for the furthering of co-creation, then concluding:

I would like to dialogue further with you on the theme. Much love to you, Andy.
Barbara Marx Hubbard

I responded:

Dear Barbara,

Delighted to hear from you. And I certainly recognize the eloquence and clarity of the Barbaramarxhubbard Vision. And for the most part, I share it as an image of where I would like for our species to be heading, for what role we might ideally play in the unfolding of cosmic evolution.

I do have one problem, though, with your statement as an answer to the question, "How should we conduct ourselves now?" in relation to our amassing and using powers over the living systems of nature.

That problem is this: how should we take into account the fact that the human world as it actually *is* right now does **not** act in a godly way? We act in shortsighted ways, depleting fisheries that we now have the power to destroy in our momentary search for profit and food. We act in callous ways, turning chickens and cows into mere machines for our exploitation in our wanting to have eggs, and milk and meat. We act quite selfishly, not taking into account the needs of future generations—in our deficit-spending not only of money, but of topsoil and climatic stability.

And if we see that *at least at present* we are acting in ungodly ways with the powers we already possess, *should that have no implications for how much permission we give ourselves to play god in the acquisition and excercise of still more powers?* **Andy**

Barbara wrote back:

The question is, since we do have these new powers, and it is very difficult, if not impossible to completely suppress or forbid them, how can we guide them toward the most beneficent use? One answer may be that if we had a transcendent vision of the meaning of these powers, which is to evolve our species toward an epoch of abundance, new vocations, new energy, new space, new knowledge, further self-actualization and freedom, that the attraction toward something good might be at least one vital factor guiding us toward the proper use of our new powers. All the best **Barbara**

In my response, I wrote:

I like the idea of nurturing a positive vision of what we might be like if we used our powers rightly. But I have a reservation. Let me put it this way:

Have you ever heard that semi-joke that the ideal person for the presidency would be a person who wouldn't seek the job? I think there's something similar about this demigod business.

I'm not sure that it is really appropriate for us to regard our ideal role as "playing God," since it seems to me that part of the qualifications for the role I think we should be playing requires a degree of humility. In other words, I think that whatever co-creation we do will be done right only if we are fully aware of the fact that we are *not* God. **Andy**

Barbara to Andy:

I am just reading a magnificent new book, not yet published, called *Relaxing into Clear Seeing*. It gives us a clear methodology to experience the nondual state of pure consciousness, springing from the work of Ramana Maharishi, and the Dzogchen teachings in Tibetan Buddhism, and others. In that teaching, to say we are *not* God is hubris, for what else could we be than God since God is everything?

If I do not identify with my individualized self, but with pure consciousness, boundlessness, the space out of which everything rises and falls, then the Eastern idea "I am God" is not hubris but humility. There is nothing but God.

Andy to Barbara:

You write that God is all there is, so that realizing that "I am God" is not hubris but humility. About which I ask: what does this have to do with the kind of "playing God" we actually see going on around us, where the players-of-God think of themselves as God, but hardly regard everything else—the stuff that they manipulate and exploit—as being God? Do you really think that humankind's present "playing God" manifests predominantly humility and not hubris?

I ask: does the fact that you are thinking of everything as God mean that you regard everything everyone does as godly? Does that include Auschwitz, or the denuding of the jungles for gold or timber? Are there distinctions to be made between behaviors (and forms of consciousness) that are in alignment with godliness and others that are not? And if so, is it not incumbent upon those who encourage humankind to move forward to lay some stress upon those distinctions?

Barbara to Andy:

As far as the idea that we are all aspects of God, of course, you are right to point out that this nondual awareness is far from common, and we certainly use our godlike powers in a god-awful manner, so often. All I am saying here is that I do not think it is unnatural that we have godlike powers. I think it is the design inherent in evolution to create beings ever more creative, with ever more awareness and freedom— witness the fifteen-billion-year trend from subatomic particles to us. I think it is natural for us to be in a kindergarten of godlings, since our big brains have just fathomed the invisible technologies of creation. *Homo sapiens* is like a two-year-old that has just learned to walk and can damage everything in sight.

What I don't like about the moral point of view is that so often it tells us what we cannot do rather than what we can do. If we were told that playing God is learning for true species immortality, that we have something great in store for us if we use our powers wisely, we might respond responsibly. I believe we need both constraints and attractions, carrots as well as sticks.

What do you think? All the best **Barbara**

Andy to Barbara:

I ask myself: what is it that is most missing from our present consciousness—the willingness to look at what our capacities are, or the willingness to entertain the idea that we should restrain ourselves?

As I look at the world around me, I see little of that mentality of six hundred years ago when it was thought that to sail out into the Atlantic beyond the Pillars of Hercules at its mouth (do I remember the name of their geography correctly?) was beyond man's proper place. I see much more of hubris and thoughtlessness in the pursuit of the human empire that Bacon launched four centuries ago, and that now recognizes no checks to the accumulation and exercise of human power.

Hence, to me, the message of humility and self-restraint seems crucial to our present need. The message of envisioning the fulfillment of godlike ambitions can be constructive, but I'd like to see it wedded to the other.

What think you of that? **Andy**

Barbara to Andy:

I agree with you about the need for us to restrain ourselves until and as we learn to act more wisely with our new powers. I may have quoted Eric Chaisson's idea that perhaps the reason we have not yet met any other high-technology species is that there are none. None has made it through this dangerous period that we are now entering with the powers of co-destruction and co-creation in a still self-centered stage of consciousness. There may be at work a principle of "cosmic selection," that selects against such species (as we are now becoming) before they make it into their universal phase. There are many who feel that we cannot learn "ethical evolution" quickly enough, and that therefore we will probably self-destruct with the very powers that could lift us toward becoming a universal species.

But in any event, we can't put the genie back in the box. We do have the powers of young godlings. We have found the Tree of Life. The flaming sword and the cherubim that protected the Tree of Life from humans have been breached or have invited us in. In any case, we are in the Garden of Co-Creation. It is the eighth day of creation, and humanity has awakened, recognizing some responsibility for the creation. My approach is to invite into the Garden as many knowers of the evolutionary potential of humanity as possible, to discover together the meaning of this power for the good.

I'm too tired to write more. Once again, it is really enjoyable to be in dialogue with you. Love and appreciation **Barbara**

Barbara has a good heart, I thought. If all us godlings had good hearts, I'd feel more sanguine.

The Mind of the Breadbaker

All this discussion of humankind's charging ahead to seize the Tree of Life percolated in my mind, and then suddenly it brought to my mind a piece I'd written a year and a half earlier. This one too had appeared in the *Christian Science Monitor* (June 7, 1996), and it occurred to me that it expressed well the difficult mixture of thoughts and feelings that swirl within me around these issues.

Here's how it went. I called the piece "The Mind of the Breadbaker."

From the time my little son was eight months old, he and I have done the grocery shopping together. When Nathaniel was a toddler, discovering at every turn what the world was about, I used to joke that I took him to the supermarket because I wanted him to know where food really comes from. It's not just something that's there when you open the refrigerator, I'd say, you've got to go to the Source—some place like Safeway, where it sits on the shelves. He shouldn't take our getting our daily bread for granted, I'd declare solemnly.

Back then we lived inside the Washington Beltway, but before our boy was four we left. I had found that my spirit was withering from living in a landscape where earth was just an occasional break from the pavement, just something allowed to exist in the interstices of the human grid. After a decade in a realm where the human element tyrannizes over everything, I yearned to have a place where the land around me was shaped less by my own kind than by the hand of living nature.

We moved out to the mountains of Virginia, and Nathaniel worked with me as we carved some terraces out of the hillside to grow our own herbs and vegetables. We carried chicken manure and horse manure down the slope to enrich the soil, we planted our seeds, we carefully monitored the moisture levels in the earth to make sure our plants had what they needed to thrive, and we kept some seeds from one year's harvest to plant the next. The idea of his knowing where our food came from was no longer just a joke.

And my spirit revived, rising back upright like some limp plant that just needed watering. I felt connected with the generations before me who lived from the yield of the earth, connected with my roots in this amazing experiment of life on this special planet.

Then I took up the baking of bread. Why not? As a writer, I work at home and can easily take a few minutes to tend its various phases. And is there anything that tastes better than bread fresh from the oven?

During the years I've been baking bread, it has gradually dawned on me what a marvelous invention this stuff is. We think of it as the staff of life, something quite basic, but really, our ancestors lived on this earth for countless thousands of years before anyone even thought of bread. You've got to gather the grain; you've got to grind it; you've got to get it moist; and then, there's the miracle of the leavening process. What kind of genius was it, I started to wonder, who first understood this whole process well enough to produce reliably the wonderful food of risen bread?

No doubt, the yeasts first entered the dough by accident, landing invisibly from the breeze, feeding on the moistened grain the way that molds will make an open tomato furry with their growing filaments if you leave it sitting on a summer countertop. But what kind of mind did it take to comprehend the living process that had occurred between the yeast and the wheat, and to be able to replicate it each day to give his or her family the staff of life?

Not long ago, as I mixed my dough, I understood: The minds of those who conceived this process of turning grain into bread had themselves been cultivated by generations of experience at turning earth into crops of food to eat. What I saw was this: the baker of bread is farming, and what he is growing is yeast.

Think of it. The farmer tills his or her soil; the baker grinds the wheat into flour, preparing a special kind of earth for a particular kind of crop. The farmer sows seed into his prepared soil; the baker adds yeast into the dough. Like the step from the primitive society's gathering of seeds for eating into agricultural society's growing of crops, the step into the baking of leavened bread also required people to grab hold of the forces of growth and reproduction: the seed that used to just fall onto the ground is now planted; the fungus that used to biodegrade the grain seed in the earth is now brought to the feast of the seed ground up for the dough.

Like the irrigator of crops, the grower of yeast must make sure that there is enough moisture in the soil that's been prepared. It's not just coincidence that leavened bread was invented about 5,000 years ago by farming people living by the Nile River, a desert area where irrigation and the control of water were vital to survival. The farmer needs warmth and sunlight for his crops to thrive; the baker puts his or her leavened dough in the warm sunlight, or by the warm stones of an oven, to rise. The farmer must be patient with the organic process of growth, waiting for the crops to mature before attempting to harvest. The baker must also bide his time, waiting at each stage for the dough to rise.

If, in his vision of the world, the baker of bread is a farmer, that also means that the baker is an engineer, engineering the growth of living stuff. The baker is one not only with the sower who drops seeds into furrows but also with the herder, who brought wild animals into a pen. We take all this for granted, but this breakthrough of mind brought about a revolution in life on earth.

I think about this revolution as I come in from the terrace with Nathaniel to remove my fresh-baked loaf from the oven. Nathaniel says he's starving, and well he might be after working the soil with me and dancing across the pumpkin vines on the slope. It is midsummer, and the vines have burst free of the terrace we built for them, spreading across the hillside so rapidly that we joke about their taking over the world. While I carve for him a steaming slice from the new, hard-crusted loaf, it comes to me that it was this breakthrough, this mind of the farmer and breadbaker—with its new conception of the relationship between the human and the living world—that laid the foundation for the human empire.

In the genius of the first bakers of bread, I realize, we find newly sprouted that vision of dominion that, cultivated and extended over five millennia, has brought us—for better and for worse—to where we are today, to that dangerous growth of human pride that has given us a globe-encompassing system of manipulation and production that threatens to choke off the living systems that sustain us.

Nathaniel savors his food, and says, "Thanks, Dad, for the great bread!" "Hey, kid," I reply, "I'm glad you love the bread. But don't thank *me*. I just work here." The breadbaker, I figure, ought to bear in mind where our food really comes from.

The One Truth and the Many
How Can Good Order Be Built from What We Can Know of Truth?

A Missing Dimension?

For a while, the forum danced around in a kind of celebration of the integration that the evolutionary framework provided by Herman, and others, seemed to offer us. Actually, it was only a handful who were celebrative. A few others were engaged, if a bit tentative. And then there were some—such as Carl and Kenneth—who were conspicuously, if predictably, absent from the conversation.

In this conversation, with those most celebrative taking the lead, an effort was made to try out this bottom-up/top-down synthesis on a few of the contentious moral issues that beset contemporary American society.

If people on the cultural left were to take seriously the idea that the natural order imposes some moral obligations on human beings, it was asked for example, how might that influence their views about abortion? If people on the cultural right, and particularly religious conservatives, were to take seriously the idea that all our truths are not skyhooks, handed down from above from some wholly superior authority beyond question, but are merely cranes, built up from the same fallible human stuff that is supposed to be ordered, how would that affect how they would discuss the issue of the tolerance versus the rejection (or even persecution) of homosexuality?

If people of the countercultural persuasion were to look at the human being as not only an end in him- or herself but also as part of a larger human order that needs to be served for the sake of all, would that have any ramifications for their views on such matters as the virtue of sacrifice, or the nurturing (or challenging) of children's self-esteem, or even issues like "welfare" and "patriotism"? And if people on the cultural right were to really grasp that a sound moral system can take as its foundation only the goodness of meeting the needs and enhancing the quality of experience of human beings (and other sentient creatures), would that have an impact on how they stand on such issues as masturbation, suicide for the suffering and terminally ill, as well as, again, self-esteem and the virtue of sacrifice?

It was a good, if inconclusive, discussion.

What then took us in a different direction was a message that arrived from Rev. George, dissenting from what seemed like a consensus, at least among those then engaged, about how satisfactory this whole evolutionary perspective was.

Several of you know me reasonably well, *Rev. George began,* and you know that I'm not the kind of guy who throws around phrases like "secular humanism" as a term of opprobrium. But I have to say, that phrase has come to my mind while I've been following—and, to a limited extent, participating in—this discussion. This great "evolutionary" integration that is being developed here, I regret to say, does not satisfy me very thoroughly. I can see that in some ways it does achieve a synthesis, it does build some bridges, but it's becoming ever clearer to me as we go along, that in some rather important ways this perspective is not an integration but is rather much more closely aligned with one part of our cultural division than with the other.

As I tune in on my own unease I realize that some elements really important to me are omitted in this "synthesis." Aside from "secular humanism," another term that's been floating to my consciousness has been "***materialism***." And what are missing, to me, are the spiritual dimension and—yes, I know, we've been through this—God.

I'm not sure just what I want from you, or what I myself want to do with this discontent. I'm not calling into question the scientific validity of evolution as an account of how life arose, and how we human beings came to be here, peering up into the heavens asking these vital questions. Evolution happened—I'll concede that and, to disclaim again, I'm not the kind of fellow who says that we should teach "creationism" in the schools. But all that notwithstanding, I feel in my guts that there's something more—something in heaven and earth that is not captured in your materialistic philosophy.

Are we really nothing more than matter and energy that somehow congealed by chance given world enough and time? In my heart, I feel that we are more than that. Surely there must have been more going on than just random events yielding self-organization out of the slime. And surely there must be more to us now than just so much gross matter so ordered as to be able to say thank you and please at the dinner table while we absorb energy from the seeds of wheat leavened by one-celled organisms. Man does not consist of bread alone, I say. There is a spiritual dimension, isn't there? I have experienced it. Others have experienced it. It is a dimension that seems unexplained by a wholly materialistic framework. It is, indeed, what leavens our existence.

And then, too, there's that transcendent dimension. There's God. For more than a century, people of a rationalist bent have been trying to "nothing but" God out of existence. "The projection of the superego" some have said. "A way of imaging our ideals," goes another. So were the prophets coming down from the mountains, then, just projecting their paternal introjects? Have the mystics just tripped out and confused themselves about their ego boundaries? I don't think so.

I can't prove my case. I can't summon up fossil evidence and do DNA comparisons to prove that something quite essential is left out of your materialistic, wholly secular perspective, but I did want to bear witness, for whatever it may contribute to this search for the truth, that I am unwilling to allow my understanding to collapse into this merely evolutionary perspective. **Rev. George**

What Rev. George got back from this was, predictably, challenging if not dismissive.

It seems indicative, *wrote Peter,* that you refer here several times to what you *feel,* as if your feelings were somehow evidence so consequential that it should outweigh what a reasoned analysis of the empirical data shows.

It is indeed true, *Peter continued,* that your desire to reestablish some place here for something immaterial, for something transcendent and God-like, does not get any support from fossil evidence or DNA chronologies. But are we not better off allowing reality—speaking to us through the evidence—to dictate what we do and do not believe? **Peter**

At this point, Cynthia took off from this on a most interesting riff. It comprised a very eloquent discourse on scientific epistemology, likening it to the very process of evolution itself, and contrasting it with the epistemology of faith that traditionally has underlain efforts to construct the theocentric worldview that science has been replacing.

As an intellectual edifice, scientific inquiry *is itself* a "crane" of the kind we were discussing earlier. With science, through the process of unfolding inquiry, the data of empirical reality—which can be seen as the substratum of a bottom-up way of knowing—allows us to arrive at provisional truths, at hypotheses always subject to questioning and revision as new data from below are discovered that challenge the existing paradigm.

By contrast, received religion is not only about enshrining a Skyhook at the heart of the basic questions about reality, but also employs a skyhook-approach to knowing. The Fundamentalist does not begin with questions, and a methodology for inquiry. He begins rather with the conclusions. The religious tradition's basic framework of knowledge hangs there as if it were self-established, self-validating. The mind, rather than open, is closed to new information that might require some modification or wholesale shift in the belief system. With beliefs cast in the form of skyhooks, the kinds of conclusions that should be the **end** of inquiry serve rather as the ***beginning,*** what should be developed and supported is rather taken as a given from which all else must follow. **Cynthia**

Cynthia's message led to a flurry of other brief messages affirming the virtues of open-minded and empirical approaches to knowledge, and opposing dogmatism and the unwillingness to question assumptions in the light of contrary evidence. John Stuart Mill was quoted saying that he who has tested his beliefs against all information, who has sought difficulties with which to challenge them, can know that his beliefs and judgment are superior to those of one, or of a multitude, who have not put their beliefs to such tests.[1]

Soon thereafter, Herman entered in, continuing the use of the skyhook-crane distinction as a way of gently but firmly disallowing Rev. George's attempts to put God back into the picture.

The wonderful thing about the evolutionary perspective, *Herman wrote,* is that it all builds up from below. With an understanding of the emergence of "cranes," we discover there's no need for skyhooks. Indeed, no place for skyhooks. Don't you see, George, that adding God is just putting something inexplicable into a system that makes excellent sense without it?

If you concede the reality of evolution, I don't see how there can be any place left there for God, or any such transcendent skyhook. Evolution is a straightforward unfolding, going from the beginning through various stages on up to the present, and then further into a future. I suppose you're right that by being resolutely bottom-up, evolution does take sides in our cultural battle, that it is—in that respect—at odds with the traditionally religious part of our culture. But on this crucial rejection of the notion of the skyhook, I hope you can see, the evolutionary perspective is at least on the side of scientific reason and empiricism.

Why inject mystery where there need be none? **Herman**

I felt immediately moved, by a recollection from my own life, to enter the conversation. Not just *any* recollection, indeed, but a recollection of what may have been my life's most crucial moment. But I hesitated for a while, and during this time of hesitation Terrence posted a message.

I appreciate George's attempt to remind us that this "evolutionary perspective" about which some of us have gotten so enthusiastic is not necessarily the last word on how we should understand our place in the great scheme of things, *Terrence wrote*. George has helped bring back to my mind an earlier discussion of ours that seemed important at the time: whatever happened to that insight we were developing about the deficiency in the "liberal" outlook in its ability to inspire in people a "passion for the whole"?

I've been listening here lately to Ralph and other liberals feeling, somewhat triumphantly, their vindication by Herman's perspective. Swimming contentedly between the rigid positions of top and bottom; figuring things out as we go along; creating little bits of man-made order as we need to so that things can be kept decent. But that need for people's hearts to be moved by an image of some transcendent Whole that commands our love and allegiance—that need has not been met by this evolutionary perspective, and it seems to me that no note has been taken here of that void.
Terrence

Just because some people may argue that we ***need*** some God, doesn't mean that there ***is*** one, *Cynthia replied*. And as Herman said, evolution as a perspective gets rid of these skyhook-deities.

It was at this point that I decided to take the plunge and tell about how my own life-changing experience might bear upon all this.

I'm reading here on the forum about how an evolutionary perspective necessarily eliminates the idea of a transcendent, God-like presence in our cosmic picture, *I said*, but my own life has hinged upon a moment of transcendent vision that seems to that calls into question that either/or picture.

On several occasions on this forum, I've mentioned that first book of mine, *The Parable of the Tribes*. I think you know that this book and the ideas embedded in it have been a pretty big deal in my life. But you might be surprised to know that this whole project began at a particular time and place, that it began with a particular experience of "Aha!" that gave me the seed of the whole vision. And perhaps you'll be more surprised still to know that this experience is remarkable not only for its having shaped pretty much the whole of my work in the world ever since, but also for being unique in a most surprising way: my envisioning of the parable of the tribes was the one moment in my life when I felt that I was being **shown** something. To put it plainly, this book grew out of what I called at the time, and have no reason now to call otherwise, a revelatory experience.

I cannot explain how this could be so, but that it was some kind of revelation seemed undeniable when I experienced it. In some ways, the truth of that felt even more undeniable than other things I believe to be true, because I experienced that truth as being more powerful and more compelling than I have experienced other truths before or since.

I was tempted to tell about this experience a while ago, when we were discussing that "passion for the whole." Kenneth had told of his own moving encounter with something transcendent—his God—and I felt the impulse to share my own intense and transformative encounter with what I sensed was something all-encompassing at the heart of things. But, for whatever reason, I held back.

Now it seems I must "testify," as some people might put it. Our conversation has drawn a clearcut dichotomy between the evolutionary perspective and the transcendent, perhaps God-oriented vision. In that context, what is striking about my experience is that it seemed to affirm both simultaneously. And though I feel confused about that possible paradox, and that confusion causes me to waver and stumble here and there, I have lived my life since then as if somehow both were true. As if, that is, the world were simply unfolding in the blind evolutionary way **and** as if there were some transcendent Something somehow connected with the whole process.

The content of my vision—at that moment, and in the book I wrote subsequently—as some of you may know, is resolutely evolutionary in its orientation. It is quite bottom-up in its Darwinian suppositions, with a view of the cosmos unfolding in some way blindly, creating on this earth a living system that does not plan for those new potentialities and dangers that blind evolutionary emergence can bring, and that has now led to a dangerous and painful experiment involving *Homo sapiens,* the emergent cultural animal.

At the same time, while I was "seeing" this tragedy in the unfolding process, I was also set aflame by the apprehension of something transcendent—something ineffably beautiful and sacred—that was showing me all this. I called it the Source and, although its nature was fundamentally mysterious, I felt that it radiated in everything around me, in the trees, in the face of my companion, in the nature of Life (or maybe Being) itself. It was **in** everything, and yet it also transcended everything.

It was a mystery, and I never felt that my mind encompassed just what it was that I had encountered. At the same time, I felt absolutely devoted to whatever It was, and when this revelation seemed to be accompanied by my being given an "assignment" to write a book articulating what I'd seen, I felt moved to undertake a solemn commitment to fulfill that assignment. I cried at the time, actually—which is not much like me—from fear of what this "mission" of mine might entail. And, as the next fourteen years before that book was published were eventually to prove, those fears turned out to be hardly excessive. But without the numinous quality of that sense of this Transcendent Source, and the transfixing energy of the relationship I formed with It at that moment, I do not believe I would have completed the work. In the absence of that special charge, I'd have faltered at any of a dozen trying points along the way, and abandoned that task.

So I feel I understand something of Kenneth's moment under the stars. And the particular nature of my revelatory moment makes me think that we should not be too hasty in rejecting Rev. George's dissatisfaction with the evolutionary perspective in the purely materialistic form in which our conversation has developed it to this point. **Andy**

Heresy

The response I got to this message took me somewhat aback. Perhaps I should have anticipated that some of my buddies would have thought me a turncoat for trying to reopen the door to what they regarded as magical or at least illogical thinking, and to the reinstatement of the banned Skyhook. Indeed, upon reflection, it occurs to me that perhaps it was the anticipation of such a response that had inhibited my sharing this experience earlier. Nonetheless, when the response came it proved, although not entirely pleasant for me to deal with, quite worth the hassle.

I'm surprised at you, Andy, *wrote Ralph, more in sadness than in anger.* I'd thought you to be "one of us," by which I mean a more or less clearheaded, empirical kind of thinker. And here you are bringing in some kind of mystical experience and asking that we treat it as illuminating something important about the nature of the cosmic order.

I don't doubt your testimony about the power of the experience, about its being beautiful and moving. But I would think you'd regard it more as some kind of physiologically unusual event—some neurological blip of some kind—rather than a glimpse about the essential nature of the cosmos. **Ralph**

Before I could respond to Ralph's lament about my lapse into magical and mystical fuzzyheadedness, another response came in, this one from Cynthia.

We just got through talking about the soundness and power of the scientific epistemology, and I'd just assumed from all your previous participation, Andy, that you also subscribed to this approach, *wrote Cynthia*. Now here you bring in some highly personal experience of yours, apparently regarding it as important evidence. What are we supposed to do with that "evidence"? This experience of yours is not replicable. Other people cannot go and reproduce the same circumstances and get the same evidentiary results. Even you yourself, I expect, could not.

Are you interested in throwing out science and replacing it with mysticism? **Cynthia**

At this point I felt quite uncomfortable with the way I was being perceived—as someone who'd extricated himself from within the fold, who'd passed beyond some kind of pale. I wanted to bring myself back within the aura of respectability in the eyes of these people, my friends, but I also wanted to respond with integrity, remaining true to this experience that—more than any other single event in my life—I had allowed to shape my destiny.

Your challenges to me are challenges that, over the years, I have posed to myself, *I wrote*. And I will confess to you that I have no completely satisfactory response to them. I make no assumption about where the truth lies here. Yet I believe that it may be you who are making the unquestioned assumptions here, and whose logic therefore contains the gaps. And so, as I respond to your challenges I want also to issue a challenge to what may be your own "unscientific" way of thinking.

Let me start by saying that I do not dismiss the possibility that my "revelatory" experience was, as you say, some kind of neurological blip. Maybe it represented some kind of dissociation, or hallucination, or other illusion-producing event. Maybe it was just components of my own psyche coming together in a moment of epiphany. And of course you are right, Cynthia, about the nonreplicability of my experience.

The fact is, however, that I am far from unique among humankind in having had such a mystical or "revelatory" kind of experience. A larger proportion than you might expect of the American public—maybe as high as a third—has apparently had **some** kind of significant religious experience. And beyond that, there have been a variety of mystical experiences, reported through history, which have been vital parts of the lives, not only of the individuals who had them directly, but of entire cultures that have placed these experiences at the center of their own worldviews. (I think of Buddha's under the tree, of Paul's on the road to Damascus, and of countless other mystics whose testimony is part of the heritage of various religious traditions.)

About all these experiences, you can say that they are nonreplicable (even though various traditions—with Hindu and Buddhist meditation practices, Zen koans,

Christian hermits with their fasts in the wilderness, etc.—have worked to find ways of replicating them). And you could raise the possibility that in all these cases nothing is happening but neurological blips, that Dostoyevsky's mysticism was "nothing but" the product of his epilepsy, that Joan of Arc must have been psychotic to hear those voices. And you might be right.

But not necessarily! That is all that I want to argue—not necessarily. Is it not conceivable that in these events—as the experience itself seems to affirm—something important and true gets glimpsed? **Andy**

Cynthia responded: Science is not about what is conceivable, but about what can be established. Science is not about the off-beat and the bizarre, but about the replicable patterns and what can be demonstrated by controlled observations.

I began my response: To me, the essence of science is not the matter of replicability or experimentation, though those deservedly play an important role in the development of the body of scientific knowledge. What is essential to the spirit of science, I would assert, is a kind of open-mindedness: "I will allow myself to be informed by the cosmos," the scientific spirit says, "without prejudice. Whatever might be the truth, I will remain open to its speaking to me."

In a science undertaken in that spirit of the unprejudiced search for the truth, the question of conceivability is a vital one. The challenge I am posing to you is this: Can you *imagine* a cosmos in which some vital dimension of the reality—perhaps some Being or some aspect of the Whole—was knowable to creatures within that cosmos only through something like mystical experience? And therefore, I ask: is it possible that there are important truths about the nature of our cosmos that you, by your rules and assumptions, are precluding yourselves from knowing? **Andy**

This is not the kind of universe that science shows us to be in, *Cynthia answered tersely*.

Now who is thinking in a circle? *I challenged back*. We've complained—rightly I'd say—about the way religious traditionalists start out with their conclusions, then admit as relevant only the evidence that conforms to those *a priori* assumptions, and conclude by declaring those original assertions to be confirmed.

Now I've asked if it is conceivable that there could be important truths about the cosmos that might not be disclosed by the usual scientific method, and the response is that the usual scientific method has not disclosed it. Hmmm.

But is there any reason why revelation *cannot* be possible? I cannot see how such a possibility can logically be excluded. And if that possibility exists, it would seem to me that any epistemology or set of assumptions that *completely forecloses the possibility* of knowledge of that vital dimension cannot be considered truly scientific.

Genuine science, in my book, does not foreclose the possibility of obtaining any important knowledge. **Andy**

Let me see what it is that you are suggesting is — or may be — true about the cosmos, *Larry's message began,* in addition to this nice and tidy evolutionary perspective that George regarded as too materialistic, and that you are saying that somehow need not be so.

I gather you were not suggesting that we reject the evolutionary view. After all, your revelation as you reported it was decidedly evolutionary in content. So if that's so, what is — or might be — that Source that you felt you made contact with? How can there be a Something All-Encompassing out there hanging around while all this evolution is going on? What's the connection between the two parts of your truth? **Larry**

To quote the late, great Tevye, *I responded,* I'll tell you: I don't know. But it is a question that I've pondered and what I've come up with, hardly to my satisfaction, is that maybe there's some kind of Whole that is emerging through the evolutionary process, and maybe there is some kind of Source from which it all has been emanating from the beginning. The first is a kind of Emergent God; the second is more like a preexistent Creator. My gut sense has been that, somehow, it is both.

And I don't know how it can all work. On the one hand, if it's a preexistent Creator, what is It doing during all these billions of years when evolution is wending its very slow way, and when there are, presumably, no little critters like us to Spill the Beans to in such a revelatory process? And if it's an Emergent God, then how did it emerge, and what is our relationship to It? Sometimes I've wondered if we are somehow components of something bigger than ourselves that's coming into existence as evolution knits together something more Whole than the fragmentary universe that first arose. And the idea that it might somehow be both is admittedly pretty mind-boggling.

I confess to being pretty clueless. **Andy**

I've always been intrigued by religious experiences, *wrote Herman.* But I do not want that kind of perspective to start undermining what we've accomplished here. And what I think we have accomplished is a clearheaded and logically consistent way of understanding the way our cosmic order works, and also of how it doesn't work. What I'm referring to is that matter of the skyhooks and the cranes.

The evolutionary perspective is emphatically unmagical in its orientation, and I want to step in here to defend that demystification of human thinking that has taken our species so long to achieve. When you, Andy, start entertaining the idea of there being some Source of everything, some preexisting Being from whom all Order and other blessings may flow, I hear "skyhook," and I want to say "No!" "No" to the illogic of something that is self-created, and something superior to us who are to be ordered. "No" to enshrining mystery at the core of our worldview.

You have made a case, Andy, for the importance of remaining open-minded to various possibilities. You have argued that one's assumptions should not preclude one from ever being able to learn important things that **conceivably could be true**. I appreciate that. But there is also, as I expect you know, the philosophical concept of "Occam's razor," according to which one should choose to gravitate to the simpler and more logically elegant explanation rather to posit something elaborate and improbable. (Among physicians, there is the somewhat kindred idea framed in terms of diagnostic conclusions: if you hear hoofbeats, don't think zebras.)

Now for us, we can admit the **conceivability** of a weird and bizarre and mysterious universe, and yet turn away from that in preference to the simple and explicable and sensible alternative that presents itself to us. I would regard your interpretation of your revelatory idea as a form of thinking "zebras," and the empirical scientific perspective as the sensible alternative that makes far more sense to entertain. **Herman**

When I undertook to respond to Herman, I worked first to center myself. I had the greatest respect for Herman, and I could tell from his message that there was a lot at stake for him in this issue. For both those reasons I wanted to be sure that I spoke with care.

I hold you in very high esteem, Herman, and I'm most sympathetic also with your relationship to the mystery of things—drawn to it but also wanting to demystify. I too experience the hunger for a world that makes complete sense, that is clear and logical, in which mysteries are to be solved and not reveled in. If the choice were as you suggest, I would probably agree with you about which side to fall toward as we slide down Occam's razor. (Ouch!)

But in my view—and many years ago, I'd have said "regrettably," but at this point, my feelings are far more complex—this is not the nature of the choice we face. It is true that my Source brings in an element of the mysterious, perhaps even one of those dread skyhooks. But what is not true, as I see it, is that your alternative is so simple and grounded and free of mystery.

The evolutionary point of view, you claim, says "Of course all this will just naturally unfold, from the ground up, with order created by nothing except cranes that emerge, themselves, along the way." But there is a preamble that is missing there. And that preamble is "Given the existence of the universe, and given its being a lawful one that behaves in an orderly way. . . ." It is by ignoring that "given" that I think you are able to see your perspective as a thorough demystification. Bring that "given" back in and look at it squarely, and I think one is confronted with what you dread: the mystery of the skyhook.

By this, I do not mean a skyhook necessarily of the God-above kind. Rather I mean this: that existence itself is a skyhook, that having an orderly universe where

$F = ma$ and $E = mc^2$ in itself constitutes a skyhook. These dimensions of being—that the cosmos exists, and that it obeys the laws science discovers—are fundamental mysteries, it seems to me, as incomprehensible and inexplicable as any others. Where did they come from?! How did they come to be, and to be the way they are? What kind of answer can even be imagined that isn't somehow a kind of skyhook with nothing beneath it to support it?

And so it seems to me that there is absolutely **no escape** from the reality that the universe is at bottom an impenetrable mystery. If I had a choice between a worldview in which the mind never got boggled, and one that incorporates some bogglers of the mind, I'd choose the former. But I don't see that we do—or ever can—have any such a comfortable unboggled choice. I'm saying that there are basic and inescapable questions to which there are no conceivable answers that would make sense to us—or, at least, that would make sense to me.

Maybe other people's minds can really grasp these ideas that are so utterly incomprehensible to me, but I am doubtful about that. This whole problem—the search for some underlying answer that doesn't raise other questions of "why?" or "how?" and that itself makes sense—reminds me of a story. I don't remember where I heard it but, as I recall, in the story a woman comes to a famous scientist after he's given a talk about modern cosmology. She tells him that he's got it wrong, that the way the universe is put together is that the whole thing rests on the back of a turtle. "And what, madam, does this turtle rest on?" "Oh, under him there's another turtle," she replies. "And beneath that second turtle?" "Below him is still another turtle." "And then, please, what is there—" "No need to ask," the woman interrupted him. "It's turtles all the way down."

To my way of thinking, science does not really get us out of that woman's problem. No matter how many cranes we uncover, we still are faced with the problem of figuring out how it can be turtles all the way down. **Andy**

The Missing Capital "T"

I must say, Andy, that like some of the others I too felt surprised to hear some of this from you, *Rev. George posted in the next message,* although in my case the surprise is a pleasant one.

I have felt a discomfort, in our recent discussion, that some of those whose voices have been important here in the past—people like Kenneth and Carl—have made themselves absent. Kenneth's experience under the stars was, as I recall, received here with some appreciation. But once a number of people started to form some consensus around an evolutionary view of the cosmos, I've wondered what that appreciation might mean. And I have worried that perhaps Kenneth—and others—

might have withdrawn in the belief that there was no place here for a worldview like theirs.

So I am glad to hear someone of your nontraditional stripe out here making a case for the possibility of there being some access to greater truths, spiritual realities, beyond those provided by the purely materialistic kind of empiricism. **Rev. George**

There came then together two messages that seemed like different sides of the same coin. One was from Kenneth.

Thank you for your solicitude, *Kenneth wrote,* but please do not group Andy and his supposed "revelation" together with my experience, and that of a great many other souls that have been saved by our Lord and Savior. It is well established that there are false prophecies as well as genuine, that people can be led astray by voices they mistakenly think to be from God but that are, in fact, from the demonic realm that works to lead them astray.

There are many beliefs, but only one truth faith. **Kenneth**

The second message came from Ralph.

I would not want for Kenneth to leave because he felt excluded, *Ralph began in a sentence that was already obsolete by the time it reached our inboxes,* or as though we were not interested in hearing what he might think or feel. But the lumping together of your experience with Kenneth's does raise a difficulty with the epistemology you're proposing, Andy. You and Kenneth may both have had "mystical" experiences, but you do not report the same findings from those experiences. And you mentioned Buddha under the tree and Paul heading to Damascus. Both had big "aha's," but the Big Truths that struck them were not identical. What kind of credence can we give, then, to any of these reports? **Ralph**

Precisely, Ralph, *Herman wrote as a rejoinder.* I would be a good deal more impressed by this revelatory way of knowing if everyone who had such experiences came back with the same reports. Then those who didn't have that experience—the singular form would then apply—could just be like people who haven't been to Hawaii, but who, because of the reports from those who have made the journey, have no reason to doubt that it's there. Or perhaps they could be like the colorblind who, though they can't tell how brilliant is the red of the rose, and perhaps cannot really quite "get" what the idea of "brilliant red" means, nonetheless could come to understand that there's something out there that's real and that, for some reason, they're not able to apprehend.

But that's not the way it is. And that in itself, it seems to me, profoundly undermines any claim of the receivers of such revelation to being in possession of genuine knowledge. **Herman**

You are right, *I acknowledged in my reply, which I posted immediately,* that this diversity of "revelations" poses an important challenge.

One way to meet that challenge is Kenneth's way, that is, to conclude that one of them is right and all the rest are wrong. It is not logically impossible that this is the case, but it certainly is suspicious that we have so many believers of different stripes taking that approach. "Our faith is the truth faith, all the rest are infidels" has served the Inquisitors of the Church of Rome and the Ayatollahs of Islamic Iran equally. (I notice that the fundamentalist rabbis of Israel are now trying to sever all forms of Judaism besides their own from the tree of the Jewish religion.) To me, it seems more reasonable to interpret the certainty of true believers as evidence of the believers' need for certainty than of their possessing good grounds for it. And more reasonable to interpret the differences in the various "revealed" truths as bearing testimony to the failure of ***any*** of them to return from the mountain with ***The Truth*** with a capital "T."

Which leads some people to adopt a second interpretive approach, along the lines of Herman's thinking, which is to reject this whole approach to knowledge as lacking in validity. "If at most one religion can be right, then the channel for attaining religious knowledge must be pretty poor, so it is reasonable to assume none of them are right." If that were the case, then humans would be pretty foolish for choosing—as people generally have throughout history—to put such knowledge at the core of their worldview.

But I don't think the Buddhists have been foolish to keep Buddha and his "truth" before their eyes, nor Christians to revere that of Jesus, and so forth. (Nor do I think my using my own numinous experience as a compass for my life has been folly.) It seems pretty clear that much understanding of tremendous value has come to humankind through such channels.

So, what I come to is a third way of interpreting this variety and inconsistency of testimony. In this interpretation, the diversity of revelations does constitute a problem, but it is not a fatal one. I would say that the key point is not that revelation's problems are mortal but that we are. Let me explain that cryptic remark.

If there ***is*** some Huge Truth out there that presents itself to us in these nonreplicable but searing moments, it may well be way over our heads, beyond our ability upon perceiving it to capture it cleanly. And that, indeed, is what the mystics have always reported: isn't that what's meant by the ***ineffability*** of the experience? It's a "Wow! What was that?!"

And so I come to the view that we are capable of a mystical apprehension of some Truth, but one that we can see but dimly, however intensely illuminated it may be, and can capture in a form inescapably contaminated by our own categories and limitations. It's like what one ant says to another in a little Sufi tale: "God is so great

He has not just two antennae but four." What I am proposing is that we should regard the testimony with which people return from their mystical encounters as being of vital importance, but unreliable, distorted, incomplete. Big truths, but no capital "T."
Andy

Fears of Chaos

You rationalists are forever being reasonable, and forever missing the Truth that is there for the having, *Kenneth wrote at that point.* You take eternal truths and, by relying upon your reason of which you have made a God, you knock them off their throne. The result is darkness. The result is chaos. By abjuring the leap of faith, you leave yourself on the crumbling ground in which you have nothing to hold onto. You say, "Everything is true," which ends up meaning, "Nothing is true." And you are left with nothing, and a world made up of people like you will crumble along with your foundationless beliefs. **Kenneth**

This led Terrence to weigh in as well.

I'm not sure that I would use the same words as Kenneth to articulate my reaction, but my response is akin to his. A few times in our discussions, the question of moral relativism has been thrown at you people on the liberal side. And my recollection is that most of you have consistently denied it. Yet the more I listen to how you paint your worldview, the more those denials ring false.

A while back, *Terrence continued,* Herman was talking about changing circumstances requiring changing moral rules. It sounded to me like saying that there are no moral absolutes, that it all depends on the situation. And when Andy was discussing the good, it sounded like he was saying (or at least implying) that there are all kinds of ways that people's needs might get met, so that how we organize things here in the United States (with our Constitution and our inalienable rights) might be matched in goodness by some other system in another part of the world that, though they didn't respect those rights, might be just as good. (Which sounds to me like the way the Communist regime in China deflects our criticism of their human-rights abuses.)

Now we hear even revealed truth reduced in status to being just another form of man-made propositions. There have been many revelations, Andy's arguing, and they all should be regarded as having some piece of the truth. Which also sounds like an argument for relativism. "Choose your own truth. None is better than another."

Do you still deny that you are tearing down all absolutes, and leaving us in the chaos of moral relativism? **Terrence**

And then, surprisingly, there was Carl back again.

The Lord God handed down ten commandments on Mt. Sinai. "Thou shalt not kill." "Thou shalt not commit adultery." "Thou shalt not covet." And the others. These were God-given truths then, and so they remain for all time, and in all places. Such truths do not change. **Carl**

It was Herman who responded first, while I was still trying to outline a cogent response.

I guess it depends on what you mean by relativism, *Herman said*. If it means that any set of moral rules must be judged to be as good as any other, then I am emphatically *not* relativistic. If relativism means denying the claim that there is only one Absolute morality—one that is right for always and everywhere—and that all deviations from that one Absolute are errors, then I would say I am a relativist. **Herman**

Herman captured the essential structure of the response I wanted to give, *I then posted*. For me, too, there is an essential distinction to be made: one question is whether there are, in some way, objective standards of truth and goodness; the other is whether any renditions of the true and the good that we humans can come up with can be the complete, a one and only fulfillment of those objective standards. My position is that though objective criteria for validity exist, our human formulations are always at best approximations.

About what is "good," my criteria involve the meeting of human needs. In that perspective, let me address Terrence's point about our society and the inalienable rights we have enshrined in our Constitution.

As an American boy, I'm glad to live in the good ol' U.S. of A., which I think does a good job—by historical standards—of meeting human needs. Our way of doing so does entail some costs, though. And because of problems like violence, and various other symptoms of social and personal stress, not all the citizens of other countries would necessarily prefer their society to be like ours. Some of these costs are connected with our individualism, with its respect for "rights," and some with our dynamism. So part of the issue has to do with trade-offs: one apparently can't have everything at once. People could rationally prefer to give up some of our liberties—in economics, in gun ownership—in exchange for a more harmonious and coherent society.

As for whether a Confucian society that has a much more authoritarian structure with much less granting of those "inalienable" rights might do as good a job at meeting human needs on balance—along the lines, say, of Singapore—that's a proposition that, whatever my skepticism in particular cases, I could not **automatically** reject. I see no basis for claiming that there can only one good way to organize a society.

But like Herman I am emphatically not relativistic in saying that no judgment can be made between the "goodness" of American society and that of, say, Zaire under Mobutu or Cambodia under Pol Pot.

Similarly with the matter of revealed truths. I confess my uncertainty about this, but I do suspect that there's a Truth out there to which we have at least occasional access, but which no one can bring back intact. But that doesn't mean that all renditions of it are equally valid, any more than any painter's rendering of a tree on his canvas would be as good as any other's, or any student's account of a lecture would be as accurate as any other's. None absolute, but not all equal.

To me, that's not being relativistic about the value of the various revealed truths that humankind has set down. **Andy**

Just man-made stuff will never do, *wrote Henry*. This is the irreducible sticking point with your bottom-up ways, even with the addition of this flabby allowance of revelation. "Revealed, but distorted. From God (whatever That is), but cast into form by man." It's still the modern project, on those same terms that can never achieve any truth that is beyond our questioning. Nothing whatever to bow down to, because everything we place on the altar is simply of our own creation. You give us idols, while we still need God. **Henry**

Once again I say, just because we may need something doesn't mean it's available to us, *Cynthia wrote in rapid reply*.

What's the matter with what has been crafted by man? *Ralph challenged Henry*. The American Constitution was put together by a group of extremely wise and able men, not by God. But the document is great nonetheless. **Ralph**

The Constitution is always sitting there, ready to be amended, *Henry answered*. People are constantly clamoring to get their hands into it and improve it, substituting their imperfect "wisdom" for that of the Founders. This is emblematic of the problem with having only the relative (and I will stick with that word) and imperfect creations of humans and not having access to something so unquestionable in its high status—a skyhook way over us, if you like—that people simply bow to it.

What is man-made, in other words, simply does not command the necessary respect. It does not have the ***authority***. And without that authority, the ultimate outcome is chaos. **Henry**

It sounds to me, *Larry wrote next,* that you've got the same kind of problem that Fred had in his anarchism. If authority works so well, how did we ever get to the modern age?

In other words, if we go back some centuries, we get to the era where kings ruled by divine right, where the established Church had a monopoly on the worldview market.

Yet out of that world emerged this modernity that you decry. Out of this impeccable order has come this chaos, pecking away at established authority. Sounds like your order wasn't so impeccable either. **Larry**

It is this worship of reason that is the undoing of the Given Order to which we should, in an act of faith, simply subordinate ourselves, *Carl wrote.*

This is indeed what reason does, it breaks everything down, *Henry affirmed.* It did the same to the Greeks. As soon as inquiry was established as the basic means of epistemology, it started dissolving the glue that held their world together.

The effort I'm about to make is probably vain, *Larry penned next,* but it's time someone stood up for reason and displayed how unreasonable your rejection of it is. I recall a previous citation of Goya's line about the "dream of reason" producing "monsters." But what about all the monsters that grow out of unreason?

The Nazis drove millions of people to the gas chambers by virtue of a three-pronged set of propositions that defy reason: first, that the best and highest people are those who are powerful; second, that the Jews are a terrible threat because, despite being a small minority, they dominate the world; and third, that the Jews are the lowest and worst of people and should be exterminated. Anyone who can hold all those three propositions together in the same head is not afflicted with an excess of reason.

I'd rather live in a world in which people feel compelled to think through the logic of their positions—and confront their contradictions—than in one where people feel free to ignore demands of rational logic. It's the latter kind of world that produces the greatest monstrosities. **Larry**

I'd like to back up a bit, leaving aside this dispute about reason and unreason, *Terrence wrote.* (Though my own position is a variant—and, ultimately, a refutation—of the "if God had wanted us to fly he'd have given us wings" view: namely, if God had not wanted us to use our reason he'd not have given us the rational faculty.)

My concern about the assertion that all our orderings—structures of authority, systems of morality, etc.—are man-made is that ***it opens the doors to unceasing iconoclasm.*** Here's where Henry seems to me to have something important to say. The liberal world of constructed truths turns, inevitably it seems, toward self-destruction of its own order.

When the Constitution is understood as just the fruit of human labors, it invites the search for the all-too-human defects in it. So a historian like Beard purports to demonstrate that the Framers of the document were really just trying to protect the economic interests of their own class.

Now, in every day's newspaper, this obsession with finding the ***feet of clay*** is carried to still greater extremes. Whoever is in the White House is fair game for this obsession.

What kind of sexual misconduct can we pin on him? How has he subverted justice for his self-interest? What laws has he broken, or if not laws, which of the Ten Commandments?

It is not just the president, of course, but anyone who might be placed on a pedestal of any kind. The press seeks to find the clay feet, to uncover the scandal that will bring low whatever is placed high.

This is how the bottom-up understanding—the vision of everything being made merely of mortal stuff—brings social disorder. **Terrence**

Well said, Terrence, *Henry applauded*. This is indeed a natural extension of the modern project, which pulls everything down to its own level. We see how this problem dawns—and correspondingly how the sun begins to set on the concept of the sacred nature of temporal authority—in Shakespeare's *Richard II*. Richard is king, but he is wondering how he can be king because he is a man. He is still struggling with the old understanding of the king as being something tinged with the divine. It is not a great leap from this character's wonderings to the assertion by Hobbes, a few generations following Shakespeare's, that the king is a thing men have made for their own sakes, that there is no species of "king."

And now, with this constant scandal-mongering, today's journalists conspire with their salacious public to besmirch everything that might have authority, to "dish the dirt" so that no one can stand before us with any moral authority. **Henry**

It does seem an interesting contradiction, *Rev. George wrote*. On the one hand, it seems that people have a thirst for authority, for something unquestionable and clear-cut to show them the truth and the way. On the other hand, as you rightly point out, Henry, there does seem to be an irresistible iconoclastic impulse in operation in today's world. How are these to be reconciled? **Rev. George**

No contradiction, *Henry replied*. People's simultaneous craving for and repudiation of authority is just another indication of the perverse nature of the beast.

I'd interpret the contradiction differently, *rejoined Peter*. People crave authority, but they are not such fools that just any authority will do. They want to know of any authority, "Can I trust you? Can I lean on your word? Will your guidance carry me safe?" So it is the very seriousness with which the issue of authority is taken that leads to the kind of testing and destruction that we see. Especially when authorities have let people down in the past, the fear of leaning on the unreliable will give some urgency to the iconoclastic project. **Peter**

This is precisely why it is so essential, *Henry wrote*, that we return to those earlier understandings of order by which the power and word of God serve as the source of all authority. **Henry**

Maybe it would be nice if it were so, *Cynthia wrote, in a reprise of what was becoming her theme.* But saying it would be nice doesn't make it so. After all, was not Hobbes right that there is, indeed, no species of king? And wasn't Jefferson right in denying that some human beings were created with saddles on their backs so that other human beings might ride upon them? **Cynthia**

I am glad you keep underscoring this inescapable truth, Cynthia, *Ralph wrote.* We may crave some Authority on high. We may crave eternal and unquestionable verities. But what we actually have, inescapably, are authorities that are made of flesh and blood, as well as rules that can be no more than merely the best attempts that such mortals as we can make to map out the course of what a good moral or political order might be. **Ralph**

Whether or not there is a species of king, *Kenneth wrote,* there is a King of the Universe. Whether or not our Constitution is crafted by moral man, and subject to amendment, we are in possession of laws that stand before us as timeless truths. The Eternal King has laid down His laws, and these are beyond question. In the Ten Commandments, to give a crucial example, we do possess moral absolutes. **Kenneth**

Again, it is argument by declaration. *Ralph's impatience was almost audible in the written words.* I will admit that in most respects most of the time most people will be well served to live their lives in accordance with most of those commandments. But I find it unpersuasive in the extreme when someone just declares that "There are moral absolutes, and here they are." **Ralph**

Your being persuaded or not is your problem, *Kenneth replied, testily.* The truth of "Thou shalt not kill" and "Thou shalt not commit adultery" stands before us clearly and, I suppose, it is another case of "Having eyes, see ye not?" **Kenneth**

Your love of simplicity gains my sympathy, Kenneth, but not entirely my respect, *Larry replied.* Let's take these "absolutes" of yours. First, "Thou shalt not kill." If I recall, we've ascertained that you are not a pacifist. And certainly neither was the Lord who handed down that commandment. So, I guess it is OK to kill the enemy. Does the enemy have to be certified by a sovereign government under whose jurisdiction one lives? Or might we, under some circumstances, rightly be entitled to declare our own enemies without official governmental approval? And how about that sovereign governmental power itself? Would it be OK to kill the agents of that sovereign government to whose power one is subject if that government was the murderous one of Nazi Germany or of Pol Pot in Cambodia? And how about self-defense?

It seems to me that there are many ambiguities and difficult situations in which it is far from clear that your absolute commandment directs one toward what is best. It seems that the commandment really boils down to "You shouldn't kill, except in those situations when it's OK to kill," which isn't all that helpful.

And then there's adultery. I'm willing to concede that, as a general rule, adultery is probably not a good idea. But I would have no difficulty thinking up various situations in which what would legally be defined as adultery would be defensible, would in fact be the cause of goodness, all things considered. If people in some conceivable situation were to sacrifice all chances for any emotional fulfillment, if they were to confine themselves to a loveless existence, for no reason other than that they bought your idea that a simple commandment was an unquestionable absolute, I would not regard that as a contribution to good order. **Larry**

I concur with Larry that the whole idea of "moral absolutes" is an illusion, *Ralph added at this point.* People have enshrined a variety of principles that may be valid or useful in the overwhelming majority of instances, but are not infallible guides to the good. If we want to know—for the actual situations in which we must make decisions—what is good and right, there is no escaping the continual need to find our way. There is no last word available to us. **Ralph**

This is moral relativism, and it is a recipe for chaos. **Henry**

A Necessity for Idols?

Even if Ralph and Larry are right about moral absolutes, *Peter began,* I think it is still possible that Henry is right about that way of thinking being a recipe for chaos, or at least for—pardon the expression—relative chaos.

Let's stipulate that these moral absolutes are really only probabilistic statements about what is usually right. What if it is the case that the proportion of time people will do what is right is much higher if those statements **are** believed (falsely) to be absolutes (word of God, or whatever) than if people recognize (correctly) that only most of the time are they guides to right conduct? Indeed, that seems to me quite likely true.

What I am suggesting more broadly is that there may be considerable danger from the recognition—even if it is valid—that none of the ordering principles by which we live is **the last word,** unquestionable and unalterable. Maybe people need to believe that the moral rules they are given are, indeed, moral absolutes. Need to believe that their traditional way of living is **the right way to live.** Need to believe that the revelation on which their cultural system is founded is **the one and only Word of God.**

Once we recognize that all our ordering principles are man-made, are subject to question and revision and to comparison with alternatives that might be their equal or superior—once we recognize all that, are we not in danger of lapsing, indeed, into the kind of confusion that Henry abhors, but that neither should the rest of us be happy to countenance? **Peter**

After Peter posted his message, I had to take off for a while. My friend and former student, Nick Biddle, and I had arranged to meet at a Burger King in Mt. Jackson just off of Interstate 81. Nick was traveling north from where he was living, in Boone, North Carolina, heading up 81 to visit his parental home in Pennsylvania, east of Pittsburgh. And the time-pressure on him made it impractical for him to take a detour out to our mountain place west of the interstate. But he wanted for us to have some sit-down time together, and I was happy enough to drive to Mt. Jackson.

On the way, I thought about what Peter had just written about people's need for their truths to be beyond question, written in stone handed down from Sinai, and I recollected a little interchange to which I'd been party over the weekend. The occasion had been a wedding in my wife's family. April's first cousin, once removed, had wedded a young woman in a Presbyterian Church in Staunton, Virginia. Staunton is only about an hour and a half from our place, but with so many of April's rellies (as they call themselves in that clan) coming in from out of town and staying in the specially arranged block of rooms at the Holiday Inn there, we'd splurged by staying there, too. The next day, after helping a little bit with the undecorating of the American Legion Hall where the reception had been held, April and I, along with the groom's parents (the mother being April's first cousin, not removed at all), went over to the home of the newlyweds to drop off some goodies from the reception. The young couple were off on their honeymoon already, but the bride's parents, being from out of state, were staying there, and it was about the conversation with the bride's mother that I was thinking.

Religion is an important part of the families of both bride and groom, and although the groom's parents are Evangelical and the bride's are Presbyterian (both father and grandfather of the bride, military chaplains, helped officiate at the wedding), I caught no whiff of any religious differences between the two families, or their offspring. Discussing with the groom's mother this father-to-son handing down of the ministry, I asked whether any of her three sons showed signs of following along that path.

"It's too soon to say, but this year, thank the Lord, the two older boys *accepted the Lord*," she responded.

My lame—and doubtless inappropriate—attempt to make a joke about the idea of "accepting the Lord" (I had in mind a famous line of Ralph Waldo Emerson's about so-and-so "accepting the universe," to which he had replied, "She had better") went mercifully unnoticed, and then the mother went on, turning to the groom's mother as well as to us, saying, "It is so good to *know* now that we'll see the children in heaven." Afterward, what April wondered about most was whether the woman simply *assumed* that we shared her belief, or whether it just didn't matter. What struck me most was that she possessed such absolute certainty and that, though this certainty seemed to me misplaced, I could easily imagine that it *would* feel good to *know* that one's children had eternity well taken care of.

By the time I was finished with these recollections, I was already passing the dumpsters on route 263 (garbage is not collected in our kind of area, but must be hand-delivered by its producers to the collection points) and thus was not very far from the Burger King. So I started thinking about my upcoming conversation with Nick.

Nick had been my student more than twenty years before when I taught for a while at Prescott College in Prescott, Arizona, but he was now a professor of history at Appalachian State University. He had invited me down to ASU to speak, which I was delighted to do. While there, I had done some preliminary events—talking to various classes, including Nick's—and then had done a university-wide evening talk. In some ways, I preferred the lesser events because, except for in Nick's class where I was asked to discuss *The Parable of the Tribes*, the conversation in those forums is generally quite improvisational and, compared with the stand-up monologue form of the evening talk, the unexpected and creative can more readily happen.

"There had been one moment in the formal evening talk, however, that had felt quite meaningful and alive to me. And April and Nick, the only people with whom I'd really had a chance to debrief, had felt the same way about this particular juncture in the evening presentation.

My talk had been the one that had become my usual in the past year or two: "Beyond Dispute: Bridging Across America's Moral Polarization." In it, I present the kind of ideas contained in that "but rabbi, how can they both be right" way of looking at the culture war, and in "The Dance of Polarization." The idea is that moral wisdom is hard to obtain, that we each tend to have only some piece of the truth (and that one distorted), and that we should learn from each other. The talk went well, and then we got to the Q & A period.

Most of the audience consisted of students, people in their very late teens and early twenties. A pattern in the questions soon became apparent. The questioners wanted me to give them some clear and final answer on one or another of the pressing and controversial issues of the culture war that I'd touched upon. The student would say, in essence, "Getting past all that stuff you said earlier, so just what is it that is the right answer about abortion, or about how we should treat criminals, or whatever?"

In each case, I started giving them an answer that explained how I myself tended to think about the question. I tried to model the process I'd been advocating, articulating what seemed to me to be correct about the point of view of one side of the controversy, and then what seemed valid in the other side, and then groping a bit for what a larger truth might look like that could integrate those truths. Needless to say, the result was not any neat and tidy package that could be boiled down to "yes" or "no," no cookbook recipe for certainty.

After the nth such question was asked, I made a shift. Instead of trying to address the question in its own terms, I went off on a riff. Having stood up on that stage until that point more as a performer than as a genuine and whole, spontaneously flowing human being, I found myself now dropping deeper into myself, getting the gooseflesh that I generally interpret as a sign of the spirit moving through me, and I waxed even eloquent.

I don't remember verbatim just what I said, but the gist of it was something like this: "You want Answers that are cut-and-dried. There aren't any, at least not any that are really honest. If you want to have everything clearly defined, the path of just how to live and what to do all laid out for you, then you should be a beaver. Chomp on the trees, build the dams. It's all in your blueprint.

"For us—*Homo sapiens*—it's different. We have to find our way. I don't have answers of the kind you seem to want but—more than that—I'm suggesting that an essential part of the answer is not to think in terms of such Answers. To be a human being, I'm saying, means that finding our way is a never-ending task.'"

It had felt very enlivening to deliver those words. They'd come from my core, and those moments had made the whole evening feel worthwhile.

I pulled into the Burger King lot at almost the same moment that Nick did, so neither of us had to wait for each other. After a warm greeting, we ordered a couple of those ninety-nine cent loss-leader quarter-pounder burgers and settled into a booth to visit for a while. We discussed our kids and other family matters, and our various writings and plans, and then toward the end of our time, I asked Nick to tell me what he could about how my visit to Appalachian State had been received. "Yeah, I was going to get to that," Nick said, "it was pretty interesting." Then, after some nice words about what some of the faculty had said about my visits to their classes, he told me about his students' reactions.

"My students thought your presentation of *The Parable of the Tribes* was really excellent. They liked the talk some, too, but a number of them didn't know what to make of it. What they said was, 'That business about his not *knowing* the answers, about the uncertainty—he was pulling our leg, wasn't he?' "

Nick looked up at me with his eyebrows raised, and I looked for a second at him with the same facial arches, and then let out a big guffaw—as if to say "They're pulling my leg, aren't they?" Nick laughed, too, and then continued.

"The way they figure it, you're the authority, we're paying you money to come and talk, so you *must* really know the answers. I talked to them a bit about Socratic kinds of teaching, but the idea seemed pretty foreign to them. They turned back to your presentation: all that talk about inquiry, about seeking, they thought it must be some kind of a ploy, and they couldn't figure it out."

After some further rumination on the meaning of that reaction of the students, and on why the Athenians gave Socrates that hemlock brew, we went to our cars, gave each other a friendly hug, and drove off on our separate ways.

Meanwhile, back on the forum, the discussion had continued from where I'd left it, with Peter's questioning whether people really could live with the recognition that their own truths did not have a capital "T," that they did not necessarily possess the one and only Word of God, and that their visions might coexist with other truths that also had validity.

That need you describe, Peter, for absolute certainty in the sphere of moral truth, *Ralph wrote,* may well characterize a great many people. But I do not believe that we need to regard that need as an inescapable trait of human nature. I know people who can hold their truths differently. These people can be committed to their visions while also regarding the truths of others with respect and some openness to learning from them. **Ralph**

The question might be asked, I guess, *Larry responded to that,* whether the humility and open-mindedness you describe, Ralph, reflects human nature, while the need for certainty is symptomatic of some kind of damage that has been done, or whether conversely, it is the need for certainty that is the default position to which humans are liable and the more open-minded state represents some kind of achievement in overcoming our natural tendencies.

I tend to suspect, regrettably, that the latter is closer to the truth. **Larry**

After a bit of bandying about on this particular question about which condition reflected human nature, and which needed explaining, a posting from Carl once again challenged us.

The Tower of Babel Problem

While you gentlemen are congratulating yourselves on your humility and your tolerance, *Carl wrote,* I would like to say that if we are agreed that "good order" is what it is that we wish to see achieved, humility of that kind is no virtue, and neither is "tolerance" something to be congratulated. If the righteous have that kind of humility, it will only disable them from acting in the world to uphold righteousness, leaving the field to the evildoers who seem never to lack for passion and purpose. And as for tolerance, I have not held with that liberal notion that tolerance is so great a thing. "Good order" is achieved by having things operating in a good way, and tolerating any other way can only encourage the breakdown into disorder. **Carl**

Tolerance is a virtue, *Ralph said,* for a number of reasons. Paramount among them is that peace is a virtue, and without tolerance there is no peace. As your Lord said, "blessed are the peacemakers."

If everyone holds his version of the truth with the attitude you are advocating, Carl, then how will they get along? I have heard this conservative attack on the liberal virtue of tolerance before. And what I like to cite on such occasions is the historic connection that the liberal idea of tolerance as a virtue grew out of the experience of seventeenth-century England, where the ruinous chaos of civil strife revealed to thinking people that it was no small accomplishment to find a way for people with different views to live in peace together. **Ralph**

My Lord also said, *Carl came back,* that he brought not peace but the sword. He did not shrink from confronting the sinful powers of his time.

Yes, and this brings us back to the question of the value of humility, *Ralph replied.* If we each felt entitled to regard himself as the Son of God, then I could see that we wouldn't have any special need for humility among the pantheon of virtues. But so long as the world is populated by people who are not Jesus Christ, I think we're better served by people who are not so sure of themselves.

Tolerance is required not only because we should have the humility to know that our version of the truth is not necessarily the only good one, but also because we should have the humility to know that neither we nor other people of flesh and blood like ourselves can be trusted to have the power to compel even those who are wrong to adhere to that one "right way" of which you spoke. **Ralph**

I make no claim, of course, to be the Lord, *Carl responded.* But I am in possession of God's word. And I do not regard it as a virtue in a society to tolerate clear contraventions of what God has enjoined us to do and to refrain from doing. Hence that liberal self-congratulation of tolerating, say, homosexuality seems to me only making a virtue of what is, indeed, a grievous fault. It is, in fact, complicity in sin. **Carl**

I have no intention of making tolerance out to be—pardon the expression—an absolute value, *wrote Ralph.* My liberalism does not compel me to tolerate murder, or rape, or armed robbery, or a host of other infringements upon the rights of other individuals. As for homosexuality, between consenting adults, I would argue for tolerance being here a virtue: the costs of not tolerating it would involve a serious infringement on the rights of those individuals, and the costs to society—such as in discomfiting people like you, Carl—seem slight in comparison.

Again, not all people are in agreement about what constitutes the word of God, the standard of goodness. And let me mention again the lesson of seventeenth-century England. Are you willing, Carl, to have religious wars fought over every point of disagreement between the similarly righteous-feeling, but dissimilarly believing? Or, if you contemplate the alternative, which is oppression of the holders of one vision by the holders of the other, are you willing to take the chance that your side may not always prevail and that your one "right way" will be the one that is *not* tolerated?

In the face of the reality of diversity in the area of beliefs, it seems to me that a rational person must recognize that a maximum degree of tolerance, consistent with maintaining a degree of order and coherence in society, is the best course to take. **Ralph**

Yes, diversity. That is the problem to which this discussion has been directing my attention since I last posted. *This was, again, Larry, who evidently was still pondering the human need for certainty, and how the gratification of that need appears to be threatened on all sides.*

Earlier, someone (I think it was Herman) was talking about how the business of revelation would be easier to credit if all the reports were identical. It seems to me that in effect, by living in a multicultural world we are all in something like that dilemma. How are we to relate to our own ways of understanding, and to those of other people, when we are compelled to live in the midst of people very different from ourselves?

It must have been so much easier back in the old days, when societies were so much more homogeneous. **Larry**

An interesting point—something I've thought about some, myself. *This was Herman.* Indeed, I have sometimes conjectured that it is no coincidence (forgive the Marxist locution) that the rise of modern consciousness and the European exploration of the world were contemporaneous. No doubt, part of the connection involves the way the modernizing changes in consciousness helped to launch the exploration: the medieval mind was not about to set out for points unknown. But what intrigues me more is the idea of the connection going in the other direction—the impact on European civilization of the sudden exposure to diverse human cultures.

By that I mean that it was when the Europeans left the culturally sheltered (meaning homogenous) environment of their own lands (where even a comparatively tiny minority of people only as different as the Jews could not really be tolerated), and came into contact with cultures and races almost completely different from their own, that their whole perspective was forced to shift.

It was then that rational inquiry grounded in empirical observation seized hold of the European mind. It was then that systematic social philosophy in Europe, grounded in explicit first principles—as with Hobbes, or Machiavelli—really began. It was then that empirical science started to take off.

My thought about the connection goes something like this. When we live surrounded only by other affirmations that our own understanding is synonymous with the nature of things, we do not experience the need to see ourselves in perspective, nor to reason out from that perspective into the existence of a level of reality that might transcend—or underlie—our own outlook. But as soon as we are compelled to see that human life can take many forms, then we are led to look at our own form in a new light. Our answers will—or may—begin to appear to us as but one of a larger species of answers, the whole array of which points to a vision still more fundamental. We are then led to ponder deeper questions of human nature and the nature of reality itself. We are driven away from taking the status quo for granted and toward inquiring into the origins and developments that lead to ourselves.

It must indeed have been a most disturbing development for those world-exploring Europeans to discover human diversity. One can always take refuge in ethnocentrism—declaring, "Ours is the one true faith! The rest are pagans and heathens to be converted. We are the bearers of civilization to the benighted!"—and certainly the Europeans indulged in a great deal of that. But they could not escape the powerful, and powerfully disturbing, pull toward letting this reality speak to them in its own tongue, rather than just reducing it to the language of their prejudices and preconceptions. **Herman**

My fear, *Larry responded,* is that the lapse into ethnocentrism is the only really probable response that people will take in response to the confrontation with diversity.

Look at what's happened recently in the former Yugoslavia: here are people who have been living in proximity for centuries, who spent decades as fellow citizens in one nation-state, and the result only seems to have been an intensification of ethnocentric passions, with everybody ready to claim everything for their own and eager to destroy those who are different.

In recent years, with the rise in America of the idea of multiculturalism, a number of people have worried about a corresponding "Balkanization" of our pluralistic society, as different tribes seem to be coalescing and pulling away from each other. And so I am torn, myself, as these cultural battles rage: should English be made the official language of the United States? Should the old Western canon be thrown out, with dead white males pushed aside to make way for new "classics" penned by representatives of groups formerly ignored? Should different standards for admission to universities or hiring for positions be used for members of one group than for members of another?

I can grant that no one way embodies all truth and virtue, but I am troubled about whether we can really live together in a spirit of multiculturalism, overturning the cultural hegemony of the white Anglo-Saxon civilization, without lapsing into the chaos of tribal warfare. **Larry**

I believe you are underestimating our capacities," *Ralph replied to Larry's concern.* These wars among peoples do not just ignite spontaneously. The conflict in Yugo-slavia—although exploiting the tinder of ancient resentments that lay about—was fueled by quite contemporary nationalist demagoguery on the part of the Serbian leader, Milosevich, beginning even before the country broke up. When I look at American history, I see tremendous grounds for optimism about the ability of different peoples to live together in reasonable harmony. We've been engaged in this "melting pot" business for many generations now, and although we've had our problems—our nativist movements, our "Irish need not apply" signs, our internment camps for the Japanese-Americans—I would say that we've shown that we can combine diversity and tolerance and social peace pretty well. **Ralph**

Most of that history was during a time when the dominance of the mainstream culture was beyond question, *Terrence interjected*. Now that this centripetal cultural force is under organized, ideological attack, that successful past you mention may afford no assurance about our future. I see serious forces of disintegration at work. There are places where one does not hear English spoken on the streets. **Terrence**

You worry about having more diversity than we can digest, *wrote Ralph*. At times I worry about just the opposite. Your comment about places where English is not spoken suggests you may have forgotten that a century ago also there were many streets where English was not the language spoken, whether it was in one Chinatown or another, or a Jewish neighborhood with Yiddish the language of daily life, or in Italian neighborhoods where new immigrants still spoke the tongue of their mother country. Those who feel that English must be forced upon everyone by legal means seem not to have noticed how readily this problem of diverse tongues solves itself. The children of the immigrants learn the dominant language of the society: Frank Sinatra spoke the tongue of Hoboken, not of Sicily, and Phil Silvers's movies were not in Yiddish.

Sooner we should worry about homogenization of all cultures, I would say. So far from needing to make English the official language of the United States, it would seem that English is well on the way to becoming the official language of the planet. **Ralph**

Yes, that homogenization is my concern, too, *Rev. George posted next*. Not so much with languages; more with fundamental visions of the human reality. I think of that Sufi story of the blind men and the elephant, each gaining his own sense of the beast from the particular part with which he'd come into contact. (The one holding the tail concludes that the thing is rope-like, the one with a leg says it's like a pillar, etc.) The story is, at one level, about the confusion that comes from the different testimonies. But at another level it also reveals an opportunity: for if they listen to one another, they are in a good position to get a better sense of the elephantine nature of the whole beast.

Cultural diversity, it seems to me, offers us such a multiperspectived understanding of our elephant. And that diversity of perspective seems to me now endangered. Will we not be terribly impoverished if the various homogenizing forces—mass media, global communications, and global commerce—give us all such a common outlook that we all become swept up in a single way of understanding? As some wrote not long ago of an "end of history," might there now be some "end of spiritual visioning," converging on some kind of consensus? **Rev. George**

It strikes me that an important element of what culture is about, and how it works, is being omitted from this conversation, *Terrence said*. You (liberals) want diversity for its enrichment of our perspective. You fear intolerance and ethnocentrism for its failure to recognize that our own truth is not necessarily the one and only truth, not necessarily the last word. You see the blind men and the elephant and you celebrate the opportunity it presents.

Let me present to you another famous story about diversity: that of the Tower of Babel. What is most germane about that story in this context is the means by which the project is destroyed: God, in giving them different languages, makes them unintelligible to one another. One does not need to say that one language is "right" and other languages "wrong" to hold the belief that "good order" among people who must live together requires that *some* language be *shared*.

Here's one piece of culture that can serve as an example. We live in a time when many people have come to believe that manners do not matter. I've given a lot of thought to how it is that manners do indeed matter. When we meet a stranger, if that person performs the various niceties that our culture has established for the ritual dance of friendly sociality—the right uses of pleases and thank yous and your welcomes, the proper handshake, the right ways of offering and accepting and refusing— we relax into a sense of comfort and familiarity with this person. The dance gives us assurance that this person will act in a way that is predictable, and more precisely, it is a predictability that conforms to our rules of consideration, propriety, fairness, and so forth.

But what if this person follows a completely different set of rules from the ones we know? Maybe he arrives at two for a lunch agreed to be at noon. Maybe you cross your legs and he is from a culture in which that is seen as a sign of disrespect. Trust is much harder to establish. Comfort vanishes in the face of unsettling surprises, and puzzlements about interpretation. It becomes difficult to work together. The Tower of Babel strikes again.

Likewise with this brouhaha in recent years about the Western canon. (As an aside, let me assert that this teaching of the tradition of our civilization can be entirely justified on good old-fashioned grounds: the fact that this is the tradition that has shaped those institutions and philosophies that define the country that we live in, and to which waves of immigrants have subsequently chosen to come, is sufficient in my view to give that tradition a privileged position. Other things can certainly be added, so that we can see that humanity has created other worthy thoughts and literature in other traditions. But the *Analects of Confucius* should no more displace Locke's *Treatise on Government* than our Constitution should be replaced by an Emperor presiding over a Mandarin bureaucracy. This is a nation with a history, and as peoples join the nation they also join in the possession of that heritage.)

In the context of this discussion, however, the relevant and important point I wish to make is that education should make sure that our citizens are inculcated with **some coherent and shared heritage**. It is not enough that everyone sees the Super Bowl or *Jurassic Park*. We need to create a shared set of experiences that are carefully selected to provide a common foundation on the basis of which we can deliberate together as citizens. And this involves, more than anything else, the conversation of values and ideas from Aristotle through the *Magna Carta* to the speeches of Lincoln—even if they all involve dead white males.

The whole idea of a canon has been under attack, and this attack reflects, I believe, a fundamental failure to understand the indispensability of cultural coherence, and the central role that shared ideas play in providing such coherence.

Here's a thought experiment. Imagine that there are five different cultures, each of which provides an excellent basis for ordering human life. Imagine a group of people from each of these different cultures, each group made up of superb specimens of its own kind, people who are the best embodiments of the virtues as understood in the cultures from which they come. Now imagine that we bring these groups together to form a society. The groups will have to live side by side. They will have to work with each other. And they will have to make policy together.

My prediction is that this combination of well-ordered people will itself not be well ordered. Instead, they will produce the disorder that comes from diversity. Even if many cultures may be valid, I believe that we need to have a single predominant culture in order to create good order. **Terrence**

I would say that these well-ordered cultures in your thought experiment, if indeed they are well ordered, will have produced in their excellent specimens the capacity to bridge their differences and work well together. **Ralph**

I do not think it is as simple as that, Ralph, *Peter wrote*. Those who are best molded to fit into their own orders are often not so well able to see beyond the confines of that order. I think of some of the rigid Fundamentalists I have known who are good and admirable specimens of their tradition, but not well equipped to deal with full respect and appreciation for people from very different points of view. **Peter**

This exploration of the Tower of Babel problem then culminated in a message from Rev. George. I thought it quite eloquent.

I agree with Peter that it is not so simple, *Rev. George wrote*. It is not so easy to see one's point of view as being only what it is. The indignation one feels when the rules one lives by are broken—"That s.o.b. said 'noon' and he kept me waiting till two!"—is not easily sloughed off. To do so requires so broad a vision of what human life is about, or could be about, that the bridging of differences Ralph is so sanguine about really represents a rather profound spiritual challenge.

As a story, "The Blind Men and the Elephant" is not so different from "The Tower of Babel." To me, the main difference is that the Sufi story contains the image of the elephant that lies beyond the different perceptions. It thus contains the seed of a higher aspiration than the contention among the blind men, or the confusion and dispersion of the peoples building the Tower.

Yet I fully acknowledge that this aspiration can be fulfilled only to the extent that we human beings achieve something spiritually rather advanced. It involves not only seeing ourselves in perspective, but requires also seeing how those sacred matters that we have placed higher than ourselves—our ideals, our commandments, our Gods—truly fit into the great scheme of things. If even our most sacred texts—our revelations—have our fingerprints all over them; if even our proudest traditions are not without flaws; if none of our answers is the last word, and thus the questions must remain somewhat open—then we are called upon to hold within our minds an enormously large place for this mind-boggling cosmos, and to hold within our hearts an extraordinary degree of humility.

Not easy tasks for creatures of mere flesh and blood—even with a generous admixture of spirit thrown in. **Rev. George**

Conclusion
Choices

Choices

My Son, My Adam

"Dad, can I play Nintendo now?" I looked up from my manuscript-in-progress for this book to see Nathaniel. He was standing in front of me, a hopeful expression on his face. "How much have you played so far today?" I asked. "About forty minutes, when I first got up," Nat answered. "And have you done any other screen-time today?" We've taken to regarding television and video games as different aspects of a single category called "screen-time," to be limited collectively. "I watched about half an hour of 'James and the Giant Peach'." I pondered a bit, setting down my book, and found a line from Goethe's *Faust* coming to mind. *"Hier steh' ich vor dem Tor,"* Faust says near the beginning, before he makes his diabolical deal, *"und weiss nicht mehr als bevor."* ("Here I stand before the door/and know not more than before.")

But then, I thought, maybe it wasn't true that I knew no more than before. "Well, kid, how would you like *this* as an answer: I'm willing to let you make the decision, so long as you promise me that you'll do what you think is best for you. Is that a deal?" Nat looked a bit quizzical, gave a little thought, and then agreed. I betook myself off to my garden, to give him a little room to decide to play Nintendo, or to decide not to.

It occurred to me, as I started doing some weeding, that—it being now July—Nat's birthday was just around the corner, and the not-yet-eight-year-old about whom I'd written in my initial "Nintendo Dilemma" inquiry was about to become a nine-year-old. The outlines of his man's body were becoming visible, almost daily more so. A month before, we'd allowed Nat to make his own choice about his haircut, knowing what he'd choose, and knowing that it wasn't what we wanted. And sure enough, he'd sacrificed the long hair he'd had since infancy, and opted for the buzz cut for which he'd been hankering. And sure enough, it was a shock to us. But I found, to my surprise, that within a few hours I'd decided that he was right, that somehow it suited him. The new haircut suited him because of what it revealed about who he now was. It was when he emerged from that haircut that I saw that the little boy was in fact becoming a man before our eyes. The long bangs had obscured the increasingly manly skull that he was wearing under that mop of straight hair, and now, here it was. I liked what I saw.

Down in the garden, the new terraces I built were still highlighted with the dramatic spears of the gladiolas I'd planted, but there was as yet no sign of the flowers presumably to come. Amidst the gladiolas was a feathery plant that I recognized. After five summers here I finally knew this plant by sight, though previously I could at least recognize it the moment I touched it and unwittingly released its sweet and pungent fragrance. These plants I'd seen used in some kind of arrangement at a church yard sale, but I had decided that as interesting as the scent was, I was going to treat these interlopers as weeds. So I plucked them up, with big gobs of my farmer-Jones topsoil clinging to them, banged off the soil, and laid the weeds above the bed to compost themselves.

My thoughts then turned to a little family meeting we'd had a couple nights before. During a recent family trip, Nathaniel had been asking at what seemed like frequent intervals if he could buy a lottery ticket (since minors cannot buy the tickets, it was we who'd have to buy a ticket on his behalf). April and I agree that the lottery is, by and large, not a healthy thing to get caught up in. Gambling in itself seems to us to teach something less than wholesome about how to make one's fortune. And I am particularly appalled by the state's luring people into what is clearly a sucker bet. For every dollar the player plunks down, chances are he'll pick up a measley four bits. To me, the two little green grooves in the roulette wheel are enough to make that bet irrational, and the state lotteries are basically roulette wheels in which half the grooves are green. And it is particularly disturbing that a disproportionate number of the most serious players of these state lotteries are poor people, those who can least afford such sucker bets. But, admittedly, gambling can be fun, and fun is worth something. So April and I were not of a mind to forbid Nathaniel the lottery experience altogether.

The solution we came up with for the lottery problem pleased us all. This was the deal: Nathaniel could play the lottery as often as once a month, but the money he used would have to be money he earned. He would not be allowed to use the easy-come money that I keep on account for him, the account that is funded by the birthday and Christmas checks he gets from April's mother. Too easy, that way, to think that the money he blows on the lottery wasn't worth anything much anyway. With earned money, we figured, he'd recognize the value and meaning of what he was spending. And to earn the dollar he used for his lottery ticket, he would have to work one half hour on some job that needed doing and that lay outside the usual realm of chores he did simply as a contributing member of the family. That night, for example, I'd given him the job of gathering up some loose metal wires that remained on one of our slopes, remnants of our predecessor's anti-deer measures. Now, at least, when he wasted his money he would have some idea that a piece of himself had gone into making that possible, and this should make it easier for him to make sensible decisions about how much weight to give to that momentary fun he would get as he scratched off the graphite with hopes of striking it rich.

When I say that this resolution of the lottery issue pleased us all, I mean April, Nat, and me. A friend who heard of it was a good deal less enthusiastic. "You seem to assume that your young fellow should grow up to embody your kind of virtue," he said. "Because you're prudent and thoughtful and frugal, you assume that Nat ought to become that kind of man. But what if it's Nat's destiny to bring to the world an entirely different kind of goodness? What if it's his nature to be bold without calculation, to follow magnanimous impulses, to be extravagant?" He capped his challenge by reminding me of William Blake's dictum that "Prudence is a rich old maid courted by incapacity."

In my response, I acknowledged fully that there were other equally valid ways of being virtuous than my style (though I question whether anyone who'd based his whole work life on being true to some vision, whatever the professional or financial consequences, could be said to have pitched his tent under the banner of "Prudence," Blakean or otherwise). And I conceded further that it was an important question to keep before me whether my way of helping Nathaniel in the development of his character was appropriate to his particular nature. But beyond those concessions, I also said that, like anyone else, I can really only teach what I know. And so, while there may be many paths, those whose fate it was to be my children are fated to learn more from their father about the approaches that have worked for me than about other approaches. It may be, I said in summation, that Johann Christian and Carl Philip Emmanuel might have become more accomplished (or more fulfilled) as painters than as the composers they actually became, but growing up in the home of J. S. Bach meant hearing the way of music more than seeing the way of painting.

The raising of a child seems a process of continual exploration, as the child explores who he or she is and might become in the world and as the parent tries to figure how to guide the child in that becoming.

That negotiation about the lottery now brought to my mind another negotiation to which I had been more silent observer than active participant. This one involved Nat's desire to purchase a video game he'd located at a good price. April had qualms about his getting this game— *Dark Forces* was its name—because it was another of the hunt-'em and shoot-'em genre that seems so predominant in the realm of video games. I had declared my observer status in this negotiation because I did not share April's discomfort, or at least not much, but I also respected that her concerns should be addressed. And I liked the deal they eventually worked out.

The deal was that Nat would be allowed to play the game for only as much time as Nat spent reading Newbury Award–winning books. April and I both felt that Nat could benefit from expanding his reading to literature of better quality, and so this was a deal that seemed to promise that Nathaniel would benefit (in one sense of the word or another) from *both* sides of the contract. Indeed, it seemed—to us, at least—that his "cost" in the deal was really his greatest benefit.

There was, however, one nagging doubt I had about that *Dark Forces* deal. My unease stemmed from writings by a friendly acquaintance of mine, Alfie Kohn, on the subject of rewards. According to Alfie, when you get someone to do something by giving them external rewards, you make it not more likely, but *less,* that in the future they'll choose to do it in the absence of such rewards. In other words, Alfie would argue that by making the reading of Newbury books a means of getting *Dark Forces* time, we were making it less likely that Nathaniel would voluntarily turn to such reading in the future. I've known of Alfie's arguments and empirical evidence on this question for some years now, and I never quite know what to do with them in my role as a father. There are some activities that a person might never try at all without some inducement, but that, once tried, demonstrate their intrinsically rewarding and enriching nature. So I've tried to lure my children into various "good activities" by non-alfiekohnian means so that they would discover through experience what they'd been missing. Anyway, Alfie had given me qualms about deals like the one April and Nat reached about *Dark Forces,* but I still thought their arrangement a good one.

Not an easy thing, being a parent. So much wisdom needed, but where to get it?

This note of parental uncertainty reminded me of a conversation that took place during the most recent visit of my daughter, Terra, to our place. During one scene when I was in the kitchen serving Nat the dessert of his choice, and Terra and Nat were on the other side of the counter, Terra ventured that I was being too stingy in the size of the serving I was giving him, and she suggested that this was just the most immediate instance of a chronic error on my part. I was up for discussing this.

I admitted that I did not know for sure whether my approach to the dessert issue—very controlled quantities, once a day—was a good one. Terra and I have our own history on the subject of sweets. She's long had an insistent sweet tooth and, when she was younger, April and I would sometimes find empty candy-bar wrappers stashed in her room— the remnants of unauthorized and illicit post-dessert indulgence. Terra sees her love of sweets as just how she is, while I have understood it, since she was a very little girl, to be a compensatory reaction to having been deprived of some other kinds of goodies in the first couple years of life. But life is a notoriously poorly controlled experiment, so who knows? In any event, Nathaniel has suffered no such deprivations, as far as I can see.

My attitude about giving sweets to my kids—or to myself either, for that matter—is tied in with a generally health-oriented attitude about food and eating: we should cultivate habits that nourish our bodies, we should eat what our bodies are asking for rather than feed our faces, with measured exceptions for the moments of indulgent enjoyments. When it comes to snacks, for example, I think that "snack foods" should be the last things one would choose. They are generally pure indulgence—fat, sugar, salt. Those things I would put as adjuncts to an otherwise healthy meal. (For example, at Nat's prodding I'll buy a small bag of potato chips about once a month, and serve a handful as an occasional side dish on his dinner plate, maybe with his cheese sandwich and broccoli.) Snacks should consist of the most elemental of foods, I say, things like a carrot, an apple, a piece of bread. Eating, as I see it, is a matter most fundamentally of giving the body what it needs.

Anyway, though I haven't heard much good scientific evidence to support the belief I'd picked up thirty years ago from Adelle Davis that sugar is bad for you, I have continued to operate on the belief that our taste for sweets, in this modern world, is one of the chief means by which we can readily be led astray by our own appetites and ensnared by the seductive food purveyors of our modern marketplace. So with my children I've tried to limit the consumption of sweets—not making them into forbidden fruit, but something around which to practice discipline in the pursuit of one's pleasures.

"Well, Nat, what do you think?" I'd asked Nathaniel when Terra had challenged my judgment. "Do you think that Terra is right, that I should loosen up on the sweets? Should I give you more? or let you choose how much you'll get?"

"I think you could loosen up some, but not leave the amount up to me," Nat said. "Maybe if you gave me 50% more, it would still be all right."

"Well, as you know, your Mom gives bigger servings than I do, so it seems that I'm out here on an extreme all by myself. Maybe I am wrong," I'd conceded.

Being a parent involves so many junctures with such uncertainties. I don't mind my kids' challenging my judgment on these parenting issues, though I also do not change my position at the drop of a hat. I may be wrong, I figure, but then again, so might the kids. April is generally very appreciative of the way I am as father to the kids, which contributes to the job's being one of the great pleasures of my life. But sometimes she, too, thinks I'm too hard on one or the other. (When it comes to violence in video games or movies, though, she thinks I'm too soft.) As I went on to another terrace and moved aside some wandering tomato plants to allow a couple of basil plants to get their full quota of sun—I've been told that without intense sunlight, the basil leaves will never develop that miraculous basil flavor in all its robustness—I thought about a recent conversation with April, in which she'd voiced one of her rare questionings of my fathering approach. The issue had been my feeling that, when it comes to the process of self-creation, Nathaniel is too lazy.

Here is the most sturdy of lads, with substantial abilities, with no apparent traumas in his past life or great difficulties in his present life. His world is peopled primarily by people who love him profoundly and well, and who also enjoy being in one another's family. He suffers no insecurities in the world in terms of the family, our ability to put bread on the table, our health; none in terms of his standing with his peers, his ability to enjoy their respect and affection, or with his teachers. Throughout his life, he's received the message that he is a wonderful creature. And in the meantime I, as his father, have also encouraged him to stretch himself, to find his passion and go for it, to make himself as much as possible into the person he, in some sense, was meant to be. He is my unwounded child, born of the marriage that stayed happy and healthy. He has come into a world that has not damaged him, has left him with all his strengths intact. As a creature, Nathaniel seems well positioned to show just what were the strengths, and weaknesses, with which he came from the factory.

Nathaniel is my Adam.

Yet, undamaged though he may be, he does not stretch himself as he could and, I feel, ideally would. He enjoys considerable comfort, it appears to me, and could take on more burden at some level of spiritual challenge without in any way overburdening himself. The job of taking stock of himself and deciding just what he wants to become and then setting out to grow in that direction—that job seems to me entirely within his reach, quite reasonable and beneficial for him to undertake, but one that he nonetheless has shown only desultory interest in taking on. One part of the role I've adopted as his father is to encourage him to take on that project as his own. He is a child with the most powerful will, and was precocious in his willpower: when he was a two-year-old, and someone gave him some Easter chocolates one morning, he astonished us when, told that he would have to wait till after dinner to eat any, he was able and content to carry those goodies around all day in their little sack. And Nathaniel also has shown, at times, a drive for mastery so powerful that I imagine he could harness to become practically whatever he wanted enough to become.

As the summer began, I had talked with Nat about what he might like to accomplish for himself with the summer, now that he was freed of the obligation to give the heart of his days to school. We'd come up with a couple of camps he was excited about: one, an overnight basketball camp for kids at a college in a part of the Shenandoah Valley further south, coached by a man of whom I'd heard great things; the other a science day-camp at the Discovery Museum in Winchester to the north. That still left eight weeks of his ten-week summer vacation. Anything else, I asked, that he might go for on his own? Would he like to collect insects? Build a fort? Anything that really caught his interest, that he'd like to study? Read biographies of people he admired? Any way he'd like to develop himself? Nat shied away from taking on any such projects, saying he'd be happy to stay home and shoot hoops, read leisure-style kid books, and have an occasional friend over. OK, I said, and I backed off, at least until I had some better idea of how to engage Nat in challenging himself.

"Lighten up," was April's comment to me about the whole thing. "He's fine," she said. "I think you expect too much of him."

"What makes it too much?" I asked.

"Nat's a good kid," she said. "So why do you feel he ought to be working to become more than he is?"

"I agree he's a good kid. Everybody thinks he's a good kid—us, his teachers, all our adult friends and family who know him. But he's coasting. Well, maybe that's putting it too strongly, but he's taking it easier than he needs to. He could strive more without being strained, I feel. And even if you don't share my sense of the importance of this in terms of achievement, I know there are some aspects of how he deals with us in the family that you *do* care about and where you'd welcome his cleaning up his act. Nat himself can recognize these places for him to grow, I think, but he doesn't choose to take on the job.

"Nathaniel has the potential to craft himself into something a whole lot more marvelous—a whole lot more valuable to the world—than just a good kid that grows up to be a good guy."

"Maybe that kind of person—one who strives to be 'all that he can be'—isn't who Nat naturally is," April replied. "I think it should be good enough that he's a good kid who's making his way well in the world."

"It is 'good enough.' But something in me says that 'good enough' is not good enough," I said, the meaning of my words somewhat cryptic even to me.

And now out in the garden—repairing some of the stone walls with which I'd made my terraces on our steep slope, as I was pondering April's admonition to me to lighten up, and pondering also my own not-yet-articulate sense that good enough is somehow not good enough—I took a hard look at myself. So much of my early writings had been a defense of human nature against that poweful strain in our civilization that has condemned us as fundamentally flawed. The Calvinist notion of our depravity I'd seen as a case of blaming the victim—an unjust view of a fundamentally beautiful creature, a view that in itself was depraved in its identification with that "angry god" in whose hands we miserable sinners dangled over the fires of damnation. Now, I reflected, here I am pressing my "good kid" of a son to stretch himself into some form other than the one he seems naturally inclined to assume. Am I the agent of the same cultural impulse I'd spent years deploring?

The thought was not a comfortable one. I did not wish to imbue my boy with any distaste for himself, making him into Nietzsche's "sick animal." I found the image a painful one: Nathaniel, laboring under the weight of unrealistic or excessive expectations, carrying a continuous discomfort within his own skin that comes from bad conscience. This was a burden that I knew from my own years of struggle to come to peace with the realm of shoulds, and it was not what I had in mind for my boy. But might that be what I'm doing? If so, I should surely "lighten up" before I truly damage this, my "undamaged" child, my Adam, before I darken both Nat's life and mine with such a crime—the infliction of injury, unintended, perhaps, but still a kind of involuntary manslaughter.

But then again, if part of our culture unjustly condemns and wars upon human nature, are there not problems also with the part of our culture that simply accepts us as just fine the way we are? Like our indulgent political culture that tells the American people that they are the fount of all truth and wisdom, and holds up to them no ideal of a democratic body politic to which they should strive to measure up. Like our market-place, where the road to riches is to give the customer, who's always right, what he wants. Give them the violent entertainments and junk foods that give them the pleasurable rush of sensation on which they can readily get hooked. I can see how easily Nathaniel—under different auspices—could roll down the hill that April and I have been helping him up, and become like so many of his fellows whose lunches in school consist of Cheetos and Twinkies with Kool-Aid to wash it down (this is no exaggeration!), and who spend hours watching the most dreadful assortment of *G.I. Joe* and *Power Ranger* programs, with occasional forrays into *Die Hard* movies.

However skewed the culture may seem to be between the poles of con-demnation and indulgence, I felt committed to find some intermediate approach, one that would challenge without injuring, and would support and nurture without indulging.

As I thought along these lines, while I worked with my hands to undo the entropic effect on the walls of the passage of time and the freezes and thaws of winter, Nathaniel came up to me.

"Shoot hoops, Dad?" he asked.

"Yeah, sounds good," I replied, "let me just put these rocks back in place."

We left the orchard, and climbed up the driveway to that space I'd created for Nat for his seventh birthday. In our quite unlevel piece of the world, I'd made a level spot for soccer and basketball, erecting on the edge a hoop on a pole, and we had grandiloquently dubbed the whole place the Sports Complex. As we walked, I spoke to Nathaniel. "I want to ask you something, and I want you to feel completely free to tell me what you really think. OK?

"You know that in a lot of ways I challenge you, trying to get you to take on some part or another of the job of becoming as good a person as you can be. Right? Now, some people think—and I can imagine they could be right—that I should lighten up on you. They say you're a good kid—and on that I completely agree—and that I should press you less about what you choose to do.

"What I want to ask you is, would you like for me to lighten up, or keep pressing you as I do, or what?"

By this point we were in the Sports Complex, and Nathaniel started shooting a few short shots off the board. He'd affirmed my little "OK?" and "Right?" leading into my question, and I could see that he was now considering the larger question.

"No, I don't want you to lighten up," he declared. "I don't feel it's too much. It doesn't hurt me any, I can take it."

"I'm glad it doesn't hurt any. But do you think it does you any good?"

"I don't know. I think so."

It was my turn to shoot now, and after missing a few I felt myself getting into a groove, hitting three or four eighteen-footers in a row. It had always mystified me how sometimes one would get into such a groove, and it would feel as though one's hands and feet and eyes knew precisely how to work, and then that feeling would disappear and one would throw up bricks for a while, and then the in-the-groove feeling would return again. Why can't one stay in the groove? I've wondered that for years.

I started missing again, and I gave the ball back to Nat for some shots, and then we adopted a "shoot till you miss" policy, which made our alternation more frequent.

"By the way, kid, what did you end up doing about the Nintendo?"

"I didn't play," Nat said. "I read *Matilda* instead."

Matilda, huh, I thought to myself. We do not regulate Nat's reading time at all, following the usual middle-class belief that reading is a good thing. Still, *Matilda* is not the book I'd have ideally have him read. For one thing, he'd read it before, as well as seen the movie—so there was nothing adventurous about that. For another, it's one of Roald Dahl's usual melodramas in which the adult authorities are unrelievedly and irredeemably evil and corrupt, as well as stupid, and the kid is the font of unadulterated truth and virtue. The book could use some subtlety. But this was one good place for me to lighten up, I figured, and besides, *Matilda* wasn't really what was interesting in Nat's answer.

"Didn't play, huh, why not?" I asked him.

"You made me promise," Nat said.

"I hope you felt you could make the choice to play," I said. "If you decided that was consistent with your promise."

"Yeah, I know. I could have played if I thought that was best for me. But I'd already played some this morning, and I could tell that playing more now wasn't really the best thing for me to do."

"If you hadn't made that promise to me, and the choice had still been up to you, would you have played?" I inquired.

"Sure," answered Nat.

I hit what used to be called my jump shot, back when my legs were young enough for my elevation to qualify as a jump, and then spoke: "So that leads me to one last question: why is it that, if you can tell that playing more was not what's best for you, you'd have chosen to play anyway?"

He thought some, and then started shooting his buzzer-beater 20-foot lunge-shot, and then replied, "I don't know."

"Neither do I, boychick. And I wish I did, because it isn't just you. It seems we humanoids often don't do what we know would be best for us." And I thought about myself and, for one example, how I know that if I did 45 minutes a day of concentrated yoga it would be wonderful for me, and how despite that knowledge I can only get myself to do little stints of 5 or 10 minutes, a couple times a day.

We May Grow

Later that day I decided I felt like dropping in on my friend, Mr. Godachi, to see how his garden was growing, and to see whether he had any reactions to the pieces of the manuscript of this book, which I'd recently given him. As it was July, Mr. Godachi's snapdragons were growing all in a swirling blaze of color around the sign at his entry way, a sign reading, "Godachi's Garden—all who enter may grow." I'd once asked Godachi if his sign was a take-off on the inscription over the arch at Harvard through which I'd walked on my way to classes during my undergraduate years: "Enter to Grow in Wisdom." During those student years, my feeling was that it was a noble purpose for entering the place, but that it had little to do with what actually animated most of the enterprises within the confines of the great Yard to which the arch led. Anyway, Godachi had laughed and denied his sign had any relation to that inscription. He made some vague allusion to some Japanese text, but I couldn't tell if he was serious or kidding.

"I've come to grow!" I called out to Godachi as I jogged down the driveway to his cottage-like house. Mr. Godachi was carrying some rich-looking compost from a heap he kept behind his place out toward his herb pathway. He turned with a smile, and when I caught up with him, he jokingly sprinkled some of the compost on my feet and said, "This ought to help." I jumped back and said, "I'm not standing around to see how you might water my feet." And we laughed.

"This line, 'all who enter may grow,' just what does it mean? Does it mean that it might or might not happen? Or does it mean that we have your permission to if we so choose, that there is no prohibition against growth here?" Godachi gave me an especially keen little twinkle of the eye, and said, "Yes!" "Well, which is it?" I insisted, "If it's from the Japanese, the ambiguity of 'may' must be absent in the original. So which way does it point?"

"I have a question for you," Mr. Godachi replied. "What do you mean with this word you just used, *'choose'*?" I looked at him puzzledly. Then he pointed at my manuscript. "No free will," he said, completing the explanation. "So I am wondering, what is the difference between the 'might-or-might-not' and the 'permitted' interpretations?"

"Do you disagree with me, then, about this question of free will?" I asked.

"No, actually I do not disagree with what you say," he responded. "I was just teasing. Well, not 'just teasing.' What you say is OK, but what you don't say—or say enough of—is also important."

I waited for him to go on, but the silence lasted long enough that I realized that he'd put the conversational ball back into my court. "Yes, well, what is it you want said?"

"That each person *does* choose. That even if the human being, as you say, does not have free will, each person nonetheless has a will, and with that will he or she can freely choose." His eyes were once again twinkly—

I imagined with his pleasure at the wording of his paradox—but there was also a rather serious tone to his words.

"Well, that's *in* there," I protested. "I fully acknowledged that we do indeed make choices, just as we experience ourselves as doing."

"Yes, I know, it's in there. Your argument against free will is intended to be applied just at that 'ultimate' level where free will could be used to justify sinners burning in hell for eternity. Other than that, you're affirming the reality and importance of our choices.

"But my fear," Godachi continued, "is that, for readers, the message of responsibility will not come through as clearly as the message of our being, as you put it, 'the fruit of the world.' And that people will come away, therefore, with the sense that the human agent has been taken off the hook. It is part of the human condition to be *on the hook*, however, and I think it important for that to come through."

"Like how?" I asked.

"You're the writer, you'll have to come up with your own literary strategies for getting the message across. But here's what I would say to someone who accepted your argument about the ways that free will is not a reality. I'd say: 'But you know, you *do* have a choice. Can you feel it, as you are sitting there? Yes, it is right there. You know there are things you *could* do, that you *should* do. You could put aside a bit more of your own ease and comfort and put your heart and energy more into taking care of the larger whole. The choice is available to you, and you could make it.

" 'You could make that decision to become a Big Brother or Big Sister, that is, to give of yourself as if you really did know that the welfare of the most disadvantaged among us matters as much as the welfare of ourselves. Forget about that question of how the will that makes that decision got formed. You now *have* that will, and there is nothing to prevent your deciding to use it for good. Experience it: you have it in your power to make the right choice. Nothing in what Schmookler argued diminishes that reality.'

"Something like that. I would want my readers to get in touch with that place in themselves where they are—quite really—free moral agents. I'd want them to envision from that place how their actual choices stack up against the best choices that are in their power to make, and thus to confront themselves with the gap between the two, and with what it is in their hearts or guts that they allow to create that gap."

"An interesting challenge for a writer," I granted, "though I'm not sure exactly how I'd go about getting people to that experiential place. But I do know what you mean by that place: I've experienced it before, myself, that cusp of a decision between the course I know is right and the one I am tempted to take anyway."

"That is a cusp on which a great deal of human life is lived," Mr. Godachi stated, "but the awareness of that moment-to-moment cross-roads is often missing."

"But what about that idea that one of the people on the forum put forward, that in some sense people are always doing the best they can?" I asked.

"It's true, at some level," Mr. Godachi answered, "but it's not very illuminating. Especially for thinking about one's own choices and con-duct. But it's of limited value even in thinking about *other* people—be-cause, as that other person on the forum countered, if it's the *only* thing they can do (seen at that level), it is just as true to say they are always doing their worst as their best. But in terms of one's relationship to one-self and one's own choices, that perspective could easily act as an obstacle to realizing one's true potential for the good. It gets in the way of con-fronting the reality that one has choices, and that one could make those choices better if one directed one's will that way."

"Hold on a second," I interjected. "Just what is it that does that 'direct-ing' of the will if not the will? Isn't there a paradox here?"

"The human landscape is strewn with paradoxes," said Godachi. "Let's put it this way: a person could make better choices if he *wanted* to. I would rather have people who choose not to do the good to confront their 'I don't want to' rather than to take refuge under an 'I can't.' The 'can't' obscures the reality of choice, while the 'don't want to' helps bring it into healthy relief."

"How do you mean?"

"Ask people about Mother Teresa's life and how it compares—in terms of service to the good—with the one they're living." This is when she was still alive. "A lot of people will say something like, 'Oh, I couldn't do what she does, I just don't have it in me.' But what if you told those same people, 'Here, I'll give you ten million dollars if you'll go and spend a year ministering to those who need it, just as Mother Teresa does'? I expect a lot of people who 'couldn't' serve as Mother Teresa does would find a way to do it. In other words, it wasn't a matter of 'can't,' it was a matter of not feeling the desire, the motivation, the will, to do it."

"It's one thing to get on a plane to India, and hand food out to the poor," I maintained, "but that's not the same as giving all that Mother Teresa gives. Some things aren't so easy to will. Some things go way beyond just getting one's body into the right location."

"Granted," Godachi replied. "But the importance of getting one's body on the right airplane should not be underestimated. And it's not just big decisions like caring for the homeless of Calcutta. It can also be little things like getting one's body off the sofa, turning off the TV, and making the call to Mom that you know will make her day."

With that food for thought, I soon took my leave from my gardener friend and teacher.

When Push Comes

That conversation with Godachi led me to reflect on a familiar question: How much should I push myself?

As often as I've pondered this question, I do not find it an easy question to answer. During my years working on *The Parable of the Tribes*, there were times I wasn't sure I could carry all I'd taken on. Then, more recently, I went through some years when I felt so dragged down and debilitated by I-don't-know-what (and neither did the doctors) that I eventually felt compelled to divest myself of the responsibilities I'd previously taken on to try to help the larger world. It seemed plenty to get myself out of bed, take care of my personal and family duties, and not be too much of a drag to be around. (This experience and my reflections on it can be found in my book *Living Posthumously*.)

Going through that time of debilitation gave me some appreciation of how difficult it can be for many people, just working to keep body and soul together. When, as a child, I saw those famous pictures from Depression-era Oklahoma, showing young women, not looking young at all, with faces haggard by worry and strain, I got my first intimation of how people can get worn out by daily life. But of course, throughout history in many parts of the world, the strain of life has been like that, and it is not because of advances in medicine and public health alone that we, the affluent of the modern world, tend to live so much longer than our ancestors.

For one thing, our immediate, personal burdens are far lighter. Although I can always find things to worry about, unlike my ancestors I do not worry whether tomorrow there will be food to put on the table, whether there will be cossacks breaking down the door, whether I will have to father six children in order for it to be likely that two might reach adulthood. Like most Americans of this era, I have it easy. I need only turn on CNN and look at the faces of refugees in the camps near Rwanda, or of the people who have endured war in Bosnia, or of the Russians with their cruel history and their pint-of-vodka-per-day consumption habits, to have it driven home how fortunate I am. How fortunate so many of us are.

We have the comfort that comes from sitting on top of the literal and metaphorical food chain. It is an achievement, the way so many people of advanced years in our society look so fresh and unworn. Seventy-year-olds nowadays can look as fresh—and have as many years of life remaining to them—as did fifty-year-olds just a couple of generations ago. But that achievement, looked at another way, may also represent a kind of indulgence: so much ease taken, over so many years, in so troubled a world. No, perhaps not so much an indulgence as a waste, the way it seems a waste when a president with very high popularity ratings in his second term makes no use of them to achieve important but politically costly purposes. That's not a perfect analogy, since the time expires on the president's term in an automatic way that it doesn't on our biological clocks. But still, there's reason to be asking the question: for what can I *use* this resource—popularity or vitality—besides looking good?

We are not only the fortunate, but in a larger perspective the fortunate of the fortunate. For our whole species has climbed its way to the top of the food chain. For thousands of years, and to an ever-increasing extent, our species has dominated the planet in a way no other species has ever done. We have become the colonial masters over practically every biosystem on earth, with the other forms of life living, increasingly, at our sufferance. Our numbers have grown, our control over the land-mass has spread, our ability to subjugate and manipulate the ecosystem for our purposes has multiplied. Unprecedented power—for what? In the society around me the predominant answer seems to be: for our comfort and entertainment and ease.

By the standards of my class in America, I live a frugal life. Our expenses for living are less than half those of many of our middle-class friends. But I ought not kid myself. To be able to live on six and a half acres of mostly wooded hillside, to have fruit trees to tend and clean air to breathe, to be able to put $150 into a Sports Complex—these are luxuries in a world of coming-onto-six-billion people. It's true that April and I give ourselves away a lot, I concede to myself, and that at the end of the day we know we've done some work. But we need only look in the mirror—the 51-year-old man who still has something of a jump shot and the 45-year-old woman who can still bicycle up the steep 1000-foot rise from the bottom of the valley to the top of our ridge—and we must know that we've got it good, that life is depleting our resources at a pace that's slow by any historical standard.

That line comes to me—one that I used to dislike for what I'd taken as the odor of snobbery—"From those to whom much is given, much is expected." I can't now remember what I'd found objectionable about it. Yes, I think, I ought to push myself. Not to the point of great pain and strain, but at least past the point of ease and comfort.

For all the creatures caught up in evolution, it then comes to me, life has never been a matter of being able to just coast along. Life has always been straining and exploring, for the whole endeavor has been a game at the highest of stakes—a matter of life and death. The protomammals that scurried under the feet of the dinosaurs did not develop into the swift gazelle and the fierce leopard by just coasting. I mean nothing Lamarckian here in saying that, but life has always been stretching and straining, selecting for those who gave the extra effort that would make the difference between survival and elimination. Life has always faced challenges, and it seems unlikely to me that the dance of life would culminate in a creature, sitting as lord of the creation, defining its life in terms solely of ease and comfort.

Terra's Visit

The next day was Friday, and as soon as she'd finished her shift at her summer job Terra would be coming to our place for the weekend. She was coming with Mike, her boyfriend, which was fine with us since we all liked Mike, and since Mike's presence would make the passage of time out here in the boonies less tiresome for my city-girl daughter. This would be the first time we'd seen Mike since our trip together to North Carolina to celebrate the eightieth birthday of my aunt Evelyn (a.k.a. Chava, Hebrew/Yiddish for "Eve") with various other members of our somewhat small clan. Family gatherings with no one her age around are not Terra's kind of thing. Terra has a shy side, and in addition she does not readily stretch herself to people different from herself to discover what might be interesting or worthwhile about them. I've understood for quite some time that she finds most of my friends "boring." And I understood, in the case of Chava's birthday celebration, that for Terra the idea of spending a whole weekend hanging out with people even older than her parents was not a great turn on.

Nonetheless, although I did not exactly command her presence, I indicated strongly that showing the flag for Chava on this occasion had a value that should weigh a good deal more heavily in her calculations than the question of what would be the most fun way to spend the weekend. And when she signed on to that way of looking at it, we sweetened the deal by getting Mike included in the invitation. As it turned out, the weekend was very enjoyable for those "young folks." There was access to a swimming pool, for one thing. There were some stretches of time during which they were free to go off on their own and check out Duke University and UNC. And there was, perhaps, something more.

One highlight of the weekend for me involved Terra. The main celebration of the weekend was a dinner at a restaurant near Chapel Hill, where we all sat at a rather long table. Terra was at the other end of this table from me, so I didn't see her much. About midway between us was an old man, long ago widowed from Chava's first cousin. Though not connected to us by blood, and though he was long since remarried, he was still a part of our family. A former professor of mathematics, this man was now severely stricken, among other difficulties that afflicted his old age, with Parkinson's disease. He was very difficult to communicate with, did not seem to be very much "with it," and appeared to be rather depressed. At one point during the long-lasting dinner, I looked up and saw that Terra was escorting this old and frail man around the room. The elderly gentleman was smiling, and seemed even a bit animated.

As I learned later, Terra had looked over and noticed that the man had withdrawn from all the conversations going on around him, and was just sitting there in a sort of somber heap. And she felt moved by this sight to go over and strike up a conversation. When she learned that he was feeling uncomfortable from sitting so long on the hard chair, but felt too unsteady to do anything about it, she offered him the little stroll together that I'd witnessed. Being on the arm of a lovely young lady, I think, made his evening. I think that the giving of this gift enriched Terra's too. And certainly mine.

Now with a couple of hours to go before Terra and Mike were due to arrive at our home in the mountains, I set aside my intellectual work and went out with Nat to carry water up to a flowerbed beyond the reach of our hoses. On the radio there had been talk of possible showers late evening, but I didn't want to take any chances, what with the astilbe looking so bedraggled earlier in the day when I'd gone up for the mail. By the second trip up with the buckets, my legs were feeling their age.

"When's Terra getting here?" Nat asked.

"I'm not expecting her before seven," I replied.

"Too long," Nat declared.

"So you're eager to see her."

"Yeah, but I wish she weren't coming with Mike. Then she'll not have any time for me."

Both Terra and her older brother, Aaron, now working his summer job in New England, had doted on their much younger brother since the day he'd been born. The sibling rivalry that had flared all too often between the older children had never in the slightest entered their relationship with Nat. It had been a pleasure, through the years, to see how the kids took delight in each other.

But not an unmitigated pleasure. Especially in recent years, as Nat ceased to be the little kid and began to be a more substantial physical and intellectual presence, he'd become something of a bull in Terra's china shop. Admittedly, Terra was partly responsible. She had developed a pattern of teasing and joking and roughhousing with Nathaniel from which Terra, as the little puppy her little brother had been started turning into the more powerful dog he was now, had been slow to break away. But in the past year or two, I'd noticed that Terra was doing less and less to encourage Nat's onslaughts and spending more and more of her time with Nat defending herself against them. Nathaniel had certainly noticed that he was getting rebuffed more often, but this did not seem to be leading to any change in his conduct. It was quite obvious, I thought, how Terra did and did not wish to be treated, and quite predictable therefore which of Nat's habitual ploys would lead to her telling him to get out. Yet for all that predictability, Nat persisted. Some piece—of whatever it would take for Nat to treat his sister with greater sensitivity and consideration—was missing.

When I had mentioned to April earlier that there were some aspects of Nat's way of acting in the family where I knew she felt he could "clean up his act," it was specifically this pattern with Terra I had in mind. In some ways, this pattern was an extension of a more general characterological trait, evident since day one, of trying in every situation to see how far he could extend his will. Far more than with either of the other kids, being father to Nat had always meant defining my boundaries and being clear with my limits. But it was especially with Terra, and especially in recent years, that it seemed that life was knocking on the door of Nat's mind and asking him to let in some new considerations.

"Nat, you remember how we were talking about how sometimes you know that you should do something different from what you're doing, but you still sometimes choose anyway to keep doing what you feel like? Well, I think you're old enough now to decide to make a different choice—for example in how you are with Terra. You know what I mean?"

"She's always telling me to back off. I'm tired of it."

"I bet you know how she'd like to be treated, don't you? I bet you know when what you are doing is something that bothers her. Am I right?"

"Yeah, I guess so."

"Do you know why you do it anyway, despite your knowing that it's something she doesn't want?"

Nat thought. "No. Well, maybe. I kind of enjoy it."

"I would like to ask you to try something this weekend. You are getting to be a young man, and that's different from being a baby. When you're a baby, it's pretty much OK to do whatever feels right to you. By the time you get to be a man, it's part of your job to take care of how other people feel, too. And along the way, you move from one of those places to the other. How about, this weekend, you take it as part of your job—with Terra—to act with her only in those ways that you really think that she would like? And to restrain yourself from doing those things you know she doesn't like? I bet she'll be pleased to have a young man like you acting that way with her. And maybe you'll find the different relationship with her more enjoyable, too."

Nat considered it. And then he agreed.

And it worked. At times, Nat acted with genuine solicitude for his sister. More than a few times, Nat's old habits reasserted themselves, and then he'd look over at me, and I'd respond with arched eyebrows, and he'd back off a bit. There was greater warmth between them, and greater peace in the house. And at the end of the weekend, with Nat's permission, we told Terra about Nat's project, and she thanked him most graciously.

Beyond the Standards of Apedom

Nathaniel *is* a good kid. Even if we did not encourage him to be more considerate of his sister—or to hold the door for his grandmother, instead of dashing through and letting it close in her face—he'd still be a basically good kid. But the question remains, "Good enough for what?"

I am carrying the gravel by the wheelbarrowful up the driveway, from the place where the rains have brought it up to the gulleys the rains have formed. As I rake in the stones to defeat the water's relentless channeling, I am thinking of these things. And I recall a line about human nature from *The Parable of the Tribes*, that it is not that human nature is necessarily "good" but that we evolved to be, by nature, "good enough" to live the lives our genetic heritage prepared us to live. Until comparatively recently, our ancestors—even after they were completely human, indistinguishable in biological endownment from ourselves—were still living lives quite continuous with those of the prehuman primates from whom they had descended (or ascended?). They lived in small family groups, essentially egalitarian bands, in relative peace apparently and without need of much foreign policy, subsisting (like other primates) on what nature spontaneously provided.

Each such human person flowered, we can imagine, into his or her own individuality—quirky, most likely, and perhaps even not trivially flawed. Why wouldn't they be flawed? Evolution, as had been said on the forum, is not required to produce perfection. The impetuous and strong-willed youth, like Nathaniel, in a paleolithic band, would have served his group's survival well, even if he was rough on his sister, and even if he neglected to help his aged grandmother with her load of berries. In that world, perhaps even some bully would have been only a minor nuisance.

If we lived still in such a world, I wondered, would I as Nat's father be less likely to press him to "be all that he can be"? Yes, I expect so. Something has happened in the past ten millennia that is quite heavy, and that makes it hard—and perhaps quite inappropriate—to lighten up.

What was good enough for an ape, or even for fully human beings living still in the basic primate pattern, became not good enough at all when civilization erupted out of the evolutionary process, bearing us upward with it into the possession of unprecedented powers. The bully who might have been tolerable in the little band represented a human possibility that could be absolutely devastating in the mighty systems of civilized society. Thus it is that we see that as civilization emerges, so does slavery. So does tyranny. So does chronic and devastating war. What might have been quirks or little flaws in apedom are magnified into deadly sins in the civilized world. It may be for good reason that, apparently, it is with the rise of civilization that the sense of sin, and the sense of evil polarized from good, also arise.

My "parable of the tribes" tried to demonstrate that the human creature's emergence out of the order of nature condemned us to an unprecedented kind of anarchy that inevitably would bring certain kinds of evil—those clustering around the quest for power—to the fore. Systemic forces, I argued, had magnified some of the worst of our human potentialities into inescapable and dominant facts of our collective existence.

But even in the absence of such a systemic pull toward such evils, simply the indisputable fact of human powers would have brought the issue of moral responsibility into the aching heart of human existence. Once we found ourselves outside of the confines of the order into which our nature had been crafted to fit, and in which therefore our merely following our nature might be good enough, we humans were challenged to create and conform to new kinds of order. And with systems that placed enormous power into the hands of some of us, the new evolutionary challenge of civilized order inevitably focused attention on the task of moving human concern further from self-interest toward a caring for the whole. Not entirely against the grain for a social animal like us, but enough further in that direction than had been required of us in our natural condition that it did strain against our natural tendencies. This strain was part of the price of our rise to the position of being the lords of creation.

And for all the strain, we have consistently fallen short. The world we have brought into being through the gift of our cultural creativity demands of us more virtue than, throughout history, we have been able to muster.

Our godly powers continue to expand. With every leap forward in such powers, the necessity for godliness in our consciousness grows also. I wonder: Are we willing to confront that challenge, are we willing to pay that price for our great advantages? Take the likely price required for an environmentally sustainable civilization. With hundreds of millions of us now consuming wealth at levels barely dreamt of even by the nobles and royalty of earlier eras, the possibility has emerged of our destroying ourselves by unthinkingly or uncaringly destroying the biosphere on which we depend. A godly creature would restrain its appetites, and thus preserve the wholeness of the larger Order. But too often it is just in our conquest of the world that we are willing to be as gods, while insisting on being just lazy primates with respect to our ordering of ourselves.

The blessing and the curse of our position are that we get to work our will on the planet and that we live on the edge of self-created catastrophes.

Yes! That's the key phrase, it occurs to me: *self-created*. That's the essence of the human condition. That we are self-created, that the world and our role in it have become the fruits of our own choices. We are the lords of creation precisely because of our creative capacities, the ability to invent and reinvent our way of life. Creativity is life at the crossroads, life as choice. And for the creative creature—the one not confined to paths laid out in any genetic code, the one who has brought an indeterminacy into the flow of life's unfolding—the challenge of life becomes inescapably a *moral* one. We make choices—choices with enormous repercussions—and that entails *responsibility*. All creatures have faced great dangers, but it is the creature whose dangers are "self-created" who must bear that special burden: *sin*.

If our choices had an impact only on our own individual lives, then we'd perhaps have merely traded one set of difficulties (lack of food, disease, predators) for another (moral pressure, bad conscience, uncertainty), and might rightly just accept our moral failure and decide we'd gotten the better of the bargain. But our moral failings are not such private matters: they can lead to persecutions of whole peoples, they can engender wars or chronic hatreds, they can leave millions who might be cared for to live in unnecessary privation, they can despoil the whole planet. So perhaps we have no right simply to accept—or disregard—our moral failures. A degree of moral effort on our parts, even of moral strain, may be an appropriately small cost to pay, given the potential size of the benefits.

But such a cost-benefit analysis will be persuasive to us only if we are making our calculations from the perspective of the larger whole. Taking the viewpoint of the whole is, perhaps, the essence of what it is to be godly. But, because being godly does not come easily to apes like us, we are more inclined by nature to focus instead on our own costs and benefits. We want what comes naturally to be sufficient. We want it to be good enough to be good enough. It is irresponsible to accept as our birthright these unnatural powers but to refuse to accept as our birth-responsibility the unnatural burdens of what is required of us morally. For the lords of creation, it seems only a degree of godliness is good enough.

That, I decide, is what I'm working to help Nathaniel to embody: whatever his godly potential is. Such a Nathaniel can help make better the Order of this distressed and endangered world. And being a father who tries to help him become that more godly Nathaniel is part of my responsibility to that larger Order also.

Progress and Entropy

That night, when I talked with April about this—to explicate that inarticulate sense I'd had before that "good enough" wasn't good enough—she had mixed reactions.

On the one hand, she agreed with me completely that humankind isn't measuring up to some important standard. When it comes to what we're doing these days on this planet, April feels even more passionately than I that our species' current sense of responsibility isn't good enough. Her love of the earth goes very deep, and it brings her a good deal of pain. The pain she feels is from the destruction we are inflicting on the earth. And it is painful for her, too, that she feels quite out of tune with most of the rest of humanity who seem to be able to proceed so blithely in consuming the earth without much thought for the rest of the biosphere, or for the future generations of our own kind either.

On the other hand, she did not want Nathaniel, her baby, to be injured by the weight of the responsibility of having to measure up to some standard of godliness. She wanted him to be free of the burdens of so difficult and challenging a morality as might be deemed necessary for "the lords of creation."

Frankly, I shared her ambivalence. But maybe, I said, it doesn't have to be such a burdensome thing. Maybe we can find a way to help him to care about all the good stuff without being injured by any of it. As we talked about this hope, though, April came back to that recurrent pain that she feels for the injured earth. This seemed to her to refute my hope about the pain-free way. But then I asked April: "If you could choose simply to be free of the pain you feel for the plight of the earth, would you take that option?" She didn't have to think very long. No, was her clear and emphatic answer. That pain is part of her contact with the sacred, and it is part of what moves her to do what she can of what needs doing. So, I asked, would you wish to spare Nathaniel some similar amount of pain that he might have to go through to do what he might do of what needs doing? And we talked about this, without her reaching any conclusion. Except that we agreed that being a human being is an interesting, and not easy thing.

In the morning, still thinking about how our going beyond apedom has necessitated our meeting some difficult moral challenges, I decided I'd reply to an e-mail I'd received a week before but had set aside unanswered. It was from a fellow named Jim, an old crony from my one disillusioning year at Yale during my radical days as a graduate student. This was 1970–1971, a time when I was newly aflame with my vision of the parable of the tribes, and more than most of my fellow graduate students this fellow Jim, who'd recently e-mailed me out of the blue, had been sympathetic with my intention of developing a thoroughgoing critique of civilization.

Andy—at least with a name like Schmookler I don't have to wonder whether you're the right one—a little Internet search I did the other day just happened to land me on your Web site. (By the way, where do you live these days?) I read through some of your short pieces on a variety of topics, and I thought I'd drop you this line. For old times' sake, mostly. And to grouse a little at you, too.

And then he went on to discuss some of the pieces I'd written in recent years on the culture war, the ones that spoke of bridge-building, of listening, of seeking a higher wisdom, and so forth.

I have to admit to some disappointment, *he summed up his reaction to these pieces,* to see that you've abandoned the ramparts of the battle against what you and I both used to recognize as oppressive systems of dominance and control. With the rest of the country having become so conservative, I am not surprised when Democrats like Clinton adopt an essentially Republican platform. But you? A fire-breathing, fundamental critic like you were? *Et tu,* Andy? **Jim**

Needless to say, I wasn't delighted with this image of me as betrayer of my previous radical vision. But Jim's message had challenged me to sort out just how I had and had not changed in my views. And now with the thoughts about apedom from the day before still fresh in my mind, I sat down to respond to that challenge.

Dear Jim, It was good to hear from you, for the most part, with some mixed feelings about the grousing. By the way, I live in Virginia, in the mountains, and so I have regular encounters with grouse. But most of these grice are not so hard on me as you, with your *"Et tu,* Andy." But hey, neither are they nearly as interesting and stimulating as you have always been.

From there, I started addressing his challenge to me. I told him about my thoughts on apedom, and then proceeded to try to connect that with his particular complaint.

Maybe what is coming up for me is a new wrinkle in my thoughts about progress. You and I, growing up in the 1950s, were both imbued with a sense that history was a matter of "onward and upward." Right? In my most purely radical days of the late '60s and early '70s, I rejected that way of understanding history. Civilization itself was, I argued, fundamentally dangerous and destructive from the outset. It was shaped by forces we didn't really control, and it consisted of power systems that were themselves as much problem as solution. I still believe all that to be true. The idea of "progress," in the form it was usually sold to us, obscured a great deal of what is important about the dynamics of history and the workings of the power systems.

But even as I rejected that old notion of progress I was still entertaining one of my own. As I saw it—correctly, I would still maintain—we were coming to the point where humankind could both envision and be in a position to construct a different kind of civilization that contained and controlled the previously free play of power, and which could restrain the human assault on the biosphere. And I was hoping that we would seize that opportunity and dismantle the oppressive systems that history had created. I hoped that—energized by our native goodness and wisdom—we would undertake the construction of the new, more humane and viable civilization I still envision as our proper task.

What has changed is that what is **native** to us has come to seem to me rather less, in moral terms, than what is **required** of us. As a consequence, I have more mixed feelings about the systems that you and I agreed were oppressive. What is fundamental here is not just that I admit more than I would have that our cultural systems need to challenge and order and control us to some extent—that, in other words, it may be necessary for our cultures to do at least some of what you and I might have labeled "oppressing." (I'm still not sure how much real oppressing, if any, is needed, and I still believe that compared with the civilization we could conceivably achieve, our historical structures of control are excessively oppressive.) But there is another important element: and that is that I have recognized the possibility of a kind of cultural entropy which could be even more oppressive, in a fundamental sense, than our cultural traditions. A lazy revolution, therefore, I regard as even more injurious than the ancien regime.

Here's what I mean. If human nature were geared entirely toward the good—that is, toward what "goodness" requires in our current earth-bestriding circumstance— then it would be safe to dismantle the old systems of control. We could imagine that while the new order is being constructed, people would behave appropriately. But if our natural inclinations are inadequate—as my argument about getting beyond apedom suggests—then our existing cultural moralities, even though in some ways oppressive—may play a vital role in maintaining a degree of goodness in the world. For without them, we could simply slide downhill toward a level that might be OK in apedom, but would be quite dangerous in our very unnatural present circumstances.

So what you regard as my cavorting with the enemy is, I would say, a reflection of my recognition that a humane world depends upon our culture giving us guidance and form. When I was focused upon the evils our our cultural inheritance, I saw in the fact that every generation arrived fresh from nature a source of great hope. Which it is. But now I am acutely aware also of how the same fresh start that creates the possibility of cultural renewal and transformation can also bring a most perilous cultural deterioration and amnesia.

Is that not part of what we see on the cultural landscape around us? Do we not see that, when cultural entropy brings the disintegration of standards and ideals and morals, people tend to be prey to their own baser impulses, and also to the base manipulations of others? Do we not see that the storming of Bastilles can, in the absence of the proper ordering principles, lead not to liberation but to a reign of terror? (And by terror, I mean, for example, the violence and degradation in our streets, and the brutalities of the fictions we enact on our movie screens.)

The old traditions, for all their flaws, erected important backstops against a downward slide of humanity. However possible better cultural structures may be for humankind, we cannot afford just to discard those we now have before we have something better to put in place. If one understands the human project as one in which we are engaged in an uphill struggle, then one will conclude that the approach that relies on just doing what comes easily is doomed to end at the bottom. And that only by careful and hard work—like climbers at El Capitan—does one make progress upward.

So it seems to me that the task of achieving good Order—with the best possible liberation of the human spirit consistent with the harmony and viability of the larger whole—is a good deal more challenging and difficult than we were inclined to see it back then, and certainly more so than the movement of which we were part acted as if it were. The human project is one that is fraught with difficulty, and our "movement" had very little to say about difficulty, about the plain old hard work and moral challenge that we must confront if this project is to succeed.

The evolution of life has borne us up to this spit of terra incognita. We think of ourselves as the beneficiaries of this evolution, while in fact we are fundamentally its channels. We're not the winners of some big Darwinian competition, entitled to spray ourselves with post-game champagne in the locker-room; we are the scouts in a march of life that's still ongoing. We thought we could somehow just enjoy the benefits of our advantages, but we didn't recognize that evolution is—as it has always been—our *job*. Like life since the beginning, we are challenged to extend and stretch ourselves. And that is hard work. And it's a matter of life and death.

And then, after a few pleasantries and friendly remarks, I signed off and sent the message.

More than Sacrifice

A few days later, we had Mr. Godachi over to our place for dinner. Though I am the usual cook in our house, April generally does the cooking for guests. On this occasion, however, I wanted to do the cooking. It felt right, somehow, to share with Mr. Godachi our daily fare. This consisted of my homemade pizza—a wheat and millet crust, topped with an herb, garlic, and olive oil sauce rather than tomatoes, lots of cut up veggies, and with only a fraction of the cheese that pizzas usually have—accompanied by a tossed salad with plenty of herbs from the garden, and my homemade olive oil and lemon-juice dressing. On this occasion, I also went down with Mr. Godachi to harvest some broccoli from my first-ever broccoli plants. (These plants were this year's gardening revelation, with their spectacular broad leaves that look just as dry the moment after they are hosed, the water beading off them, as they did before.)

While I did the dinner preparations, Mr. Godachi sat at the counter across from me, in the same seat where Terra had sat for our discussion of my stinginess with Nat's desserts. Putting the pizza up to bake, I told him some of my thoughts since leaving his place earlier in the week. His remarks had raised the question of how much we should push ourselves, and from there I'd put the challenges we face into an evolutionary perspective and concluded that, having achieved great power over the large wholes of which we are part, we need to stretch ourselves to become more aligned with the whole. Doing what comes easily and naturally might have sufficed for a human living still like a primate but was no longer an adequate standard for a creature operating in full-blown civilization. I concluded with the idea that only as much godliness as we could realize within ourselves was good enough, and that this had clarified my understanding of my role as Nathaniel's father. At which point, I looked at Mr. Godachi expectantly.

"I see," he said, "that there is still something unsettled for you in this. No?"

"Well, of course," I replied, "having said all that I still have to struggle to make every decision, to balance one thing with another, to know how to go about things."

"That's it? No, I don't think so," Godachi said, "You're not bothered by this 'being a human being is difficult' business. That's become you're bread and butter. No, there's some other discomfort I'm detecting."

"Hmmm. Yes, I think I know what it is," I realized. "Like April, I have mixed feelings about burdening my boy. There's a part of me that still wants good enough to be good enough. I don't like the idea that the greater good may require his pain.

"Here's the image. I've never joined in the applause for the biblical Abraham, for his readiness to obey the Lord's order to him to sacrifice his beloved son, Isaac, up there on the mountain. My feeling has been that Abraham should have told Yahweh to go get Himself another chosen guy, if a readiness to slaughter an innocent child was a requirement for the position. Anyway, while I've been wrestling with this whole issue, the image of Abraham about to sacrifice Isaac to his God has popped discomfitingly into my mind.

"I do believe in this virtue of godliness. But I don't want to hurt my boy, even if the larger whole requires that we humans get put onto some morally transforming rack. I want to have my cake of nurturing a happy child and also be able to eat our doing our part to make things whole too. I'm not reconciled to having to choose between those."

"Ah, yes." Mr. Godachi smiled. "Let me tell you how I see it. Perhaps it will give you some comfort."

Mr. Godachi leaned back on his stool, tilted his head back slightly and closed his eyes. At this moment, he looked radiant and I thought perhaps my previous alarming perception of him as having aged greatly had been an illusion. "I like your use of the word 'godliness' in this context. 'To be like God.' What does it mean? Aligned with the good order of the whole, you've suggested. But a good order is also one that is at peace. Here is where you see a tension: because if it is the nature of the human *not* to be sufficiently aligned with the whole, then becoming godly in the first sense—responsible, morally structured, pulled away from excessive self-interest—means to be pulled out of alignment with one's own inner peace.

"So you end up with an image of sacrifice. For the sake of God, the child that comes from Nature must be sacrificed up on the mountain.

"But what if there is a kind of magic that greatly mitigates—even if it does not wholly eliminate—that need for sacrifice?"

He paused long enough for me to realize I'd better speak if I wanted the water to keep coming up from the well. "But what kind of magic can there be?" I asked.

"*Can* there be? Ha! The thing about magic is, there *can* be *any* kind of magic." He chuckled a minute over this. I thought it amusing in a theoretical kind of way, but did not feel moved to join in. I wanted that magic delivered.

"Take the yogi," Mr. Godachi resumed. "He practices an exacting and difficult discipline. He must work. He must subordinate his energies to his wisdom, to the wisdom of his tradition. But then, once he does that, this discipline enables him to let go of the places within him where the pain and tightness have pulled him away from his true human form. He opens up the body, achieves an aspect of the 'union' that is at the root of the Sanskrit word '*Yoga*' and becomes a creature at peace with himself. He has also become godly, because the realization of the full health and openness of the organism is part of a creature's way of godliness.

"Do you see the magic? The discipline is the means of liberation. Hard work is the route to genuine relaxation."

"Yes, I know what you mean," I replied. "I've experienced something of the sort myself. But intuitively, I question whether you've delivered me from my dilemma or not. Let me see if I can articulate this. . . .

"Oh, yes. With the yogi, the whole process of alignment and harmonizing has to do with his own body. I find it easily comprehensible how a kind of natural godliness of this kind would be unproblematic. But a great deal of the moral challenge we face has to do with bringing ourselves into alignment with a much larger whole than we ever used to need to take into consideration. It goes beyond the scale of order that comes naturally to us. We are now in this unnatural position, because of our nongenetic evolutionary eruption into this unnatural scope of our powers, and I don't quite see how the yogi's comfort and well-being can reassure us about meeting the demands of this other kind of godliness."

"Yes, good move," Mr. Godachi chortled, as if we were in a chess game and I, his student and opponent, had made the move he'd been waiting for. "So, just as you see the sense of sin as having arisen with the unnatural condition of civilization, so also, I gather you are saying, the sense of some overarching whole, some positive relationship with a larger order, some orientation to a pervasive dimension that might be called God—all this you also believe is extrinsic to human nature, is an adaptive response to humankind's recent and unnatural state of civilization? Do I understand you correctly?"

"Yes, I think so. With civilization we get these great all-ruling deities, who make demands, who hand down laws, who cleave right from wrong."

"Here's another piece of magic that might do the trick," Mr Godachi resumed. "If the human striving for godliness were indeed only an artifact of this evolutionary upsurgence of the past ten thousand years, then your conundrum might indeed have no good solution. But it appears that this is not the case.

"It appears that human beings had a mystical life, of some kind, well before civilization. In other words, even when—in your terms—the species was still living in some kind of continuity with the primate past, when it had not erupted into this new evolutionary status of civilization, even then there was a vital channel open to some relationship with the larger whole. The art in the caves suggests that spirituality long antecedes the new unnatural demands. Mysticism is found among the shamanistic, so-called primitive societies. Indeed, the mystical experience is so profound—not as frequent as, say, sexual orgasm, but universal across human societies and just as total when it does occur—that the conclusion is inescapable that the mystic capacity is built deeply into human nature.

"The turning toward a connection and alignment with the whole, it therefore seems not too far-fetched to believe, is therefore a *natural inclination* in the human creature. The striving for harmony, for beauty, for harmony are, I would say, built into the animal. Godliness is not some

new and alien value, I am suggesting, but—at least in some dimensions—
a fundamental human aspiration.

"What is magical about this," Mr. Godachi continued, "is that it suggests that even before it was needed—the kind of need that civilization's new challenges created—there was an orientation in the human animal toward wholeness, toward alignment, toward a mystical oneness. How did it get there? Why was it there? A good mystery—considering both your suggestion that a primate-like life had no need for concern about how the larger whole is ordered, and the idea that evolution is not supposed to be able to anticipate future needs.

"Perhaps this mystical capacity was a by-product of the creative spark that was already well entrenched in the nature of this unusual animal. After all, by the time civilization began, it had already been many thousands of generations since humankind's embarkation upon the experiment of shaping life according to culturally created meanings. Perhaps the indeterminacy had already made it advantageous for this creature to have some kind of compass available to orient it with respect to the larger systems. Even hunter-gatherer bands might have needed to avoid "sinful" choices that would have placed them out of alignment with the requirements of life. And then, perhaps the answer is just in terms of still more magic, some kind of Hand that fashioned in this emerging creature something in the Maker's own image. Ha!"

He laughed again, and then continued more seriously. "And there is one more piece that I can offer that should help with your dilemma. And it concerns these two points of yours: you have observed, correctly I think, that godliness does not develop easily in a human being, and then you conclude that therefore the work of achieving godliness must be sacrificial. What takes discipline and hard work, the assumption is, must go against the grain and thus bring pain.

"But there is much evidence that your unhappy conclusion does not follow from your correct observation. I am not going to deny that *some* aspects of the challenge of godliness may entail genuine sacrifice. Your argument has its valid applications. But in many vital ways, embodying godliness fulfills the godly person as much as it serves the surrounding Order.

"Across cultures and religious traditions, it seems that the deepest fulfillment is found by those who somehow do achieve a measure of godliness. That mystical experience of oneness with the One, or the All, is universally reported to be blissful, enraptured, beautiful. It is in Mother Teresa's face, not in John D. Rockefeller's, that we can discern joy and satisfaction in life. It is the disciplined and ordered music of Bach, not the screeching of subway wheels on the rails, that gives listeners peak experiences. It is the person who looks upon his or her life and sees that it has been lived in accordance with sacred principles who feels contentment. The heart that's filled with love, not the hate-filled one, is happy.

"These are some of the dimensions of godliness, and the evidence suggests—to my reading of it, at least—that the path toward godliness and that toward one's own deepest fulfillment are not opposed, but rather are in quite close alignment. Hard work, certainly. But, in its essence, the task of making oneself into the very best human being one can be, into the godly person, is not one of great sacrifice. And it is certainly the case that meeting these challenges can be very difficult work, just as the comfort of yoga does not come without discipline."

"If I understand you," I ventured at that point, "you are saying that godliness—or alignment of oneself with Good Order—is indeed a demanding task that takes discipline, that must work uphill against what just naturally flows with no effort. (Even if—as in yoga, or meditation— it is the effort and discipline of learning to make no effort!) But that even if we must stretch and push and top-down-order ourselves in some ways, the fruit of that work—in at least many relevant dimensions—is not pain but a greater fulfillment. Godliness then is not so much a matter of sacrifice as of enlightened self-interest?"

"Yes, you understand what I am saying," Mr. Godachi said. "Though sacrifice may be part of the picture, and humankind is certainly challenged to undertake very difficult work in the realization of its godly potential, the benefits of that work include not just a viable overarching order but also the reward of life's deepest fulfillments.

"Thus, Andy, if you help your boy become more godly—and do so in wise ways—you are not sacrificing him like some feast for the gods. Rather, you are helping him to come to the table of the gods to feast, himself, on life's truest foods."

At this point, the pizza in the oven was done, and I called the family to the table to eat with our guest, whose words, I figured, I'd be spending much of a lifetime digesting.

Notes

Chapter 4

1. Derived from Kuhn, Helmut, "The Case for Order in a Disordered Age," in Kuntz, Paul G., editor, *The Concept of Order* (Seattle: University of Washington Press, 1968), p. 445.

Chapter 5

1. Michael Walzer, "The Communitarian Critique of Liberalism," in Etzioni, Amitai, *The New Communitarian Thinking* (Charlottesville, VA: University Press of Virginia, 1995), p. 69.

2. Quoted in Stanislaus Andrzejewski, *Military Organization and Society* (London: Routledge and Kegan Paul, 1954), p. 131.

3. William Galston, "Value Pluralism and Political Liberalism," in *Report from the Institute for Philosophy and Public Policy,* College Park, Maryland, Summer, 1996.

4. Quoted in Carl J. Friedrich, *Tradition and Authority* (New York: Praeger, 1972), p. 30, emphasis added.

Chapter 6

1. Sir Edward Coke, *Institutes: Commentary Upon Littleton.* First Institute, 97b, quoted in *The Oxford Dictionary of Quotations* (Oxford: Oxford University Press, 1980), p. 154.

2. Quoted in Stephen L. Collins, *From Divine Cosmos to Sovereign State* (New York: Oxford University Press, 1989), p. 30.

3. Carl J. Friedrich, *Tradition and Authority* (New York: Praeger, 1972), p. 100.

4. Andrew Bard Schmookler, *The Parable of the Tribes: The Problem of Power in Social Evolution* (Albany, NY: SUNY Press, 1995), p. 21.

5. Sheryl L. Burkhalter, "Completion in Continuity: Cosmogony and Ethics in

Islam," in Lovin, Robin W. and Frank E. Reynolds, editors, *Cosmogony and Ethical Order: New Studies in Comparative Ethics* (Chicago: University of Chicago Press, 1985), p. 229.

6. Draws heavily upon a column entitled "Commandments not about restriction, but giving freedom." by Rev. Tom Berlin in the *Shenandoah Valley Herald* (Woodstock, Virginia, August 1996).

Chapter 7

1. Cited in Carl J. Friedrich, *Tradition and Authority* (New York: Praeger, 1972), p. 30.

2. Quoted in Theodore Lowi, *The End of Liberalism* (New York: W. W. Norton, 1969), p. 285.

3. Rudolf Dreikurs and Loren Grey, *Logical Consequences: A New Approach to Discipline* (New York: Hawthorn Books, 1970), p. 12.

4. Edmund Burke, quoted in Friedrich, Carl J., *Tradition and Authority*, p. 28.

5. Quotes appear in Jacob Viner, *The Role of Providence in the Social Order: An Essay in Intellectual History* (Philadelphia: American Philosophical Society, 1972), pp. 99–101.

6. Herbert Spencer, cited in Rudolf Dreikurs and Loren Grey, *Logical Consequences,* p. 63.

7. Eugene D. Genovese, "Over the Rainbow," *The New Republic,* July 15 and 22, 1996.

8. Story cited in Norman J. Girardot, "Behaving Cosmogonically in Early Taoism," in Lovin, Robin W. and Frank E. Reynolds, editors, *Cosmogony and Ethical Order: New Studies in Comparative Ethics* (Chicago: University of Chicago Press, 1985), pp. 89–90.

9. Ranulf, Svend, *Moral Indignation and Middle Class Psychology* (New York: Schocken Books, 1964).

10. Horace, *Epistles* I.x.24.

Interlude: Handling Wild Creatures

1. Quoted in Alice Miller, *For Your Own Good* (New York, Farrar, Straus and Giroux), frontispiece.

Chapter 8

1. Quoted in Alan Watts, *Tao: The Watercourse Way* (New York: Pantheon Books, 1975), p. 37.

2. Ibid., p. 55.

Chapter 9

1. In Michael J. Sandel, "Moral Argument and Liberal Toleration: Abortion and Homosexuality," in Etzioni, Amitai, *The New Communitarian Thinking* (Charlottesville, VA: University Press of Virginia, 1995), pp. 75–77.

2. See Jeffrey Abramson and Elizabeth Bussiere, "Free Speech and Free Press: A Communitarian Perspective," Ibid., p. 221.

3. Jean Bethke Elshtain, review of *It Takes a Village* by Hillary Rodham Clinton, in *The New Republic,* March 4, 1996, p. 33.

Chapter 10

1. Quoted in Arthur W. H. Adkins, "Cosmogony and Order in Ancient Greece," in Lovin, Robin W. and Frank E. Reynolds, editors, *Cosmogony and Ethical Order: New Studies in Comparative Ethics* (Chicago: University of Chicago Press, 1985), p. 292.

2. See Adkins, in Lovin and Reynolds.

3. See, e.g., Robin W. Lovin, "Cosmogony, Contrivance, and Ethical Order," in Lovin, Robin W. and Frank E. Reynolds, editors, *Cosmogony and Ethical Order: New Studies in Comparative Ethics,* p. 333.

Interlude: A Hand in the Miracle

1. Fred Turner, *Shakespeare and the Nature of Money: A Moral Economics for the Twenty-first Century* (Oxford: Oxford University Press, forthcoming).

2. *Christian Science Monitor,* August 6, 1996.

Chapter 11

1. Daniel C. Dennett, *Darwin's Dangerous Idea: Evolution and the Meanings of Life* (New York: Simon and Schuster, 1995).

2. Lynn Margulis and Dorion Sagan, *Microcosmos: Four Billion Years of Microbial Evolution* (New York: Pantheon Books, 1974).

3. Gerhard Roth and Helmut Schwegler, "Self-Organization, Emergent Properties and the Unity of the World," in Wolfgang Krohn, Gunter Kupper, and Helga Nowotny, editors, *Self-Organization: Portrait of a Scientific Revolution* (Dordrecht, Boston: Kluwer Academic Publishers, 1990).

4. Quoted in Stephen L. Collins, *From Divine Cosmos to Sovereign State* (New York: Oxford University Press, 1989), p. 44.

5. See Stephen L. Collins, *From Divine Cosmos to Sovereign State,* p. 6, and Joseph M. Kitagawa, "Chaos, Order, and Freedom in World Religions," in

Kuntz, Paul G., editor, *The Concept of Order* (Seattle, WA: University of Washington Press, 1968), p. 287.

6. Quoted in Eugene Genovese, "Ideas Had Consequences," in *The New Republic,* June 17, 1996.

7. Frank Salter, "Political Science," in *National Review,* June 3, 1996.

8. Sheryl L. Burkhalter, "Completion in Continuity: Cosmogony and Ethics in Islam," in Lovin, Robin W. and Frank E. Reynolds, editors, *Cosmogony and Ethical Order: New Studies in Comparative Ethics* (Chicago: University of Chicago Press, 1985), p. 233. Internal quote from Toshihiko Izutzu.

9. Quoted in H. Ronald Pulliam and Christopher Dunford, *Programmed to Learn: An Essay on the Evolution of Culture* (New York: Columbia University Press, 1980), p. 98.

10. See Stephen L. Collins, *From Divine Cosmos to Sovereign State,* chapter 2.

11. Stephen Macedo, *Liberal Virtues: Citizenship, Virtue, and Community in Liberal Constitutionalism* (New York: Oxford University Press, 1991), pp. 41–42.

Chapter 12

1. John Stuart Mill, cited in Stephen Macedo, *Liberal Virtues: Citizenship, Virtue, and Community in Liberal Constitutionalism,* p. 281.